Skirball Cultural Center
Library
2701 N. Sepulveda Blvd.
Los Angeles, CA 90049

Monographs of the
Hebrew Union College
Number 20

———

"Were Our Mouths Filled With Song"
Studies in
Liberal Jewish Liturgy

Skirball Cultural Center
Library
2701 N. Sepulveda Blvd.
Los Angeles, CA **90049**

An I. Edward Kiev
Library Foundation Book

Monographs of the Hebrew Union College

1. Lewis M. Barth, *An Analysis of Vatican 30*

2. Samson H. Levey, *The Messiah: An Aramaic Interpretation*

3. Ben Zion Wacholder, *Eupolemus: A Study of Judaeo-Greek Literature*

4. Richard Victor Bergren, *The Prophets and the Law*

5. Benny Kraut, *From Reform Judaism to Ethical Culture: The Religious Evolution of Felix Adler*

6. David B. Ruderman, *The World of a Renaissance Jew: The Life and Thought of Abraham ben Mordecai Farrisol*

7. Alan Mendelson, *Secular Education in Philo of Alexandria*

8. Ben Zion Wacholder, *The Dawn of Qumran: the Sectarian Torah and the Teacher of Righteousness*

9. Stephen M. Passamaneck, *The Traditional Jewish Law of Sale: Shulḥan Arukh, Ḥoshen Mishpat, Chapters 189-240*

10. Yael S. Feldman, *Modernism and Cultural Transfer: Gabriel Preil and the Tradition of Jewish Literary Bilingualism*

11. Raphael Jospe, *Torah and Sophia: The Life and Thought of Shem Tov ibn Falaquera*

12. Richard Kalmin, *The Redaction of the Babylonian Talmud: Amoraic or Saboraic?*

13. Shuly Rubin Schwartz, *The Emergence of Jewish Scholarship in America: The Publication of the Jewish Encyclopedia*

14. John C. Reeves, *Jewish Lore in Manichaean Cosmogony: Studies in the Book of Giants Traditions*

15. Robert Kirschner, *Baraita De Melekhet Ha-Mishkan: A Critical Edition with Introduction and Translation*

16. Philip E. Miller, *Karaite Separatism in Nineteenth-Century Russia: Joseph Solomon Lutski's Epistle of Israel's Deliverance*

17. Warren Bargad, *"To Write the Lips of Sleepers": The Poetry of Amir Gilboa*

18. Marc Saperstein, *"Your Voice Like a Ram's Horn": Themes and Texts in Traditional Jewish Preaching*

19. Emanuel Melzer, *No Way Out: The Politics of Polish Jewry, 1935-1939*

20. Eric L. Friedland, *"Were Our Mouths Filled With Song": Studies in Liberal Jewish Liturgy*

"Were Our Mouths Filled With Song"

Studies in Liberal Jewish Liturgy

Eric L. Friedland

Hebrew Union College Press
Cincinnati

© Copyright 1997 by the Hebrew Union College Press
Hebrew Union College-Jewish Institute of Religion

Library of Congress Cataloging-in-Publication Data

Friedland, Eric L.
  "Were our mouths filled with song" : studies in liberal Jewish liturgy / Eric L. Friedland.
p. cm. – (Monographs of the Hebrew Union College; no. 20)
Includes bibliographical references and index.
ISBN 0-87820-419-9 (cloth : alk. paper)
  1. Reform Judaism – Liturgy – History. 2. Judaism – Liturgy – History. I. Title. II. Series.
BM660.F68'   1997
296.4'5046—dc21   96-51937
                                                                                        CIP

Printed on acid-free paper
Manufactured in the United States of America

Dr. I. EDWARD KIEV
1905–1975

DISTINGUISHED RABBI, CHAPLAIN, AND LIBRARIAN

In September 1976, Dr. Kiev's family and friends established a Library Foundation bearing his name to support and encourage the knowledge, understanding, and appreciation of scholarship in Judaica and Hebraica.

In cooperation with the Hebrew Union College Press, the foundation presents the present study by Eric L. Friedland as an I. Edward Kiev Library Foundation volume.

To the memory of three twentieth-century ḥasidey ashkenaz:

Rabbi David Dagobert Nellhaus
Professor Nahum Norbert Glatzer
Professor Jakob Joseph Petuchowski

והמשכילים יזהירו כזוהר הרקיע

Daniel 12:3

אִלּוּ פִינוּ מָלֵא שִׁירָה

כַיָּם וּלְשׁוֹנֵנוּ רִנָּה כַּהֲמוֹן גַּלָּיו

וְשִׂפְתוֹתֵינוּ שֶׁבַח כְּמֶרְחֲבֵי רָקִיעַ

וְעֵינֵינוּ מְאִירוֹת כַּשֶּׁמֶשׁ וְכַיָּרֵחַ

וְיָדֵינוּ פְרוּשׂוֹת כְּנִשְׁרֵי שָׁמָיִם וְרַגְלֵינוּ

קַלּוֹת כָּאַיָּלוֹת אֵין אֲנַחְנוּ מַסְפִּיקִים

לְהוֹדוֹת לְךָ יְיָ אֱלֹהֵינוּ וֵאלֹהֵי אֲבוֹתֵינוּ

וּלְבָרֵךְ אֶת־שְׁמֶךָ

Contents

Preface

The making of Jewish prayerbooks began more than a millennium ago and continues today, seemingly without end. Similarly, affirmation of the human need to create ever more authentic, heartfelt, and precise communication with the divine informs our liturgy today, just as it informed the venerable *nishmat* prayer of the Shabbat and Festival *shaharit* service:

> Were our mouths full of song as water fills the sea
> And our tongues as tireless as the ocean's waves
> Were our lips full of praise as wide as heaven's dome . . .
> Never could we praise You enough, Eternal One, our God, and God of those who preceded us.

This volume explores how that need has been identified and fulfilled in the non-Orthodox Jewish liturgy from the mid-1800s through the latter part of our century. Most of the chapters originally appeared as separate articles in a journal, annual, collection, or Festschrift in the last twenty-five years but have been inaccessible to those desiring primary research material on the dynamics of liturgical development and innovation: the complete Judaicist, the student of comparative liturgics, the theologian, the sociologist of religion, the rabbi of a congregation, the seminarian, the prayerbook compiler-to-be, or simply the Jew looking for alternative paths in prayer.

The collection as a whole is a concerted multiple approach to the polychrome phenomenon of what Jakob J. Petuchowski called "prayerbook reform." That is to say, we are investigating a goodly number of the countless ways that the Siddur, Mahzor, and Passover Haggadah have been adjusted, amplified, or transformed so as to faithfully mirror modern Jews' understanding of themselves, their place in society, and their sancta.

A single method of procedure is scarcely sufficient to consider such matters, which also encompass the purpose, doctrinal makeup, philosophical outlook, posture towards tradition, the respective roles of Hebrew and the vernacular, the overall literary execution and quality, and the the short-term and long-range outcomes of such protean liturgical creations. Thus some studies focus on the efforts of individual liturgiographers; others examine the history and development of the liturgy of a specific ideology, congregation, or national Jewish community. In other instances, innovative approaches toward specific holy days, hallowed rituals, or classical religious beliefs are charted.

One recurrent metaphor for the Jewish Prayerbook has been the image of the cathedral. Largely because for centuries Jews were prevented from expressing their artistic gifts in the construction of edifices *ad majorem gloriam Dei,* the creative drive was channeled into textual/conceptual directions. One need but recall, especially from the Byzantine era through the eve of Jewish Emancipation, the tremendous midrashic productivity, the reformulation of halakhic codes and their endless glosses, breathtaking mystical-metaphysical speculations, poignant melodies, and limitlessly intricate poetic effusions. These took the place of the golden candlesticks, rock crystal reliquaries, the enameled caskets, opulent mosaics, and splendid cupolas of edifices such as St. Mark's Cathedral in Venice. In both there is a marvelous harmony of exuberant composition.

The siddur is certainly no exception to that kaleidoscopic verbal aesthetic. With the help of the illuminating histories and textual studies of scholars such as Seligmann Baer (1825–1897), Israel Davidson (1870–1939), Ismar Elbogen (1874–1943), Louis Finklestein (1895–1991), Ezra Fleischer (1928–), Daniel Goldschmidt (1895–1972), Joseph Heinemann (1915–1978), Abraham J. Heschel (1907–1972), Lawrence Hoffman (1942–), Abraham Z. Idelsohn (1882–1938), Eliezer Landshuth (1817–1887), Jakob J. Petuchowski (1925–1991), Jefim (Hayyim) Schirmann (1904–1981), Eric Werner (1901–1979), and Leopold Zunz (1794–1886), one can easily see how the Prayerbook became, as it were, the Jew's resplendent cathedral surrogate.

Only a handful of the above have included the latterday adaptations of the Prayerbook within their purview. Those few have been more willing than the others to view the revision and layering of the past century and a half as modern counterparts to the liturgiographical achievements of the past: the ancient Rabbis' setting forth the structural groundwork of Jewish prayer after the collapse of the sacrificial system; the medievals' learned rhapsodies; the codifiers' regulations of tefillah, the Kabbalists' theurgical disciplines; and the folk expression of religious emotion among the Hasidim. Elbogen, Idelsohn, and Petuchowski broke much new ground in giving proper recognition to the more recent exertions on behalf of intellectual integrity, cultural congruity, group and individual self-redefinition and honest speech in Jewish prayer—all of which certainly form an equally legitimate area of study. It is hoped that our efforts here advance their efforts even further.

The work of research could never have been completed without the archival and bibliographical resources of the American Jewish Archives, Cincinnati; American Jewish Historical Society on the campus of Brandeis University; Leo Baeck College, London; Leo Baeck Institute, New York City; Boston Public Library; the library of the Harvard Divinity School; the library of the Hebrew [Teachers] College, Brookline; the Klau Libraries of the Hebrew Union College-Jewish Institute of Religion; the National Library of the Hebrew University, Jerusalem; the Library of Congress, Jewish Division; the Judah L. Magnes Memorial Museum, Berkeley; the library of the Jewish Theological Seminary; the New York Public Library, Jewish Division; and the Asher Library of the Spertus College of Judaica, Chicago. The tireless cooperation of their respective staffs is gratefully acknowledged. Many unexpected treasures turned up in synagogue libraries, such as those of Congregation Emanu-El of New York City; Temple Israel of Boston; Congregation Keneseth Israel of Philadelphia; Temple Oheb Shalom and Sinai Temple, both of Baltimore. Our thanks go to them as well.

But a special sense of indebtedness is naturally felt towards friends and colleagues who without stint provided gentle criticisms, helpful insights, and much needed prodding over the various stages of this work's composition. Let me here express my abiding gratitude to Mr. Yehuda Berger, of New York City, for ever pointing to the latest creative endeavors on the liturgical scene; Dr. David Ellenson, of the Hebrew Union College-Jewish Institute of Religion, Los Angeles, for his always heartening learned and collegial support; Dr. Shmuel Klatzkin, of Dayton, Ohio, for periodically calling to mind an overlooked halakhic usage and clarifying a Hasidic doctrine or practice; Professor Murray Lichtenstein, of Hunter college, for his unfailing sense as a *Wissenschaftgelernter* and poet; Professor Jonathan Magonet, co-editor of the Reform Synagogues of Great Britain's *Forms of Prayer* series, for generously illuminating its rationale and method; Rabbi John D. Rayner, prayerbook compiler extraordinary of British Liberal Judaism, for his graciously instructive pointers; Rabbi Chaim Stern, premier editor of the American Reform *Gates* series, for elucidating points of detail; Professor Richard Sarason, of the Hebrew Union College, Cincinnati, for being the main spur and stimulus behind the publication of this work; and Rabbi Victor and Eleanor Zwelling, of Dayton, Ohio, for their infectious love of Torah and wonderfully sustaining friendship.

My heartfelt thanks go to Wright State University, College of Liberal Arts, Dayton, which kindly furnished funds for optical scanning, and to the Jewish Federation of Greater Dayton, which helped defray the costs of typesetting the long Hebrew passages. The generosity of Dr. Alvin and Donna Denman, Dr. Ivan and Sonia Goldfarb, and Bruce and Fran Rickenbach funded the indices, which were expertly prepared by Lee Raubvogel. The patience and professionalism of two topnotch secretaries, Joanne Beirise, of the University of Dayton, Religious Studies Department, before her recent retirement, and Rebecca Steele, formerly of Wright State University, the Department of Religion, certainly should not go unmentioned.

I am grateful to Professor Michael A. Meyer, chair of the Publications Committee of the Hebrew Union College, for his clearheaded editorial judgment, and to Barbara Selya, managing editor of the HUC Press, whose diligence, ingenuity, and wit made all our labors light.

It was Ḥazzan Emeritus Gregor Shelkan, of Congregation Mishkan Tefila, Newton, Massachusetts, whose poignant cantorial renditions instilled within me, as a preteen, a lasting enchantment with the classical Jewish liturgy and the glorious music of the synagogue.

Finally, I cannot forget three influential teachers, *zikhronam li-verakhah.* Librarian Rabbi David Dagobert Nellhaus opened the world of books to me. Professor Nahum N. Glatzer demonstrated that the prayer texts of the Jewish people, in all lands and ages, are peerlessly *keley qodesh,* vessels of holiness. And Professor Jakob J. Petuchowski showed me in numberless ways that the liturgical undertaking today too has its valid and sacred place in the *seder tefillot yisra'el.*

Introduction:
Jewish Worship Since the
Time of Its Standardization

Even as one is continually aware of the timeless qualities of the Jewish Prayerbook through the centuries, there was hardly a time when it was not somehow in a state of flux. The Jews' worldwide wanderings may explain some of this liturgical malleability. Despite fidelity to, and pride in, a tradition that harks back to a past, immediate and remote, the Jewish people has tended generally to be open to new ways of approaching that venerable tradition, notably in eras and societies not given to restrictive or discriminatory excesses. This pattern in evident in the Middle Ages, given the qualifications mentioned, not much less than in our highly mobile, changeful age.

The High Middle Ages in France and Germany

Just as the liturgical compilations of Amram (ninth century),[1] Saadiah (882–942),[2] and Moses Maimonides (1135–1204)[3] in the East went a long way toward consolidating the labors of the past in the area of worship, so *Siddur Rashi*[4] (by Rabbi Solomon ben Isaac of Troyes [1040–1105]) and *Maḥzor Vitry*[5] (by Simḥah ben Samuel of Vitry [died before 1105], a leading disciple and possibly colleague of Rashi) were to pave the way for similar efforts in the West. While depending heavily upon earlier non-European efforts *(Seder Rav Amram* in particular), both *Siddur Rashi* and *Maḥzor Vitry* are indigenously Franco-German. Although *Siddur Rashi* provides only the halakhot for prayers, *Maḥzor Vitry* stipulates these rules and regulations and furnishes the prayer texts as well.

The high Middle Ages thus gave rise to a series of geographically specific volumes representative of regional rites, each known as a *minhag:* for instance, *minhag Rhinus* (the Rhineland rite) or *minhag Österreich (Böhm)* (the Austrian or Bohemian, i.e., eastern European, rite). These rites are generally conceptualized as belonging to larger families, particularly *minhag Sefarad* (the rite of the Iberian Peninsula) and *minhag Ashkenaz* (the rite of northern Europe). *Minhag Sefarad* eventually made its way throughout

I

the Mediterranean, via Jewish refugees from the Spanish Inquisition and Expulsion of 1492, just as *Minhag Ashkenaz* was carried by successive waves of Jewish migrants from western and central Europe to eastern centers like Poland and Russia.

The medieval period witnessed not only a gradual crystallization of the Prayerbook but also the composition of many new poetic works *(piyyutim)* beyond those written by perdurable Palestinian poets of the earlier Byzantine age such as Yannai and Kallir. Two types of *piyyut* that dominated the Ashkenazic orbit were the *selihah* (forgiveness), for penitential services,[6] and the *qinah* (lament), for days commemorating national or communal tragedies. These received their impetus in Italy and were developed in Jewish communities along the Rhine by the Kalonymide family, among others. Without doubt, the vulnerable position in which the Jews as a minority and as adherents of a despised faith found themselves—and their all too frequent persecution and martyrdom—were conducive to the mood and mindset responsible for the composition of such heartrending *selihot* and *qinot*.

Penitential piety reached its high point in eleventh- to thirteenth-century Germany in the movement known as German Hasidism *(hasidey ashkenaz),* which reinforced and deepened devotional life by intensifying and interiorizing Jewish moral teaching. Its founder, Judah ben Samuel he-Hasid ("the Pious"; died 1217), and his key disciple, Eleazar ben Judah of Worms (1165–1238), taught meditation, mystical prayer, and asceticism. Theurgy and theosophical speculation formed important parts of the belief system upheld by these pietists.

German Hasidic worship could be simple and direct at one moment and theologically complex the next. On the one hand, the value of simple, sincere prayer was recognized, as is attested by this moving utterance of the cowherd "who knew not how to pray":

> Master of the universe,
> It is revealed and known to Thee,
> That if you had cattle and gave them to me to tend
> For everyone else I tend expecting pay
> But for Thee I would tend for free
> Because I love Thee.[7]

The pietists would have had no difficulty endorsing that mystical aphorism: *tefillah beli kavvanah ke-guf beli neshamah* ("Prayer without sincere intention, or proper inwardness, is like a body without a soul").[8] On the other hand, they created a textured hymnody that shows both literary and theological sophistication, particularly in the Hymns of Unity *(shirey ha-yihud)* to be recited on successive days of the week. The best known of these, the Hymn of Glory *(shir ha-kavod)* also known as *ani'm zemirot* ("Sweet Hymns and Songs Will I Recite"),[9] is customarily sung in Orthodox synagogues towards the end of services on Saturday morning. Interestingly, the text of *ani'm zemirot is* found, in toto or in part, in the prayerbooks of every American non-Orthodox rite since the 1940s.

Unlike any other contemporary rite, traditional or otherwise, the 1945 edition of the Reform *Union Prayer Book* II reproduced, in English rendition, portions of the Hymn of Unity appointed for Sunday:[10]

How shall I come before God, the Most High? And how shall I bow before the God of old?

If the mountains were an altar, and all the wood of Lebanon laid thereon;

If all the cattle and all the beasts were slain, and lain as a sacrifice upon the wood;

All Lebanon would not suffice for fuel, nor all the beasts for burnt-offering—

Lo! all these were not enough to serve, to come therewith before the God of glory,

For Thou, our King, art exceedingly glorious; how then should we bow before our Lord?

Verily none living can honor Thee—how can I, Thy servant?

For Thou hast multiplied good things for me—For Thou hast magnified Thy mercy unto me.

Great are the debts I owe Thee for the good Thou hast wrought for me.

I have not served Thee in accordance with Thy benefits: one in ten thousand I have not repaid Thee.

If I say, I will declare their number, I know not how to count them.

And what shall I return unto Thee, seeing that Thine are the heavens, and the earth also is Thine?

It is written: I, the Lord, will not reprove thee for lack of sacrifices or thy burnt-offerings.

Concerning your sacrifices and your burnt-offerings I commanded not
    your fathers.
What have I asked, and what have I sought of thee but to fear Me?
To serve with joy and a good heart; behold, to hearken is better than to
    sacrifice,
And a broken heart than a whole offering. The sacrifices of God are a
    broken spirit.
I will build an altar of the broken fragments of my heart, and will bow
    my spirit within me.
My broken spirit—that is Thy sacrifice; let it be acceptable upon Thine
    altar.
I will proclaim aloud Thy praise; I will declare all Thy wonders.

The Influence of Kabbalah

The Jewish mystical tradition reached its culmination in the publication
of the Zohar, a major part of which was written in Spain pseudonymously
by Moses de Leon (1250–1305). The influence of the Zohar on the theology of prayer has been incalculable. One's "state of contemplation" during
the recitation of prayer was held to impinge inescapably upon the sephirotic realm of divine emanations, that is to say, upon the various manifes-
tations of divinity itself.[11] For all that, specific selections from this classic
of the Kabbalah are scarcely found in the Sephardic and Ashkenazic rites.
One rare example is the Aramaic *berikh shemeih* invoked in front of the
open ark before a Torah scroll is taken out for a public reading:[12]

> Blessed be the name of the Lord of the universe! Blessed be Thy
> crown and Thy dominion. May Thy good will ever abide with Thy
> people Israel. Reveal Thy saving power to Thy people in thy sanctu-
> ary; bestow on us the good gift of Thy light, and accept our prayer in
> mercy. May it be Thy will to prolong our life in happiness. Let me
> also be counted among the righteous, so that Thou mayest have com-
> passion on me and shelter me and mine and all that belong to Thy
> people Israel. Thou art He who nourishes and sustains all; Thou art
> He who rules over all; Thou art He who rules over kings, for domin-
> ion is thine. I am the servant of the Holy One, blessed be He, before

whom and before whose glorious Torah I bow at all times. Not in man do I put my trust, nor do I rely on any angel [literally: 'son of God'], but only in the God of heaven who is the God of truth, whose Torah is truth and whose Prophets are truth, and who performs many deeds of goodness and truth. In Him I put my trust, and to His holy and glorious name I utter praises. May it be Thy will to open my heart to Thy Torah, and to fulfill the wishes of my heart and the heart of all thy people Israel for happiness, life, and peace.[13]

The stage that followed the Zohar in the development of the Kabbalah, however, was to have a pivotal impact on Jewish worship. This stage came into being in Safed with the promulgation of the teachings of Isaac Luria (1534–1572), popularly known by the acronym of his name and title, *Ari*. We witness a breathtaking efflorescence not only of new mystical doctrines rooted in the Zohar and its antecedents but also of novel approaches to the standard liturgy and the creation of extraliturgical practices and hymnody. Luria was behind the institution of (1) special preparatory meditations called *kavvanot,* intended to induce the proper inner state in the worshiper so as to effectuate change on the cosmic level, and (2) *yihudim,* prayers designed to achieve "unity" among the manifold aspects of the Godhead, which kabbalistic theology held to have been fragmented in the process of God's creation of the cosmos. Luria set up nocturnal vigils *(tiqqun hatzot)* as well, particularly on the night of fateful occasions, one a semifestival and the other a major festival, Hoshana Rabbah and Shavuot, respectively. In addition, both he and his many disciples produced a rich store of hymns that in time were disseminated the world over. A surprising number of the Sabbath table songs that continue to enchant emanated from the Lurianic circle.

To give a slight idea of the style and attitude found in this eruption of postbiblical devotional prosody in the Hebrew language, we reproduce in the fairly literal translation of the *ArtScroll Siddur* a now-popular love song to God by a Safed Kabbalist in his own right and author of the important *Sefer Haredim,* Elazar ben Moses Azikri (1533–1600). Normally sung just prior to the commencement of the public worship on Shabbat Eve, the amatory hymn of longing and healing is called *yedid nefesh* ("Beloved of the Soul").[14] Its mystical significance lies in the fact that the four Hebrew letters beginning the four verses spell the sacrosanct four-letter name of God (YHVH). While reciting this love poem to God, the mystic concentrated on the four letters unifying the divine name and hoped that fragmented divinity itself would again be unified.

> Beloved of the soul, Compassionate Father, draw Your servant to Your will. Then Your servant will hurry like a hart to bow before Your majesty. To him Your friendship will be sweeter than the drippings of the honeycomb and any taste.
>
> Majestic, Beautiful, Radiance of the universe—my soul pines for Your love. Please, O God, heal her now by showing her the pleasantness of Your radiance. Then she will be strengthened and healed, and gladness will be hers.
>
> All-worthy One—may Your mercy be aroused and please take pity on the son of Your beloved, because it is so long that I have yearned intensely to see the splendor of Your strength. Only these my heart desired, so please take pity and do not conceal Yourself.
>
> Please be revealed and spread upon me, my Beloved, the shelter of Your peace. Illuminate the world with Your glory that we may rejoice and be glad with You. Hasten, show love, for the time has come, and show us grace as in days of old.

Polish Hasidism

During the first half of the eighteenth century in Poland, the Lurianic phase of the Kabbalah underwent a popularizing process. Kabbalah's elitism and esotericism were blunted; its teachings, streamlined and transformed, were brought to the masses. This new phase, Polish Hasidism—not to be confused with the earlier German Hasidism—was founded by Israel Ba'al Shem Tov (acronym: *Besht;* c. 1700–1760), who preached simplicity, fervor, and hope in the aftermath of the Chmielnicki massacres and the Sabbatean fiasco. In 1648 Chmielnicki had led a peasants' revolt that decimated the Jewish population in Poland. That same year the most famous of the medieval false messiahs, Shabbetay Zevi, had declared himself. In 1665 Shabbetay Zevi converted to Islam, crushing the hopes of Jews worldwide.

In the wake of these events, this new form of Hasidism invested prayer with new dimensions.[15] It offset, as well, the academic formalism of the

Lithuanian yeshivot and the inaccessibly arcane quality of Lurianic Kabbalah as it had evolved until the start of the eighteenth century. In its place, *hitlahavut* (enthusiasm) became a primary criterion for bona fide worship. One's heartfelt commitment and total involvement might be expressed in worship through somersaults, dance, zesty melodies, and the like. (Parallels in revitalization drawn from American religious history include such enthusiastic utopian-communitarian nineteenth-century movements as the Shakers.)

A crucial factor in the success and cohesiveness of the Hasidic movement was the emergence of the charismatic figure of the tzaddiq (the righteous one) or rebbe. Dynasties—"galaxies" might not be an inappropriate term—of such spiritual leaders appeared. Each rebbe in the generations succeeding the Besht had his own particular style and placed his unique stamp on his group or conventicle within the larger movement—all the while maintaining a recognizably common Hasidic mode. In his exquisite short manual of select Hasidic aphorisms, *Ten Rungs,* Martin Buber includes a modest number of penetrating statements on prayer (one of the "rungs") such as the following:

> This is how the words of prayer: "Hear us, when we call for help, hear our cries, Thou who knowest what is hidden," are expounded:
>
> We do not even know how we are supposed to pray. All we do is call for help because of the need of the moment. But what the soul intends is spiritual need, only we are not able to express what the soul means. That is why we do not merely ask God to hear our call for help, but also beg Him, who knows what is hidden, to hear the silent cry of the soul.[16]

Buber also includes this poignant reworking of the ancient Rabbinic version of the Parable of the Prodigal Son:[17]

> A king's son rebelled against his father and was banished from the sight of his face. After a time, the king was moved to pity for his fate and bade his messengers go and search for him. It was long before one of the messengers found him—far from home. He was at a village inn, dancing barefoot and in a torn shirt in the midst of drunken peasants. The courtier bowed and said: "Your father has sent me to ask you what you desire. Whatever it may be, he is prepared to

grant your wish." The prince began to weep. "Oh," said he, "if only I had warm clothing and a pair of stout shoes!"

See, that is how we whimper for the small needs of the hour and forget that the Glory of God is in exile!

Two of the premier tzaddiqim, Shneur Zalman of Liadi (founder of the highly visible Lubavitcher group) and Naḥman of Bratslav, developed well-defined approaches to Hasidism and hence towards prayer and the accompanying inner preparations. The Lubavitcher rebbe combined mainstream kabbalistic thought, particularly its Lurianic phase, with the staunch philosophical endeavors of Moses Maimonides. This intellectualist brand of mysticism is much in evidence in Shneur Zalman's treatment of prayer and *kavvanah* in his *Tanya*.[18] Naḥman of Bratslav, on the other hand, though certainly no antinomian or nonconformist when it came to statutory prayers and ritual observances, broke new ground, both in what he encouraged and in what he did himself. Solitude *(hitbodedut)* in prayer, especially in a rustic setting, received a fresh emphasis; so did spontaneous prayer in the vernacular, in this case Yiddish, touching on matters of immediate, pressing concern to the individual.[19] Some of his deepfelt extraliturgical private meditations, as recorded by his key disciple and amanuensis, Nathan of Nemirov, have, not surprisingly, found their way into the most recent official prayer books of the Reform and Conservative movements in the United States[20] and their counterparts in Great Britain. In its "Passages for Silent Devotion," for example, the editors of the British Reform *Forms of Prayers for Jewish Worship* included this example of Naḥman's outpourings of the soul:[21]

My Father in heaven,
Save and help me from this moment to be in the fields every night . . .
To cry to You from the depths of my heart . . .
To set forth all the burdens and negations that remove me from You,
    Light of Life,
And give strength to strengthen myself in spite of everything—
With happiness that has no end,
Until my heart lifts up my hands to clap, to clap, to clap, and my legs
    to dance until the soul swoons, swoons.
And help me ever make a new beginning and to be a flowering well of
    Torah and prayer,

To work always with quickened spirit,
And to stand with powerful strength against the scoffers and mockers,
Who go about in our days—days of double darkness . . .
But oh, against all the troubles and burdens,
Your joys and Your delights are strong and powerful . . .
O, our great Father, home of delights and wellspring of joy.

Reform in Germany

Meanwhile, in eighteenth- and nineteenth-century central and western Europe, Jewish communities underwent their own earth-shattering changes. The French Revolution and ensuing Emancipation from the ghettos in major cities freed Jews from concomitant medieval disabilities. While the lifting of former restrictions was obviously a welcome turnaround, it was not without hazard. A goodly number of Jews felt ineluctably attracted to the cultural and religious values of the non-Jewish society to which they were newly exposed, and the traditions in which they had been reared paled by comparison. There were those who shucked their ancestral ways completely. Others knew that concessions of various kinds and degrees were going to have to be made if Jewish identity was to be maintained and Judaism to survive. Reform became the catchword of the day; and no segment of Jewry in western or central Europe remained untouched. Even Orthodoxy was profoundly affected.[22] Theology, prayer, and styles of worship were thus enormously reshaped by historical and socioeconomic events from the close of the seventeenth century throughout the nineteenth.[23]

One of the byproducts of the Emancipation was the introduction of liturgical scholarship in a new key. No longer were prayer texts commented upon solely with devotional or homiletical intent. Critical tools now came to be applied for the triple purpose of ascertaining the correct text, determining its historical background, and finding out the actual intended meaning of each prayer unit. At the forefront of such endeavors were the grammarians/copyists/expositors Wolf Heidenheim (1757–1832), Eliezer Landshuth (1817–1887), and Seligmann Baer (1825–1897). And the first to put liturgiology on a sure scientific footing was the luminary Leopold Zunz, whose path-blazing works are still very much in use.[24]

At the same time, a small group of Jews in Hamburg introduced changes of public worship by (1) abridging prayers, particularly the medieval accretions (many of which were no longer understood), (2) according a prominent place to the vernacular alongside (or occasionally in place of) the Hebrew, and (3) introducing the organ and choir, as part of a larger effort to transform Jewish worship into a model of western decorum. The synagogue they established was the Hamburg Temple (1817), where they introduced what is generally referred to as the Hamburg *Gebetbuch* (Hamburg, 1819).

The next generation, marked as it was by rabbis who had joined the laity in its Reform cause, was dissatisfied with piecemeal practical reforms and sought to revise the Prayerbook according to theologically consistent principles in addition to contemporary aesthetic sensibilities. The deliberations of the progressively-minded 1840s Rabbinic Conferences on matters of liturgy and halakhah provided helpful guidelines to rabbis and congregations.[25] By then the lines were clearly drawn from left to right: (I) the extreme Reform position articulated by the *Reformgemeinde* in Berlin and its eventual pastor Samuel Holdheim, (2) the moderate, gradualist Reform—or, as the term came to be, Liberal—one formulated by the likes of Leopold Stein and Abraham Geiger, (3) the Conservative stance adhered to by Michael Sachs, Zacharias Frankel, and Manuel Joel, and (4) Neo-Orthodoxy, created by Samson Raphael Hirsch.

Reform in North America

In the middle of the nineteenth century, the second major wave of Jewish immigration to the United States was comprised largely of those fleeing persecution from German-speaking lands. Many brought with them their reforming tendencies, and their rabbis sought to implement the new ideas concerning worship that had sprouted on European soil. They ranged from moderate Reform (Leo Merzbacher, Adolph Huebsch, Isaac Mayer Wise) to traditionalist Reform, or what I would call *proto-Conservative* (Benjamin Szold, Marcus Jastrow, Alexander Kohut, and Aaron Wise) to enlightened Orthodox (Isaac Leeser and Sabato Morais).

The bold and principled David Einhorn was a notable exception to the nearly universal temperate tendency in American Jewish liturgy at the time. Believing that compromising with Orthodoxy would be fatal to Judaism in the long run, Einhorn composed his brilliantly restructured prayerbook, *Olath Tamid,* which synthesizes the theology, ritual consensus, and aesthetics of Reform in a truly astonishing fashion. Chapter one fully analyzes that work and places it in the context of its liturgical predecessors.

Rejecting Einhorn's elitism, Isaac M. Wise proved himself the pragmatist in drafting a rite, *Minhag Amerika,* that would appeal to a broad spectrum of non-Orthodox views as they pertained to belief, choice of language during public worship, ritual observance, and liturgical preference. Chapter two considers those features in *Minhag Amerika* that rendered it unique among non-Orthodox prayerbooks. A generation later, in the 1890s, the time was ripe to venture a single liturgy for all Reform congregations in the United States. Isaac S. Moses, who in the course of his long rabbinic career used a variety of revised prayerbooks, including those by Einhorn and Wise, laid the foundation for the amalgamated rite in the form of a draft. Kaufmann Kohler, son-in-law of David Einhorn and premier theologian of the Reform movement at the turn of the century, served as chief editor of the 1895 publication. He and the others on its editorial commission worked with Moses's draft, combining the best features of *Olath Tamid* and *Minhag Amerika* (and others as well) to create the *Union Prayer Book,* which became the longest-lasting non-Orthodox rite anywhere in the world.

In another direction, while loyal to the rhythms and ambience of the traditional service, proto-Conservative Marcus Jastrow took discrete editorial and translational liberties with predecessor/collaborator Benjamin Szold's more traditional *Abodath Israel* to reflect more expressly the American scene and mood at the time, sociologically and politically as well as theologically. Chapter three explores Jastrow's philosophy, methods, and aims in that important undertaking.

Hebrew Creativity

One of the many traits shared by the majority of the prayerbook revisers throughout the nineteenth century—when philology reigned supreme— was their facility with the Hebrew language. With discerning eyes for alternative classical texts (biblical, Rabbinic, and medieval) that accorded with contemporary literary, ethical, and religious sensibilities and framed new prayers in the sacred tongue, they skillfully retouched the transmitted liturgical text to make it consistent with their modified doctrinal outlook. The era marked an extraordinary burst of American Hebrew creativity in an unexpected quarter. Chapter four explores that period of intensive Hebrew liturgical creativity, providing examples of its most successful applications. One of the most fascinating is the focus of chapter six—a little known revision of the ubiquitous *eyn k-eloheynu* hymn by Leo Merzbacher, the moderate Reformer who served as rabbi at what is now New York's Temple Emanu-El in the 1840s and 50s.

Robust Hebrew creativity was at the same time also evidenced in the liturgy of British Reform. Examining examples of that rite's consistent and largely successful efforts to pen new prayers in Hebrew rather than in the vernacular, chapter five traces the development of the British rite from the movement's founding in 1841 to the present day, focusing as well on its Anglican influences and creedal modulations.

Theology in the Maḥzor

The High Holyday maḥzor is undoubtedly the primary rite to which the majority of today's Jews are exposed—thus justifying the tremendous expenditure of time, effort, and talent that goes into the preparation of these manuals. Further, I would suggest, these rituals for the Days of Awe provide an accurate glimpse of how Jewish communitites here and abroad experience the sacred, cogitate on the deeper issues of life, and communicate with God. Chapter seven explores in depth the nineteenth-century American Yizkor Services by Merzbacher, Einhorn, Wise, Huebsch, and Krauskopf, on the Reform side, and those by Szold and Jastrow on the Positive-Historical (later to become Conservative) school. In briefer fashion the twentieth-century Conservative, Reform, and Reconstructionist High Holy Day Memorial Services in their various stages are considered, with revealing comparisons drawn with their nineteenth-century antecedents.

Also dealing with the *yamim nora'im,* chapter eight focuses on the *Gates of Repentance* (1978) and its companion commentary, *Gates of Understanding* (1984), to observe the shifts in late twentieth-century theological and ethnic commitment. In doing so, it traces some of the ways in which certain basic prayers or sections of the High Holy Day liturgy came to be as they are.

Not long after the appearance of the standard maḥzorim of the North American Conservative and Reform movements in the seventies, the Reform Synagogues of Great Britain and the Movement for Progressive Judaism in Israel issued their respective High Holy Day prayer manuals, *Seder ha-Tefillot, Forms of Prayer for Jewish Worship: Prayers for the High Holy-days* (1985) and *Kavvanat ha-Lev* ("Devotion of the Heart") (1989). Chapter nine shows how both liturgies, sharing common features, bear the unmistakable imprint of the American rites. At the same time, it highlights those areas in the layout, content, theological orientation, literary quality, and mood of the two maḥzorim that reflect their dissimilar liturgical sensibilities.

The Denominational Siddur

By the end of the nineteenth century, siddur production moved increasingly out of the congregational sphere into the denominational orbit. Much is revealed sociohistorically and theologically about a religious movement by the ways in which a denominational prayerbook takes shape over the course of time. Chapters ten through twelve focus on three of these prayerbooks. *The Gates of Prayer* is considered in the context of its earlier American (and British) influences, then evaluated critically to determine where it succeeded and where it fell short in that collective endeavor of the American Reform rabbinate

Similarly, ever since their *Shir Ḥadash* (1939) and *New Hagaddah* (1942), the Reconstructionists have been at the forefront of liturgical creativity, willing to try the new and unventured while reactivating material long forgotten. Chapter eleven examines its latest siddurim, *Kol Hane-shamah for Shabbat Eve* (1989), *Kol Haneshamah for Shabbat Vehagim* (1994), and *Kol Haneshamah: Daily Prayer Book* (1996), and evaluates their success in meeting the twin challenges of their considerable legacy and the demands of the last decades of the twentieth century.

Relying on their own resources and on the liturgical creativity of their American and British counterparts, Israeli religious progressives issued a noteworthy siddur of their own in 1982, *Ha-Avodah sheba-Lev.* Chapter twelve traces that rite's liturgical influences and analyzes its structural approach and its stance on, among others, issues of gender, the Diaspora, and the ultimate Redemption.

Thematic Studies

In treating Liberal Jewish liturgies thematically, the final five chapters survey both nineteenth and twentieth-century prayerbooks for those commonalities and divergences that determine the state and direction of liturgical change. Chapter thirteen sheds light on the early attraction to certain Sephardic features in text and conduct of worship within the non-Orthodox branches of American Judaism. Chapter fourteen traces the changing stance of Progressive prayerbooks toward the mystical component in the Jewish tradition. Recognizing that the need for a more intimate relationship with God is an ongoing one, liturgical revisers have been reevaluating the merit of their rich kabbalistic legacy and reappropriating many an abandoned prayer in the newer rites, often with good results.

More problematic are those areas where traditional attitudes conflict with modern sensibilities. Chapter fifteen examines Reform, Conservative, Reconstructionist, and Polydox haggadot to trace what non-Orthodox Jews, both observant and non-observant, have asserted concerning the age-old messianic hope that informs the haggadah, especially those sections that by design resonate messianically—the *ha laḥma anya,* the Cup of Elijah, and the *nirtzah* at the close of the Seder. Chapter sixteen questions the appropriateness of the collective desire for vengeance (*neqamah*) expressed at irregular intervals in sources ranging from the Bible to the newest post-Holocaust siddurim. And chapter seventeen explores liturgical approaches to the commemoration of the Ninth of Av, suggesting that even an ancient fastday can recover relevance, credibility, and authenticity for Liberal Jews in the postmodern era.

An earlier version of the first part of this chapter appeared in *The Making of Jewish and Christian Worship,* ed. Paul F. Bradshaw and Lawrence A. Hoffman. © 1991 by the University of Notre Dame Press. Reprinted by permission.

1. See A. L. Frumkin, *Seder Rav Amram ha-Shalem* (Jerusalem, 1912); E. D. Gold-schmidt, *Seder Rav Amram Gaon* (Jerusalem, 1971).

2. See Israel Davidson, Simhah Assaf, and B. I. Joel, eds., *Siddur Rav Saadja Gaon . . .* (Jerusalem, 1963).

3. See E. D. Goldschmidt, ed., *Seder Tefillah shel ha-Rambam al pi Ketav-Yad Oxford,* from the seventh volume of the *Makhon le-Ḥeqer ha-Shirah ha-Ivrit* (Jerusalem, 5719 [1959]), pp. 158–213; Jacob I. Dienstag, "The Prayer Book of Moses Maimonides," in Menahem Kasher, ed., *The Leo Jung Jubilee Volume* (New York, 1962), pp. 53–63.

4. See Solomon Buber and J. Freimann, eds., *Siddur Raschi* (Berlin, 1911); reprint ed. (Jerusalem, 1963).

5. See Simḥah ben Samuel, *Maḥzor Vitry,* ed. S. Hurwitz (Nuremberg, 1923); E. D. Goldschmidt, *"Nusaḥ ha-Tefillot shel Maḥzor Vitry lefi Ketav-Yad Reggio,"* in *Meḥqarei Tefillah u-Fiyyut* (Jerusalem, 1979), pp. 66–79.

6. See Abraham Rosenfield, ed., *The Authorized Selichot for the Whole Year,* 2d ed. (London, 1957). It was of such heartfelt collective outpourings that Leopold Zunz remarked in his *Die synagogale Poesie des Mittelalters* (Berlin, 1855), as translated in the Conservative *Sabbath and Festival Prayer Book* (1946): "If there are ranks in suffering, Israel takes precedence of all the nations: if the duration of sorrows and the patience with which they are borne ennoble, the Jews can challenge the aristocracy of every land; if a literature is called rich in the possession of a few classic tragedies—what shall we say to a National Tragedy lasting fifteen hundred years, in which the poets and the actors were also the heroes?"

7. The prayer of the uneducated cowherd in *Sefer Ḥasidim* may be found in Nahum N. Glatzer, *Language of Faith* (New York, 1967), pp. 72–73.

8. Isaiah Horowitz, *Sheney Luḥot ha-Berit* I, 249b.

9. Jakob J. Petuchowski, "Speaking of God," *Theology and Poetry: Studies in Medieval Piyyut* (London, 1978), pp. 31–47.

10. The individual Hymns of Unity for Sunday through Friday may be found, with helpful explanation, in Seligmann Baer, *Avodat Yisrael* (Roedelheim, 1868, repr. ed. 1937), pp. 133–49. As yet there is, regrettably, no complete English rendition of all of the *shirey ha-yiḥud,* perhaps because, practically speaking, there is so little time on regular workday mornings to give them the full devotional concentration they amply deserve. A continuing desideratum is a translation of all these wonderfully luminous/numinous hymns into an English that captures at least a fraction of the layered meaning contained in the Hebrew.

11. See Isaiah Tishby, ed., *Pirkey Zohar* II (Jerusalem, 1969), pp. 79–144.

12. The Aramaic prayer, *berikh shemeih,* has this rubric before it: "Rabbi Shimon said, 'When they take the Torah scroll out in the congregation for reading therein, the heavenly gates of compassion are opened and they arouse love above, and one is requested to say this: "Blessed be His name etc." until "for life and for peace"' (Zohar, *parashat vayaqhel,* 369). Another, less familiar Aramaic passage is *ke-gavna de-innun* on Shabbat Eve before the *barakhu* (Zohar, *parashat terumah,* 163b)

13. The translation here is by Philip Birnbaum, *Ha-Siddur ha-Shalem: The Daily Prayer Book* (New York, 1949). For a discussion of the indirect polemic concerning a major tenet of the Christian faith contained in *berikh shemeih,* see Daniel Chanan Matt, *Zohar: The Book of Enlightenment,* Classics of Western Spirituality (Mahwah, NJ, 1983), pp. 18-19.

14. Nosson Scherman, *Siddur Imrey Ephraim: The Complete ArtScroll Siddur* (New York, 1985), pp. 340–41. See the present-day Conservative *Siddur Sim Shalom* (New York, 1985), pp. 252–53, and the Reconstructionist *Kol Haneshamah: Shabbat Eve* (Wyncote, PA, 1989), pp. 8–11, for a mellisonant and perhaps more evocative if not quite so literal English versification by Zalman Schachter-Shalomi (reproduced in chap. 12, p. 248) Cf. the bit more literal but degenderized rendition in the Reform *Gates of Prayer* (New York, 1975), p. 159.

15. Perhaps the best comprehensive scholarly treatment of the subject of prayer in Hasidism is Louis Jacobs, *Hasidic Prayer* (New York, 1973). For a summary of the differences between the prayer-centered Hasidim and the learning-centered Mitnaggedim, see Norman Lamm, "Study and Prayer: Their Relative Value in Hasidism and Misnagdism," in *Samuel K. Mirsky Memorial Volume* (Jerusalem and New York, 1970), pp. 37–52.

16. Martin Buber, "The Rung of Prayer," *Ten Rungs* (New York, 1947), pp. 27–33.

17. For the original Rabbinic story, see *Pesikta Rabbati* 184b-185a; one translation of it appears in Claude G. Montefiore and Herbert Loewe, eds., *A Rabbinic Anthology* (Cleveland, New York, and Philadelphia, (repr. 1963), p. 321, no. 835.

18. Shneur Zalman, *Likkutey Amarim {Tanya}*, trans. Nissan Mindel, I (New York, 1972), ch. 38, pp. 224–32, for example. The recovery of the intellectual strain should not by any means be taken to mean any outright rejection of feeling. It was, after all, the same Zalman who prayed, "My Lord and God, I do not desire Your paradise; I do not desire the bliss of the world to come; I desire only You Yourself."

19. Nathan of Nemirov, *Rabbi Nachman's Wisdom,* ed. Zvi Aryeh Rosenfeld, trans. Aryeh Kaplan (Brooklyn, NY, 1973), pp. 9–16, 179–82, 305–7.

20. E.g., the same entreaty for peace in *Gates of Prayer,* p. 694, and in *Siddur Sim Shalom,* pp. 416–17. All of the moving supplications by the Bratslaver rebbe in the present abovementioned American Reform and Conservative rites come from his *Liqqutey Tefillot,* ed. Nathan Sternhartz of Nemirov, via the British Liberal *Service of the Heart,* ed. John Rayner and Chaim Stern (London, 1967), p. 282; and Glatzer, *Language of Faith,* pp. 314–15.

21. Lionel Blue and Jonathan Magonet, eds., *Forms of Prayers for Jewish Worship* (London, 1977), p. 349.

22. Hardy protagonist of Orthodoxy as Hirsch was, he was scarcely immune to all the arguments of his Reform coevals. In his synagogues he introduced a choir (all male, as would be expected, and without musical instruments) and, provoking a good bit of controversy, did away with the sacrosanct Kol Nidrey formula chanted on Yom Kippur Eve. He strongly endorsed the classical Reform doctrine of the Mission of Israel to all humankind. See Noah H. Rosenbloom, *Tradition in an Age of Reform* (Philadelphia, 1976), pp. 69–70.

23. The authoritative history of Reform Judaism is Michael A. Meyer, *Response to Modernity* (New York and Oxford, 1988).

24. Leopold Zunz, *Die synagogale Poesie;* and idem, *Die Ritus des synagogalen Gottesdienstes* (Berlin, 1859), among others.

25. The best—and only—detailed survey of all the Reform, Liberal, and Progressive liturgies in Europe since their beginnings is Jakob J. Petuchowski, *Prayerbook Reform in Europe* (New York, 1968).

1

David Einhorn and *Olath Tamid*

Kaufmann Kohler, David Einhorn's illustrious son-in-law and a preeminent figure in American Reform Judaism at the turn of the century, spoke of the author of *Olath Tamid* as "the uncompromising champion of Reform."[1] An adulatory tribute, the phrase does to a large degree encapsulate Einhorn's zestful and tumultuous career as preacher, liturgist, editor, controversialist, abolitionist, and leading theoretician of American Reform.

Born in Dispeck, a small village in Bavaria, on November 10, 1809, Einhorn came under the tutelage of Rabbis Wolf Hamburger and Joshua Moses Falkenau at the famed yeshivah of Fürth, where many of the leading German rabbis of the century received their training. He obtained his *morenu* diploma at the age of seventeen and later attended the Universities of Würzburg and Munich, where the ideas of Friedrich Schelling, the German Romantic philosopher, were in vogue. The impact of the secular and academic world became evident in Einhorn's mounting attraction to liberal principles in political and philosophical, as well as religious, spheres. His adoption of those principles and his steady demand for intellectual and theological rigor soon involved him in controversy, even before he assumed his post as *Landesrabbiner* (district rabbi) in Birkenfeld in 1842. During his tenure at Birkenfeld, Einhorn participated in the last two of the *Rabbinerversammlungen* of the middle 1840s: in the Frankfurt-am-Main Conference, as member of the commission on liturgy; and in the Breslau Conference, as chair of the commission on the dietary laws and as referee for the commissions on the Sabbath and on the status of women. In both conferences he made known his liberal views, particularly with regard to the use of the vernacular and the inclusion of the sacrificial cult, the levitical rites, Zion, and messianism in the liturgy.[2] It was at that time that he announced his position on the Sabbath, regarding it as a more authentic *ot*—sign or embodiment of the Covenant—than *milah,* since women are not left out of the observance of the former institution.[3]

Einhorn acceded in 1847 to the post of chief rabbi vacated by Samuel Holdheim in Mecklenburg-Schwerin[4] and in 1849 was recommended by Holdheim[5] to serve the Reform congregation at Budapest, where his religious and political views aroused the suspicions of the Austrian govern-

ment and the opposition of the Orthodox.[6] The result was the closing of
the Reform synagogue in 1852 and an enforced leisure for Einhorn, during
which he wrote the first volume of his formative *Prinzip des Mosaismus und
dessen Verhältnis zum Heidenthum und rabbinischen Judenthum* (Leipzig, 1854).

Even in his beloved America, on whose shores he landed in 1855 to
assume the pulpit of the Reform Har Sinai *Verein* in Baltimore, Einhorn
was to arouse controversy because of his convictions. Not long after his
arrival, he entered the fray with his rejection of the platform of the 1855
Cleveland Conference convened by Isaac M. Wise, Max Lilienthal, and
others for the purpose of striking a modus vivendi with the traditionalist
camp. Since the Talmud was to act as the standard and, thus, a bond of
unity, Einhorn and like-minded colleagues rose in arms and staunchly
refused to yield on principle. This opposition marked the beginning of a
rift in the Reform movement that lasted until virtually the end of the
nineteenth century, when people like Einhorn's spiritual successor, Kaufmann Kohler, with pen and in person, performed a labor of reconciliation
between the Einhorn and Wise factions.[7] And back in Baltimore, the congregation that gave Einhorn free rein to experiment in the area of theoretical and practical Reform (including the publication of *Olath Tamid* and the
outspoken monthly *Sinai),* tactfully denied him freedom of the pulpit on
the slavery question.[8]

The innovative years of Einhorn's life work in the rabbinate reached an
apex in Baltimore. They were followed by an anticlimactic period (aside
from his active part in the Philadelphia Conference of 1869) beginning in
1861, when he fled from Baltimore for his pro-abolition stance and
assumed the pulpit at Kenesseth Israel in Philadelphia. In 1866 he left
that position for Adath Yeshurun of New York City, where he served until
his death on November 2, 1879.

The impression generally gained from such a cursory review of Einhorn's life is that of an unbendingly consistent, intrepid reformer. It is
important to bear in mind, however, that terminological connotations do
shift and today's radical could easily turn into tomorrow's conservative—
and vice versa. Hence, Einhorn's reforming career calls for closer scrutiny,
reassessment or, at the very least, some qualification. For instance, he
labeled the platform of the Frankfurt *Reformverein, the* radical Jewish group
within Germany in 1843, as a "confession of unbelief."[9] Despite his aver-

sion to making the Talmud the norm,[10] as proposed at the Cleveland Conference, Einhorn was clearly no Karaizing anti-Talmudist. His declaration

> However strong our belief in [the Talmud's] veracity may be, we must refuse and reject such deification; we address the Talmud in these words, "Israel believes thee, but not in thee; thou art a medium through which the divine may be reached, but thou art not divine"[11]

should be proof enough of that. Einhorn was no uncritical supporter of Holdheim's conception of the Sabbath as merely symbolic. Nor was he as ready, as his elder colleague was, to permit any transfer of the day to Sunday.[12] Moreover, intermarriage was plain anathema.[13]

As the few examples above suggest, and the analysis of his liturgical work to follow will attest, the Reform Einhorn strove to cultivate was an expansive and open-minded one that invariably grounded itself in and presupposed an undiminished concern for form and structure. The edifice of Judaism was to be refurbished inside and out, according to given specifications and carefully thought-out criteria, so that it might truly and resplendently abide until the messianic time. An examination of Einhorn's magnum opus, *Olath Tamid,* should help clarify this approach.[14]

The Title

It is unusual for a title of a Reform prayerbook to bear the sacrificial, cultic overtones that *Olath Tamid* does. Siddurim would often carry titles indicating authorship *(Tzelota de-Avraham),* place of origin *(Maḥzor Vitry),* or simply the fact that this was a prayerbook *(Hegyon Lev).* Less common, particularly among Liberal prayer manuals, was the use of a title pertaining to the ancient Temple worship—*e.g. Qorban Yehudah* or *Olat Re'ayah.* What, then, moved Einhorn to utilize the unmistakably cultic "continual burnt offering" for the designation of his liturgical work?

The answer lies in Einhorn's theory of Mosaism in contradistinction to Rabbinism, as presented in his aforementioned *Das Prinzip des Mosaismus.* Einhorn drew a sharp line of demarcation between the Mosaic cult, which is of only passing, pedagogic, and symbolic value, and the Mosaic theology and ethics, which comprise eternal truths. For Einhorn—and for Isaac M.

Wise, too—the revelation at Sinai was a real and epoch-making event, even though the scriptural details depicting it are peripheral, subsidiary to the momentous encounter between God and Israel. Those details, however, serve to illuminate both the physical and spiritual implications of that event in the life of the people.

Einhorn was in touch with the findings of biblical criticism of his time and not at all averse to integrating its results in his system. But they did not impinge upon what was for him the Pentateuch's unshakeable core, the central phenomenon of the revelation at Sinai and the concomitant determination of Israel's destiny. The Torah was fundamentally and manifestly the word of God,[15] to be revered as a reliable testimony of Israel's divine appointment.

This reverence is attested in Einhorn's craftsmanlike handling of biblical texts in the course of his sermons and in his original prayers. The triennial cycle adhered to in Einhorn's congregation covered the entire contents of the Pentateuch just as the one-year cycle does, in contrast to the haphazard, faulty reading of snippets that obtains in many Reform temples today. For Einhorn and his nineteenth-century confreres, the Torah was clearly divinely ordained, and the sacrifices mentioned in Torah could not be irreverently tossed out as utterly worthless.[16] The third article of the Philadelphia Conference's platform reads:

> The priestly service of the Aaronites and the Mosaic sacrificial cult were only preparatory steps for the true priestly service of the whole people which in fact began with the dispersion of the Jewish nation. For inner devotion and ethical sanctification are the only pleasing sacrifices to the All-Holy One. These institutions which laid the groundwork for higher religiosity went out of existence once and for all when the second Temple was destroyed. And only in this sense have they educational value and may they be mentioned in our prayer.[17]

In a similar vein, Einhorn's choice of the phrase is informed by the hope he harbored—that his prayerbook would aid the worshiper in rendering a *Ganzopfer,* a perfect offering most pleasing to God. The other sacrifices, such as the peace-offering, were only partially consumed upon the altar, the remainder to be eaten by the priests and the one who brought the offering. Only the *olah* was to be completely consumed on the altar, "an offering by fire of pleasing odor unto the Lord." So were man's offerings of the heart to be free of admixture, of deception—*tamim yaqrivenu.* It was Einhorn's wish that his prayerbook, stripped of anything that might be found objectionable, no longer tenable, or conflicting with the deep-seated beliefs of the modern Jew, would prove a true *olah.*

It is perhaps also significant that the name by which Einhorn's Baltimore congregation chose to designate itself was *Har Sinai.*[18] The "perpetual offering" described in the biblical citation (Numbers 28:6) that Einhorn selected for his epigraph was presented on Mount Sinai. His title, then, might also have been an affectionate, though indirect, reference to that congregation.

In the structuring of his new rite, Einhorn had several earlier efforts before him to serve as guides. He used the 1819 Hamburg Temple *Gebetbuch* and Holdheim's 1848 *Gebetbuch für jüdische Reformgemeinden* as practical and concrete models and Leopold Zunz's *Die gottesdienstliche Vorträge* as a theoretical model.

Borrowings from the Hamburg Gebetbuch

As in the Hamburg Temple *Gebetbuch,* the pagination of *Olath Tamid* is from left to right (and not from right to left as in the traditional Prayerbook), and all the services of the year are contained within one volume— beginning with the Sabbath, on through the Festivals, the New Year, the Day of Atonement, and the weekday, and terminating with matrimony, funerals, and a triennial lectionary. Unlike the *Gebetbuch,* however, *Olath Tamid* omits circumcision. The Mecklenburg controversy with Franz Delitzsch in 1847 over the sine qua non character of *berit milah* may or may not explain the absence of the initiatory rite from the Einhorn work. On the other hand, services for confirmation and the admission of proselytes, both nonexistent in the *Gebetbuch,* gain prominence in *Olath Tamid.* And whereas the Hamburg book provides for the Ninth of Av service, complete with *eli tziyyon ve-areha, Olath Tamid* offers a novel service embodying Einhorn's understanding of the day as the Messiah's birthday.[19]

To give prominence to the Morning Services, Einhorn places all Evening Services towards the end of his volume—except those for Rosh Hashanah and Yom Kippur. Although the compilers of the Hamburg *Gebetbuch* modified the traditional sequence when they put the Sabbath and Festival services at the beginning of the book—as Einhorn also did—they introduced these sections with *arvit* or the Evening Service. (For daily worship, however, the German revisers started, as in the Orthodox siddur, with *shaharit* or the Morning Service, and ended with *arvit.*)

As envisioned in *Olath Tamid,* Simḥat Torah was to be celebrated once every three years, in accordance with the triennial cycle of Torah readings. Einhorn's *Ausheben* (taking out of the Torah) for the Festival is but a slight modification of the Hamburg version. It begins with the chanting of Psalm 24:9–10. The lesson is followed by the choral singing of Psalm 150 and the Reader's recital of Joshua 1:8–9 in Hebrew. Apparently Einhorn forgot that these verses from Joshua were chosen for special recital in the Hamburg Temple *Gebetbuch,* since that book provided for no haftarot. Inasmuch as he calls for the reading of Joshua 1 as the prophetic reading after the Genesis lesson, these added sentences are redundant.[20]

Borrowings from Holdheim's Prayerbook[21]

Although Einhorn regarded Holdheim's *Gebetbuch* as too nonconformist and arbitrary,[22] the idea of a separate service for each of the Pilgrimage Festivals, the dropping of the *musaf,* and the limitation of the Yom Kippur *amidot* to three (for the Evening, Morning and *ne'ilah* Services only), all owe their origins to the Berlin manual. This is not to say that Einhorn went as far as Holdheim in emptying the interval between the Morning and *ne'ilah* sections.[23] On the contrary, Einhorn found suitable replacements for the *musaf* and *minhah* repetitions, without necessitating the long afternoon recess.

Einhorn emulated Holdheim's brevity. The focus of the Berlin prayerbook upon the Shema and the *amidah,* with newly-composed paragraphs before the Intermediate Benediction, also occurs in *Olath Tamid.* But on the whole, Einhorn proceeded with caution compared with Holdheim's unrestrained editing of the old *seder.* In cases where restructuring served no purpose except to satisfy the tastes or whims of a given congregation, it was to be avoided. Not only was it disruptive, but many more links with universal Israel would be severed. But when innovation enhanced the familiar order, Einhorn raised no serious objection. Of this latter type is Holdheim's shift of *ashreynu mah tov* from the early morning Shema to the statutory Shema, lending further dramatic emphasis to the cardinal tenet of Judaism. Einhorn followed Holdheim's example with a significant change, typical of the former's sense of Israel's mission.

From:

Und so ist es an uns, Dir zu danken, Dich zu preisen und zu verherrlichen. Heil uns, wie schön ist unser Theil, wie glücklich unser Loos, wie beseligend unser Erbtheil. Heil uns, die wir ausrufen:

to :

Heil uns, den Priestern Deiner Lehre! Wie schön ist unser Theil, wie glücklich unser Loos, wie beseligend unser Erbe, Heil uns, die wir ausrufen: . . .

[In the Einhorn/Felsenthal rendition it comes out as] Happy are we, the priests of thy law [*Lehre* is, however, *teaching,* not *law*]; beautiful is our portion, charming our lot, and blissful our inheritance; happy are we who proclaim: Hear, O, Israel . . . [This is, of course a subtle but significant adaptation of *ashreynu mah tov ḥelqenu*]

A matter of conjecture is whether either liturgiographer was aware of the corresponding introduction to the Shema in the Septuagint read in the Alexandrian Synagogue.[24]

Finally, it is interesting to note the rubric in the Holdheim book directing the congregation to rise after the sermon for the preacher's benediction. Einhorn has the exact same wording for his Protestant-derived institution.

Structural Concepts from Zunz's Gottesdienstliche Vorträge[25]

Although the Hamburg Temple *Gebetbuch* possessed admirable features, many of which Einhorn himself took up, the book had not gone far enough in the direction of Reform, and its structure and ideology left him unsatisfied.[26] The Hamburg revisions concentrated upon the external aspects of worship, with the introduction of decorum and aesthetic appeal. Aside from the excision of certain prayers or the recital of others in the language of the people, the prayerbook contained little of a positive nature that bespoke Reform.

Holdheim's prayerbook for the *Reformgemeinde* could not meet with Einhorn's wholehearted approval either. The outspoken expression of Reform within the liturgy and the brevity of the service, helped by the abrogation of *musaf,* were worthy of adoption, but its peculiarly Jewish character was missing. Although Holdheim did much to correct the "*halbjüdisch*" character of the *Reformgemeinde's* original liturgy, the Berlin rabbi's rewrite still bore the earmarks of the congregation's earlier arbitrary, unhistoric attempt. With all his reformatory goals, Einhorn wanted a prayerbook that was "*echt jüdisch.*"

Leopold Zunz's hypotheses as to the dating and original wording of the prayers afforded an invaluable opportunity. Einhorn was not one to take refuge in older usages and texts and thus claim respectable antiquity for Reform. However, if older usages did exist that agreed with Reform, how much the better. Legitimatization was not only added to the armory of the non-Orthodox, but the bonds with universal Israel were strengthened.

Thus, Einhorn was adhering to Zunz's surmised aboriginal *yotzer* when he reduced it to forty-five words.[27] *Olath Tamid* incorporated the *Gottesdienstliche Vorträge's* 63-word *ahavah rabbah*[28] supplemented by *ki ve-shem qodshekha,* possibly because of its trusting note. Zunz's putative *ge'ullah*[29] is similarly reproduced: *emet she-attah, shirah hadashah,* and *hatimah.* Not favoring any accumulations of synonyms, Einhorn omitted *malkenu* until *avoteynu,* from the forty-five word *ge'ullah* in *Gottesdienstliche Vorträge.*

On similar grounds Einhorn felt justified in applying the shears to the *amidah.*[30] Because of their conjectured greatest antiquity, the Introductory and Concluding Benedictions were invariably included when an *amidah* was read. This, in part, accounts for the liberties Einhorn took with the different Intermediate Benedictions, while leaving the remaining six intact. A notable example is the *berakhah emtza'it,* cast solely in the vernacular, for the House of Mourning. Although Zunz grouped *retzeh vimenuhatenu* together with *attah qiddashta, yismah mosheh,* and *attah ehad,* without suggesting any chronological stratification, Einhorn did make the distinction. Employing the same criteria that Zunz did for placing the antiquity of the Initial Three and the Concluding Three (that is, their regularity), Einhorn attached greater importance to the *retzeh vi-menuhatenu.* which was met with at all Sabbath services. He kept it, or its counterpart *ve-hasi'enu* for the Festivals, while dropping the once-appearing proems *yismah mosheh, attah ehad,* etc. Since these proems were presumably later compositions[31] and variable, Einhorn dispensed with them and replaced them with German compositions of his own,[32] culminating in either the Sabbath *retzeh vi-menuḥatenu* or the Festival *ve-hasi'enu.*

Einhorn's Architectonic

The Hamburg and Berlin Reform prayerbooks gave Einhorn material to work with, but it took the creative genius and religious fervor of an inspired liturgist to mold a new *oeuvre* out of earlier scattered efforts. The structure of the liturgy was given new life in his hands.

The arrangement of his services is fairly uniform throughout, whether for Sabbath or Weekday, Tish'ah be-Av or Festival. The differentiating marks are the Intermediate Benediction of the *amidah,* the choice of psalm, and the inclusion or non-inclusion of the *hallel* and the Torah reading. All Morning Services have the Hamburg selections from the *birkhot ha-shaḥar: mah tovu,* German hymn, *adon olam* (in Holdheim's translation), *elohay neshamah* (the Hamburg Temple *Gebetbuch* has *yehi ratzon* too), *ribbon kol ha-olamim,* and *attah hu.* This division is followed by the Shema and its Benedictions, mostly in Hebrew. Whereas the older edition of *Olath Tamid* placed the psalm, selected by Einhorn himself for the specific day, between *ahavah rabbah* and the Shema, the later editions put it directly—and more fittingly—before the *barekhu,* the original location of the psalmodic section (*pesuqey de-zimrah*). After the *ge'ullah* comes the *amidah,* which is a *birkat sheva* for all services, including Rosh Hashanah and Tish'ah be-Av and excepting the weekday one, which has twelve instead of the traditional eighteen or nineteen Benedictions. The *hallel,* consisting of Psalms 113, 117 and 118 only, is inserted for the New Moon, Hanukkah and *ḥol ha-mo'ed. Ausheben, Einheben* (return of the scroll to the ark), Mourners' Kaddish, *aleynu,* and *Schlussgesang* (closing hymn) follow consecutively.

However, Einhorn went beyond mere imitation of models. He restructured in startling new ways. The Day of Atonement service is a prime example. First is the already-mentioned conflation of *musaf* and *minḥah* into a single *Nachmittagsgottesdienst,* under which are subsumed *u-netanneh toqef* (Einhorn's version), the *avodah,* a *Todtenfeier,* and the Afternoon Torah Service. Consistently enough, Einhorn refused to supply this section with as much as a single *amidah,* since he did not have a *musaf* or *minḥah* anyway.

To provide these expressly for the Day of Atonement would only mar the architectonic coherence of his liturgical design. No harm is done in filling in the interval between the Morning and Concluding Services with the liturgical highlights of the intervening *musaf* and Afternoon Services in a new setting. The *u-netanneh toqef* and the *avodah* are lifted out of their *amidah* matrices and planted alongside an embellished Memorial Service and a postmeridian Torah Service. In this way the Scylla of endless traditional *amidah* repetitions with their respective confessionals and the Charybdis of a Holdheim afternoon-long rest period are avoided. The High Holy Day volume of the *Union Prayer Book* follows precisely this pattern.

The question posed at the Brunswick Conference in 1844 as to the manner in which the shofar blasts should be conducted was answered decisively by Einhorn. He reduced the blowing to three notes alone, to be produced not by a ram's horn, but by the *"Horn und Trompetenklang."* While the exchange of the shofar for modern wind instruments was an extreme measure, it was, at any rate, less radical than Holdheim's total removal of the blasts.

Germane to our discussion of *Olath Tamid's* ground plan is how Einhorn handled the text accompanying the repeated series of blowings. The absence of the *musaf* could present insurmountable difficulties to one with lesser liturgical skills or sense of symmetry. Rather than allow the whole arrangement of *malkhuyot, zikhronot,* and *shofarot* to collapse, as Samuel Adler did in his revision of Merzbacher's *Order of Prayer,* Einhorn distributes them, in German paraphrase, among the different parts of the New Year service: *melokh* affixed to *u-ve-khen ten* in the Evening and Morning *amidot; attah zokher* with *attah vehartanu* in the Morning *amidah;* and the *attah nigleyta,* directly after the prophetic lesson, culminating in the three blasts. The last section, the *shofarot,* is not altogether out of place here, since traditionally this is where the *teqi'ot meyushav* are sounded.

Einhorn's Four Special Sabbaths

The primary service in *Olath Tamid* is the one for Saturday morning.[33] It is the pared-down version along the lines of the putative mishnaic original deduced by Leopold Zunz in his *Die gottesdienstlichen Vorträge der Juden.*[34]

The service for the festival or weekday morning is mapped out essentially according to the same plan. The Zunzian/Einhornian format has been the basis for the services in the American Reform *Union Prayer Book* ever since the appearance of its premier edition in 1894.[35]

Superficially, the service is all but skin and bones. What saved it from the emaciated look—and, above all, what assured the rite as such and its near immortality through its countless spinoffs—were Einhorn's moving prayers in the vernacular. In addition, lending variety and color were the assorted special prayers (as for newlyweds, the recently bereaved, the dangerously ill, etc.—such prayers meant more in those days when communities were more closely knit than most synagogues tend to be today) and those appropriate prayers for the Special Sabbaths that fall yearly, in harmony with the Jewish calendrical and liturgical cycle.

According to the traditional list of scriptural lections in the synagogue, the Sabbaths before and after Tish'ah be-Av have special haftarot. On the three Sabbaths before the fastday, the prophetic readings are shot through with chastisement *(shalosh de-furanuta)*. Those assigned after the Ninth of Av—seven Sabbaths and seven haftarot in all—are more consolatory in character *(sheva de-nehamata)*. As noted earlier, although Einhorn prepared a distinct service for the day of abstinence, he redefined and transformed the holiday in keeping with his notion of a present eschatology-in-the-making. Because of his changes, the traditional complex of readings for the period before and after the fastday no longer applied, and so had to be dropped.

On the other hand—in contrast to other nineteenth-century American liturgical reformers, whether of a radical or a traditional bent[36] —Einhorn did retain that part of the Jewish calendar of Torah readings called *arba parashiyyot*. These are four (supplementary) pericopes for the four consecutive Sabbaths starting with Shabbat Sheqalim—the Sabbath before, or coincident with, the New Moon of Adar (the month in which Purim falls). The second Sabbath, Shabbat Zakhor, falls just before Purim. The third, the next week, is called Shabbat Parah, and the last, Shabbat ha-Hodesh, is marked on the Sabbath just before the New Moon of Nisan, the month during which Passover occurs.

Einhorn included in his prayerbook the full Hebrew text of the pericopes chosen for these Sabbaths as the *sole* readings from the Torah, in accordance with the mishnaic ruling[37] before the days of set weekly con-

secutive readings. (They are treated as *additional* in the Traditional synagogue.) The pericopes are followed by non-pentateuchal citations he
picked to have read as haftarot. Then, after the scriptural readings, *Olath
Tamid* offers prayers composed by Einhorn himself in lofty, vigorous, allusive German touching on the significance of the Special Sabbath for the
contemporary Jew. Each prayer is introduced in German with the name of
the Sabbath in question in Hebrew, *e.g.*, *"Gebet für den Sabbath,* פרשת
החודש.*"*

It is here that we fully witness Einhorn at work as a theologian, homilist,
and—one might with some justification add—a latter-day *payytan* in free
verse. There are two translations of *Olath Tamid,* a rather uninspired one in
1872 on which Einhorn received help from a sympathetic disciple with a
mind of his own, Bernhard Felsenthal (1822–1908),[38] and a later and occasionally paraphrastic[39] one in 1896 by his son-in-law, Emil G. Hirsch
(1851–1923), an eloquent spokesman for social justice. The only one of the
Four Special Sabbaths Hirsch saw fit to save in his rendition of *Olath Tamid*
was the Sabbath before Purim, which was not observed on its proper date in
his congregation. The following, for Shabbat Sheqalim, is an example of
Einhorn's flowing original prayers and the Einhorn/Felsenthal translations—Latinate and clumsy as they sometimes are.

> Andächtigen Gemüthes, O Gott, gedenken wir heute Deines, durch
> Moses verkündeten Wortes, das Jeden in Israel, arm wie reich, verp-
> flichtet, sein halbes Schekel darzubringen für's Heiligthum, zur
> Bestreitung der höheren Gemeindebedürfnisse als Lösegeld für seine
> Seele. Mit Stolz und Jubel gedenken wir ferner frommen Bereit-
> willigkeit, womit Israel zu allen Zeiten diesem Deinem heiligen
> Willen nachgekommen. Nicht blos damals, als der Heilige Tempel
> noch stand, wurden alljährlich—kurz vor dem ersten der Monde, in
> welchem unser Stamm das Gedächtniss seiner Geburt als Gottes-
> und Priestervolk feiert, neue Opfergaben zum religiösen Heile der
> Gesammtheit gespendet—auch während der vielen, vielen Jahrhun-
> derte unserer Zerstreuung nach allen Theilen der Erde fand Dein
> Gebot einen mächtigen Wiederhall in unserer Mitte. Und nicht blos
> aus einem halben Schekel bestand das Opfer in diesen zahllosen
> Jahren schweren Druckes, sondern im unermüdlichen Erdulden der
> bittersten Lebensverkümmerung, in der willigen Hingabe von Gut

und Blut für die Erhaltung Deiner Lehre. Lass, O Herr, diesen beispiellosen Opfermuth der frommen Voreltern uns, ihren glücklicheren Nachkommen, zum leuchtenden Muster und zur ernsten Mahnung werden. Gieb, dass jedes Mitglied unsere Gemeinschaft in dankbarem Gefühle Deiner Huld, die uns bessere Tage hat erleben lassen, mit Freudigkeit die ungleich geringeren Opfer darbringe, welche die Gegenwart für die Förderung der religiösen Interessen Israels fordert, dass Jeschurun, indem es das Fett der Erde geniesst, nicht das vergesse, wofür unsere Ahnen auf alles Erdengut verzichteten und Mauern von feindlichen Heeren durchbrachen. Einst werden vor Deinem erhabenen Richterstuhle wir alle gemustert und unsere Thaten gezählt und gewogen. Möchten dann die Gaben, die wir zur Verherrlichung Deines Namens dargebracht, nicht zu leicht befunden werden! Amen.

Devoutly, O God, we think of this day of that commandment of thine, announced through Moses, which obliged every man in Israel, whether rich or poor, to bring the tribute of half-a-shekel for the sanctuary, for sacred purposes common to the congregation, and a ransom for the soul. And with pride and exultation we think of the pious willingness with which Israel at all times fulfilled this duty. Not during that time alone when thy temple stood were new offerings, for the religious benefit of the community, contributed every year—shortly before the first month, in which our people solemnly commemorates its birth as a devoted priest-people; but even during the long, long centuries of our dispersion over all the parts of the world thy commandment never ceased to meet with a powerful echo in our midst. And the offering during the numberless years of crushing oppression was not half-a-shekel; it consisted in the unwearied endurance of the most cruel blasting of life, in willingly sacrificing fortune and blood for the maintenance of thy law. May that sublime self-sacrificing spirit of our ancestors be a guiding example and solemn admonition to us, the children of a happier age. Grant that every member of our community, in gratitude for thy loving kindness, which has allowed us to see so much better days, may joyfully offer the incomparably lighter tribute now demanded for the promotion of the religious interests of Israel; that Jeshurun, while enjoying the abundance of

earth's blessings, may not forget that good for which our forefathers
were ready to give up all earthly treasures, and to defy the mightiest
of hosts. We are all to be mustered on some future day before thy sublime judgment seat, when all our deeds will be counted and weighed.
May then the offerings which we shall have laid down for the glorification of thy name not be found to *{sic!}* light. Amen.

By referring to the behest in the Torah concerning the half-shekel (Ex.
30:17), Einhorn accomplished four purposes: (1) he reminded the worshipers of the self-denying generosity of their ancestors amid severe hard-
ships, (2) he suggested through this reminder that the present-day congregants, living now in far easier circumstances, be no less ungrudging and
benevolent in supporting the institutions of Judaism, (3) he intimated that
they would be held accountable before the Divine Judge for their acts of
charity or nonperformance of them, and (4) he called to their attention
that before long Passover would be coming.

In short, the prayer serves at once as a pedagogic reminder, a notice of
an upcoming event, and a charity appeal. It is plain that this prayer and
the one for Shabbat Parah were intended as much for the congregation's
instruction as for God's hearing.

The entreaty for Shabbat Parah (based on the prescription in Numbers
19:1–13) reflects more faithfully Einhorn's own literary and rhetorical
skills. Here the master preacher/liturgist takes the purificatory/contami-
nant qualities of the ashes of the red heifer (the *parah* in question) as a
point of departure for an "updated" allegorization that neither loses its historical sense nor bypasses the physicality of the ancient and, in many ways,
enigmatic ritual.[40]

> True, the statute ordering such external purification after directly or
> indirectly coming into contact with a corpse has lost all binding force
> and significance for us *(alle Kraft und Bedeutung verloren);* but the more
> intensely must we feel the obligation of keeping our souls unstained
> by rottenness, unsullied by thoughts and desires repugnant to thee
> *(vom Schlamme eines Dir widerstrebenden Sinnens und Trachtens).*

Again the worshiper is notified of the imminence of Passover, this time by
being told that the period before the festival was the time the Jews of the Second Commonwealth prepared themselves by resorting to ceremonial purifica-

tion. It is obvious that this reference is meant to reinforce the earlier reminder that Pesaḥ, the season of Israel's liberation from Egyptian bondage and birth as a priest-people *(Priestervolk,* cf. Exodus 19:6), is just around the corner.

> And thus, as during the time of the second temple the community was admonished, at every approach of the festival of deliverance *(beim Herannahen der Erlösungsfeier),* to use the purifying waters in preparation for the offering of the passover-sacrifice *(Überschreitungsopfer),* in the same way we hear a powerful admonition within us *(so waltet auch in unserer Mitte die mächtige Sehnsucht)* to meet the anniversary festival of Israel's birth with the bright garb of spiritual purity *(im Schmucke der Seelenreinheit)* upon us.

One may ask why a Reformer of Einhorn's "low-church" leanings would take the trouble to single out these Four Special Sabbaths and give them a place of prominence in his prayerbook. In the various later editions of the *Union Prayer Book,* other Sabbaths are made to stand out: the Sabbath of Passover, the Sabbath during Tabernacles, the Sabbath of Repentance, and the Sabbath during Hanukkah—in addition to the Sabbath before Purim. It is fairly common knowledge that the latter Sabbaths were selected because otherwise those holidays might go unmarked. From the larger perspective of the entire Jewish liturgical year, however, the Four Special Sabbaths to which Einhorn elected to accord prominence seem scarcely all that important. Why then did our uncompromising radical Reformer bother to highlight them at all?

One consideration is Einhorn's uncommon sense of, and flair for, the architectonic and the dramatic in his restructuring of the liturgy. The retention of the Four Special Sabbaths, then, might be a reflection of his responsiveness to the rhythms of the Jewish year.

Another consideration could well be the lavish attention shown these Sabbaths in the Ashkenazic Orthodox synagogues of Central Europe in the nineteenth century. For example, Seligmann Baer, in his monumental *Avodat Yisrael* (Rodelheim, 1868/Jerusalem, 1937), devotes forty-three pages, with explanatory glosses, to *piyyutim* that were to be inserted at various points in the service on precisely these Sabbaths. It is possible that Einhorn and his congregants nostalgically recalled their younger days in the old country when certain late winter Sabbaths during the month or so before Pesaḥ were celebrated with just a bit more festivity than usual to help hasten the coming of spring.

Finally, it is noteworthy that all the selections from the Torah for the Four Special Sabbaths are essentially the same as the traditional supplementary ones except for (1) one to four verses that are either added or subtracted, and (2) the replacement of the established Deuteronomy 25:17–19 with Einhorn's preferred Exodus 17:8–16 for Shabbat Zakhor. The substitute reading, dealing as it does with the same subject as the conventional one, does not sound as bitter or vengeful.[41] Interestingly enough, although Einhorn denominates his pre-Purim prayer as *"Gebet für den, dem Purimfeste vorangehenden Sabbath פרשת זכור"* the rubric above his Torah extract reads only *"Für Sabbath vor Purim"* —the obvious reason being that his chosen pericope does not open with the expected *"Zakhor et . . . Amalek."*

In the case of the haftarot, the most significant changes in *Olath Tamid* are those for Shabbat Zakhor from I Samuel 15:2–34 to Esther 3, and for Shabbat ha-Ḥodesh, where the highly cultic Ezekiel 45:16–46:18 is supplanted by the soul-stirring Isaiah 44:1–24. Curiously enough, although the *Union Prayer Book* omitted the lectionary for the Four Special Sabbaths, the first edition of the prayerbook provided two scriptural readings within the context of the Intermediate Benediction of the Sabbath Morning *amidah* (of all places!), one from Deuteronomy 25:17–19[42] and a second from Esther 9, both for Shabbat Zakhor. The subsequent editions of the *Union Prayer Book* dispensed with any special Torah reading for the Special Sabbath, relying instead exclusively on the regular weekly portion, but always continuing to draw from the Book of Esther for the haftarah (7:1–10; 8:15–17; or 9:20–28).[43]

As if to come full circle, in the Table of Scriptural Readings at the end of *Gates of the House* (Central Conference of American Rabbis, 1977) as well as in *The Torah: A Modern Commentary* (Union of American Hebrew Congregations, 1980), the Four Special Sabbaths come back into their own. Each of the special Torah pericopes that Einhorn treated as the one and only Torah reading for the day now comprises the supplementary reading from a second scroll, in correspondence to age-old, though post-mishnaic, usage. All the Reform haftarot are now identical with the Orthodox ones (usually slightly shortened), excepting of course the one for Shabbat Zakhor. For the Sabbath before Purim, the present American Reform lectionary turns back to Einhorn's example in exchanging the rancorous I Samuel 15:2–34 for one or more auspicious chapters of Esther.[44]

The Relative Positions of Hebrew and the Vernacular in Olath Tamid

At odds with Zacharias Frankel, who regarded the Hebrew language as indispensable to Jewish worship, Einhorn was in full accord with the majority opinion at the 1845 Frankfurt Conference, where he participated in the stormy debate on the question of Hebrew:

> The introduction of the vernacular into the service is necessary. Hebrew is the language of the study of the Law, but it is not the organ wherewith to express the feelings of the people. Aforetimes prayer was only the cry of pain: scarcely intelligible expression sufficed for this; but now the people need a prayer that shall express thoughts, feelings and sentiments; this is possible only through the mother tongue. . . .[45]

Einhorn entertained an almost idolatrous love for the German language—and the culture and literature of which it was the vessel. Hebrew gave us Mosaism; German, Reform. For Einhorn, the relevance of Judaism for modern man hinged upon education in the German literary classics and philosophies. Without German, Judaism was thought to be doomed to moribundity and irrelevance.

Later, in the seventh article of the 1869 Philadelphia Platform, Einhorn's sentiments were virtually unchanged.

> The cultivation of the Hebrew language, in which the divine treasures of revelation have been couched and in which the immortal monuments of our literature have been preserved (the commanding influence of which extends to all educated nations), must in our midst be considered as the fulfillment of a sacred obligation. However, this language has in fact become incomprehensible for the overwhelming majority of our present day co-religionists, and therefore in the act of prayer (which is a body without a soul unless it is understood) Hebrew must take second place behind a language which the worshipers can understand insofar as this appears advisable under prevailing circumstances.[46]

What is striking is not so much Einhorn's giving a prominent place to the vernacular or his concession on the partial retention of the Hebrew language. It is his exaltation of German, which knew almost no bounds.

Take away from Reform Judaism the German spirit, or what is the same thing, the German language, and you have torn away from it the mother soil and it must wither away, the lovely flower. The English sermon can have for its mission nothing else than to utilize the treasure of the German spirit and German literature for our religious life and therewith enrich it. In a word, where the German sermon is banned, there the reform of Judaism is nothing more than a brilliant gloss, a decorated doll, without heart, without soul, which the proudest temples and the most splendid theories cannot succeed in infusing with life.[47]

Although Einhorn obtained many of his ideas from the *Rabbinerversammlungen,* the number of liturgical models carrying out Conference resolutions was still too small to serve as a seasoned basis for his own revisions of the standard liturgy. But he drew considerably upon the few creations that were available.

The concept of an Evening Service predominantly in the vernacular, as in the Hamburg Temple *Gebetbuch,* was put to good use by Einhorn, and he went along with the Hamburgers in recasting the Benedictions surrounding the Shema, leaving Israel's watchword and the appendant paragraphs intact in Hebrew. He was not prepared, however, to accept an exclusively German *amidah,* which the Hamburg rite proffered for its Evening Service. That book had the benefit of a counter-balance in Hebrew of the *birkat me'eyn sheva,* which *Olath Tamid* did not. Therefore, the Evening *amidah* had to be given in Hebrew, because of its principal position along with the Shema. As noted before, the *birkhot ha-shahar* in *Olath Tamid* are, in imitation of the Hamburg pattern, presented in German, and the same usage of the vernacular for the last-named came to be imitated in the *Union Prayer Book.*

Other borrowings from the Hamburg manual are the choral introductions to the *ge'ullah* section, "Ewige Wahrheit ist es für uns . . .," and the idea of *elohay netzor* in German after a Hebrew *amidah.* For the most part, however, Einhorn avoided the *Gebetbuch's* German text because of its wooden literalism. He wanted his prayers to take wing, to soar; and undeviating adherence to this book's heavy-footed translation would only dampen the liturgist's muse. If German was to assume a central role, it had to prove fit for the task, to be a worthy instrument for carrying Israel's prayers aloft before the heavenly throne.

Holdheim's translations were more to Einhorn's liking. Under no circumstances, however, did Einhorn allow the Berlin Reform prayerbook to influence his new compositions. Whatever the propinquity between the two men on issues practical or theoretical, as on the definition of *ot* or on messianism, enough differences existed between them to force Einhorn to write prayers on his own, compositions that reflected his peculiar fusion of chosenness and messianism. Although Holdheim could bring himself to pray on behalf of his parishioners, "Du hast Israel erkoren aus allen Völkern," his *amor Israel intellectualis* was marked by a hesitancy that Einhorn, with his newly evolved understanding of the Jews' mission, felt no need to entertain.

Among the Holdheim translational imports are *adon olam* ("Der Herr des Weltalls"), *elohay neshamah* ("Herr, die Seele, die Du mir {Einhorn: *uns*} gegeben.."), *ribbon kol ha-olamim* ("Herr aller Welten"), *modim* ("Wir danken Dir.."), *sim shalom* ("Gieb Frieden, Segen.."), and *elohay netzor* ("Mein Gott, bewahre meine Zunge vor Bösem. . . . Nimm im Wohlgefallen auf die Worte meines Mundes").[48] The text of the *Einheben* (Ps. 19:7–8) is the same for both rites.[49] And the concluding *aleynu,* which Holdheim himself used for but a few of his "cycles" (services), became a fixed feature in *Olath Tamid.*[50]

The Role of Hebrew in Olath Tamid

A commission appointed by the 1845 Frankfurt Conference proposed that the Hebrew part of the liturgy be restricted to the *barekhu* and its response, the Shema and the first of its accompanying paragraphs, and the initial and concluding Benedictions of the *amidah*. The Torah reading was also to be conducted in Hebrew.[51] We have already seen in the case of the Morning Service in *Olath Tamid* that this sharp reduction of the Hebrew was relieved by Einhorn's introduction of Zunz's theorized primitive *yotzer, ahavah,* and *ge'ullah* in their historic tongue.[52] The commission's proposals were, however, accepted for *Olath Tamid's* Evening Service, where only the suggested portions are in Hebrew and the intervening sections are in German.

The curtailment of Hebrew notwithstanding, Einhorn did not share the exclusive monolingualism of Holdheim or of any of the latter's imitators in the American Reform rabbinate. Despite Einhorn's almost inordinate love for German, in *Olath Tamid* one finds numerous Hebraisms, such as "Olah ihres Dankes" (for the mother visiting the synagogue after her confinement) and "der Vorbeter hebt die Thora von der Bimah und spricht . . ." (at *Einheben*). In like fashion the holidays are called by their Hebrew names: *Pesachfest, Atzerethfest* and *Sukkothfest,* etc. In juxtaposition, however, appear these: *Neujahrsfest, Hüttenfest* (when *Sukkothfest* is not used), and *Wochenfest.* A similar inconsistency is evident in the use of biblical names in the "Thora-Abschnitte" as well as in the Torah-Haftarah lectionary at the end of the volume. On the one hand, one encounters the Hebrew proper names in their unaltered form: Jecheskel, Jehoschuah, Jehudah, Kenaan, Koheleth, Menascheh, Mizraim, Moscheh, and Peleschet. On the other hand, Septuagint-derived spellings are also in evidence: Hoseah, Jesaias, Job, Pharan, Phareo, Salomon, and Samuel.[53]

All of which, in conjunction with the abundant midrashic allusions in the original tongue in his sermons, suggests that Einhorn was hardly negatively disposed to the language that he was inclined in large measure to displace. The repeated charge that Einhorn was an out-and-out Reformer can thus be qualified. With his avid espousal of German as the most important vehicle for philosophical and religious expression—perhaps to a certain degree because of this espousal (cf. Hermann Cohen's famous equation of *Deutschtum und Judentum*)—Einhorn was eager to maintain the historical solidarity with all Israel.

In two numbers of his periodical *Sinai*[54] prior to the publication of *Olath Tamid,* Einhorn explained some of the principles underlying his revisions of the Hebrew text of the Siddur. It is illuminating to look at a few of those revisions, ranging from the barely perceptible to the drastic. One of the most thoroughgoing occurs in Einhorn's Benediction Two of the *amidah.*[55] It will be noted that the eulogy—rather than the Benediction per se—was ultimately carried over into the *Union Prayer Book.* The subject of the traditional prayer is, of course, the resurrection of the dead. The Reformers were not alone in their objection to the literal, corporeal sense of the benediction. Indeed, the medieval rabbis toned down its physical significance in favor of the Greek-inspired Arabic notions of the immortality of the soul.[56] Einhorn's revision rests on

their support and on the Bible's reticence in the matter.[57] The text runs
as follows:

אתה גבור לעולם ה׳. רב
להושיע. מכלכל חיים בחסד. פודה
נפש עבדיו ממות ברחמים רבים
סומך נופלים ורופא חולים ומתיר
אסורים ומקיים אמונתו לישני עפר:
מי כמוך בעל גבורות. ומי דומה לך
מלך ממית ומחיה ומצמיח ישועה:
ונאמן אתה בכל דבריך. בא״ה
נוטע בתוכנו חיי־עולם:

Einhorn's *ya'aleh ve-yavo*—fixed in one location only for all services of a
festal character, that is, in the *avodah* section, before *retzeh*—is devoid of
references to the "remembrances" of Jerusalem and the Davidic Messiah.
This is as would be expected in any Liberal prayerbook. But setting off
Einhorn's *ya'aleh ve-yavo* from the others is his unique application of the
epithet "Messiah" to Israel: *ve-zikhron kol amkha beyt yisra'el meshiḥekha*[58]—
which expresses Einhorn's understanding of Israel's vocation.[59]

A change that would probably escape the notice of most readers is contained in the precentor's introduction to the priestly benediction, the
birkat kohanim. Instead of *kohanim am qedoshekha*, Einhorn has *kohaney am
qedoshekha*[60]—a grammatical construction less likely to jar one's historical
sensibilities, since the priests were in fact not so much an entire people as
an elite tribal division of it. Moreover, the expression *kohanim am
qedoshekha* never occurs in the Bible. Baer (p. 102) notes the appearance of
an analogous phrase in the Talmud:[61] *u-veney aharon am qedoshekha*. (It is
interesting to note that, as Baer observes, R. Joseph Kimḥi regarded the
phrase *kohaney am kedoshekha*, later used by Einhorn and others, as wrong.
The priests are priests of the Lord, not of the people.) But Einhorn was not
the first to find fault with the formulation as it stood in the Siddur. Kimḥi
proffered *kohanim be-am qedoshekha*, while a Roman variant gave *ha-amurah
le-aharon ule-vanav kohanim le-am qedoshekha*.[62]

The 1858 German edition of *Olath Tamid* kept the usual *sim shalom* —
with the exception of the *ḥatimah*, which was the Palestinian *oseh ha-shalom*.
The first English translation (1872), however, saw a universalization of the

prayer. Instead of asking for peace and well-being "for us and all Israel," the entreaty is broadened to embrace all mankind *(aleynu ve-al kol banekha; le-varekh et kol ha-ammim)*.

In the same vein, the ubiquitous Hamburg Kaddish was emended. The last two lines are generalized in *Olath Tamid* to *aleynu ve-al kol amenu* and *aleynu ve-al kol banav.* In his autobiography, *My Life as an American Jew,*[63] David Philipson tells that it was a prominent Jewish layman who suggested universalizing the last sentences of the Kaddish in *Olath Tamid.*[64]

Einhorn's *u-netanneh toqef* is also divergent, rejecting anything savoring of the supernatural or the mythological. No longer do we behold angels trembling at the call of judgment, or God enthroned in lofty splendor conducting His heavenly assize. Instead, we envisage humankind passing through the Shepherd's tally before its fate is decreed. The old court of appeal, based on repentance, prayer, and *caritas,* gives way to the less Damoclean notion of Psalms 8: 5–6, which casts human beings as both lowly and *engelgleich.* That biblical paradox is a recurrent theme in *Olath Tamid,* which often juxtaposes the child-of-earth image with the loftier child-of-God one.

What Einhorn seems to be suggesting is that as prone as man is to sin, he does have the capacity to transcend his sensual bounds and attain a worthy spiritual state. Although this bifurcated view in *Olath Tamid* may seem to be more Christian than Jewish, in all fairness to Einhorn, the Paulinian-Augustinian contempt of the things of earth is nowhere evident in *Olath Tamid.* Einhorn's strong Jewish sensibilities did not allow for a Manichean scorn of the material and the physical, which, after all, "God saw was good."[65] Indeed, it is somewhat surprising that Einhorn, known for his rigorous consistency, even bothered to include Meshullam b. Kalonymos' *piyyut,* with its sense of foreboding out of tune with *Olath Tamid's* overall optimistic tendency. But the popularity of the prayer, particularly of its *mi yihyeh u-mi yamut* sequence, doubtless accounts for its longevity even in a uniformly "rationalist" Reform liturgy.

Einhorn's Choice of Piyyutim in Olath Tamid

The sorrow-laden paytanic products of medieval Ashkenazic Jewry clashed with Einhorn's visionary optimism concerning Israel's career among the nations. Being obsessed with the persecution-ridden past meant taking a short-sighted view of Jewish history. The sobs of the old poems had to give way to exuberant songs of trust in the favorable outcome of Israel's mission.

For this reason, and for reasons of stylistic simplicity, the liturgical poems of Spanish Jewry take the place of the sadder Ashkenazic lyrical outpourings. Another explanation for the inclusion of Sephardic *piyyutim* lies in their suitability for congregational recitation or singing, particularly in lighter, less ponderous pieces such as *adonay honnenu va-haqimenu, el nora alilah,* and *be-terem shehaqim va-araqim.* Similar considerations prompted the replacement of the Ashkenazic *el male rahamim* with the Sephardic *mah rav tuvkha* and *menuhah nekhonah.*

The *piyyutim* in the Hamburg Temple *Gebetbuch* were hardly sufficient for Einhorn. Why were other products of Israel's poetic talents not being tapped? In addition, the Hamburg book fell into the habit, established by the traditional prayerbooks, of repeating prayers. Its *elohenu sheba-shamayim, honnenu va-haqimenu, and be-terem shehaqim va-araqim,* to cite a few examples, were reiterated several times on Yom Kippur.

To expand the selection, Einhorn retrieved manuscripts of old *piyyutim* from dusty oblivion. In his *Vorwort* to *Olath Tamid* he acknowledges Sachs's *Poesie* as the source of such poems as ibn Gabirol's *shikhehi yegonekh,* Ibn Ghayyat's *yonah hafesah,* and Halevi's *barekhi atzulah.* All the other non-Hamburg imports not cited in the *Vorwort* also come from the Sachs collection: *shimah adon, elohim eli attah, barekhi nafshi, shihartikha be-khol shahar, se'i ayin,* and *sesoni rav bekha.* In each case, the translation is Einhorn's own.[66]

Einhorn's Passover Haggadah

Einhorn's all-German domestic service for Passover Eve *(Hausandacht am Vorabend des Pesachfestes)* appears inconspicuously at the end of *Olath Tamid,* just before the Torah-haftarah lectionary. It merits close examination as a convenient capsule summary of the author's liturgical and theological method.

Although the service is stark in its simplicity and leanness, largely by dint of a ritual iconoclasm, it is clearly rooted in the textual forms of the old Passover haggadah. The characteristic landmarks—the wine, candles, Seder plate, etc.—all but universally common in today's observances, traditional or liberal, are absent. Conversely, Einhorn's *Hausandacht* adheres to the classical pattern by building up to *lefikhakh,* followed by the first two Psalms of the *hallel* and culminating in the benediction *asher ge'alanu.* The meal accompanied by the usual preceding and succeeding *Tischgebete,* i.e. *birkat ha-mazon,* ensues. The entire proceedings for the evening end with a German rendition of *addir hu,* which is spoken rather than sung! Since there is no singing interspersed among the prayers in Einhorn's revision (*dayyenu,* for example, just does not exist here) and any subsequent lengthy disquisition by the *Familienhaupt* would only have a deadening effect on a festive family affair, Einhorn adapts the traditional Four Questions asked by the youngest at the commencement of the Seder by spreading a new set of inquiries throughout the haggadah in fitting spots. Now it is either a *Familienglied* or the *Gesellschaft* that is assigned the role of asking.

As anti-ceremonial as Einhorn may have been, he showed a careful regard for the text and sought to preserve as much of it as possible—provided it did not conflict with his theological thinking or his sense of architectonic. Since he believed ceremonial usages, whether of biblical or of Rabbinic derivation, were no longer mandatory or necessarily expressive of the divine will, he could not in good conscience maintain those *berakhot* that contained the formulaic phrase "who hast commanded us . . ." (even though he entertained scarcely any qualms about preserving the *Stammgebete-complex* or benedictions in similar categories, such as *birkat ha-mazon,* the nocturnal *ha-mapil ḥevley shenah,* or the matrimonial *birkat erusin*—these apparently entailed no sacrifice of principle or disruption of his reconstituted fabric). Accordingly, not only are the benedictions regarding wine (including the prefatory Kiddush), *karpas,* and handwashing omitted, but Rabban Gamliel's triple sine qua non for the proper observance of Passover is given short shrift textually. Nonetheless, the *berakhah*-structure of the non-"commanding" variety stays, specifically in the climactic *asher ge'alanu* and in the grace before and after dinner.

Thus far we have concerned ourselves chiefly with the structural framework of Einhorn's Passover *Hausandacht.* How does he flesh out this bare outline? Here is where the man shows his true visionary colors, his literary and religious inspiration. The body of the text represents a lofty (*schwungvoll*) exegesis of the Passover event that is markedly and peculiarly Einhorn's. The emancipation from Egypt is placed in the broader historical context of Israel's long career checkered by travail, persecution, wandering and deliverance. Verses from Psalms 124 and 137 (most unusual selections for Passover) are midrashically woven into an almost sermonic dissertation on Israel's woeful past leading on to a glorious messianic future. In this haggadah, then, *yetzi'at mitzrayim* is really simply one station on the Jews' fateful journey to the *eschaton*.

In terms of content, Henry Berkowitz's lilting English paraphrase in the 1923 version of the *Union Haggadah* (pp. 115–17), "And It Came to Pass at Midnight," captures precisely what Einhorn was trying to say. In fact, the biblical phrase *Nacht der Wache* is employed repeatedly in Einhorn's version, making it indeed the leitmotif of the evening celebration for Einhorn. It is interesting to see in this connection how Einhorn interprets the meaning and purpose of *maror*. (His treatment of unleavened bread as *Priesterbrod* as well as the expected *Brod des Elends* excites notice, too, particularly in light of Einhorn's conception of Israel's priestly service to humanity.) The bitter herbs are to remind the Jewish people of the never-ending task of waging a hard and bitter combat *(einem schweren und bitteren Kampfe)* on behalf of God's doctrine and law among the nations of the world.

The culmination of this inspired if rambling piece is, as mentioned earlier, the traditional *asher ge'alanu*, recast slightly to underscore Einhorn's belief in mission-messianism-universalism. It reads in part as follows:

> . . . Mögest Du uns viele Feste bereiten und Israel schauen lassen das Fest der Erlösung der ganzen Menschheit, auf das wir Dir ein neues Lied singen mit allen Völkern der Erde! Gelobt seist Du, Gott, Erlöser Israels.
>
> "O, grant us still many festive periods, and allow Israel to see the day of the redemption of all mankind; that we may sing to thee a new song, with all the nations of the earth. Be praised, O God, Redeemer of Israel." [Einhorn/Felsenthal translation]

Einhorn's *Hausandacht* was not to lie buried forever in *Olath Tamid* or in oblivion. The 1908 *Union Haggadah* bears Einhorn's imprint quite noticeably, as in the aforementioned breakup of the Four Questions among the different parts of the Seder. And subtle vestiges lingered on later in the revised edition of 1923, as in the passage below:

> This very night which we, a happy generation, celebrate so calmly and safely and joyfully in our habitations was often turned into a

night of anxiety and of suffering for our people in former times. Cruel mobs were ready to rush upon them and to destroy their homes and the fruit of their labors. But undauntedly they clung to their faith in the ultimate triumph of right and of freedom. Champions of God, they marched from one Egypt to another—driven in haste, their property a prey to the rapacious foe, with their bundles on their shoulders, and God in their hearts.

which corresponds to the original

Ja, gerade diese Nacht der Wache, die wir, die Glücklichen, so ruhig und sicher, so fröhlich und wohlgemuth in unseren Wohnungen feiern, brachte oft unsägliches Weh über unsere Glaubensgenossen, diente oft dem grässlichen Scheusal der abscheulichsten Verleumdung, welche Tücke und Glaubenshass jemals ersonnen, zur Enthüllung. Und dennoch hielten sie, die Geliebten, unerschütterlich fest an Gottes Verheissung, die uns Sieg und Freiheit verkündet. Unermüdet zogen sie als Streiter Gottes, von einem Mizraim ins—andere, eilends vertrieben, die reichste Habe dem raubgierigen Feinde preisgebend, ihre Bündel auf der Schulter und ihren Gott im Herzen.

The growing "normalization" of the *Union Haggadah,* as of all CCAR publications, should not by any means obscure for us Einhorn's underlying inspiration. To be sure, *berakhot* for both biblical and Rabbinic ordinances have made their way back into the text, and Hebrew was found on virtually every page of the liturgy of the Seder. (The 1908 edition of the *Union Haggadah* even included a contemporary *piyyut,* unfortunately plagued by a faulty meter!) But although Einhorn's all-German Romantic flights of rhetoric, his occasional verbosity, and his apparent distaste for ceremony were largely abandoned, his theology remained. He would have gladly endorsed the hope voiced in the *nirtzah* of the 1923 edition (p. 78):

May He who broke Pharaoh's yoke forever shatter all fetters of oppression, and hasten the day when swords shall, at last, be broken and wars ended. Soon may He cause the glad tidings of redemption to be heard in all lands, so that mankind—freed from violence and from wrong, and united in an eternal covenant of brotherhood—may celebrate the universal Passover in the name of our God of freedom.

This chapter combines earlier versions of articles that appeared in the *Hebrew Union College Annual* XLV (1974): 307–32 and in the *Journal of Reform Judaism* ["David Einhorn's Four Special Sabbaths"] (Summer 1987): 43–52. Reprinted with permission.

Abbreviations Used in the Notes

Al—Benjamin Szold, *Abodath Israel,* rev. Marcus Jastrow, Philadelphia, 1873.

GV—Leopold Zunz, *Die gottesdienstliche Vorträge der Juden historisch entwickelt,* 2nd ed., Frankfurt am Main, 1892.

Hamburg GB—*Seder ha-avodah: Gebetbuch. . . . nach dem Gebrauch des Neuen Israelitischen Tempels,* 2nd ed., Hamburg, 1841.

JG—Ismar Elbogen, *Der Jüdische Gottesdienst in seiner geschichtlichen Entwicklung,* 3rd ed., Frankfurt am Main, 1931.

JPSA—The Jewish Publication Society of America

MA—Isaac M. Wise, *et al., Minhag Amerika, Daily Prayers,* Cincinnati, 1872.

OP—Leo Merzbacher, *Seder Tefillah, The Order of Prayer for Divine Service,* 3rd ed. Samuel Adler, New York 1864.

OT—David Einhorn, *Olath Tamid, Gebetbuch für Israelitische ReformGemeinden,* Baltimore, 1848.

SRSG—Israel Davidson, *et al., Siddur Rav Saadiah Gaon,* 2nd ed., Jerusalem, 1963.

UH—Central Conference of America Rabbis, *The Union Haggadah,* Cincinnati, 1923.

UPB—Central Conference of American Rabbis, *The Union Prayer Book for Jewish Worship.*

WUPJ—World Union for Progressive Judaism.

1. Kaufmann Kohler, "David Einhorn, The Uncompromising Champion of Reform, A Biographical Essay," *CCAR Yearbook* XIX (1909): 215–70.

2. David Philipson, *The Reform Movement in Judaism,* rev. ed. (New York, 1931), pp. 167, 175, 215.

3. Kohler, op.cit., p. 240. Compare Kohler's two sermons, "Are Sunday Lectures Treason to Judaism?" (1888) and "The Sabbath Day and the Jew" (1891), both of which are to be found in *A Living Faith* (Cincinnati, 1948), pp. 19–41.

4. In Mecklenburg-Schwerin, Einhorn provoked a storm of controversy when he blessed a male infant in the synagogue even though the father had refused on principle to have the child circumcised. Franz Delitzsch, a Lutheran professor of theology and missionary to the Jews, gave notoriety to the event by pointing out the illicit character of publicly sanctioning the choice made by the father not to circumcise his child. A lively exchange, with the inevitable battery of biblical and Rabbinic texts, then ensued *(Sinai* 2 [1857], 735ff.). Einhorn's sardonic clincher was "Professor Delitzsch aims by his insistence on circumcision to force the Jew to knock at the door of the Christian Church for emancipation from the yoke of the Law" (Kohler, "Uncompromising Champion of Reform," p. 238). Incidentally, the entry on David Einhorn in the *Encyclopedia Hebraica,* IV, 918, includes the assertion *ve-afilu hetif le-vittul ha-milah,* which none of my reading in Einhorn thus far substantiates. On the contrary, Kohler tells us: "Dr. Wise's proposition to admit proselytes

without circumcision, Einhom opposed for the reason that Judaism is not a proselytizing religion and desires to admit only such elements as would join it from a purely religious motive" (ibid., p. 263).

5. Even with the strong affinity between Holdheim and Einhorn, two strong-willed and restless men, in the professional, theological, and liturgical realms, differences soon began to assert themselves. It was a case of a disciple going beyond the teachings of his master and forging his own outlook. The estrangement notwithstanding, Holdheim's imprint lasted, although he did not hold his prize follower in thrall. This development in the relationship between the two will become more readily apparent in the comparison below of the respective liturgies of Holdheim and Einhorn.

6. "After the supression of the revolution and the collapse of the Kossuth movement the reactionary elements were in power, and reform of whatever kind found little favor with the government" (Philipson, *The Reform Movement,* p. 282) .

7. Wise did, however, attend the Philadelphia Conference initiated by Einhorn.

8. Salo W. Baron, *Steeled by Adversity* (Philadelphia, 1971), p. 145; W. Gunther Plaut, *The Growth of Reform Judaism* (New York, 1965), pp. 15–17.

9. Philipson, op.cit., p. 123.

10. Philipson, ibid., p. 69; Plaut, *The Rise of Reform Judaism* (New York, 1962), pp. 119–22; Plaut, *The Growth of Reform Judaism,* pp. 14–15.

11. Quoted in Philipson, op.cit., pp. 69–70.

12. Bernhard N. Cohn, "David Einhorn: Some Aspects of His Thinking," *Essays in American Jewish History* (Cincinnati, 1958), pp. 320–21; Philipson, op.cit., pp. 206, 344; Cf. Holdheim's understanding of the Sabbath in Plaut, *The Rise of Reform Judaism,* pp. 190–95.

13. Baron, *Steeled by Adversity, p.* 378. CCAR, *Rabbi's Manual* (Cincinnati, 1928), p. 175, n. 1.

14. *Olath Tamid* first appeared in Baltimore in May 1856 and was published in complete form in 1858.

15. Cohn, op.cit., pp. 317–20; Kohler, "Uncompromising Champion of Reform," pp. 248–49. Philipson, op. cit., pp. 344–48.

16. The depth of Einhorn's attachment to the Torah was reflected in his scriptural portions for Yom Kippur: the lesson for the Morning Service is the same as the traditional one, Lev. 16; for the Afternoon Service, Lev. 19 is read in its entirety. The matutinal excerpt is not all that surprising: practically every Reform prayerbook at the time had it! It is the completeness of the afternoon reading that comes as a surprise. Szold's and Jastrow's *Abodath Israel,* a proto-Conservative work, for example, gave just Lev. 19:1–18. The Festival lectionary in OT is invariably given in Hebrew, accompanied by a literal German translation. AI reproduces the Hebrew text alone, and then only for the High Holy Days.

17. This translation is taken from Plaut, *The Growth of Reform Judaism,* p. 30.

18. Charles Rubinstein, *History of Har Sinai Congregation* (Baltimore, 1918).

19. Cf. Yer. Berakhot II, 4.

20. Only in recent years has the UPB I (1940) recreated for this day a unique Simḥat

Torah Service—replete with *haqqafot* and a modernized *kol ha-ne'arim,* which is a consecration of children just starting religious school. Our attention is directed to the revival of the Hamburg-OT Joshua quotation in the UPB after *ve-zot ha-berakhah.*

To be sure, the Sephardim had long been using these verses prior to the Return of the Scroll along with others of a hortatory nature. Of these passages the Hamburg Temple GB preserved just the one from Joshua for Simḥat Torah.

21. An excellent description of the liturgy of the Berlin *Reformgemeinde,* before and after Holdheim, may be found in Jakob J. Petuchowski, *Prayerbook Reform in Europe* (New York, 1968), pp. 58–66.

22. Einhorn was not prepared to go to the same lengths as Holdheim did in his *Das Ceremonialgesetz im Messiasreich* (1845). In criticism of the last-named work, Einhorn said. "We have passed the stage of negation. We want a constructive Reform." (Quoted in Kaufmann Kohler, *Studies, Addresses and Personal Papers* [New York, 1931], p. 524.)

23. JG, p. 423. Einhorn's solution was later adopted in the UPB.

24. The prelude as found in the Septuagint reads: "And these are the statutes and ordinances which the Lord commanded to the Children of Israel, as they went forth from Egypt." The Nash Papyrus has a similar arrangement. The Hebrew document from Egypt (c. 150 B.C.), discovered at the turn of the century, is of no use for determining possible influences on nineteenth-century Reform liturgy; but studies in the Septuagint were under way in Jewish circles during the early years of Reform.

25. Although Kohler notes Einhorn's dependence on GV, it is surprising that Einhorn himself never acknowledges his debt to the liturgiologist. Kohler, "The Uncompromising Champion," p. 254; Lou H. Silberman, "The Union Prayer Book: A Study in Liturgical Development," *Retrospect and Prospect,* (New York, 1965), p. 77, n. 38. Zunz's other groundbreaking liturgical studies, on the *seliḥah,* the *piyyut,* and the different rites appeared in *Die synagogale Poesie des Mittelalters* (1855), *Der Ritus des synagogalen Gottesdienstes* (1859), and *Literaturegeschichte der synagogalen Poesie* (1865).

26. Cf. Abraham Geiger's critique in his *Der Hamburger Tempelstreit, eine Zeitfrage,* (Breslau, 1842); and Ludwig Geiger, *Abraham Geiger: Leben und Lebenswerk* (Berlin, 1910), p. 44.

27. GV, p. 382; cf. Saadiah's in SRSG, p. 11. The UPB restored Ps. 104:24 to the Zunzian base.

28. GV, p. 382.

29. Ibid., pp. 382–83.

30. A word about Einhorn's *amidah.* In *Olath Tamid* the prayer appears under its alternate title: *tefillah.* Nonetheless, the rubrics call for the congregation's standing for the opening Three Benedictions, possibly since these form a class of their own, namely as *birkhot shevaḥ* "blessings of praise." Other rites, such as Al, followed this usage; but the UPB since the 1895 edition has required standing only for the Sanctification. The British *Service of the Heart* (1967) was the first in the twentieth century to reinstitute the Einhornian practice (with regard to both posture and title) in its rubrics.

31. GV, pp. 384–85.

32. As a rule, the 1940 UPB I follows this arrangement, as on pp. 20–23, 45–46, 58,

and 128–39. However, for the Festival services, the additional English composition comes after the *berakhah emtza'it,* which was the usual sequence in 1895 and in 1918 editions of UPB I. The solitary exception is the placement of the extra prayer beween the *birkat kohanim* and *sim shalom* in the 1895 UPB Festival Morning Service. The 1894 and 1922 UPB II arrangements are confused; and the 1945 one, a disorderly attempt to rectify the hopeless muddle left by previous editions. The OT imitators were evidently unaware of Einhorn's blueprint or the scholarly basis of his design.

33. Departing altogether from the customary sequence in the siddur, Einhorn rearranges the services in *Olath Tamid* in the following order: Sabbath Morning, Festival Morning, Rosh Hashanah Eve, Rosh Hashanah Morning, Yom Kippur Eve, Yom Kippur Day (Morning, Aftenoon, Memorial, and Concluding Services), Tish'ah be-Av Eve (or, as Einhorn put it, *Abendgottesdienst für das Fest der Zerstörung Jerusalems),* Sabbath Eve, Festival Eve, Weekday Morning, etc. The disposition of the services in *Olath Tamid* doubtless tells us something about their frequency of use in the congregations that attached themselves to Einhorn's rite.

34. Frankfurt am Main, 1892, pp. 382–85.

35. See above, pp. 23–25 for a discussion of the foreshortened contours of the *matbe'a shel tefillah* that distinguish OT in the context of Zunz's surmises as to the tannaitic paradigm in the Mishnah.

36. Even though Benjamin Szold (1820–1902), of the Positive-Historical School, mentions the *arba parashiyyot* among the "Ausgezeichnete Sabbathe" in the appendix (p. 9) to his *Hegyon Lev: Israelitisches Gebetbuch für die häusliche Andacht* (Baltimore, 1867), he does nothing with them liturgically here or in his *Abodath Israel* (Baltimore, 1867).

37. Megillah 3:4–6. Hence, as a matter of course, for none of the services in *Olath Tamid,* as for a Festival or High Holy Day, does Einhorn ever make provision for the use of more than one scroll, e.g., a second or third scroll for the *maftir.*

> As for the reading from the Torah and the *haftarah,* even these are ancient customs; and in the Mishnah the number of those called [to the Torah, i.e., *aliyyot}* for each occasion and the lections *{parashiyyot}* read on the festivals and on special Sabbaths—a few of which are unlike our current-day usage (Megillah 3:4–6; 4:1–2) had already been fixed. But on a regular Sabbath during the days of the Tannaim they apparently did not read *a parashah* or an order of a known extent in a uniform manner everywhere, but they read no fewer than 20 verses, and on the following Sabbath they continued from where they had left off. After the reading of each verse they translated it (orally) in Aramaic. (Joseph Heinemann, *Ha-Tefillah bi-Tequfat ha-Tanna'im ve-ha-Amora'im* [Jerusalem: 1964], p. 24 [translation mine].)

It was thus not until some time after the mishnaic period that we learn about the distinction between the Babylonian-rite annual Torah lectionary and the Palestinian-rite triennial version.

38. New York, 1872.

39. Chicago, 1896.

40. Einhorn's method of allegorization is not unlike that of his master, Samuel Hold-

heim. Compare, for example, with Holdheim's sermon, "Die Symbolik des mosäischen Gesetzes oder die sittliche Reinigung des Menschen," in his *Predigten über die jüdische Religion* (Berlin, 1853).

41. Another possibility is that Einhorn was aware of the requirement that "one who reads the Torah may not read fewer than three verses" (Megillah 4:4), and the traditional lesson for the Shabbat Zakhor (Deut. 25:17–19) barely makes it.

42. Ironically, the Deuteronomy passage was the very one with which Einhorn was so uncomfortable that he sought to relieve it with an extract he found more congenial.

43. Hence the remark, "In the Reform ritual some of these Sabbaths (*e.g.,* Zakhor, Parah) are not observed" (in "Special Sabbaths," *Encyclopedia Judaica* 14:574) is not entirely true.

44. The Special Sabbaths accorded individual prayers of their own in the various editions of the UPB reveal somewhat the shifting estimations of the holidays. It is interesting, for example, that the "Sabbath coincident with the New Moon" (1895) falls by the wayside (1918, 1940), while Hanukkah and Purim are given the ascendancy. The relative newness of the prayers appropriate for the Sabbath during Passover and during Tabernacles reveals these Sabbaths' role as partial surrogates for the Festivals themselves.

45. Quoted in David Philipson, "The Religion of the Prayerbook," *Journal of Jewish Lore and Philosophy* 1(1919): 75.

46. Plaut, *The Growth of Reform Judaism,* p. 31.

47. Quoted in David de Sola Pool, "Judaism and the Synagogue," in *The American Jew: A Composite Portrait,* ed. Oscar I. Janowsky (New York, 1942), p. 45.

48. A comparison between Holdheim's moving German rendition of *elohay netzor* and the current UPB paraphrase of the same reveals the mediating role played by OT:

Holdheim	*UPB (1940)*
Mein Gott. bewahre meine Zunge vor Bösem, meine Lippen vor Trug. Verleih' mir Sanftmuth gegen die, die mir übel wollen. Pflanze Demuth in meine Seele und Gottvertrauen in mein Herz. Sei mein Hort, wenn ich in Schmerz verstumme, mein Trost, wenn meine Seele gebeugt ist. Lass mich wandeln in Deiner Wahrheit. Leite mich, denn Du bist mein Gott und meine Hilfe, auf Dich hoffe ich all-täglich. Nimm in Wohlegefallen auf die Worte meines Mundes, die Regung meines Herzens komme vor Dich. Gott, mein Schöpfer und Erlöser! Amen.	O God. keep my tongue from evil and my lips from speaking guile. Be my support when grief silences my voice, and my comfort when woe bends my spirit. Implant humility in my soul. and strengthen my heart with perfect faith in Thee. Help me to be strong in temptation and trial and to be patient and forgiving when others wrong me. Guide me by the light of Thy counsel, that I may ever find strength in Thee, my Rock and my Redeemer. Amen. May the words of my mouth . . .

49. This simple psalmodic example was later to become part of the UPB's ampler, more traditional, and more Hebraic "Return of the Scroll."

50. The first paragraph of the regular Holdheim-Einhorn *aleynu* reads, for *shelo asanu,* predictably enough, "dass Er uns befreit hat von der Finsterniss des Irrglaubens, und uns gesendet hat das reine Licht der Offenbarung." The *aleynu* prefacing the *avodah* on Yom Kippur runs, in a vein perhaps more typical of Einhorn:

שבחר בזרע אברהם
למען יתברכו בו
כל משפחות האדמה

While no kneeling is required here, it is called for during the climactic recitation of *va-anaḥnu kor'im* before the closing Shema, etc., at *ne'ilah.*

51. *Protokolle und Aktenstücke der Zweiten Rabbiner-Versammlung,* Frankfurt am Main, 1845, pp. 60–72.

52. The Morning Services for Sabbaths and Holy Days in the UPB have in the main preserved Einhorn's quantitative balance between the Hebrew and the vernacular.

53. It is important to observe that all that is given in Hebrew was read in that tongue and not in translation. This can readily be ascertained by the fact that in the latter part of the volume, for the Evening Services ushering in the Sabbaths and Festivals, *shaḥarit* for the weekday and *Halbfesten,* Service in a House of Mourning, and the private morning devotions, the Hebrew texts are unaccompanied by translation. The Hebrew was present in OT not for the sake of mere historical reminiscence; it played an active part in the service. The only services rendered wholly in the language of the people were for matrimony, conversion, grace before and after meals, and the Passover Seder. Even here the Hebraic stamp is unmistakable, and the *matbe'a shel tefillah* largely preserved.

54. I (1856): 97–100, 129–39.

55. An error crept into the otherwise superb notes to the aforementioned *Service of the Heart.* In n. 58 the change from "Redeemer" to "Redemption" in Benediction I is said to have begun with the 1858 edition. Startling as it may seem, *go'el* is kept in that edition, though translated as *Erlösung.*

56. Cf. Mishneh Torah, Hilkhot Tefillah Vlll:2. Joseph Albo *Sefer ha-Ikkarim,* ed. Isaac Husik (Philadelphia, 1946), vol. IV, pp. 267–72.

57. *Sinai* I (1856): 134—37.

58. This version was perpetuated in the 1923 UH. Cf. the verse in Einhorn's *avinu malkenu: harem qeren yisra'el meshihekha*—which fits Einhorn's conception of Israel's vocation. Staunch anti-nationalist that Einhorn was, his utterances on the messiahship of the Jewish people bear a striking resemblance to Adam Mickiewicz's view of Poland as a messianic nation and to Dostoyevsky's pan-Slavic idea of Russia as the messiah of humankind.

59. Philipson, *The Reform Movement, p.* 248; see also *Sinai* I (1856):132–33.

60. MA adopted this wording as well.

61. Yoma 41b.

62. Elbogen (JG, p. 72) erroneously calls him David Kimḥi. Cf. SRSG p. 42, n. 12.

63. Cincinnati, 1941; pp. 39–40.

64. The only one to adopt Einhorn's liberalized Kaddish was Max Landsberg. The

tremendous hold this prayer has had on Jews dampened the revised prayer's potential popularity even among OT-imitators. Startling is Krauskopf's eccentric Kaddish, which opens with *yitgaddal* until *rabbah,* continues with Job 14:1–2, Eccles. 3:20b, c, Job 3:17–19a. Eccles. 12:7, Prov. 12:28, and concludes with the Hamburg *al yisra'el* and *oseh shalom* until *aleynu* (without *ve-al kol yisra'el)*—then, *ve-imru amen.* Here an assortment of stray Wisdom observations on death attempts to displace the sublime affirmation of faith in the centuries-old Kaddish. The Reformers usually knew that philosophical ruminations on death cannot approximate the measure of comfort offered by the resignation-in-hope implied in the time-honored doxology. Witness the ephemeral character of the various pre-Kaddish meditations in modern rites. Few mourners seem to miss them if they are not read. Emil G. Hirsch ("A Memorial Oration," *David Einhorn Memorial Volume,* ed. Kaufmann Kohler [New York: 1911], pp. 479–80) notes that Einhorn would not permit them in his prayerbook.

65. Whereas Einhorn presented his entire *u-netanneh toqef* in Hebrew, Landsberg reproduced it mostly in English.

66. Is it mere coincidence that these very choices (of Einhorn's) from Sachs's collection were also utilized by Szold and Jastrow in their *Abodath Israel?*

2

Isaac Mayer Wise and *Minhag Amerika*

Because of a growing sentiment that the multiplicity of *minhagim* only engendered confusion and unnecessary division within the far-flung and still fragile Jewish community in the United States, the Cleveland Conference in 1855 commissioned Isaac M. Wise and others to prepare a uniform liturgical text that would appeal to conservative and liberal congregations alike.[1] The revisers were animated at once by loyalty to Reform and to the traditional halakhah. Although pains were taken to keep Orthodox and Reformer within the same camp, the compilers of the envisioned union prayerbook surrendered scarcely any of their convictions in the creation of a compromise text.

Wise, for instance, expounded a style and grade of Reform that partook of a moderation somewhat typical of what might perhaps be called the Breslau-Bohemian school. Doctrinally, the contents of *Minhag Amerika*[2] differ insubstantially from what was being taught by the more radical Eastern sections, as represented by David Einhorn, Samuel Adler, and others. Ritually and liturgically, however, the new *minhag* was rather respectful of the old forms.

After the Conference shelved the proposed prayerbook and disbanded for lack of common ground between the traditionalist and liberal factions, Wise himself adopted the text and later took greater liberties with it—in part because there was no longer an Orthodox presence to accommodate to and in part because his own peculiar brand of Reform underwent modification. His shift from a cautious, middle-of-the-road position to one that shows little, if any, equivocation becomes quite obvious if one compares the *Minhag Amerika* of 1857 to the 1872 edition.

As startlingly inventive and innovative as Wise proved to be, he did have before him various liturgical models to imitate, appropriate from, or take as a point of departure for his own work. The *Rabbinerversammlungen* of the mid-1840s gave him a theoretical foundation and a fund of practical pointers on the matter of liturgical revision. Wise derived much inspiration, too, from the Sephardic handling of the transmitted texts. A few of these had been mediated through the influential *Gebetbuch* conceived and issued in 1819 by the Hamburg Temple, whose rite left a considerable imprint not only on the architectonic of *Minhag Amerika* but on its hymnody as well. In the last analysis, these revisions are by and large what one might expect to appear in a typical Liberal siddur, particularly of the category that Petuchowski aptly called "Reform from within."

We address ourselves now to a consideration of those features in *Minhag Amerika* that rendered it unique among non-Orthodox prayerbooks. The dyed-in-the-wool rationalist that Wise was, he revealed, both in his *Minhag Amerika* and in his countless written works, a kind of scriptural fundamentalism, a Karaitic tendency as it were. A distinction must be drawn here. Given his deistically-tinged rationalism and his historical sense, Wise's scripturalism did not so much reflect a supernaturalist literalism[3]— which is far from the case—as much as a Haskalah type of renewed, literary appreciation of the Hebrew Bible. That appreciation was enhanced by the near-bibliolatry of nineteenth-century American Protestantism and by Wise's desire to ease the yoke of Rabbinic law by harking back to a simpler, pristine biblicism, itself a source of legitimation not likely to be questioned. Wise's quasi-Karaizing bent is illustrated in the way the *berakhot* for Rabbinic ordinances are couched[4] and in his predilection for prolix passages from the Tanakh in place of those—usually pertaining to the Levitical cult—chosen by tradition.[5]

All the same, the partiality shown by Wise to the biblical word over the Rabbinic should by no means be construed as utter disregard for the Talmud. His unstated theory would seem to be formulated thus: could streamlining of the system of commandments be obtained by resorting to Scripture, that too would constitute a valid path to be followed by Reform.

Minhag Amerika became widespread in the latter half of the nineteenth century, but, significantly, did not last more than a few decades. In contrast, Benjamin Szold and Marcus Jastrow's *Abodath Israel,* a contemporaneous liturgical work of approximately the same degree of Reform as *Minhag Amerika* but not nearly so eccentric, endured for close to a hundred years and continues to this day in a slightly altered form in Max D. Klein's *Seder Avodah* (I, 1951; II, 1960). One explanation lies in the fact that upon the appearance of the *Union Prayer Book* in 1894, Wise withdrew his own work in favor of the new rite. The dream of a unified American Israel was one that never had really left him, from the days of the Cleveland Conference on.

Another explanation for *Minhag Amerika*'s relative shortlivedness may well be its many idiosyncrasies, some of them outgrowths of Wise's ingenious, fertile mind. A goodly number of the prayers sanctified by centuries of use were so emended as to lose any recognizable affinity with the originals. In addition, *Minhag Amerika* contains a number of unconventional services: a private Yizkor designated for individual use either during a period of mourning or for *Jahrzeit* (but not *hazkarat neshamot*); and a lengthy, all-vernacular *Seelenfeier* (Memorial Service) on Yom Kippur Eve.[6] (There is vaguely similar usage among the Sephardim.)[7]

Wise's treatment of the *avodah* on Atonement Day is also *sui generis* and evidence of the author's literary skill and flair in the Hebrew language.[8] An omnivorous reader and scholarly maverick autodidact, the man's prolific outpouring of the pen, in English and in German, was a remarkable achievement—although his English style would suffer occasional lapses, particularly during the period of his editorial labors on *Minhag Amerika.* These slipups, rare and insignificant as they were, would hardly do for the non-immigrant next generation.

Nonetheless, several characteristic highlights in *Minhag Amerika* were to attain permanence, especially in the *Union Prayer Book,* which is basically a derivative of its rival prayerbook, *Olath Tamid.* The overall pattern of Wise's famous and moving *Seelenfeier,* with its haunting choral refrain, "What is man, O Lord?" was taken over in the High Holy Day volume of the *Union Prayer Book* and situated, more strategically and familiarly, between the Afternoon Service and *ne'ilah.* The Yizkor Service framed by Morris Silverman in our time for the Conservative mahzor[9] is in part Wise's version, updated and Hebraicized.

Similarly, the choice of *piyyutim* for Yom Kippur in the *Union Prayer Book* II is all Wise's; so is the manner in which the *aleynu,* or Adoration, is worked over.[10] The particularist *she-lo asanu,* offensive to many a nineteenth- or twentieth-century Liberal Jew, was deleted outright and the opening paragraph replaced with a subsequent passage, *she-hu noteh shamayim* until *hu eloheynu eyn od,* followed by *va'anahnu kor'im* and the continuation from *emet malkenu.* Wise's rewrite was ultimately the *Union Prayer Book's,* too, in translation generally and in the original language as a dramatic prelude to the *avodah* on Yom Kippur.

And of course the most felicitous case of borrowing is the 1918 *Union Prayer Book's* (and the earlier Reconstructionist prayerbooks')[11] Hebrew text of *sim shalom* from the 1857 edition of *Minhag Amerika,* which blends the particular with the universal, the Ashkenazic with the Sephardic, and the traditional with the liberal, in a prayer for peace. With the Sephardic and Liberal wording underlined, the petition reads as follows in Wise's translation:

> Our Father, whose goodness, blessing, favor, grace and mercy is with us, and *all who venerate Thy name* bless all of us unitedly with the light of Thy presence; for, O God our Lord, by the light of Thy presence Thou hast given us the Law of life, the love of grace, justice, blessing, mercy, and life and peace.

> Mayest Thou be pleased, to bless Thy people, Israel, *and all other nations with the fullness of Might and Peace.* Praised art Thou, God, *source of Peace.*

An earlier version of this chapter appeared in *Hebrew Abstracts* XIV (1973): 89–92. Reprinted with permission.

1. A brief discussion of *Minhag Amerika* in its antecedent phases may be found in Michael A. Meyer, *Response to Modernity: A History of the Reform Movement in Judaism* (N.Y./Oxford, 1988), pp. 233–35.

2. The full title of Wise's rite is *Minhag Amerika: Tefillot Beney Yeshurun/Daily Prayers* (Cincinnati, 1857). The revised edition has the slightly modified wording, *Minhag Amerika/The Daily Prayers for American Israelites* (Cincinnati, 1872). Both editions were published by Bloch and Co.

3. In the 1872 version of his prayerbook, Wise deleted from the *modim* prayer in the *amidah* the pregnant phrase *ve-al nissekha shebe-khol yom immanu* ("for Thy miracles daily with us"). Since the 1857 edition, the *al ha-nissim* inserts for Hanukkah and Purim have been missing their prefatory sentence, "We thank Thee also for the miracles, for the redemption, for the mighty deeds and saving deeds wrought by Thee, as well as for the wars which Thou didst wage for our fathers in days of old, at this season," starting instead directly with *bi-ymey mattityahu* and *bi-ymey mordekhay ve-ester.*

4. The blessings for a number of the biblical commandments are kept intact in the first edition of *Minhag Amerika,* as for tzitzit, tefillin, mezuzah, lulav, and 'dwelling in the sukkah.' By the 1872 edition, these *berakhot* fall by the wayside. However, in the blessings for Rabbinic ordinances (*mide-rabbanan*), to wit, for kindling the Hanukkah lights and reading the Megillah, the formulaic *asher qiddeshanu be-mitzvotav ve-tzivvanu* is abandoned for doctrinal reasons. In their place Wise offers, in Hebrew, an unusual conflate of two customary benedictions: "Blessed art Thou, O Lord our God, King of the universe, who hath kept us in life, sustained us, and enabled us to reach this season to kindle the light of

Hanukkah [or to read the book of Esther]," followed by the benediction *she-asah nissim* (thereby contradicting the anti-miraculous tendency mentioned above in n. 3!). This unconventional rearrangement appears in both the "traditionalist" 1864 edition and in the more freehanded 1872 one. Cf. Jakob J. Petuchowski, *Prayerbook Reform in Europe* (New York, 1968), chap. 10 ("Reform Benedictions for Rabbinic Ordinances").

5. For instance, in lieu of the cultic reading from Numbers 28:26–27 during the Festival *musaf amidah* on Shavu'ot, Wise furnishes for the same spot verses from Deuteronomy (4:9–13) recounting the climactic Sinai event.

6. See chap. 7.

7. Cf David de Sola Pool, ed., *Tefillot le-Yom Kippur/Prayers for the Day of Atonement According to the Custom of the Spanish and Portuguese Jews* (New York, 1984), pp. 32–34.

8. See chap. 4.

9. Morris Silverman, ed., *Maḥzor le-Rosh ha-Shanah ule-Yom ha-Kippurim/High Holiday Prayer Book* (Hartford, 1961), pp. 321–30.

10. See chap. 8.

11. In the current Reconstructionist *Kol Haneshamah: Shabbat Veḥagim* (Wyncote, Pennsylvania, 1994), *sim shalom* has become a fusion of the Conservative *Sabbath and Festival Prayer Book* (N.Y., 1946) version (*sim shalom, tovah u-verakhah* ba-olam) and the old Wisean formula (*levarekh et ammekha yisrael* ve-et kol ha-ammim be-rov oz ve-shalom).

3

Marcus Jastrow and *Abodath Israel*

The original creator of *Abodath Israel* (German ed., 1863; English ed., 1865) was Benjamin Szold. Although doctrinally somewhat progressive, the rite was fundamentally no different from the other nineteenth-century German Liberal prayerbooks.[1] In converting *Abodath Israel* into an American Liberal prayerbook (1873), however, Marcus Jastrow creatively modified the classical contours of the Siddur preserved in Szold's version and added many new prayers. Without minimizing Szold's significant role and initiative in originating the rite, our attention in this chapter focuses on the man who virtually re-created *Abodath Israel* and in so doing contributed significantly to the development of American Jewish liturgy. It was, after all, Jastrow's version that lasted well through the twentieth century and engendered similarly-oriented prayerbooks such as Barnett Elzas' various liturgical works and Max D. Klein's *Seder Avodah* (2 vols., Philadelphia, 1951 and 1960). In our treatment of Jastrow, we shall concentrate on his philosophy, aims, and methods—and only incidentally on the details of his textual reforms.

Born on June 5, 1829 in Rogasen, Posen, then a province in Prussia, Jastrow received secular training at the gymnasium concurrently with his rabbinic studies. He went on to the University of Berlin and later earned his doctorate at Halle, after which he obtained his first rabbinic post in the Liberal congregation at Warsaw (1858).

Jastrow's congregation consisted chiefly of the German Jewish element of the community, to which was joined the Polonizing intelligentsia. During his ministry a rift developed between the German majority and a Polish minority, but the young rabbi succeeded in reconciling the two elements and subsequently increased attendance at the once-divided synagogue. The experience of pacifying disagreeing parties was to stand him in good stead in his later work: infusing the traditional prayerbook with the new spirit of Liberal Judaism.

During Jastrow's stay in Warsaw, the Poles were chafing under the autocratic rule of their czarist overlords. Having thrown himself completely into the study of Polish life and language to integrate himself into his newly adopted surroundings, Jastrow, the religious liberal, joined the dean of Polish Orthodoxy, Dov Berish Meisels, in espousing the cause of the young Polish patriots in their revolutionary activities. When the first insurrectionists fell, the two Jewish clergymen stood shoulder to shoulder with their Christian counterparts in a funeral-demonstration against Russian tyranny.

Along with Meisels and other community leaders, Jastrow was imprisoned for three months, then expelled from Poland for participating in the short-lived uprising.[2] He assumed a pulpit at Mannheim, in Baden, but when the edict of banishment was revoked gave in to the importunings of his Warsaw congregation and agreed to return to his post there. When the revolt erupted anew and he was forced to abandon his homeward journey, he accepted a call from the renowned congregation at Worms, in Hesse-Darmstadt. The reactionary Bismarckian government, however, refused to ratify his appointment there because of his earlier political activities. Fortunately, he soon received a munificent offer from Congregation Rodeph Shalom in Philadelphia, which he accepted in 1866.

It would be out of place here to review the history of the congregation that was the object of Jastrow's spiritual care for the remainder of his life.[3] Instead, our attention will be focused on those factors, both personal and congregational, that ultimately led to further alterations in the Reform rite.

Scholarly Influences on Jastrow's Direction of Reform

To understand what predisposed Jastrow to embrace the cause of moderate Reform, it is illuminating to consider how he came to calibrate, as it were, the midpoint of the arc at the ends of which stand inelastic Orthodoxy and radical Reform.

One early influence must have been the eloquent preacher Michael Sachs, the protagonist of moderate Reform from Berlin. Although there is no record of any immediate relationship between the two, it is hard to imagine that Jastrow, a pedagogue at the religious school attached to Sachs's synagogue, was unaware of the controversies that raged between the fiery Sachs and the equally formidable Samuel Holdheim, leader of the *Jüdische Reformgemeinde.* The issues aired during their fervent exchanges could not have left the young Jastrow unimpressed.

Jastrow must also have known of Sachs's commitment to the continuity of Israel's historic identity and opposition to innovations inconsistent with the genius of Judaism, as well as his research in and translation of medieval Hebrew poetry. Sachs had already begun work on his monumental nine-volume *Festgebete der Israeliten,*[4] a poetical translation of the maḥzor. Thus Sachs's work must have served as a standard and model for Jastrow's verse reproductions of the Yom Kippur *piyyutim* in English.

Jastrow's historiographical proclivities were doubtless also influenced by contacts with Heinrich Graetz. Indicative of Jastrow's own chronicler's bent and well-developed critical sense is Graetz's eight-colume *Vier Jahrhunderte aus der Geschichte der Juden, von der Zerstörung des ersten Tempels bis zur makkabäischen Tempelweihe* (Heidelberg, 1865). Later, when Jastrow was on the editorial board of the Jewish Publication Society of America, he agitated for the publication in English of Graetz's *Geschichte der Juden* (1848).[5] In turn, it is noteworthy that Graetz was instrumental in advancing Jastrow's budding career. It was upon Graetz's recommendation that Jastrow was appointed preacher at the Warsaw Congregation mentioned above and later received the call to Mannheim.

Jastrow's allegiance to the moderate Reform, proto-Conservative camp was also cemented by his association with Manuel Joel (three years his senior) in the gymnasium and university, as well as in later years. Best known for his pioneering investigations of Jewish religious philosophy, Joel applied his critical acumen and skill with medieval texts to authoring a revised prayerbook for Abraham Geiger's former congregation at Breslau.[6] Joel's *Gebetbuch* —published in 1871, the same year as Jastrow's first revision of *Abodath Israel*—reverts in many cases to the traditional formulation in preference to Geiger's adaptation. The clear note of Reform is sounded throughout, however, within the framework of the traditional service. In some instances, Joel revises hallowed texts to the extent that the original is barely obvious. The Tenth Benediction of the *amidah,* for example, is drastically reworded in the following exalted manner:

תקע בשופר גדול לחרותנו
וקול דרור וישועה יישמע באהלינו
בא׳׳ה משמיע ישועה לשארית ישראל:

Of course, changes of this type are confined for the most part to the week-day *shemoneh esreh.* And each time the rewritten version appears, the traditional formula is furnished as well, in small print, for the benefit of

those attached to the established text. Withal, the contours of the traditional service abide, and a penetrating eye is needed to detect the modifications.

Many of Jastrow's early associates, as we can see, were advocates of the
tenets propounded by the Breslau school, although not all of them attended or taught at that city's Jewish Theological Seminary. These men recognized the necessity of Reform, and indeed fought valiantly on its behalf.
All the same, they had become wary of the drift of the *Rabbinerversammlungen* of the mid-forties, whose overall goal seemed to be to completely
reconstruct the religious life and worship of the Jew according to contemporary models.

In opposition to this tendency, Zacharias Frankel and his confederates of
the Positive-Historical school thought incessant temperature-taking of the
modern cultural environment a dubious procedure and that those elements
of Judaism that are eternal should not be so readily surrendered to the
mood of the hour. Distinctions had to be drawn between the permanent
and the accidental: it made little sense to remodel the timeless faith of
Israel according to the all-too-transient canons of the latest cultural fash-
ions and the evanescent dictates of current philosophical systems. If
changes were to be instituted, they had to be accomplished from within,
according to the innate genius of Judaism, and not imposed from without,
in conformity to alien standards.

Further proof of where Jastrow's sympathies lay can be surmised from
his various contributions, on historical and etymological subjects, to
Zacharias Frankel's *Monatsschrift* and to the Orthodox Abraham (Adolph)
Berliner's *Magazin für Wissenschaft des Judenthums.* Unlike most of his
American clerical counterparts of reformist tendencies, Jastrow emulated
his teachers of the Breslau trend by engaging in disinterested *Wissenschaft
des Judenthums.* David Einhorn and Isaac M. Wise were also scholars, but in
their scientific labors, which yielded occasional flashes of insight and
inventiveness, the polemical strain almost invariably had the upper hand.
All three men received tutelage in the traditional lore of Israel and in the
contents of the Talmud, Midrash, and Codes. Not all, however, submitted
to the discipline of rigorous objective scholarship. Attempts in that direction were often weakened by special considerations and partisan zeal. Like
his colleagues Szold, Huebsch, and Kohut, however, Jastrow did not allow
pulpit rhetoric to color his scholarly efforts.

Nor was the tendency among some "Breslauers" to pit *Wissenschaft des*

Judenthums against the devotional life to be tolerated by Jastrow. Moderate Reform was not to be charged with inconsistency or vacillation. It was to be grounded on principles as least as watertight as those of radical Reform. Many Romanticists of the Schleiermacherian variety were susceptible to strong doses of Rationalism. To a degree greater than his fellow prayer-book compilers, however, Jastrow implemented the ideals of analytic, objective scholarship to both advance the cause of the Positive-Historical party and to strip it of excessive Romantic elements—those elements that, in his opinion, only weakened its defensive position against the onslaughts of radical Reform.

The radical Reform group was not above manipulating occasional historical tidbits or eccentric halakhic practices to justify and legitimize their non-conformist practices or non-practices. In contrast, the members of the Positive-Historical party, with its characteristic reluctance to depart from established usage, sustained a unitary, corporate view of Jewish life and history. They felt no compulsion to avail themselves of deviant halakhic practices. Nor did they feel obliged to explain away such practices or to effect any forced, labored reconciliations. No harm was done in recording them or integrating them into the larger view of Judaism. Hence, the disciples of Frankel sensed no contradiction between an impersonal, detached study of the people and faith of Israel and a passionate commitment to that totality. Without accepting Geiger's radical inferences, they could heartily adopt his convictions as to the undeniable good that might accrue from such impartial inquiry. Although the all-out Reformers included the learned Geiger in their pantheon, they rarely subscribed to his program of dispassionate Jewish scholarship, believing that it bore too much of pedantic antiquarianism. The exclusively forward-looking posture of out-and-out Reform left little room for such disinterested musings about the past; scholarship would have to be subservient to one primary end: Reform.

But Jastrow did not consider it imperative to plunge into the depths of antiquity in order to yield something of immediate utilitarian value. He appreciated the value of Judaism in all of its phases: past, present, or future. Nor did he evade the demands of the hour; he faced controversial issues bravely, resolutely, and without either truckling under the demands of radical Reform or yielding meekly to long-standing usage.[7] His lexicographical *chef d'oeuvre,* twenty-five years in the making, may be said to have run against the current of on-going Reform, but to him scholarship was more important than ideology. He undertook the gigantic task of compiling his *Dictionary of the Targumim, the Talmud Babli and Yerushalmi, and the Midrashic Literature,*[8] familiar to English-speaking students of Rabbinic literature. Unstintingly he gave of his time and energy to the Maimonides College (1866–1873) as "Professor of Talmud, Hebrew Philosophy and Jewish History and Literature." During the last eight years of his life he served as chief editor of the Jewish Publication Society's *Holy Scriptures;* and from 1900 to 1903 as editor of the section on Talmud for the *Jewish Encyclopedia.*

All of these aspects of Jastrow's personality comes through in his 1871 German revision of *Abodath Israel.*[9] The technical apparatus of the prayerbook is faultless. The insertion of additional *piyyutim,* the metrical reproduction of the same in English (in the 1873 edition), and the composition of new prayers in the author's native and adopted languages all reveal his considerable literary and linguistic talents, as well as his mastery of Jewish learning.[10] There is no dissociating Jastrow the liturgist from Jastrow the scholar.

Jastrow's Pedagogic Interests

On perusing the contents of Jastrow's edition of *Abodath Israel,* one is surprised at the paucity of the expository or the informational. The Torah readings for the New Year and the Day of Atonement stand in the Hebrew text alone, as in Szold's 1863 original, unaccompanied by the expected English translation. This deficiency is curious in view of Jastrow's active participation in the translation of the Hebrew Bible and his replacement of the prescriptive Leviticus 18 with the loftier chapter 19 as the selection for the Yom Kippur afternoon Torah lesson. The didactic tenor so pronounced in today's Conservative prayerbooks is noticeably absent in the Jastrow revision. Frequent Hebrew transliteration is not resorted to, and such fundamental terms as *Torah, mitzvah* and *berakhah* are scarcely used. In this respect Jastrow hardly differed from his more radical Reform colleagues. Like them, he attached greater weight to the ethical teachings of Judaism, which, as set forth in *Abodath Israel,* are buttressed by Kant's categorical imperative. The only hint of the praiseworthiness of a life lived according to the requirements of the ritual law is the incidental mention of fasting in a few of the *piyyutim* read on the Day of Atonement.[11]

It is noteworthy that Issac M. Wise assumed that more than a few of his parishioners at K. K. Bene Yeshurun of Cincinnati could read unvocalized Hebrew.[12] Perhaps Wise entertained hopes of seeing congregations thoroughly versed in the holy tongue, at a level where the vowel points would become unnecessary. Jastrow was less sanguine and felt that only a minority would be able to appreciate the sources of Jewish tradition, including the prayerbook, in the original.[13] We know of his manifold activities on behalf of Jewish education, but are always struck by an undercurrent of despair in his view of the state of sound Jewish learning in America.

Nevertheless, Jastrow's artistic sensibilities got the better of him, and he could not resist introducing Rodeph Shalom worshipers and allied congregations to the treasures of medieval Hebrew liturgical poetry—much as Michael Sachs had done in the *Festgebete* for his Berlin flock. Jastrow revealed a decided predilection for those *piyyutim* that were in use in the Spanish-Portuguese rite,[14] to the extent of omitting some of the Ashkenazic *piyyutim* in Szold's edition, such as *melekh elyon el dar ba-marom, imeru lelohim, enosh eykh yitzdaq peney yotzero, omnam ken,* and *be-motza'ey menuhah.* Apart from such cherished pieces as the *ya'aleh* and *u-netanneh toqef,* the *piyyutim* in Jastrow's 1873 *Abodath Israel* are, in the main, Sephardic—although they are much more varied than those in the Hamburg *Gebetbuch,* which expressed a similar Sepharadizing tendency.[15]

While the credit for the spade-work is due to Szold, it was Jastrow who brought these medieval *piyyutim* to the attention of American Jewry by means of his tasteful poetic translations. Here the scholar, teacher, and litterateur in Jastrow combined to supply a worthy and gifted rendition of the creations from the Golden Age of Spanish Jewry. The following is an example of Jastrow's chaste expression, in a translation of Isaac ibn Ghayyat's *qerovah, yonah hafesah bi-netot ha-yom:*[16]

> The dove seeks shelter at the day's repose,
>> Beneath the Rock she hides herself at eve.
> She glances round, lo, soon the day will close,
>> She makes thy dwelling-place her nest at eve.
> She has been crying all this day in Woes,
>> "When shall I rise to God ? How slows the eve !"
> Pour out on her thy grace—the daylight goes,
>> Command thy love to rest on her this eve.

And as in prayer to thee this day she rose,
    Accept her, Lord; she waits from morn to eve.
O turn to us in love! the day fast flows,
    Long-stretching are the shadows of eve.

An examination of the Hebrew reveals Jastrow's fidelity to the underlying text, in spite of his usual habit of taking considerable liberties in his English renditions of statutory prayers. Jastrow aimed at cultivating the literary tastes of his congregants and leading them on the paths of virtue and righteousness, without reference to either halakhah or aggadah.

Whatever may be said of Eleazar Qallir's (possibly eighth century) obscure style, that prolific *paytan* from the age of Byzantium strove both to teach his listeners and to praise the *shome'a tefillah*.[17] By comparison, Jastrow's translations—many of them estimable in an age given to exaggerated, grotesque periphrasis—appear as literary diversions. In this, Reform has made itself felt.[18] Jastrow implemented many of the suggestions made at the Reform synods that convened since Szold wrote his first edition of *Abodath Israel*. Of course, such innovations were more possible two decades after the initial work of Reform had been done. Jastrow was to complete the task by actualizing the resolutions adopted at the Leipzig Synod of 1869: providing prayers and meditations in the vernacular to "be introduced into each of the four services on Yom Kippur as time permits"; recasting the intermediate sections of the *avodah* Service;[19] and restoring the one-year lectionary cycle, albeit abbreviated, in place of the triennial cycle that he and Szold had originally adopted.[20] Jastrow was even able to carry out the defeated resolution of abolishing the custom of calling congregants to the Torah.[21] He supplied a shortened *lekhah dodi* with three stanzas, plus refrain—but heeding the suggestion of Leopold Stein of Frankfurt am Main,[22] he proffered an alternative rubric after the table of contents: "English hymns may be inserted: In the Service for Sabbath Eve, in place of 'Lechah Dodi.'. . ."

With all his vast erudition in Rabbinic literature, Jastrow succumbed to contemporary criticism or reserve about the rabbis of the Talmudic age—who, for him, as for his liberal contemporaries, possessed a lesser degree of sanctity. Only those commandments that were biblically-derived (*mide-orayeta*) could be attended by a *berakhah* (*asher qiddeshanu be-mitzvotav*). The Rabbinic ordinances (*mide-rabbanan*) were not to be so accompanied. The

1841 edition of the Hamburg *Gebetbuch,* for example, conforms to this procedure. And in Jastrow's *Abodath Israel,* the Megillah-reading and candlelighting at Hanukkah are introduced with *she-asah nissim* and *she-heḥeyanu.*[23] The *hallel* is neither begun nor concluded with a *berakhah.*

A Change of Heart

Jastrow's theological interest in Reform can be traced as far back as 1865, as evidenced by this statement from his *Vier Jahrhunderte,* with its dilation upon the mission of Israel (the translation is Isaac Leeser's):[24]

> . . . to diffuse the knowledge of the sole, incorporeal, holy God; with this doctrine is connected that of purest philanthropy towards all men without any distinction, of the equality and unity of all men, whose value depends only on their moral conduct, the doctrine of Providence, which leads mankind to continually progressing improvement of morals, until at length all shall acknowledge and love the sole and only One, until the love of fellow-beings shall have taken possession of all, when war shall cease, peace shall prevail and God will judge between all the nations.

Jastrow's Reform principles—the degree and definition of his Reform—are precisely defined in his *Antwort an Herrn I. M. Wise* (1867), in the form of a *syllabus errorum.* Without going into the details of the controversy, which became bitter and personal, we are indebted to it for having forced Jastrow to itemize his theory of Reform in the form of a *sic et non* summary:

1. I am for any reform that is able to influence the moral enhancement of the Jews.
2. I am against any reform that issues out of a mere desire toward assimilation or grasping after innovation without its being a means toward moral elevation.
3. I am for any reform that is compatible with the spirit of Judaism.
4. I am against any reform that denies this spirit.
5. I am for any reform that confers the outer appearance of Jewish thought-content with beauty and worth.

6. I am against any reform that ascribes all worth to outer appearance.
7. I am for any reform that links itself with the historical development of Judaism.
8. I am against any reform that severs its connection with the past.
9. I am for any reform that makes it possible for all Jews still to find themselves in our houses of worship in spite of many changes.
10. I am against any reform that dissolves this link with co-religionists.
11. I am for any reform that arouses the consciousness and keeps it aware that outer forms are vehicles of inner thought.
12. I am against any reform that rejects those vehicles as unnecessary.
13. I am for any reform that is, without strain, consistent with the Bible and its oldest traditional interpretation, as set down in the Talmud.
14. I am against any reform that arbitrarily creates new interpretations, inasmuch as I know I cannot do without the traditional guide in the practical implementation of the biblical commandments.
15. I am for any reform that removes the old-fashioned prayers that came into being during the Middle Ages.
16. I am against any reform that touches or alters the older portions of the prayers.
17. I am for any reform that concerns itself within the above-cited limits with the maintenance of peace with the congregation.
18. I am against any reform that threatens peace and promotes dissension.

This itemized platform helps us to understand the criteria underlying Jastrow's revision of *Abodath Israel* and the ritual reforms executed in his synagogue. The blend of tradition and change enunciated in the *Antwort* is embodied in the *"minhag* Jastrow"; but, in real life, with the growing progressivism and exclusivism of American Reform, Jastrow had to either take a stand against the movement's drift or violate his convictions.

His intensifying opposition to Reform as it was represented by Wise, Kohler, and others is attested by a letter, dated Philadelphia, January 4, 1886, to Jacob Ezekiel. In it Jastrow takes exception to the appointment by the Hebrew Union College of the "congregational-leader-editor" Wise as its provost, and notes[25]

. . . the indignation, too, against the Pittsburgh Conference, an indignation more general than the *American Israelite* seems to admit, arose not merely from the principles there proclaimed but more from the whole tone and temper displayed. It is felt that the whole Conference was a piece of machination against the attempt at reconciling all factions if possible, through the personal contact and unostentatious meetings held by the Ministers' Associations—attempts which, if continued, will lead to cooperation in maintaining and strengthening the "religious sense" in the people, no matter whether in "orthodox" or "reform" direction.

A little over a year before the framing of the Pittsburgh Platform, Jastrow was harking back to the particularistic aspect of Judaism, without denying its universalistic features—and thus setting himself apart from the more radically-disposed Reformers. To his congregation Jastrow expressed his sentiments in the following sermon, in a style redolent of the Rabbinic Midrash:[26]

Israel was chosen from among the nations for a peculiar mission, and in the furtherance of that mission, special laws were enjoined. Can we ourselves then preserve our truths best by giving up our peculiar laws? Let us learn from nature . . . Here is a well renowned throughout the land for its medicinal properties; to it the weak and afflicted flock from all parts, drink of its soothing waters and return strong, renewed in strength and spirit. The wiseacre suggests: "Why should these weak and afflicted ones be made to go through long and weary distances to drink of the healing waters? Remove the borders of the well, dig channels that these waters may flow through the land, bringing with it happiness to all." But he forgets that the waters pure and clean obtain much of their virtue from the nature of the ground in which it lies; that if the borders of the wall are removed and the waters flow from their accustomed place, not only may its original power be dissipated, but it may gather foreign qualities in its course baneful to those whose health it was expected to restore.

So it is with Israel's religion . . .

Jastrow's congregation, Rodeph Shalom, withdrew from the Union of American Hebrew Congregations in 1884, in the wake of rash and irresponsible remarks made by Wise regarding *kashrut* and other theological and halakhic matters. It rejoined the Union eleven years later, at the prompting of Henry Berkowitz, one of the first graduates of the Hebrew Union College and Jastrow's successor to the pulpit. (Jastrow was made rabbi emeritus in 1892). With a view toward adopting the *Union Prayer Book* and at Berkowitz's suggestion, on May 31, 1895, a Sabbath Eve Service was held using the newly-created rite. Predictably, Jastrow did not take kindly to the action, and in a communication to the congregation voiced his strong opposition to its adoption.[27]

The better part of Jastrow's life had been spent in trying to effect a modus vivendi between what he believed to be the inherent nature of Judaism and the just demands of Reform. Although his position led inevitably to difficulties and tensions, his reworking of Szold's *Abodath Israel* shows the extent of his success. The 1871 and 1873 editions remain remarkably free, textually speaking, of theological dissonances and aesthetic incongruities.[28]

Jastrow's own Rodeph Shalom, one of the first congregations to adopt the *Union Prayer Book,* did not prove loyal to its leader's rite. Others, however, were. As late as 1932, Morris Silverman noted in a "Report of Survey on Ritual" that four Conservative congregations were still using the Jastrow *Abodath Israel.*[29] A last edition was printed in 1954, making it the longest-lasting of all the American Reform prayerbooks.[30]

Nevertheless, Jastrow was bitter about his congregation's defection, and made no secret of his feelings to the press.[31] He was now irrevocably in the traditionalist camp. Despite the propensity of the wealthier members of the temple—and even the not so wealthy—for lavish funerals, for example, Jastrow put himself on record against costly funeral trappings, perhaps as a final act of defiance against his congregation's refractory ways:[32]

> It is my will that my funeral be conducted in the plainest and least expensive way. Let the coffin be plain and entirely unornamented . . . I wish to be buried in a plain white shroud. At my funeral nothing but the ritual shall be read . . . In expressing these wishes it is my object to set an example of simplicity, as against the burdensome extravagances now in vogue at funerals, which rests heavily upon those who feel forced to go beyond their powers for the sake of appearances . . .

Sadly, proof of Jastrow's total alienation from both his congregation and his earlier commitment to liturgical renewal was his repudiation of *Abodath Israel* in favor of the Orthodox Singer volume for his own private worship.[33]

An earlier version of this chapter appeared in *Texts and Responses,* ed. Michael A. Fishbane and Paul R. Flohr (Leiden: E.J. Brill, 1975), pp. 186–200. Reprinted with permission.

1. A particularly important German Liberal influence on Szold's book was Leopold Stein's *Seder ha-Avodah, Gebetbuch für Israelitische Gemeinden* (Frankfurt am Main, 1860).

2. Ismar Elbogen, A *Century of Jewish Life* (Philadelphia, 1960), pp. 64–66; Simon Dubnow, *Divrey Yemey 'Am 'Olam,* trans. Baruch Karu (Tel Aviv, 1952), p. 632; *Encyclopaedia Britannica,* 1959 ed., XIII, 143.

3. Eduard Davis, A *History of Rodeph Shalom Congregation* (Philadelphia, 1926); Jeanette W. Rosenbaum, "The Hebrew German Society Rodeph Shalom in the City and County of Philadelphia (1800–1950)," *Publications of the American Jewish Historical Society* 41 (September 1951-June 1952): 83–93.

4. Second ed. (Berlin, 1855–56).

5. Jastrow's historical aptitude asserts itself transparently in his long Tish'ah be-Av prayer, which is a schematic recapitulation of Israel's past.

6. Max Wiener, *Abraham Geiger and Liberal Judaism: The Challenge of the Nineteenth Century* (Philadelphia, 1962), pp. 47–49.

7. E. Davis, op. cit., pp. 82, 84–85, 86, 90–91, 95.

8. 2 vols. (London and New York, 1886–1903).

9. Jastrow's first revision of *Abodath Israel* (1871) was in German; his subsequent revision (1873) in English.

10. In his study "Bachya and 'The Duties of the Heart' " *(Sermons, Addresses and Studies* [London, 1958], Vol. III, pp. 337–38), Joseph J. Hertz discusses the mystic moralist's *tokheḥah, barekhi nafshi,* quoting "a few sentences in the noble version of Dr. Jastrow."

11. Mention is made in *malki mi-qedem po'el yeshu'ot,* by Mordecai ben Shabbetai, read during *musaf,* where the verse

וראה צומו ונפשו כי רוח אין בו.
כי לא אכל לחם כל היום:

is rendered:

"See their afflicted souls, as they abstain
From food all this day."

(This supplicatory *piyyut* has had remarkable staying power in the Afternoon Service of UPB II, from the 1894 edition all the way to the 1978 *Sha'arey Teshuvah.* The verse in question has, interestingly, never appeared in any of these editions.) This almost unexpected allusion to abstinence from food and drink is overshadowed by its absence in the prayers and meditations in the vernacular, which speak of the soul's "exhaustion." One wonders, however, whether this is from fasting. In the stirring *ya'aleh* hymn Jastrow, following Szold, gives us *ya'aleh atiratenu me-erev* instead of the customary *ya'aleh innuyenu me-erev*. (Klein departs from his *Abodath Israel* predecessors and, for grammatical reasons, goes back to the older wording.) Even the Feast of Tabernacles, with its rich symbolism, is described in an introductory English prayer simply as "a feast of joy for thy protecting care"—with hardly a word about the sukkah or the Four Species—although there is a benediction before the waving of the lulav prior to the *hallel* and the requisite *hoshanot* after the *musaf amidah*. The mandatory character of the Law is blurred, as in this prayer for the Feast of Weeks:

> ". . . our hearts rejoice in the inestimable privilege of having been chosen to spread the pure knowledge of thee, O God, and the love of man over the whole face of the earth; and we pray thee to accept these joyful emotions as our offering of thanks, now and evermore."

12. The 1857 and 1872 editions of *Minhag Amerika* contain *dinim ha-shayyakhim le-hilkhot tefillah,* which are sundry inspirational sentences—rather than ritual directions as the title would seem to imply—relating to prayers from the Talmud and the *Shulḥan Arukh,* solely in Hebrew, and unpunctuated at that!

13. Cf. E. Davis, op. cit., pp. 90–91; Moshe Davis, *Yahadut Amerika be-Hitpatḥutah* (New York, 1951), pp. 179–80.

14. Acquaintance with the Hamburg *Gebetbuch,* Sachs's *Die religiöse Poesie der Juden in Spanien* (1845), and Isaac Leeser's Sephardic *Siddur Siftey Tzaddiqim* (2d ed., Philadelphia, 1853) doubtless helped reinforce *Abodath Israel's* Sepharadizing tendency from its inception.

15. It is to be recalled that the Leipzig Synod of 1869 had urged greater selectivity with regard to the High Holiday *piyyutim.*

16. It is not inconceivable that Jastrow's inclusion of this fitting *qerovah* for *ne'ilah* was actuated by Einhorn's use of the same in *Olath Tamid.* (Szold did not include it.) Einhorn himself borrowed the "überaus liebliche" *yonah ḥafesah* from Sachs's *Poesie.*

17. Leopold Zunz, *Die Gottesdienstlichen Vortrage historisch entwickelt* (Frankfurt am Main, 1892), 395–402; Jefim Schirmann, "Hebrew Liturgical Poetry and Christian Hymnology, *JQR* 44 (1953): 138–46.

18. Just as the *piyyutim* in Jastrow's *Abodath Israel* are rendered more faithfully than the statutory prayers, the translation of the High Holy Day prayers in *Union Prayer Book* II has tended to be more literal than that of the Hebrew pieces in *Union Prayer Book* I.

19. David Philipson, *The Reform Movement in Judaism* (rev., New York, 1931), p. 303.

20. Ibid., p. 302.

21. Ibid., p. 303; *Ismar Elbogen, Der Jüdische Gottesdienst in seiner geschichtlichen Entwicklung,* 3rd ed. (Frankfurt am Main, 1931), p. 429.

22. Philipson, *The Reform Movement,* p. 138. The shortened version of *lekhah dodi* was later adopted in the 1940 edition of the *Union Prayer Book*

23. It would be interesting to know whether Jastrow and his colleagues did not have in mind the Talmudic dictum concerning the Hanukkah lights (B. Shabbat 23a), which, admittedly, would act as a very weak support.

24. *Occident* 44 (1866): 70–71. The passage is taken from Jastrow's first lecture in his *Vier Jahrhunderte*, p. 6.

25. American Jewish Archives, Box 1278.

26. "National and Universal Judaism," *Jewish Messenger* 55 (Feb. 15, 1884); Moshe Davis, *The Emergence of Conservative Judaism* (Philadelphia, 1963), pp. 306–7, 463, n. 53.

27. E. Davis, op. cit., pp. 96, 106–8.

28. Bernhard Felsenthal observed concerning *Abodath Israel,* ". . . es gewährt dem Referenten besondere Freude, sagen zu können, dass, vom Standpunkt der Bearbeiter aus, das Werk also ein ganz gelungenes bezeichnet werden kann." "Ein neues Gebetbuch," *The Jewish Times,* Deutscher Theil 3 (Dec. 29,1871): 733–34.

29. *Proceedinsgs of the Rabbinical Assembly* 4 (1932): 322; cf. Moshe Davis, op. cit., p. 178, n. 51.

30. Temple Ohabei Shalom, Boston's oldest Reform congregation, was still using the "Minhag Jastrow" as late as the 1950s.

31. E. Davis, op. cit., p. 105.

32. *The Jewish Exponent,* 37 (Oct. 16, 1903).

33. Moshe Davis, "Benjamin Szold u'Marcus Jastrow," *Sefer ha-Shanah li-Yhudey Ameriqah, The American Hebrew Year Book* 6 (1942):427–39.

4

Hebrew Liturgical Creativity
in Nineteenth-Century America

Nowadays within the United States new Hebrew liturgical compositions are pretty much taken for granted. Running the gamut from traditional non-Orthodox rituals to the avant garde to specially written services for Yom ha-Sho'ah or Yom ha-Atzma'ut, hardly a prayerbook has been issued in recent years that does not contain an innovative prayer in the sacred language of the Jewish people.

This was not always the case. In the nineteenth century, American Jewish liturgical activity limited itself to reconciling standard Hebrew texts with contemporary thought and temper, to condensing services, and to drafting new prayers in the vernacular. Aware that large-scale changes in the liturgy would drive away some worshipers and that unnecessary division could wreck a young and still-fragile American Jewish community, those who shaped non-Orthodox American siddurim of the mid-nineteenth century proceeded with caution. (*Olath Tamid,* symbol of a kind of *Austrittsreform,* was a conspicuous exception, as discussed in chapter one). By the last decade of the century, even greater liberties were taken with the transmitted prayer texts and a larger role assigned to the vernacular, on occasion to the virtual displacement of Hebrew in non-Orthodox services.

Before the Anglicization of Jewish worship accelerated, however, a period of substantial and creditable Hebrew liturgical creativity intervened for about twenty years and recurred again in the middle of the present century. Interestingly, the majority of the nineteenth-century liturgists, including the most Hebraically-minded among them, were scarcely animated by the Zionist ideal in any of its pre-Herzlian configurations, much less after it was to ripen into a full-scale movement. The only prayerbook revisers to cast their lot with the Zionist camp were Benjamin Szold (1829–1902) and his colleague and collaborator, Marcus Jastrow (1829–1903).

Hebrew Creativity in the Shemoneh Esreh

One of the likeliest targets for Hebrew textual rewrites in the early period was the weekday *shemoneh esreh.* The recensions extend from the barely detectable to the drastic. As an illustration of the diverse ways one passage has been revised, for Benediction Ten in *Order of Prayer* (1855), Leo Merzbacher (1809–1856) substitutes the following, in which universalism and particularism mesh and fuse: (English translations are as they are supplied in the rites, unless otherwise noted):

חרות

תקע בשופר גדול לחרות עמים. ושא נס לקבץ גליות. וקרב פזורינו.
ונפוצותינו כנס מירכתי ארץ. וברך לאמים יחד. בברית שלום
ושלוה. אהבה ואחוה: ברוך אתה יי מקבץ נדחים:

> Sound the great shofar proclaiming the freedom of peoples. Raise the banner to gather in exiles, and assemble our scattered kin and dispersed ones from the ends of the earth. Bless the nations together in a covenant of peace and tranquility, love and brotherhood. Blessed art Thou, O Lord, who gatherest the dispersed. [Translation mine]

Interestingly, Merzbacher's successor at the congregation that later became Temple Emanu-El in New York, Samuel Adler (1809–1891), saw fit to rule out *ve-qarev pezureynu u-nefutzoteynu kannes mi-yarketey aretz* and leave the rest, including *ve-sa nes le-qabbetz galuyot,* this time interpreted broadly to mean all humankind's exiles. In the 1873 edition of Szold's *Abodath Israel,* Jastrow redrafted the benediction—keeping, however, the rhythm and pacing of the traditional locution and underlining the outer thrust of the Jews' raison d'être, their mission to the world.

תקע בשופר גדול לחרות עולם. ושא נס עמך ישראל בארבע כנפות
הארץ. ברוך אתה יי מרים נס עמו ישראל:

> May liberty be enjoyed throughout the whole earth, and grant that thy people Israel, in all quarters of the globe, may be recognized and appreciated for their efforts towards the advancement of truth and enlightenment. Blessed be thou, O Lord, who exaltest on high the banner of Israel.

Wise's emendation of the same benediction in both the 1857 and, more especially, the 1872 editions of *Minhag Amerika* decidedly blunts Israel's special capacity as agent of divine revelation to the world:

תקע בשופר גדול לחרות כל־העמים ושא נס ליחדם בברית שלום
וקרבם אליך לעבדך באמת. ברוך אתה יי חובב עדת לאמים:

Let resound the great trumpet for the liberty of all nations; lift up the banner to unite them in the covenant of peace, and bring them nigh unto Thee, to worship Thee in truth. Blessed be Thou who lovest the community of nations.

The general accord reached by the nineteenth-century prayerbook compilers on the ever-besetting *golah/galut* question brings us to a consideration of how Zion and Jerusalem fit into their scheme of things. Although some of the aforementioned rabbis advocated in unqualified terms a return to Israel's ancient homeland, all but Adler and Wise have a special place for Jerusalem in their rituals. For instance, in his Fourteenth Benediction, Merzbacher envisions the city as a kind of *civitas dei* and includes an apposite citation of Zechariah 1:3:

ירושלים

ולירושלים עירך ברחמים תשוב. ותשכון בתוכה כאשר דברת.
ונקראה ירושלים עיר האמת. והר יי צבאות הר הקדש: ברוך אתה
יי בונה ירושלים:

Return in mercy to Jerusalem, thy city, and do Thou dwell in her midst, as Thou hast spoken: "And Jerusalem shall be called the faithful city, and the mountain of the Lord of Hosts." Blessed art Thou, O Lord, who rebuildest Jerusalem. [Translation mine]

Jastrow in this same benediction provides a simple, low-keyed Hebrew wording; its English paraphrastic rendering is Ahad Ha'amist in tone:

ולירושלים עירך ברחמים תשיב זיוה. ולכבוד תהיה בתוכה כאשר
דברת. כי מציון תצא תורה. ודבר יי מירושלים. ברוך אתה יי בונה
ירושלים:

May the glory of Jerusalem, thy city, be restored as the spiritual center, whence sprung forth all divine ideas, in accordance with thy promise, that from Zion the law should go forth, and the word of the Lord out of Jerusalem. Blessed be thou, O Lord, who didst rear up Jerusalem as the center of religious ideas.

Of all the alterations, perhaps the most extravagant is the Wisean 1872 overhaul of Benediction Fourteen. Although the Hebrew is hardly idiomatic in a liturgical sense, it is fairly clear what Wise was trying to say. With the dispersion of the Jewish people, the Shekhinah is no longer seen as circumscribed or concentrated in any single spot or shrine:

שכון בקרבנו יי אלהינו ורוח קדשך הופע עלינו כאשר נתת אותנו
לברית עם לאור גוים. קדש את־שמך על מקדישי שמך. ברוך אתה
יי הנקדש בנו לעיני הגוים:

God, our Lord, let Thy dwelling be in our midst, and let the glory of Thy holiness shine upon us, as Thou hast made us the people of the covenant into the light of the nations. Sanctify Thy name upon those who sanctify it. Praised be Thou, God, who art sanctified by us before the nations.

Gilluy shekhinah here would intimate for Wise diffusion/disclosure rather than banishment of the Divine Presence.

In connection with our discussion on the reworking of individual benedictions in the weekday *tefillah,* it is interesting to note a significant restructuring carried out by Benjamin Szold in his exquisite and well-proportioned domestic companion volume to *Abodath Israel* called *Hegyon Lev, Israelitisches Gebetbuch für häusliche Andacht* (1867). For the private Morning Service, Szold preserves the scaffolding of the tannaitic *Stammgebete,* including the Shema and its attendant benedictions, yet offers an extraordinary revision of the *tefillah.* Not only is the *havinenu,* with small adjustments, enlisted in place of the usual thirteen Intermediate Benedictions (since it is already an abstract of them), but the Introductory Three and the Concluding Three are likewise condensed after the pattern of the customary *birkat me'eyn sheva,* or *magen avot,* on Friday night. The following is Szold's abbreviated private *shemoneh esreh,* with his accompanying German translation:

ברוך אתה יי אלהינו ואלהי אבותינו. אלהי אברהם אלהי יצחק
ואלהי יעקב. האל הגדול הגבור והנורא. אל עליון קונה שמים
וארץ. מגן אבות בדברו. מחיה מתים במאמרו. האל הקדוש שאין
כמוהו. ברוך אתה יי האל הקדוש:

הביננו יי אלהינו לדעת דרכיך. ומול את לבבנו ליראתך. סלח לנו
חטאינו. וגאלנו למען שמך. רחקנו מחולי ומכאוב . ודשננו בשובע
ברכותיך. נפוצותינו תקרב לעבודתך. והתועים ישפטו על דעתך.
יעלצו בך אוהבי שמך. וישמחו בבנין עירך. הרם קרננו בישועתך.
ואל תשיבנו ריקם מלפניך. טרם נקרא אתה תענה. ברוך אתה יי
שומע תפלה:

לפניך יי אלהינו נעבוד ביראה ופחד. ונודה לשמך בכל יום תמיד.
מעין הברכות. אל ההודאות. אדון השלום. ברוך אתה יי עושה
השלום:

Gelobt seiest Du, Ewiger, unser Gott, und Gott unserer Väter, Gott Abrahams, Gott Isaaks und Gott Jakobs;—grosser, allmächtiger und ehrfurchtegebietender Gott!—Herr in den Höhen!—Schöpfer des Himmels und der Erde! Der ein Schild war unseren Ahnen mit seinem Worte, und durch seinen Anspruch die Todten belebt, der heilige Gott, dem Keiner gleicht. Gelobt seiest Du, Ewiger, heiliger Gott.

O, gib uns Einsicht, Ewiger, unser Gott, Deine Wege zu erkennen und öffne unser Herz Deiner Ehrfurcht. Vergib uns unsere Sünden und erlöse uns um Deines Namens Willen. Halte uns fern von jeglichem Leid und Weh und erquicke uns mit der Fülle Deiner Segnungen. Bring' unsere Zerstreuten Deinem Dienste näher und leite die Irrenden nach Deiner Einsicht. Lass frohlocken in Dir Alle, die Deinen Namen lieben, und sich erfreuen an dem Aufbaue Deiner Gottesstadt. Erhöhe unsere Würde durch Dein Heil und lass uns nicht leer weggehen von Deinem Angesichte. Bevor wir rufen, mögest Du uns erhören ja das Gebet aus jedem Munde in Barmherzigkeit. Gelobt seiest Du, Ewiger, Erhörer des Gebetes.

Vor Dir, Ewiger, unser Gott, stehen wir im Dienste, in heiliger Scheu, und im Schauer der Andacht. Wir danken Deinem Namen täglich und unaufhörlich, o Urquell der Segnungen, Gott der Dankeslieder und Herr des Friedens! Gelobt seiest Du, Ewiger, Schöpfer des Friedens.

Szold's rendition in German is rather close to his Hebrew formulation. My English translation below is a literal one of the German:

Praised be Thou, Eternal, Our God, and God of our fathers, God of Abraham, God of Isaac and God of Jacob;—great, almighty, and awesome God!—exalted Lord!—Creator of heaven and earth! Who was a shield to our ancestors with His word, and who at His bidding reviveth the dead, the holy God, whom none resembleth. Praised be Thou, Eternal, holy God.

O, give us insight, Eternal, our God, to know Thy ways and open our heart to Thy reverence. Forgive us our sins and redeem us for Thy name's sake. Keep far from us every sorrow and pain and quicken us with the fullness of Thy blessing. Bring our scattered ones closer to Thy service and lead the wayward toward Thy judgment. Let those that love Thee exult in Thee, and rejoice in the building of Thy holy city. Raise our dignity through Thy salvation and let us not go away emptyhanded from Thy presence. Before we call, mayest Thou hearken unto us; for Thou hearkenest in mercy unto the prayer of every mouth. Praised be Thou, Eternal, hearer of prayer.

Before Thee, Eternal, our God, we stand in service, in holy fear, and in awe of devotion. We thank Thy name daily and unceasingly, O Source of blessings, God of thanksgiving and Lord of peace! Praised be Thou, Eternal, Maker of peace.

This abridgement does not, however, dislodge the full weekday *amidah* for public daily worship. Szold's capsule is in all likelihood designed for the benefit of the worshiper needing to be at work on time, much like the traditional *havinenu.*

The Avodah Service on Yom Kippur

Another example of Hebrew liturgical creativity was the *avodah* section of the Additional Service for the Day of Atonement. Merzbacher, Wise (1857), and Szold each furnished an *avodah* in Hebrew. Einhorn's and Jastrow's were in German and English respectively—both reserved the Hebrew exclusively for the high-priestly confession ([*ve-khakh hayah omer}* *ana ha-shem*), whether twice or thrice said.

A common practice among the nineteenth-century Reformers was to replace R. Meshullam b. Kalonymos' virtuoso *amitz koaḥ* with the easier to understand and mellifluent Sephardic preamble to the *avodah, attah konanta.* Szold followed suit, incorporating some fresh additions of his own for the sake of brevity and clarity. Between the High Priest's three confessions, he substituted the appropriate verses from Leviticus 16 (describing the priestly Atonement service) for the poetic paraphrases of the relevant sections in Mishnah Yoma (whence the literary material for the *avodah* derives). In so doing, he underscored the priest's rank as teacher (after the portrait in Malachi 2:7) and model for the Jewish people as emissaries of ethical monotheism to the whole human race.

Szold intromitted several explanatory paragraphs in pure Hebrew and gave his own novel version of *ashrey ayin,* just as several of the great medieval *paytanim*—Solomon ibn Gabirol, Judah Halevi and Abraham ibn Ezra—did. Let one of Szold's own verses of the same speak for itself, this one shortly after the third and last confession by the *kohen gadol:*

כל אלה בהיות ההיכל על יסודותיו. ומקדש הקדש על מכונותיו.
וכהן גדול עומד ומשרת. דורו ראו ושמחו:
אשרי עין ראתה כל אלה.
הלא למשמע אזן דאבה נפשנו:
אשרי עין ראתה מכהן כהן וחק דתותיו בפיהו. ועולה לא נמצא
בשפתיו.
אשרי נוצרי עדותיו:
אשרי עין ראתה שכינת אל בדבירו. וכהן ומלכים ילכו לאורו.
אשרי שאל יעקב בעזרו:
אשרי עין ראתה הדרת קדש בקרב עמו. וכהן אמריו ירב.
אשרי תבחר ותקרב:

אשרי עין ראתה חזות מאוד נוראה. וחוט שני הלבין להראות קו
פליאה.
אשרי נשוי פשע כסוי חטאה:
אשרי עין ראתה זכים במקדש מעוני. בשוב יי את שיבת ציון לעיני.
אשרי הגבר אשר יבטח ביי:
אשרי עין ראתה קהל האל מריע. בצאתו חפשי ישועה משמיע.
אשרי המחכה ויגיע:

All these rites were performed while the Temple, with its Holy of
Holies, remained on its site, the High Priest standing forth to minister. His generation saw and rejoined. (Traditional maḥzor)

Happy the eye that saw these things. How doth our soul grieve at
their recounting.

Happy the eye that saw the High Priest officiate and impart laws by
his mouth. "And no wrong was found on his lips." (Mal. 2:6)

"Happy are those who keep His testimonies." (Ps. 119:2)

Happy the eye that saw the Presence [Shekhinah] of God in the inner
sanctuary. Priest and kings shall come to His light.

"Happy is he whose help is the God of Jacob." (Ps. 146:5)

Happy the eye that saw the beauty of holiness in the midst of His
people and the Priest speaking eloquently.

"Happy is he whom Thou dost choose and bring near [to dwell in
Thy courts.]" (Ps. 65:5)

Happy the eye that saw a truly awesome sight, a scarlet thread turning white, thus showing a wondrous judgment.

"Happy is the one whose transgression is forgiven, whose sin is covered."(Ps. 32:1)

Happy the eye that saw the pure ones in the holy abode, when the
Lord restored the fortunes of Zion before mine eyes.

"Happy is the man who trusteth in the Lord."(cf. Jer. 17:7 and Ps. 40:5)

Happy the eye that saw the congregation of God making joyful noise
when he came out free, announcing salvation.

"Happy is he that waiteth and cometh." (Dan. 12:12)

[Translation mine.]

Wise may not have been quite as respectful of the tripartite architectonic of the *avodah* as Szold: the author of *Minhag Amerika* supplied only
one set of *ve-kakh hayah omer* and *veha-kohanim veha-am* paragraphs, the
High Priest's confession on behalf of the entire congregation of Israel. But
he certainly took no less heed of the grand dramatic quality of this section
of the *musaf* service. In contrast, Adler seemed eager to finish the *avodah* as
quickly and painlessly as possible: he devoted only three pages to it
(Merzbacher had seven).

In addition to reproducing two of ibn Gabirol's verses, *aromemkha
ḥizqi ve-ḥelqi* and *ashrey ayin,* for the beginning and conclusion of
the *avodah,* Wise furnished a new version of *amitz koaḥ* in flawless biblical Hebrew. In it, he retained Meshullam b. Kalonymos' *incipits,* or
introductory phrases (*amitz koaḥ* and later *nilvim elav* [that is, the
High Priest] *nevonin yeshishey sha'ar,* here altered to *nilvu elekha* [that is,
God] *avraham, yitzḥaq ve-ya'aqov ha-temimim),* reviewing Israel's pri-
mordial beginnings as a priest-people and reducing the cultic aspect to
the barest minimum.

Wise's metrical and scripturally-inspired finish to his distinctive rendition of *seder ha-avodah* aptly encapsulates the liturgist's understanding of
the ancient institution of sacrifice. (Note: in the following Hebrew
excerpt the *ḥet* stands for the officiant [*ḥazzan*] and the *qof* for the congregation [*qahal*])

ח' שש אנכי על אמריך. ואני באתי בדבריך : **ק'** כי כתוב לא על
זבחיך אוכיחך: **ח'** על דבר זבח ועלותיכם. לא צויתי את אבותיכם:
ק' מה שאלתי ומה דרשתי ממך. כי אם ליראה אותי: **ח'** לעבוד
בשמחה ובלבב טוב. הנה שמוע מזבח טוב: **ק'** ולב נשבר ממנחה
טהורה. זבחי אלהים רוח נשברה: **ח'** זבח ומנחה לא חפצת. חטאת
ועולה לא שאלת: **ק'** מזבח אבנה בשברון לבי. ואשברה אף רוחי
בקרבי: **ח'** רום לב אשפיל ואת רום עיני ואקרע לבבי למען אדני: **ק'**
שברי רוחי הם זבחיך. יעלו לרצון על מזבחך:

I rejoice in Thy precepts, and approach Thee with Thy words, as were written: "I will not admonish thee on account of sacrifices or burnt offerings"—"I have not given commandments to your parents, on account of sacrifices and burnt offerings."—"What I ask and what I require of thee, it is nothing except to fear me, to worship with gladness and a happy heart; for obedience is better than sacrifice."— "And the contrite heart is more acceptable to me than the pure offering." The repenting soul sacrifices to the most High. Thou desirest neither offering nor sacrifice, Thou askest not for gifts or presents. I will erect an altar to Thee of my broken heart, and humiliate thereon my haughty mind. I will subdue my vain heart and my evil propensities; I will prostrate myself before my God. Repentance and remorse are the sacrifices which are most acceptable on Thine altar.

Hoshanot

At a time when most American non-Orthodox rituals left out the colorful usages specific to Sukkot—Wise's *Minhag Amerika* was a happy exception—Szold made a point of retaining them, so long as they were decorously handled, in both theology and execution. When Szold's *Abodath Israel* first came out in 1864, it contained all the *hoshanot* for the seven days of Sukkot, including Hoshana Rabbah. In fact, they are all essentially the same as in the standard Ashkenazic rite.

In *Abodath Israel,* however, Hoshana Rabbah itself undergoes something of a facelift. While the expected seven *hoshanot* are said (*"Am siebenten Tage {Hoschana-Rabba} werden sämmtliche Stücke gesprochen,"* as the rubric has it), the traditional apotropaic "beating of the willow" is done away with, in conformity with the esthetic of the German Liberal synagogues at the time. Likewise, the semi-festival loses its penitential character—along with its generous helping of *piyyutim*—carried over from the High Holy Days.

In any event, Szold keeps the special *hoshana* for the day, the sparkling *tittenenu le-shem veli-tehillah,* with the sting taken out of its almost flagrant chauvinism. A second type of *hoshana* traditionally follows, each verse beginning *ke-hoshatta* ("As Thou hast saved . . .") and ending with the refrain *ken hosha na* ("So save Thou us!")

In his magisterial *Maḥzor le-Sukkot,* published in 1981 under the auspices of the Leo Baeck Institute, Daniel Goldschmidt has shown us the many variations of this second *hoshana* that exist within the Ashkenazic rites alone. The commonest in use is the highly allusive *ke-hoshatta elim be-lud immakh,* chanted every day during the week of Tabernacles. It is precisely here that Szold breaks new ground by composing an original *ke-hoshatta* litany free of knotty references and intricate *jeu de mots* and yet manageable for the Hebraically-taught worshiper, who will find it uncluttered and polished.

The customary *hoshi'ah et ammekha* then concludes Szold's *hoshanot.* This innovative *piyyut* has enjoyed robust durability both through Jastrow's 1873 abridgement of *Abodath Israel* and its heir apparent, *Seder Avodah* (1951) by Max D. Klein. What follows below is Szold's unlabored, graceful *ke-hoshatta avraham be-har ha-moriyah* and an English redition "contributed by a friend and colleague" of Jastrow's. Klein's additional Hebrew verses, reflecting the modern-day realities of the Shoah and the State of Israel, appear, with a translation, in brackets.

כהושעת אברהם בהר המוריה.

כן הושע נא: עניתו משמי עליה.

כהושעת יצחק בנו יחידו.

כן הושע נא: מנעתו משלוח לו ידו.

כהושעת יעקב איש תמימך

כן הושע נא: בשרתו ישע ממרומך

כהושעת אהוביך זרע ידידים.

כן הושע נא: הוצאתם מבית עבדים.

כהושעת משה בארץ ציה

כן הושע נא: הנחלתו דת ותושיה.

כהושעת אהרן מכהן באלמך.

כן הושע נא: פארתו באוריך ותומיך.

כהושעת במדבר בני אמוניך.

כן הושע נא: כלכלתם לשבע במנך.

[וכהושעת ציון עיר קדשך.

כן הושע נא: ונתת שלום לבניך.

כהושעת עמך משני אריות.

[:כן הושע נא]   ונהלתם על־מי מנוחת.

כהושעת מאז יגיעי כח.

בשבתותיך המצאתם מנוח.

כן הושע נא:

As thou didst save they servant Abraham,
And on Moriah's mount didst answer him,
   So save us now!

As thou didst save his son, his only one,
And didst withold the hand raised 'gainst his life,
   So save us now!

As thou didst Jacob save—the upright man,—
And cheer him with glad tidings of thy grace,
   So save us now!

As thou didst save the seed of thy beloved,
Delivering them from Egypt's servile yoke,
   So save us now!

As thou didst Moses save 'mid wastes untracked
And make thy glorious law his heritage,
   So save us now!

As thou didst Aaron save—thy Temple's priest,
And deck him with the shield of Light and Truth,
   So save us now!

As thou didst save, midst the desert's drear,
And feed thy people with celestial food,
   So save us now!

[As thou didst help Zion, thy holy town,
And gavest peace to thy exiled children;
   So, we pray thee, help us thou.

As thou didst help thy people from the teeth of their foes,
And didst lead them beside quiet waters.
   So, we pray thee, help us now.]

As thou didst save the wearied at all times,
In offering the Sabbath's joyful rest,
   So save us now!

Making this innovatory *ke-hoshatta* even more remarkable is the fact that, apart from the official rites of the Conservative Movement and the prayerbook of the Brazilian Liberal congregations in Rio de Janeiro and Sao Paulo, there is today not a single Progressive prayerbook that holds fast to a second *hoshana* in any way. In this regard, Szold and Jastrow added a novel twist to the traditional pattern with pleasing results.

Tish'ah be-Av

Surprising as it may seem, recalling Reform's quondam coolness if not sheer antipathy toward the Jewish national idea, Tish'ah be-Av, one of the most national of Jewish holidays, received rather extended treatment in the early editions of the non-Orthodox rites. At first Szold and Wise clung to the customary observance with little or no deviation. The table of contents prefacing the first edition of *Minhag Amerika* offered the reader some seven items for the fastday. And all in all, Szold's arrangement tallied with Wise's.

By the eighteen-seventies, however, Szold's *Abodath Israel* as modified by Jastrow and *Minhag Amerika,* which had undergone much verbal change meanwhile, gave up the traditional format all but completely. Szold's version made way for Jastrow's lengthy prayer-disquisition embodying the notion of the Jewish people "as the nation chosen . . . to be the standard bearers of eternal truth before the sons of men," while the second edition of *Minhag Amerika* displayed not a trace of the holiday itself.

Among these diverse nineteenth-century treatments of Tish'ah be-Av in the liturgy, Einhorn's *Olath Tamid* is unique. Apprehending the Jews' function on earth in eschatological terms both as *Priestervolk* and Messiah, Einhorn seized upon the Rabbinic representation of the Ninth of Av as the Messiah's birthday and wrought a thoroughgoing transformation from its conception as a day of mourning to one of historical recollection and present and future rejoicing. He utilized, in typological manner, Psalm 80 for the psalmodic portion and singled out Deuteronomy 10:12–22 and Zechariah 7 and 8:16–20 as the Torah and haftarah lessons.

Despite what appears at times his fervent Germanophilia, Einhorn was obviously no stranger to the Hebrew language. The following is his climactic *berakhah emtza'it* after the *qedushah* for the Anniversary of the Destruction of Jerusalem, at the end of a long oration on the world-historic significance of the day:

אתה נגלית מלכנו על הר ציון לעם קדשך ותשמיעם את־הוד קולך
ודברות קדשך מלהבות אש להודיע בארץ דרכך בכל־גוים ישועתך.
הרם קרן ישראל עמך לתת להם פאר תחת אפר. שמן ששון תחת
אבל. מעטה תהלה תחת רוח כהה. בנה ביתך אשר בית תפלה
יקרא לכל־העמים. וכסאך מהרה תכון. ותמלוך אתה לבדך על־כל־
הארץ. ברוך אתה יי בונה חרבות עולם.

Du hast Dich, unser König, auf dem Berge Zion Deinem heiligen Volke geoffenbart; aus Feuerflammen hast Du es die Majestät Deiner Stimme, Dein hochheiliges Wort vernehmen lassen, dem weiten Erdenrunde Deinen Weg zu verkünden, alle Völker Dein Heil erkennen zu lassen. Erhöhe doch das Horn Deines Volkes Israel! Verleih' ihm Schmuck statt Asche, Freudenöl statt Trauer, ein Prachtgewand statt betrübten Gemüthes. Erbaue Dein Haus, das einst das Bethaus aller Völker wird gennant werden; errichte Deinen Thron in Bälde, dass Du allein regierst über die ganze Erde. Gelobt seiest Du, Gott, der Du die Trümmer der Welt aufbauest

The following English translation is by Emil G. Hirsch, Einhorn's son-in-law:

Thou, O King, didst reveal Thyself on Mount Zion to Thy holy people; they heard Thy majestic voice, Thy holy word, out of flames of fire; Thou didst appoint them to make known Thy way in the earth and among all nations Thy help. Give triumph to Thy people Israel! Let them be wrapped in beauty and not garmented in sackcloth and ashes. Give unto them joy for mourning; courage for despondency. Build Thou Thy house—the house of prayer unto all the nations. Establish speedily Thy throne; and reign Thou over the whole earth. Praised be Thou, O God, who rebuildest the waste places of the ages!

Death and Mourning

With no exception, the nineteenth-century manuals mentioned above have a Hebrew *vidduy shekhiv me-ra* or *Sündenbekenninis* (deathbed confession) and a *tzidduq ha-din* (burial service). Wise has for both editions of *Minhag Amerika* an out-of-the-ordinary *tefillah la-avelim u-le-Jahrzeit* comprised of Psalm 90, *adonay mah adam, ezkor* (the old Yizkor prayer put into the first person!), *shivviti,* and *mah rav tuvekha.* From the lack of rubrics it is hard to determine whether this service was to be said in private, recited in the House of Mourning, or conducted as a Memorial Service. Most likely Wise had it in mind for all such occasions.

Another type of innovation, an unobtrusive insert, was introduced by Adler in his revision of Merzbacher's *Order of Prayer.* This piece, meant to be recited in the House of Mourning, is situated in the *shemoneh esreh* between the Seventh and Eighth Benedictions. Entitled *neḥamah* (comfort), this unpretentious prayer is inspired by three older usages: 1) the reflective Talmudic benediction for mourners, *attem aḥeynu ha-meyugga'im,* which closes with *barukh menaḥem avelim* (Ketubot 8b), 2) the traditional interpolation in the weekday *tefillah* for fastdays, *anenu,* and 3) the personal entreaty on behalf of the sick, suitably interjected in the Eighth Benediction. Adler's apt accessory *berakhah* deserves quotation for its eloquence and neoclassical brevity:

נחמה

עננו יי עננו. ואל תתעלם מתחנתנו. היה נא קרוב לקוראיך. שלח
מרפא לתחלואי ידיך. יהי נא חסדך לנחם האמללים ולחבש שבר
לבבם. כי אתה יי [כשמת האב: אבי יתומים ודין אלמנות אתה]
תמחץ וידיך תרפאנה. ברוך אתה יי מנחם אבלים:

Hear us, O Lord! hear us, and reject not our prayers. Be near to those who seek for thee in their sorrow, and send help to those whom thou hast stricken. Mayest thou send consolation from thy bountiful source of mercy to the orphans, and heal their wounds of grief; for thou, O Lord! (*if for the death of a husband or a father:* art a father to the orphan and a protector to the widow) Thou woundest and healest. Blessed art thou, O Lord! who consoleth the mourner.

Adler's unique *neḥamah* was to hold out up to the preliminary drafts of the *Union Prayer Book* (1892) through the mediation of Isaac Moses (1847–1926), an important but unsung figure in American Jewish liturgical development. In the Evening Service for the House of Mourning, this novel *birkat avelim* became the main benediction after a compression of the First Three Benedictions. Three years later the CCAR issued a special booklet, *Evening and Morning Services for Week Days,* which expanded on the foregoing by adding a modified *havinenu* and exchanging Adler's creation for a longer and more ruminative one of its own:

אנא יי מלך מלא רחמים אשר בידך נפש כל־חי ורוח כל־בשר איש.
אליך נשא לבבנו בליל עמל ויגון: הנה הובלנו למנוחת עולמים
את־מחמד נפשנו. כי אתה צוית: פרוס עליו (עליה) סכת שלומך.
הסתר את־נשמתו (ונשמתה) בצל כנפיך: ואנחנו לא נתלונן על מדת
שפטך. כי צדיק אתה בכל דרכיך. ונתחנן אליך לאמר. תן בנו כח
לשאת את אשר נטלת עלינו: השכיבנו יי לשלום גם כי לבבנו נשבר
ונדכה. האר אלינו אור פניך למצוא ארח חיים. ונלכה בה עד הקץ
אשר שמת לנו: הן ידענו כי לכל־לילה בקר. ומקץ כל־נשף אור
יומם: העמידנו מלכנו לחיים. ונעשה איש איש חקו כאשר צויתנו:
מודים אנחנו לך על הנפש הזאת. אשר בחסדך נתת לנו. ובצדקתך
לקחת ממנו: הורנו את־דרכיך ותגבר צדקתנו על עמל נפשנו: אנא
יי מוריד שאול ויעל. רפא נא בברכת שלומך את־לבבנו הנשבר:
מחה דמעה מעל פנינו. ככתוב בלע המות לנצח. ומחה יי דמעה
מעל כל־פנים: ונאמר. הזורעים בדמעה ברנה יקצרו: ברוך אתה יי
מנחם אבלים:

In the night of sorrow we turn to Thee, o God, who dwellest with the contrite of heart. At Thy command we have laid to rest one to whom we clung with all the fibres of our being. Spread over him (her) the sheltering booth of Thy peace. We would not murmur at Thy inscrutable decree, but pray Thee for strength to bear what Thou hast put on us. Where can we find support but in Thee? Let us lie down in peace, though our hearts are sorely rent; let, in the night which enshrouds us now, Thy light shine upon us, that we may still find the path of life, and willingly pursue it to the goal which Thou appointest to each of Thy children. We know that every night has its morning: that after the hours of darkness come again the hours of daylight. Grant that we, too, may remember that the seed, oft sown in tears, ripens into a harvest to be gathered in joy.

We thank Thee for the life which in Thy love Thou hast given, and in Thy wisdom hast taken away. Make us to know Thy ways, that in our love we triumph over selfish woe and grief. Blessed art Thou who lowerest into the grave, but bringest up again, who woundest, and bindest up. Let the balm of Thy assurance be distilled into our troubled spirits, that athwart our tears may arch the rainbow of Thy eternal promise. Praise be to Thee, O God, who comfortest the mourners. Amen.

Conclusion

It is clear that all of the major nineteenth-century American agents of liturgical change were very much at home in the Hebrew language and saw no reason not to try their hand at formulating new prayers in it. Indeed, all of the editors of the rites we have had occasion to look into were inured in the traditional disciplines of the European yeshivot as well as university-trained. Consequently they had more than a passing familiarity with the classics of pre-modern Hebrew literature and possessed current aesthetic awareness and sensibility.

From the Positive-Historical or proto-Conservative school (Szold and Jastrow) through the respectful, gradualist expression of Reform (Merzbacher, Adler, and Wise) to Reform at its most thoroughgoing (Einhorn), these leaders sought to naturalize, one might say, their advanced understanding of Judaism by putting it in the natal language of the Jewish people. To do such was to lend a kind of authenticity to the enterprise of bringing the tradition into accord with contemporaneity. Of course, it no doubt says something too about the level of expectations and state of preparation of their respective congregations, willing as they obviously were to sponsor and adopt such rites.

Not all the prayerbook revisers succeeded equally. Perhaps the most accomplished stylistically were Merzbacher, in his smooth emendation of individual benedictions in the *shemoneh esreh,* and Szold, in his graceful domestic summary of the daily *amidah* and his shortlived *piyyut* for the *avodah.* Probably least fortunate literarily were Wise's attempts, which were marked by a fitful eccentricity and a certain studied and forced biblicism—the design and genius of the Siddur is, after all, Rabbinic, not biblical. The key exception is doubtless his first-rate *sim shalom,* quoted earlier—and ironically, the only nineteenth-century Hebrew composition to survive into the twentieth.

As demonstrated in chapter one, Einhorn was no doubt the most creative in recasting the structure of the prayerbook so as to reflect his novel conceptualization of Judaism, even though his own Hebrew compositions were few and far between (e.g., the liturgical centerpiece of his *amidah* for the Ninth of Av). In contrast, the other liturgists' innovations were paramountly in Hebrew, with occasional prayers and hymns in either German or English—which all goes to show that any correlation between the degree or extent of liturgical reform espoused and the love and mastery of the Hebrew language is at best weak or incidental.

The picture that emerges from the data we have examined is that in the nascent days of creativity in the United States, an earnest effort was made by the leading practitioners of Jewish prayerbook reform to frame new prayers in the language hallowed by millennia of reverent use. Going beyond their European counterparts, who generally limited themselves to replacing Ashkenazic *piyyutim* with the more lilting and engaging Sephardic ones, preparing new prayers in the language of the country they lived in, and in modifying, however slightly, existing Hebrew texts, these immigrant *mesadderim* sought to revitalize both the liturgy and the Hebrew language by composing anew, whether in prose or in paytanic form.

The modest surge of Hebrew liturgical creativity from the 1850s to the 1870s did not abate completely, as illustrated by the aforementioned *birkat avelim* and in a passable Hebrew lyric by the Jewish historian Max Margolis in the 1908 edition of the *Union Haggadah.* And several decades later, Hebrew liturgical creativity came into its own again—as evidenced by Louis Ginzberg's celebrated and much imitated Prayer for the Government in the Conservative *Festival Prayer Book* of 1927, and by the various Reconstructionist siddurim, the Reform *Sha'arey Tefillah,* and the emerging feminist rites.

An earlier version of this chapter appeared in *Modern Judaism* 1 (December 1981): 323–36. © 1981. The Johns Hopkins University Press. Reprinted with permission.

5

Hebrew Creativity in British Reform

To be sure, liturgical creativity in the Hebrew language has been around for some time,[1] but it was primarily channeled into the adjustment of traditional liturgical texts so that they harmonized with contemporary thought, as in the many restatements of the *musaf* and the introductory paragraph of the *aleynu*.[2] Generally, new prayers were written in the vernacular and not in Hebrew. The only rite to depart from this prevailing pattern all but systematically for close to a century and a half has been the *Forms of Prayer for Jewish Worship* of the Reform movement in England.

Since the movement was founded, in 1841,[3] its mother congregation, the West London Synagogue for British Jews, has always emphasized the primacy of the Hebrew language in its liturgy. As its founding minister, David Woolf Marks (1811–1910),[4] wrote in the introduction to the first edition of *Forms of Prayer,* of which he was the editor, "The suitableness of the sacred language and of its style, as extant in the Holy Writ, for devotional purposes, is acknowledged beyond need of demonstration."

A young man when he was invited to assume the pulpit there, Marks was in actuality an informed layman formerly engaged by an Ashkenazic Orthodox synagogue as a *ba'al qeri'ah* (Torah reader).[5] The founders of the synagogue Marks was to lead for forty-seven years wanted an abbreviated service, begun at a reasonable hour, conducted amid decorum and with dignity and restraint—without breaking with the preponderance of the British Jewish community. Unfortunately, their efforts resulted in the issuance of a *ḥerem* by the London rabbinate, brought about by the congregation's decision to abrogate the second day of the Festivals.[6]

Marks's position can be said to bear some resemblance to the earlier approach of his contemporary Isaac Mayer Wise (1819–1900) vis-à-vis biblical legislation over against Rabbinic halakhah. Perhaps because of his prior position in an Ashkenazic synagogue and his association there with Sephardic dissenters, his own absorption in the Bible, and even his lack of formal training in a yeshivah, Marks felt at liberty to forge a new hybrid ritual. Its main contours and wording—and selection of *piyyutim* for the High Holy Days—were recognizably Sephardic, but he added some items from the Ashkenazic rite (*e.g.* the chanting of the Shema after the Torah scroll is taken out of the ark) and deleted "distasteful" pieces that had no biblical warrant, such as the martyrological and vindicatory *av ha-raḥamim* prayer.

In essence, without dismissing outright the teachings and usages of the Talmudic Sages, Marks considered the *torah she-be'al peh* (Oral Law) man-made, hence not unalterably binding, but the Bible altogether divinely-inspired and everlastingly true.[7] In its early stages, British Reform staunchly upheld the eternity and divinity of the Pentateuch. It followed then that it maintained observance of such scriptural commandments as *pidyon ha-ben,* the Priestly Benediction (*dukhanen*),[8] the Counting of the Omer, and days of mourning like the Ninth of Av and the Seventeenth of Tammuz. The reading of the Megillah and the kindling of the Hanukkah lights continued to be carried out, although without being prefaced by the benedictions enjoining their enactment *(asher qiddeshanu be-mizvotav ve-tzivvanu)* for the simple reason that these customs were postbiblical or Rabbinic in origin *(mi-de-rabbanan)* and not of the same rank or compulsory character as the "Mosaic" ordinances.[9]

At first glance the premier edition of *Forms of Prayer* is no more than the Sephardic rite, streamlined by fits and starts. A closer look divulges individual features that bear careful study. One of the most conspicuous examples is the Aramaic Kaddish Hebraized from beginning to end,[10] the original of which is again the Sephardic version, with its inclusion of "the sprouting of salvation" *(ve-yatzmaḥ purqaneih* becomes *ve-yatzmiaḥ yeshu'ato),* its explicit mention of the Messiah *(vi-yqarev meshiḥeih* becomes *vi-yqarev meshiḥo),* and its expansive penultimate verse *(yehei shelama rabba min she-mayya, ḥayyim ve-sava vi-yshu'ah ve-neḥamah* becomes *yehi shalom rav min ha-shamayim, ḥayyim ve-sava vi-yshu'ah ve-neḥamah . . .).* This striking all-Hebrew formulation was to be reproduced in all the subsequent editions of *Forms of Prayer* and adjunct volumes until the 1977 edition, where it was moved to an appendix (next to a *qaddish de-rabbanan*) as a kind of historical curiosity and keepsake. Similarly, the old Aramaic Kaddish in its Ashkenazic recension resurfaces in a pair of intervening British Reform volumes, *The Evening Service* (1952) and *Prayers for the Pilgrim Festivals* (1965), after having been hushed up for over a century. In the latter volume, Marks's off-beat Hebrew transcription is demoted to a subordinate position, no doubt as a concession to those congregations still wedded to the Hebrew wording.

Circumcision and Prayers for Women after Childbirth

Marks and his assistant, A Loewy[11] (1816–1908), a native of Moravia, put together an adaptation of the text for the circumcision ceremony, introducing a reading of Genesis 17:9–14 in the central portion of the ceremony. After the recitation of the pertinent blessings by the *mohel* and the father, and after the actual circumcision itself, the *mohel* recommences with the blessing over the wine, all according to custom. In place of the prescribed blessing *asher qiddesh*[12] and the ensuing prayer for the naming of the boy, however, our authors provided a new prayer, more spiritual in tone and ethical in emphasis, expressing hopes and expectations for the child. This textual stand-in was no doubt intended also to offset the jarring "sanguinary" note in the traditional formula prompted by the citation from Ezekiel 16:6. The new formula reads:

אלהינו ואלהי אבותינו קים את הילד הזה לאביו לאמו ויקרא שמו בישראל
(פלוני בן פלוני): לב טהור ברא לו אלהים והוליכהו מעלה מעלה באורח צדקה
ואמת למען ישמח בו אביו ותגל יולדתו: תן בלבו רוח נכון ויראה לשמור
חקיך ותורתיך ולהתהלך באמתך ובנגה ישעך כי אתה תברך צדיק יי כצנה
רצון תעטרנו :

O God, and the God of our fathers, preserve this boy to his parents, and suffer his name to be called in Israel (N. N.). Create in him, O God, a pure heart, and lead him to perfection through the path of righteousness and truth! Make his father to exult in him, and cause her who bare him to rejoice in her offspring! Implant in him a spirit of fervent piety, so that he may keep thy Law and thy behests, and walk in thy truth, and in the light of thy salvation: for thou, O Lord, dost bless the righteous, with favour dost thou encompass him as with a shield.

Both the 1843 and 1931 editions of *Forms of Prayer,* incidentally, conclude the ceremony with Psalm 127, in step with Sephardic usage. However, the 1977 edition recasts a new *qayyem et ha-yeled* with a subtle exhortation to the parents as well as a wish for the child to be a blessing "to his family, the family of Israel and the family of mankind." By comparison. the prayer authored by Marks and Loewy is far more biblical sounding and stately.

Marks and Loewy filled in a gap in tradition by making available a "Prayer for a Woman, on attending Divine Service, after Child-birth." In his introduction to the first edition of *Forms of Prayer,* Marks wrote:

> As the House of God is the fittest place for offering up sacrifices of thanksgiving on all occasions of life, and as no moment is so full of intense interest to the Jewish parent, as that which ushers into existence a new claimant of the "inheritance of Jacob," we have supplied the deficiency of a prayer for such an occasion, by instituting a formula, the wording of which, being a faithful transcript of biblical language, cannot but convey devotion and comfort to the Hebrew mother for whom it is intended.

The style is of a high literary order. Many phrases are either drawn straight from the Hebrew Bible or reminiscent of it. Interestingly enough, the prayer ends with the *birkat ha-gomel,* which is traditionally said by one called to the Torah after having weathered an ordeal or mishap. Since Marks had done away with *aliyot,* it is to be wondered how a congregant, including the mother of the newborn child, would be expected to recite the blessing publicly.[13] *Forms of Prayer* offers hardly any instructions here. Perhaps the mother said the prayer in the privacy of her pew in the women's gallery and ended it with her own *birkat ha-gomel.* In all likelihood the practice of "the churching of women" in the Church of England[14] influenced *Forms of Prayer* in this regard, giving greater attention, however limited, to women in the synagogue.

שמח לבי ותגל נפשי באומרים לי בית יי נלך. כי כאיל תערוג על אפיקי
מים. כן צמאה נפשי לאל חי. נכספה וגם כלתה נפשי לחצרותיך. להלל
שמך יי בתוך עדת מישרים. לזמרך עליון. ולהודות לך על כל הטוב והחסד
שעשית עם אמתך: אין בידי להקריב לפניך קרבן כאשר צוית על ידי משה
עבדך. כי חרב בית מקדשנו. ואין לנו כהן בעבדתו. לכן. יהי רצון מלפניך יי
אלהים. מלך רחמים. שתקבל תפלתי היום כאלו הקרבתי את הקרבן.
ככתוב ונשלמה פרים שפתינו:

יי אלהים אתה ברכתני בפרי בטן. הלבשתני רוח גבורה. עת צירים וחבלים
אחזוני. אתה היית למשען לי. הודעתני אורח חיים בעברי בעמק הבכה: הם
לבי בקרבי. בהגיגי תבער אש. ובלשוני אין מלה. אך למה אביע אומר אחוה

דבר לנשוא קולי בתודה. הלא אתה אלהים בוחן לבות וכליות חפש כל חדרי
בטן. ממך לא נעלמו רגשות נפשי: אתה ידעת כי רחש לבי דבר טוב. בך עלץ.
בישועתך שמחתי:

ועתה יי אלהים נא אל תרף ידך מאמתך. חסדך ואמתך המה יצרוני. וכאשר
היית לימיני עד הנה. כן יהי רצון מלפניך למלאות את בקשתי:

(לנער) לחסתיר את הנער הזה בצל כנפיך. לברכהו. לחזקהו. ולאמצהו. אורך
חיים תודיעהו. למען יתברכו בו אבותיו. וימצא חן ושכל טוב בעיני אלהים
ואדם: יפרח כעץ שתול על פלגי מים. ועלהו לא יבול: האר פניך עליו. ונחה
עליו רוח יי. רוח עצה וגבורה. רוח חכמה ודעת.   ויראתך תהיה אוצרו. אמן:

(ולנערה) להסתיר את הנערה הזה בצל כנפיך. לברכה.   לשמרה. ולחזקה. אורך
חיים תודיעה. ותהי לאשת חיל. נא. תן תורת חסד על לשונה. ויראתך
תהיה אוצרה. אמן:

ברוך אתה יי אלהינו מלך העולם. הגומל לחיבים טובות. שגמלני כל-טוב:

Verily, my heart rejoiceth, and my soul is glad, when I enter thy
house, O Lord! for as the hart panteth after the refreshing springs, so
my soul thirsteth after God; it yearneth to enter thy courts; to praise
thy name in the midst of thy congregation; to glorify thee, O Most
High, and to thank thee for all the good and manifold mercies thou
hast vouchsafed to extend to thine handmaid. Alas! I can no more
offer a sacrifice as thou hast commanded by thy servant Moses, for
our holy temple is destroyed, and we have no officiating Priest;
therefore, may it be thy gracious pleasure, O Lord God, king of
mercy, to receive the prayer I offer up before thee, this day, as though
I had brought an offering, for it is written, "the prayers of our lips
shall be accepted, as the offering of bulls."

Lord God! thou hast blessed me with offspring, thou hast endowed
me with strength: in the hour of pain and suffering, thou wast my
support; yea, thou didst guide me in the path of life, whilst I passed
through the valley of tears. My heart is expanded, my mind is excited,
but my tongue faileth me; yet why need I search for words, or make

use of speech to give utterance to my thanks, whilst thou, O my God, provest the inward parts and the heart, and examinest its inmost recesses? From thee the feelings of my soul are not hidden, for thou art mindful of the mute eloquence of the heart; in thee it exulteth, in thine aid it rejoiceth. And now, O Almighty God, I beseech thee, withdraw not thy protection from thine handmaid! but let thy mercy and thy truth, which have hitherto sustained me, be henceforth and for evermore my support; and may it be thy gracious will to be favourable to my supplication.

(For a Boy.) O protect this boy under the shadow of thy wings, vouchsafe to bless, strengthen, and preserve him. Bestow upon him length of days, that in him his progenitors may be blessed, and that he may find grace and good liking in the sight of God and man. O may he flourish as a tree planted by the water's side, whose leaf does not wither. May thy countenance shine upon him, so that the spirit of the Lord rest upon him, the spirit of counsel and might, the spirit of wisdom and knowledge, and may the fear of thee be his best treasure. Amen.

(For a Girl.) O protect this girl under the shadow of thy wings; bless, strengthen and preserve her, and bestow upon her length of life, that she may grow up a virtuous woman. May thy mercy and thy law for ever guide her, and the fear of thee be her best treasure. Amen.

Blessed art thou, O Lord, our God, King of the universe, who bestowest benefits on the undeserving! for on me hast thou bestowed all good.

Not to be outdone by the Reformers, Herman Adler (1839–1911), the Chief Rabbi of the British Empire before Joseph H. Hertz, thereupon drew up in Hebrew and in English a "Thanksgiving to be offered up by Women after their Confinement" at the synagogue. After parts of Psalm 116 are read, the *birkat ha-gomel* is said by the mother herself, followed by a newly composed prayer to be read by the minister, and, then, the Priestly Benediction. Revealingly, Psalm 116 is the same selection as in the *Book of Common Prayer!*[15]

Other Anglican influences can be detected in *Forms of Prayer.* First of all, there is an uncustomary recital of the Ten Commandments,[16] here in front of the open ark before the scroll is taken out, carried in procession to the *bimah,* and elevated. Second, for the Afternoon Service of Shemini Azeret (replacing Simḥat Torah, an hour or so away and on the following day) when the West London Synagogue celebrated its completion of the Torah-reading cycle and the start of a new one, Marks attached the portions from the end of Deuteronomy (33–34) and the beginning of Genesis (1–2:3), the traditional lections for Simḥat Torah. Not only did the officiant ("minister") do all the readings but he was the one who said all of accompanying *berakhot,* and once only, even when he read from a second scroll, as on a Festival. To keep the readings from Deuteronomy and Genesis discrete, Psalm 150 is interspersed.[17] This can be compared to the provision in the *Book of Common Prayer* for a psalm—the "gradual," as it is termed—between the reading of the Epistle and of the Gospel. Other illustrations of likely Anglican influence and reinforcement in subsequent editions of *Forms of Prayer* will be discussed below.

Blessing of the Seasons and the Hoshanot

In Marks's preface to *Forms of Prayer* he states his intention, "in order to reduce the forms of the service to the length required," to avoid "those frequent repetitions of some of the finest prayers which seemed to us to weaken their effect." The first edition of the rite abridged the *musaf* instead of dropping it altogether and, on the Pilgrimage Festivals, subjoined thereto a virtuoso amphibious *berakhah* to take the place of the prayer for *tal* (Dew) and *geshem* (Rain) This new all-inclusive *berakhah* was designed to serve all Three Festivals, hence the title *birkat ha-mo'adim.*

From a literary standpoint, Marks's novel piece is fairly respectable but in need of the kind of emendation Loewy accomplished in the second edition. Without blotting out the reference to Jerusalem or blurring the doctrine of the Return to Zion *(ve-zakkeh otanu kullanu yaḥad lire'ot ir qodshekha bi-khevodah ha-rishon uve-tiferet godelah ki-ymey qedem),* Marks's prayer acknowledges indigenous climatic needs in the different Diaspora communities *(Zekhor adonay otanu ve-et admatenu, u-fetaḥ lanu et otzarekha ha-tov et ha-shamayim, ve-natenah ha-aretz et yevulah ve-etz ha-sadeh yitten piryo. Zekhor adonay gam et beney ammenu, ha-nefotzim ba-yam u-va-qedem u-va-tzafon u-va-negev):*

ברכת המועדים

יי אלהי צבאות הנוטה שמים ויוסד ארץ. אתה נתת את השמש לממשלת
ביום ואת הירח וכוכבים לממשלות בלילה: גבול שמת לים. וחק העתים
עשית בשחקים להשיב הרוח ולהוריד הגשם ולהשקות את הארץ מטל
השמים: בכל זמן ומועד הודעתנו נפלאות מעשיך. ומדי חג בחגו קראתנו
לבקש עזרך בקדש ולהודות לך בקהל רב. כי טוב ומטיב אתה: על כן
באנו היום לחלות פניך. ולערך משאלותינו לפני כסא כבודך:

זכר יי אותנו ואת אדמתנו. ופתח לנו את אוצרך הטוב את השמים. ונתנה
הארץ את יבולה ועץ השדה יתן פריו: זכר יי גם את בני עמנו. הנפוצים בים
ובקדם ובצפון ובנגב. והקרובים אלינו בכל מרחקי־ארץ בגשתם יחדו לקרא
בשם קדשך ולעבדך בלב אחד: ברכם בכל עת. ושמחם בכל מושבותיהם
ונחמם אתנו בנחמת ירושלים. וזכה אותנו כלנו יחד לראות עיר קדשך
בכבודה הראשון ובתפארת גדלה כימי קדם: הפלה חסדיך לנו ולכל
המיחלים לך.ושלח לנו שנת חיים ושבע. שנת ברכה ושלום. כי אתה
תשביע את כל העולם מטובך. ותמלא ידינו מברכותיך: ברוך אתה יי. מברך
המועדים:

O Lord God of Hosts, who has stretched out the heavens and laid the
foundations of the earth, thou hast appointed the sun to rule by day,
and the moon and the stars to rule by night. Thou hast set a bound-
ary to the sea, and a law for the seasons hast thou ordained on high:
the wind and the rain obey thy behests, and the dew of heaven
descends at thy bidding unto us thy wondrous works; and from festival to festival thou hast called us to invoke thy help in the sanctuary
and to praise thee in public congregation, for thou art gracious and
beneficent: we come therefore this day to supplicate thee, and to lay
our petitions before the throne of thy glory.

O Lord, remember us and our country, and open unto us thy goodly
treasury of heaven, that the earth may yield her produce and the tree of
the field give forth its fruit. Remember, also, O Lord, the children of
our people, who are scattered east and west, north and south, and who,
though distant from us, unite with us in proclaiming thy holy name
and in serving thee with one accord. Bless them at all times, and make

them joyful in all their dwelling-places: cheer them and us with the consolation of Jerusalem, and account all of us worthy to see thy holy city in its former glory and in its ancient splendour. Show thy marvellous lovingkindness unto us and unto all that hope in thee, and send us a year of life and plenty, a year of blessing and peace; for thou satisfiest the whole world with thy goodness, and fillest our hands with thy blessings. Blessed art thou, O Lord, who blessest the seasons.

Loewy's finished and unlabored rewrite wore well. Indeed, it was included in all subsequent editions through the 1965 *Prayers for the Pilgrim Festivals,* where the *berakhah* underwent a few minor stylistic changes. Its importance over the years may be attested by the following incident, which occurred on Shavu'ot morning in 1947. Because of Confirmation exercises being conducted on that day, the American-born Rabbi Harold F. Reinhart (1891–1968), at the time senior minister of the West London Synagogue, apparently felt constrained to skip the *birkat ha-mo'adim.* This decision prompted a disgruntled congregant to write to *The Synagogue Review,* then the organ of the Association of Synagogues in Great Britain (of which the West London Synagogue was the key member):

In common with a large congregation I was very delighted with and thoroughly enjoyed the Pentecost Service, which was combined so well with a really lovely confirmation service. I was at a loss, however, to understand why, in these difficult days for English Jewry, when we should try to retain as much tradition as possible, the Additional Service at the end was cut so short. Surely the congregation who had listened to such a moving sermon as the Senior Minister gave to the three charming confirmands, would not have minded staying an extra five or ten minutes to hear the beautiful blessing of the Season [sic!]—surely as much a part of the Pentecost Service as of any of the festivals—followed by such a traditional tune as *"En kelohenu"?* I strongly deprecate the speeding up of any of our beautiful festival services to finish to a timetable at 12:45 p.m., which is the common practice now-a-days, and I'm sure that none of our big congregation would mind having lunch a little later, so to hear the service really carried out and not rushed through towards the end

Yours faithfully,

C. H. D. S. HALEY[18]

After the Blessing of the Seasons, on Tabernacles, *hoshanot* were performed. Traditionally in all rites, the litany begins in alphabetical order with *Hosha'na! Le-ma'ankha eloheynu, hosha na. Le-ma'ankha bor'enu, hosha na. Le-ma'ankha go'alenu hosha na. Le-ma'ankha doreshenu, hosha na.*[19] In all rites on each day of Sukkot a different *hosha na* antiphon accompanies the circuit with the lulav and etrog.

To curtail the profusion and lengthiness of the *hoshanot,* Marks drew up a single one to avail the entire length of the Festival *(af be-eleh shiv'at yemey ḥaggenu).* While elevating in its own way, the new piece of verse is quite unlike any of its established counterparts of any rite in that the refrain *hosha na* or variations thereof are kept to a minimum and historical recollections or allusions nowhere made. Rather, an ethical note is expressly sounded. Marks even revealed the comfortable economic circumstances of the early British Reformers, with mention of its "slaves and maidservants"*(Nismaḥ lifney adonay eloheynu im baneynu u-venoteynu, avadeynu va-amateynu* [sic!]).

Below are examples of Loewy's introduction, for the better, of changes in phraseology[20] into Marks' prayer, which as a whole still brings to mind benevolent paternalism no less than genuine charitable instincts.

הושענא. הושענא: למענך אם לא למעננו. הושענא:

Save us! O save us! For thy sake, if not for our sake, save us!

אל הישועה. ביראתך נערוך תפלתנו לפניך. לשועתנו הטה נא אזנך: בכל יום ויום נברך ונקדש שמך. על חסדך ועל אמתך. בכל בקר ובקר בקומנו נשחרך. להכין לבנו ונפשנו אליך. בכל לילה ולילה בשכבנו נודך. על רב נסיך ונפלאותיך. וכן נגדלך בשבעת ימי חגנו. אשר נשמח לפניך יי אלהינו. עם בנינו ובנותינו: אנא יי צור ישענו. הטה לבנו בימי מועדנו. להרנין לב יתום ואלמנה בתוכנו. ולשמח נפש עני וגר בשערינו. מאשר תשיג ידנו. וכאשר תברכנו יי אלהינו:

הושענא. הושענא:

כהושעת מאז עדתך. עם נושע ביי. כן הושענא: צוה ישועות יעקב. וראו כל אפסי הארץ את ישועת אלהינו. הושיעה את-עמך וברך את-נחלתך. ורעם ונשאם עד העולם: ומלאה הארץ דעה את-יי. כמים לים מכסים: למען דעת כל עמי הארץ. כי יי הוא האלהים. אין עוד :

O God of Salvation, we devoutly supplicate thee: incline thine ear to our prayer. As every day we bless and sanctify thy name for thy mercy and thy truth; as every morning at our rising we implore thee to prepare our hearts for thy service; as every night when we lie down, we thank thee for thy abundant and wondrous goodness: even thus we extol thee during these seven days of our Festival, in which we, together with our sons and our daughters, rejoice before thee, O Lord our God. We beseech thee, O Rock of our Salvation, so to dispose our hearts at this holy season, that we may cheer the fatherless and the widow among us; and that we may make glad the poor and the stranger within our gates, according to the substance with which thou, O Lord our God, blessest us.
Save us! O save us!

As thou hast ever shielded thy congregation, the people saved by the Lord, so save us now. Command the salvation of Jacob, and let the ends of the earth behold the salvation of our God. Save thy people, and bless thine inheritance; tend them, and exalt them for evermore. Let the earth be filled with the knowledge of the Lord, as the waters cover the sea; that all the peoples of the earth may know that the Lord is God, and that there is none else.

Changes under Reinhart and Simmons

The next major revampment of *Forms of Prayer,* appearing under the imprint of Cambridge University Press, came out in 1931 during the ministry of Rabbi Reinhart and Rev. Vivian Simmons. The closest doctrinally to the prevailing Reform outlook,[21] the new rite steered a middle course liturgically between the Marks-Loewy prayerbook and the 1918 edition of the American *Union Prayer Book,* with the main lineaments of the older British Reform rite still perceptible.

Rabbi Morris Joseph (1848–1930)[22] wrote graceful new English prayers reflecting an unfeigned and hushed spirituality. More than any of his successors at the West London Synagogue's helm, Reinhart, himself a prolific writer of prayers, contributed his share of eloquent, moving pieces here too.[23] One of his compositions is the opening prayer on Shabbat Eve between *mah tovu* and *lekhah dodi;* and on Saturday morning six more new ones, not by Reinhart, are placed between the introductory *mah tovu* and the Preliminary Benedictions (*birkhot ha-shaḥar*), such as they are in this edition.

What makes these prayers unique is that each is accompanied by a Hebrew translation. Though not without occasional nice turns of phrase, the Hebrew is in large part beset by a stiltedness and some outright linguistic/grammatical blunders that obscure the chaste, serene style of the English original. While having words of praise for the work as a whole ("The new Prayer Book is altogether a noteworthy performance"), Theodore H. Gaster belittled the effort to Hebraize:

> [It] must be mentioned with infinite regret that the potentially valuable introduction of new prayers in Hebrew in the Sabbath Morning Service has failed of its high promise. The Hebrew is a mere translation into words of the Hebrew lexicon of thoughts framed in English. Much in these prayers would be unintelligible, in sheer point of language, to any Hebrew prophet.[24]

Happily the Reconstructionists came to the rescue by enlisting the services of Rabbi Joseph Marcus (1897–1974), an adept Hebrew stylist and specialist in medieval Hebrew poetry and Genizah research. Marcus repaired some of the clumsy Hebrew in *Forms of Prayer* and also Hebraized some of the English pieces by Morris Joseph and others in its appendix.[25]

Marcus' sonorous renditions every now and then outshine the English! For purposes of comparison we present two prayers, in English and in Hebrew, as found in *Forms of Prayer,* followed by Marcus' accomplished transfiguration of the same commissioned for the Reconstructionist *Sabbath Prayer Book* (New York, 1945) and the movement's liturgical volumes to come. First, the prayer assigned for Friday night and then a piece to be read at the beginning of the Sabbath Morning Service:

(1)

FORMS OF PRAYER

אב הרחמים מקור כל־הברכות שעה־נא לתפלתנו בליל־שבת זה: כטל
נחומים ללב נשבר כן יבוא ענג השבת לששת ימי־המעשה: בשבח והודיה
נשא לבנו אליך לחלותך לקדש את יום המנוחה הזה: אנא מרק ברחמיך

מה שחטאנו לפניך וכוננה מעשה ידינו עלינו: זכך את־לבנו מרעיונות זדון
וחדש את־שאיפותינו וגעגועינו לכל־יפה ואמת: האר־נא בשבת הזאת את־
מחשכי נפשנו והבא ברכה לבתינו ולכל היקר לנו: למען נשמור את־בריתך
מעולם ונצעד מישרים למצוא חן בעיניך תמיד: אמן:

Our Father, Source of all blessings, be with us on this Sabbath eve.
Thou hast ordained for us times and seasons, so that every day
brings its opportunities, and each Sabbath its beneficent power.
Even as joy succeeds to sorrow, so does the Sabbath peace follow the
turmoil of our workaday lives. With gratitude and with hope we lift
up our hearts to thee, and ask thee to sanctify this day of rest. Bless
our toil in the days just gone: for that wherein we have failed, do
thou forgive us; and that which we have achieved do thou make
pure. Purge away our vain self-seeking, and renew in us our strivings after truth. Send the light of joy and peace into our homes on
this Sabbath day, so that its holiness may illumine the coming
week. Unite us with our dear ones in thine all-hallowing love. So
may we keep faith with thine ancient covenant, and find acceptance
in thy sight. Amen.

SABBATH PRAYER BOOK

אב הרחמים מקור כל הברכות שעה־נא לתפלתנו בליל שבת זה. אתה
תכנת עתים וזמנים לימי חלדנו. יום יום ויתרונו. שבת שבת ורוחתו. וכמו
שסוף אנחה הנחה כן יבא־נא אלינו שלום השבת כטל־נחומים אחר שאון
ימי המעשה והמונם. אליך אלהינו נשא לבבנו בהודיה מלאי צפיה
שתקדשנו ביום המנוחה הזה. שלח־נא את־ברכתך במעשינו בימים אל זה
עברו. ויהי נעמך עלינו בימים הבאים לקראתנו לשלום ומעשי ידינו כוננה
עלינו. טהר לבנו וזכך את־נפשנו מיהירות־הבל. וחדש בקרבנו רוח נכון
השואף לאמת וצדק. שלח אורך ואמתך ששונך ושלומך אל תוך בתינו ביום
השבת הזה. ותשרה נא רוח קדשו עלינו כל־ימי השבוע הבא. אנא יחד
לבנו באהבתך הקדושה העוטרת הכל. למען נלך תמימי דרך באמונתך
ובבריתך ונמצא חן ושכל טוב בעיניך ובעיני כל־רואינו. אמן:

(2)
FORMS OF PRAYER

אב הרחמים נודה לך על שנתת לנו את־שבת קדשך. וההזדמנות להביע
לפניך תודותינו ותקותינו ושאיפותנו. על ששמחתנו בעבודתך וקרבתנו
לשמך הגדול. והראית לנו את־רחמיך והסדיך חדשים לבקרים. על ששמתנו
בעולם נפלא ונהדר. על שחוננתנו במתנת רוח ודעה. וזכיתנו בנפשות יקרות
שאהבתן היא חסננו ואוצרנו: ועל כלם יתברך וישתבח שמך הגדול והקדוש:
אמן:

Merciful Father, we thank thee for this Sabbath day. We thank thee
for the opportunity of uttering our praise and our gratitude, our
hopes and our desires. We thank thee for the joy of worshipping
thee, for the privilege of drawing near to thy holy presence. O God,
thy mercies are new every morning. Not a day passes without leaving
with us some token of thy lovingkindness. Thou hast given us life
with all its delights. Thou hast placed us in a wonderful and beautiful world. Thou hast given us the joys of the mind and the spirit.
Thou hast given us dear ones whose love is our stay and our treasure.
For these and all our blessings we praise thy holy Name. Amen.

SABBATH PRAYER BOOK

אב הרחמים מודים אנחנו לך שנתת לנו את־יום השבת הזה אשר בו נוכל
להשמיע שיר ושבחה ולהביע משאלותינו ומשאות נפשנו. שבח והודיה לך
ששמחתנו בעבודתך וקרבתנו לשמך הגדול והראית לנו חסדיך ורחמיך
הרבים חדשים לבקרים. את־נעימות החיים נתת לנו. בעולם פלאות שמתנו.
במתנות לב ורוח חוננתנו ותזכנו בנפשות יקרות אשר אהבתן היא אוצרנו
ומעזנו. ועל כלם יתברך וישתבח שמך הגדול והקדוש. אמן:

Supplicatory Prayers after the Haftarah

After the reading of the haftarah and before the return of the Torah
scroll(s) to the ark, *Forms of Prayer* provides a series of supplicatory prayers
that are successful in locution and content, both in Hebrew and in Eng-

lish. Praying for the monarchy and the empire, the bereaved, the sick, and "this holy congregation, together with all other holy congregations," this block of entreaties has stood firm for more than half a century, with a minimum of significant changes.

In the last of the supplications, a *mi she-berakh* for the community, *Forms of Prayer* combines the Ashkenazic and Sephardic texts, and in the case of the latter the few phrases in Aramaic are switched over to Hebrew. Here is the version in the sixth edition:

אלהינו שבשמים באנו לפניך להתפלל בעד

Our Sovereign Lady, Queen ELIZABETH, ELIZABETH the Queen Mother, PHILIP Duke of Edinburgh, CHARLES Duke of Cornwall, and all the ROYAL FAMILY.

אנא ברכם ושמרם: תן למלכתנו וליועציה דעת ובינה לעשות מלוכה כרצונך
ויהי חפצם לשום צדקה ומשפט בארץ: תן בלבנו לאהבה את־ארצנו ולדרש
שלומה בכל־עת ובכל־שעה: הורנו ונדע כי צדקת כל איש ואיש בתוכנו היא
חכמתה לעיני העמים: מהר והביא היום אשר יקבלו כל־בשר עול מלכותך
עליהם ושלום ואהבה יכוננו לנצח בעולם: אמן:

אב הרחמים חמל־נא וחוס־נא על אבות ובנים האבלים בקרבנו: נחם
אותם בחסדך הגדול חזקם בתקות אלמות לחזות בנעם ברכותיך בחיי־
הנצח: יקבלו בהכנעה את־מוסרך ויעשו רצונך כרצונם: אמן:

אל מלך נאמן הרופא לשבורי לב ומחבש לעצבותם שלח רפואה שלמה
לחולי עמך: ידעו כלם כי זכרונם לפניך תמיד ואתה הוא מגן ומושיע לכל
החוסים בך: אמן :

מי שברך אבותינו. אברהם יצחק ויעקב. הוא יברך את־כל־הקהל הקדוש
הזה. עם כל־קהלות הקדש. הם ובניהם ובנותיהם וכל־אשר־להם: מלך
עולמים הוא יברך אתכם. ויזכה אתכם. וישמע קול תפלתיכם. ויפדה ויציל
אתכם מכל־צרה וצוקה. וחסד יי יהי בסעדכם. ויגן בעדכם ויפרוש סכת
שלומו עליכם. ויטע ביניכם אהבה ואחוה. שלום וריעות. יהוה אלהי
אבותיכם יסף עליכם ככם אלף פעמים. ויברך אתכם כאשר דבר לכם: וכן
יהי רצון ונאמר אמן:

Almighty God, we pray to thee for our Sovereign Lady, Queen Elizabeth, Elizabeth the Queen Mother, Philip Duke of Edinburgh, Charles Duke of Cornwall, and all the Royal Family. We beseech thee to bless and keep them. Grant the Queen and her counsellors wisdom to govern the Empire in accordance with thy holy will, so that it may help to set righteousness and justice in the earth. Strengthen our love for our country, our desire to serve it, our power of self-sacrifice in the things that make for its welfare. Cause us to see ever more clearly that its high place among the nations is in the keeping of all its citizens. Hasten the time, we beseech thee, when thy rule will be accepted by all mankind, and when the reign of peace and love will be established on earth. Amen.

Father of mercies, whose all-embracing love is our refuge and hope, sustain in tenderness the sorrowing hearts among us. Comfort them in the hope of union with their dear ones in eternal blessedness. Grant them faith and courage, and submission to thy chastening hand. Amen.

O God, may it please thee to send healing to those who are in pain or in anxiety. Be thou their refuge through their time of trial. Make them secure in the knowledge that they will never be forgotten by thee, for thou art the Shield of all who trust in thee. Amen.

May he who blessed our ancestors, Abraham, Isaac, and Jacob, bless this holy congregation, together with all other holy congregations, them, their children, and all that are dear to them. May the supreme King of kings be gracious unto you, and account you worthy. May he hearken to the voice of your supplications, and redeem and deliver you from all trouble and distress. May God in his mercy uphold and shield you, spread the tabernacle of peace over you, and plant among you love and brotherhood, peace and friendship. The Lord God of your fathers make you a thousand times as many as ye are, and bless you as he hath promised you. May such be the divine will, and let us say, Amen.

In the 1950s an insert containing a supplication on behalf of the State of Israel was attached to the last page of the prayerbook to be read between the paragraph concerning the queen, the royal family, and the commonwealth, and the paragraphs on behalf of the ailing and the grieving.

PRAYER FOR THE LAND OF ISRAEL

אלהינו ואלהי אבותינו. שלח נא את ברכתך על מדינת ישראל ועל ישביה.
יהי רצון מלפניך. שתדריך מנהיגי האמה ויעציה בעצה טובה. ותחכימם
ותאמצם בשפעת עזרתך.
תנה נא לעם השכן בציון להכריז ולהודיע תורת צדק ושלום לכל בריותיך:
למען יכירו וידעו כלם.
כי מציון תצא תורה ודבר ה׳ מירושלים. אמן.

O God and God of our fathers we ask thy blessing upon the land of
Israel. May her leaders and counsellors be guided by thy wisdom and
strengthened by thy help. May the people of Israel proclaim the message of righteousness and peace to all mankind so that out of Zion
may go forth the law and thy word from Jerusalem. Amen.

Apart from those editions of *Forms of Prayer* in which A. Loewy played a
major editorial role, the 1965 *Prayers for the Pilgrim Festivals* may be
regarded as grammatically, idiomatically, and orthographically the most
faultless to date. Hence in the set of petitions described above, the 1965
compilers emend *av ha-rahamim, hamol-na ve-hus na al avot u-vanim ha-avelim be-qirbenu* to a more precise *av ha-rahamim hamol na ve-husah na al ha-
avot* **veha**-*banim ha-avelim* **shebe-tokhenu.** In the next prayer, for those who
are infirm or unwell, the verb **oleh** is intromitted between *zikhronam* and
lefanekha for clarity's sake in the phrase *yed'u khullam ki zikhronam lefanekha
tamid.* For some unstated reason, these refinements were completely overlooked in the 1977 edition of the first volume and 1985 edition of the
High Holy Day prayerbook, both of which went back to the original 1931
Hebrew wording.

There are, however, totally new prayers for Britain and Israel in the later
volumes. The most recent *Forms of Prayer* for Sabbath and weekday worship (1977) and for the High Holy Days (1985) overhaul the semibiblical-
sounding prayers for both countries to more accurately reflect modern
geopolitical realities. Great Britain functions now within a global context
a good deal larger than itself and its former holdings. The new prayer
acknowledges a worldview more modest and, in a sense, more embracing
than the Victorian or Edwardian dream of *Pax Britannica,* and the language is less stately, classical, or assured. In a similar vein the entreaty for

Israel's wellbeing trades in its sense of ethereal invincibility for a more realistic awareness of physical insecurity, hostility without, and division within. Thus the Hebrew idiom is clearly Israeli and the mindset contemporary and guarded.

Two fleeting cases of cacography failed to catch the attention of the proofreaders [יחדיו *yaḥdav* with *yod* and vowels] and [אמיתי *amiti* with *dot* in *tav*] are spelled simultaneously using the *ketav male* and the *ketav ḥaser*—a pesky redundancy.

אלהינו שמלכותו מלכות כל־עולמים יברך

May He whose kingdom is an everlasting kingdom bless
  Our Sovereign Lady, Queen Elizabeth,
    and all the Royal Family, her advisers and her counsellors.

יתן לנו כח למלא חובתנו באהבה. כך שצדק ונדיבות ישררו בארצנו. יהי שלום בלבנו. אנשי־קהלות־הממלכת יתודעו בהכרה הדדית. יהיו מאחדים באהבת־הטוב ומאלימות וריב ירחקו. עם כל־אמות־העולם יחדיו נשאף לשלוה ולצדקה. ובשלום נחיה אנו ובנינו. אז תזכה מלכותנו לכבוד אמיתי ולגדלה לקראת הגאלה ולהקמת־מלכות־השמים על־הארץ. אמן:

אלהינו ואלהי אבותינו שלח־נא ברכתך על־מדינת ישראל ועל־כל־יושביה. שלח־נא אורך ואמתתך למנהיגי־העם והדריכם בחכמה ובתבונה כדי שישרור שלום בגבולותיה ושלוה בבתיה. רוח־אחוה והבנה הדדית תרפא כל־פצע וחבורה. תקות־עמה ועבודת־בניה תגשמנה את־חזון־הנביאים: כי מציון תצא תורה ודבר־יהוה מירושלים. אמן:

May He give His wisdom to the government of this country, to all who lead it and to all who have responsibility for its safety and its welfare. May He give us all the strength to do our duty, and the love to do it well, so that justice and kindness may dwell in our land. May His peace be in our hearts, so that every community of our nation may meet in understanding and respect, united by love of goodness, and keeping far from violence and strife. Together may we work for peace and justice among all nations and may we and our children live in peace. So may this kingdom find its honour and greatness in the work of redemption, and the building of God's kingdom here on earth. May this be His will. Amen.

Our God and God of our fathers, we ask Your blessing upon the State of Israel and all who dwell in it. Send Your light and Your truth to the leaders of the people, and guide them with wisdom and understanding, so that peace may reign on its borders and tranquillity in its homes. May the spirit of friendship and understanding remove all fears and heal all wounds. There, may mercy and truth come together for the good of all mankind, so that Your promise is fulfilled: "for Torah shall come out of Zion and the word of the Lord from Jerusalem." Amen.

This unexpected run of petitions is quite different from what one would be accustomed to seeing in an Orthodox siddur, or even in Marks's *Forms of Prayer*.[26] To be sure, the practice of praying for the welfare of the community and the country is a well-established one; but wherefore the special mention of the mourners and the poor in health? Two possibilities might be considered and perhaps even reinforce one another. The Sephardim have long been in the habit of reciting at this point during the service the *hashkavah* to memorialize the departed,[27] a practice that could easily lend itself to invoking God to send consolation to the bereaved. At the same time in the service, individual *mi she-berakh* prayers of various kinds might be offered. Since neither the *hashkavah* nor the *mi she-berakh* was ever really a part of the British Reform liturgy in this context, an alternative influence might have been the liturgy of the Anglican Church.

There, after the readings from Scripture, the Creed, and the sermon, the pattern is to offer up an intercession called "the Prayers of the People" ("Let us pray for the whole state of Christ's Church and the world"). According to the rubrics of the American *Book of Common Prayer* (1977), prayer is offered with intercession for:

The Universal Church, its members, and its missions
The Nation and all in authority
The welfare of the world
The concerns of the community
Those who suffer and those in any trouble
The departed (with commemoration of a saint when appropriate).

With modifications, of course, a similar configuration is visible in *Forms of Prayer,* the key difference being that in the Jewish rite the sermon is delivered *after* the entreaties.

No doubt another major influence of the *Book of Common Prayer* was the 1931 decision to include a major portion of the Psalter in *Forms of Prayer,* paralleling Archbishop Cranmer's deployment of all 150 for the initial edition of the Anglican rite (1549; 1552)—a feature that has been maintained in all subsequent ones. Although in every edition of *Forms of Prayers* the Psalms appear in an appendix, they occupy as much as half the prayerbook and thus permit a wider range of choice than is usually offered in a traditional siddur—although only the current Festival and High Holy Day volumes prescribe which psalms are to be read and when.[28]

It is certainly appropriate to include the Psalms, Israel's first prayerbook—or hymnal—in a siddur. The original creators of *Forms of Prayer* no doubt thought it sadly ironic that a daughter faith would be at home in this psalmody while the posterity of its original composers had only a peripheral awareness of its scope and richness. They wished to expose the Jewish worshiper to the full gamut of its literary skill and religious emotion, believing that by doing so, they could both cultivate the Jewish spirit and abate monotony in various services. Further, they chose to adopt the method only sparsely followed in Jewish prayerbooks before the 1930s, that of rendering all the Hebrew psalms in verse alignment, enhancing the worshiper's esteem for this long-used religious poetry. The editors of the 1977 revision reinstated still more of them, translating afresh all those included earlier. Happily, they have succeeded in recapturing the directness, passion, and poignancy of the original Hebrew.

The 1952 Memorial Service

The 1952 *Forms of Prayer: Evening Prayers* was created for daily Evening Services at the West London Synagogue and for the House of Mourning. The text is fundamentally the 1931 liturgy with a few pregnant additions, such as a service for the Outgoing of the Sabbath, including *havdalah* with wine, spices, and candle.[29] There is also a noteworthy adaptation of the benediction after the reading of the Megillah on Purim (in addition to the three before, which had already been resuscitated in the 1931 edition), with the phrases calling for revenge deleted and the incorporation instead of lines from *shoshanat ya'aqov:* "Thou hast been our help forever and our hope in all generations. They that trust thee shall never be confounded nor put to shame."

Perhaps the most noteworthy feature in *Evening Prayers* is the provision of an unstrained and sound Hebrew translation of a Memorial Service Reinhart composed in English for the 1931 edition.[30] Medieval phrases are included, such as *ilat-reshit le-khol nimtza* ("Thou Source of all being") and a modification of a line in the Song of Songs (8:6): *azzah mi-mavet ahavah ve-emet gaverah mi-she'ol* ("Love does not die, and truth is mightier than the grave.")

הזכרת נשמות

ענה עני שפל כל־השפלים. ושא חטאו מקבל התפלות: והארך־נא ברחמיך שנותיו. וצוה כל־שאלותיו למלאות: והאל המקבל התפלות. שמע קולי אשר ישמע בקולות:

יי אלהי־העולמים. עלת־ראשית לכל־נמצא ומקור־החיים. מה־נאמר לפניך הראה ויודע הכל: בחכמתך כוננת תבל: ובאהבתך תכלכל את כל־ברואיך: אין־לנו בלתי־אם להכיר ולהודות כי אתה כל־יכל. לקבל ברב־תודה את כל־טובתיך. ולהחזיר לך לפי משפט צדקך את אשר בא לנו מידך:

יי אלהים. האר־נא לנו באור־פניך בהיכל קדשך בלב שבור ובהתאבלנו על מות _____ אשר אספת את (נפשו) (נפשה) אליך: רצה־נא ברחמיך הרבים את־(חייו) (חייה) עלי־אדמות אחרי בא קצם: ובחמלתך הגדולה תן (לנשמתו) (לנשמתה) היקרה לנו מחסה תחת כסא כבודך:

מודים אנחנו לך על כל־הטוב והנעלה אשר העניקת (לו) (לה) (בחייו) (בחייה): הערה־נא עלינו (למענו) (למענה) מאורך ומעזך: עזרנו־נא להקדיש את־אבלנו לעבודתך באהבה:

יי אלהי־העולם. היה־נא בעזרנו למען נוסיף דעת ובינה כי עת ומקום לא יכילו את כל־הנמצאים: אמנם קצרו עיננו מראות: אך למדנו־נא להשכיל בינה כי נשמת (הנפטר) (הנפטרה) (היקר) (היקרה) לנו לא נכרתה מן־החיים: עזה ממות אהבה ואמת גברה משאול: וכשם שאנחנו מתיחדים בשעה קדושה זאת (עמו) (עמה) באהבה ובזכר (מעשיו) (מעשיה) הטובים כן

יהי רצון מלפניך כי נעלה מעלה על כנפי־האמונה ונזכה לחזות חיי־אלמות:

יי אלהי־עזנו. עזרנו־נא ברפיוננו: נחמנו ביגוננו: הורנו דרך במבוכתנו:
בלעדיך חיינו הם אין ואפס. ועמך מלא־חיים לעדי־עד: אלהי־הרוחות וצור־
העולמים. תמכנו־נא כי בך בטחנו:

יהיו לרצון אמרי־פי והגיון־לבי לפניך יי צורי וגאלי:

MEMORIAL SERVICE

Answer the frail and humble worshipper, and forgive his sin, O thou, who hearest prayer! Prolong his years in thy mercy, and grant him the fulfilment of all his petitions. O God, who hearest prayer, hearken to my voice, thou who hearkenest to every voice.

O Lord God, thou Source of all being and Fountain of life, what can we say unto thee who seest and knowest all? In thy wisdom thou didst establish the universe, and in thy love thou dost provide for thy creatures. What can we do, but acknowledge thine omnipotence, and accept with gratitude thy gifts; and, in accordance with thy decrees, give back to thee thine own.

O Lord God, shed the light of thy presence upon us as we gather here with hearts bowed down by the loss of _____, whom thou hast taken to thyself. Accept thou in thy great mercy the earthly life which now is ended, and shelter with thy tender care this soul that is so precious to our hearts.

We thank thee for all that was gentle and noble in (his) (her) life. Through (his) (her) name inspire thou us with strength and light. Help us to consecrate our very grief to acts of service and of love.

Help us to realise more and more, O thou everlasting God, that time and space are not the measure of all things. Though our eyes do not see, yet do thou teach us to understand that the soul of our dear one is not cut off. Love does not die, and truth is mightier than the grave. Even as our affection and the remembrance of the good (he) (she)

wrought unite us with (him) (her) in this holy hour, so on the wings of faith may we be lifted to the vision of the life that knows no death. O God of our strength, in our weakness help us; in our sorrow comfort us; in our perplexity guide us. Without thee our lives are nothing; with thee is fulness of life for evermore. O infinite Spirit, uphold us, for we put our trust in thee.
Let the words of my mouth and the meditation of my heart be acceptable in thy sight, O Lord, my Rock and my Redeemer.

The 1965 Prayers for the Pilgrim Festivals

Beyond question the influx into England during the thirties and forties of German Liberal rabbis, with their classical training and schooling in *Wissenschaft des Judentums,* had a hand in raising the quality of the Hebrew both in *Evening Prayers* and *Prayers for the Pilgrim Festivals* (Hebrew title: *Maḥzor le-Shalosh Regalim),* printed in Amsterdam and Tel Aviv and issued in 1965. Drawing upon the scholarly studies in Jewish liturgy (one need only mention the seminal labors of Ismar Elbogen), the Festival volume is less textually idiosyncratic than the 1931 volume. Several prayers jettisoned in times past are restored—notably a full *qedushah,*[31] the *haqqafot* during Simḥat Torah, *havdalah* during the Kiddush on the eve of a Festival coinciding with the Outgoing of the Sabbath, and the placement of all of the morning psalms between *barukh she-amar* and *nishmat.*[32]
Nevertheless, the 1965 rite provides an up-to-date and more palatable translation and has taken pains to maintain grammatical and orthographic precision in the Hebrew text, which is equipped throughout with aids to correct pronunciation, symbols to indicate which syllable is to be stressed, and when the *qamatz* is to be sounded as a short 'o.' This phonetic aspect is, by the way, discontinued in succeeding volumes of *Forms of Prayer,* no doubt because of the extra work involved for later publishers, English and American.
Particularly noteworthy in the Festival prayerbook are three new Hebrew prayers, two short and one long. The first, to be recited after the benediction of the Festival (and Sabbath) lights in the home, invokes God

as the light of the world and incorporates two apposite scriptural phrases (Psalms 36:10 and Isaiah 35:10):[33]

אל שדי, אור־העולם. ברכנו בברכה שלמה מלפניך. רצה־נא בנו והאר
את־עינינו באורך ובאמתך, כמו שהדלקנו לפניך את־נרות {השבת ו} החג,
והשכן בנאותינו רוח אמונים ואהבה: הדריכנו באור פניך, ובאורך נראה
אור. שלח־נא את־ברכתך לכל־בית בישראל ובעולם כלו ותן שלום ושמחת
עולם על ראשם. אמן.

Almighty God, who art the light of the world, grant us Thy heaven-ly blessing. May the radiance of these lights, kindled in honour of this *{Sabbath and}* Festival, illumine our hearts, and brighten our home with the spirit of faith and love. Let the light of thy Presence guide us, for in Thy light do we see light. Bless also with Thy spirit the homes of all Israel and all mankind, that happiness and peace may ever abide in them. Amen.

Then the single *hoshana* for Sukkot is once more reconstituted to evoke the flavor of the traditional *hoshanot* and make more obvious use of the antiphonal *ken hosha na*. The final biblicist *hoshi'ah et ammekha* is of course the standard one found in Ashkenazic and Sephardic rites.

אני והו, הושיעה נא.
כהושעת ממי מבול את־נח, וימצא בתבה מנוח,
כן הושע נא.
כהושעת אברהם עם המלכים, בהלחמו, וכרת ברית עמו,
כן הושע נא.
כהושעת יעקב מיד לבן הארמי, ותאמר: גם בניך יקראו בשמי,
כן הושע נא.
כהושעת את־אבותינו בכל־עת צרה, כי שמך עלינו נקרא,
כן הושע נא.
אני והו, הושיעה נא.

הושיעה את־עמך וברך את־נחלתך, ורעם ונשאם עד עולם. ויהיו דברי

אלה, אשר התחננתי לפני יי, קרבים אל־יי אלהינו יומם ולילה, לעשות
משפט עבדו ומשפט עמו ישראל דבר־יום ביומו: למען דעת כל־ימי הארץ,
כי יי הוא האלהים, אין עוד.

O Lord, save us, we beseech Thee.

As Thou from the flood of waters Noah didst save,
And a resting place in the Ark for him ensure,
   So save Thou us.

As Thou in his wars with kings Abraham didst save,
And then with him an everlasting covenant make,
   So save Thou us.

As Thou Jacob from Laban of Aram didst save,
And declare: 'Thy children also shall bear My name,'
   So save Thou us.

As Thou our fathers in times of trouble didst save,
For Thou hast upon us Thy divine name invoked, So save Thou us.

Help Thy people and bless Thine inheritance; and tend and sustain them forever. And let these my words, wherewith I have entreat-
ed the Lord, be nigh unto the Lord our God day and night, that He
may uphold the cause of His servant, and the cause of His people
Israel, day by day; that all the peoples of the earth may know that the
Lord He is God; there is none else.

All that remains then of the Marks-Loewy re-creation is the substitution of the preamble hoshana; *le-ma'ankha eloheynu, hosha na* with

הושע נא, הושע נא.
למענך, אם לא למעננו, הושע נא.

Save us, we beseech Thee,
Save us, we beseech Thee.
For Thy sake, if not for ours, save us, we beseech Thee.

The most extensive Hebrew liturgical creativity in the *Prayers for the Pilgrim Festivals* is the expansive memorial prayer to be said during the

hazkarat neshamot, just after the Yizkor prayer itself. The English text appeared for the first time as one of several inserts pasted into the 1958 reprint of the seventh edition of *Forms of Prayer: Prayers for the Day of Atonement.* From its contents and style, my guess is that its composer was none other than Reinhart himself.

The prayer blends a lofty idealism with warm spirituality, the particular with the universal. Eloquent and moving as the English is, the Hebrew is undeniably classical, with many biblical and liturgical phrases. While a fairly faithful rendering of the original, the Hebrew prayer hardly ever deserts its modern dynamic and hits its mark as only a few of the others in all the editions of *Forms of Prayer* in the last century and a half.

אלהינו ואלהי אבותינו, באהבתך אלינו נתת לנו חיים. אל חי וקים לעולם ועד, עומדים אנו לפניך בשעה זו בזכרנו את־נשמות כל־אלה היקרים, הנאהבים והנאמנים שהלכו ממנו לחיי עולם. זוכרים אנו לפניך גם את־כל־חכמי אמות העולם ומנהיגיהם שהורו אותם את־הדרך אשר ילכו בה.

זוכרים אנחנו כיום את־גבורי ישראל וקדושיו שקדשו שמך ברבים ואף נזכר את חסידי אמות־העולם – עדים נאמנים לרוח קדשך השוכנת בקרבנו. אבינו שבשמים, בשעת הזכרת נשמות זו, מודים אנחנו לך על־כל־אלה שעזרו בחייהם להביא שלום וברכה לדור ודור, ובמותם קדשו את־שמך הגדול בעולם. ומצדיקי הרבים הללו כזוהר הכוכבים יזהירו.

אל מלא רחמים, זוכרים אנחנו לפניך את־כל־היקרים לנפשנו: אם, אב, אשה, בעל, בן, בת ו יד יד של כל־אחד ואחד ממנו: נפשנו תשתוחח ותהמה במקדש קט זה, בזכרנו לפניך את־שמותם ואת־מדותיהם הטובות. זכותם תגן עלינו וצדקתם תאיר את־דרכנו ותדריכנו לשמור פקודיך ונצליח להשכין בתוכנו מגמת חיים טובים וישרים.

אלהינו ואלהי אבותינו, עזרנו נא וחזקנו להיותנו ראויים לעמוד לפניך ולקים מה שהבטחנו ללכת בדרך טובים וישרים, ותוחלת מחמדי נפשנו שהלכו לעולמם לא תכזב.

אנה האל, בזכרנו את־כל־היקרים האלה נמצא נא תנחומים ובהגותנו במדותיהם הטובות וחייהם המסורים נכירה נא ונדעה את־כל־הטובות שהיטיבו עמנו.

אב הרחמים, אמץ נא את־רוחנו הנכאה להבין את־גזרתך שגזרת על כל־
בריותיך בבוא קצם: תן ברוחנו להבין שמץ־דבר של סוד־המות הגדול
והנעלם מתבונת כל־חי. חננו מאתך בינה ובאמונתנו נתחזק להודות ולהלל
את־שמך הגדול. אמן.

O Lord our God, through whose love we have our being, and in whose presence is eternal life, in this solemn hour we remember before Thee all those whose lives in this world claim our love and affection, admiration, respect and gratitude, and whom Thou hast now taken to eternity. We recall the great of mankind who in signal measure have pointed the way as leaders of men and nations. We think of the heroes and the martyrs, especially of the house of Israel, but also of all the families of the earth, the witnesses to Thy holy spirit in the world.

O Lord, in this hour of remembrance, we thank Thee for all those who have contributed to the peace and blessing of future generations, and whose passing to eternity glorifies Thy holy name. May their names shine as the stars in heaven for ever and ever.

O merciful Father, we recall before Thee, each one of us, those who are nearest and dearest to us: mother, father, wife, husband, son, daughter, friend. In the quiet of the sanctuary, the names and the qualities of them all are counted over with tender longing. Each capacity, each merit, and each grace shines before us now as a crown to a treasured name and as an incentive to rich and noble living. O Thou, God of our fathers, help us to be worthy of our finest memories and true to our highest resolves to emulate noble examples and to fulfill the hopes of our dear departed ones.

May memories, though poignant, provide us with some comfort. May the contemplation of their personalities, which renews our knowledge of their lives, heighten our sense of the blessings they have bestowed upon us.

May the voice of reason speak to our troubled spirits of the essential place of death in the scheme of life. May the light of faith pierce the shadows that enfold us. May we be wise enough to sense the over-mastering mystery which no human mind can penetrate. With a little understanding, and with growing faith, may we be strengthened to glorify Thy name. Amen.

The 1974 *Funeral Service*

The next prayerbook to appear under the auspices of the Reform Synagogues of Great Britain was the *Funeral Service* (1974, Hebrew title: *Tzidduq ha-Din),* which has all of the liturgical passages, old and new, in Hebrew and in English, except for a prayer at the reading of the inscription during the "Consecration of Memorial," or, in American parlance, the unveiling, which appears only in English.

Throughout this edition, the English is spare, unaffected, and vigorous. In no way redolent of the Elizabethan or Victorian mode, it sets the pattern for the 1977 edition of "the daily, Sabbath, and occasional" prayerbook and the 1985 High Holy Day one. In contrast, the Hebrew is pedestrian and flat. Laudable as the effort is to translate all Jewish prayer into the historical language of the Jewish people, the outcome in *Funeral Service* falls short.

During the obsequies before the Mourner's Kaddish, four new prayers for the deceased reveal British Reform's creedal loyalties. All of the new-minted prayers, as well as the traditional ones, affirm belief in life beyond the grave. A comparison between the old and new versions of the first prayer (the only one related to one in previous editions of *Forms of Prayer*) will suffice. Making its debut in the 1841 edition, the prototype of the prayer was meant to be said by the minister on the Sabbath after the funeral in place of the expected Sephardic *hashkavah.* The prayer is infused in biblical idiom, its phrases distilled from the Hebrew Bible and deftly strung together.

אלהי העולמים, בידך נשמת כל־חי ורוח כל־בריה. אנו פונים אליך ביגון
ובשמחה כי עמנו חסדך לעולם, ואהבתך ואמיתתך סועדים אותנו בכל־עת
ועת. גם כי נלך בגיא צלמות לא נירא רע כי אתה עמדנו שבטך ומשענתך
המה ינחמונו. יהוה אלהינו לקחת מאתנו את־ . . . . וברחמיך תקח אתה
לחיי עולם. יהי זכרון חייה וזכרון פעליה לברכה ולנחמה לכל־המתאבלים
עליה. זכרון זה יאמץ ויחזק אתם להמשיך בחיי יום יום ולהאמין בך
בלבבם.

אלהי הרחמים תהי לעזרה לכל־האבלים, ונחמם ביגונם. האר חשכתם
ונחמם בצערם. שנאמר: כאיש אשר אמו תנחמנו אנכי אנחמכם. לא יבוא
עוד שמשך וירחך לא יאסף כי יהוה יהיה־לך לאור עולם ושלמו ימי אבלך.

O Eternal God, in whose hand is the soul of all living and the spirit
of all flesh, to thee we direct our eyes, whether in grief or in joy; for
thou dost never withdraw thy tender mercies from us, but dost continually sustain us with thy grace and thy truth. Though we walk
through the valley of the shadow of death, we will fear no evil, for
thou art with us, thy rod and thy staff will be our consolation. Thou,
O Lord, hast been pleased to lead thy servant (N. N.) to the rest of
everlasting life; act we beseech thee towards him (her) according to
thine infinite mercy, and grant that his (her) portion may be in life
everlasting. Protect him (her) under the shadow of thy wings, so that
he (she) may behold the radiance of thy countenance, and exult in the
plenitude of thy goodness which thou hast treasured up for those
who fear thee. And do thou also grant that the remembrance of his
(her) name may prove a blessing and a comfort to those who mourn
for him (her): may it incline their hearts to remain firm in their faith,
and to walk in the path of Piety, Justice and Virtue. Deign, O Lord,
to regard those who are sorrowing, and to consider their grief of spirit; cheer their darkness, and bring consolation to them and to every
mourner in Israel. Amen.

Thy sun shall no more go down, neither shall thy moon withdraw
itself; for the Lord shall be thine everlasting light, and the days of thy
mourning shall be ended; and it is said, As one whom his mother com-
forteth, so will I comfort you, and in Jerusalem shall ye be comforted.

The closing sentences are from Isaiah 60:20 and 66:13, respectively. Marks
doubtless derived the idea of tapping these Isaianic verses from the
hashkavah, where they are spoken to the bereaved at the end of the mourning period. In the 1931 edition the prayer is moved to the funeral service
itself, with minimal verbal alterations.[34] The Reconstructionist *Sabbath
Prayer Book* adopted it, as the rubric has it, "to be said in behalf of mourners on the Sabbath following their bereavement" in the synagogue just
before the Mourner's Kaddish.[35] It could well be that for the compilers of

the 1974 *Funeral Service,* the long-lived version by Marks was too orna-mental for their taste. All the same, to the liturgically attuned ear, the adjustment in the present volume falls far short of the original.

יי אלהינו אשר בידך נפש כל חי ורוח כל בשר איש. לך עינינו מיחלות
אם בדמעות אם בשמחות. כי לעולם לא תכלא רחמיך ממנו. חסדך ואמתך
תמיד יצרונו: גם כי נלך בגיא צלמות לא נירא רע. כי אתה עמנו שבטך
ומשענתך המה ינחמונו: אתה יי נהלת את עבדך (פלוני) אמתך (פלונית)
למנוחת חיי העולמים. עשה עמו (עמה) כרב חסדך. ותן חלקו (חלקה)
בחיים וגורלו (וגורלה) בנעימים. והסתירהו (והסתירה) בצל כנפיך לחזות
בנעם פניך ולהתענג ברב טובך אשר צפנת ליראיך: ויהי נא זכר שמו (שמה)
לברכה ולמשיב נפש לאבליו (לאבליה) ויכין לבם להחזיק באמונה וללכת
בארח צדקה ומשפט ומישרים. ואתה יי הבט וראה מרת נפשם והאר חשכם
ושלם נחומים להם ולכל אבלי ישראל. אמן:

לא יבא עוד שמשך וירחך לא יאסף. כי יי יהיה לך לאור עולם ושלמו ימי
אבלך: ונאמר. כאיש אשר אמו תמחמנו. כן אנכי אנחמכם ובירושלם
תנחמו:

Eternal God, in Your hands are the souls of the living and the spirits of all creatures. We turn to You in grief as well as in joy, for Your mercy is always with us, and Your love and truth support us at all times. Though we walk through the valley of the shadow of death, we fear no harm, for You are beside us; Your rod and staff they com-fort us. Lord, You have taken from us. . . . In Your mercy bear her to life everlasting.
May the memory of her life and her good deeds bring blessing and comfort to those who mourn for her. May it give them the courage and strength to continue bravely in their daily life, trusting You in their hearts. God of mercy, help those who mourn, and comfort them in their grief. Lighten their darkness, and console them in their sor-row. It is said: "As a mother comforts her child so will I Myself com-fort you. Never again shall your sun set, nor your moon withdraw its light, because the Lord shall be your everlasting light, and the days of your mourning shall be ended."

Unfortunately, a similar prosaicism preys on the other three preludes to the concluding Kaddish.

The 1977 Forms of Prayer

Three years later, in 1977, *Forms of Prayer* was subjected to a major facelift. The editors held fast to much of the 1931 edition, but branching out in different directions, created much that was unprecedented. They loyally followed in the footsteps of the editors of that early edition—as in providing ten new prayers with which to commence Sabbath worship, four for Friday evening and six for Saturday morning. But the prayers are neither repeats of the 1931 ones nor of the Reconstructionist adaptations. The second selection for Shabbat Eve, however, is a simplified and slightly expanded rewording of the single introductory prayer for the same spot in the 1931 prayerbook.

רבון־הרחמים ומקור־הברכות. שעה־נא לתפלותינו בליל־שבת זה: ענג־
השבת בא לאחר ששת־ימי־המעשה ולבותינו המטרדים מגיעים אל־שלותם
ואל־מנוחתם: בתפלות ובהודיות נבקשך לקדש עלינו את־היום הזה: מחה
פשעינו ברחמיך וחזק מעשינו לטובה: טהר לבנו מהאנכיות ותן בלבנו
לשאוף ליפה ולאמת: האר את־החשך השרוי בתוכנו וברך את־בתינו ואת־כל־
אוהבינו: אז נבטח בעזרתך ונשמור בריתך לעולם:

לא עלינו לבד תבוא ברכת־שבת זו כי־אם על־כל־ברואי־עולם כי בנתננו
ישבע רצוננו בשרתנו נשתחרר חרות־אמת. ובברכנו אחרים נתברך: בנו
תתקים אמרתך ונברכו בך כל־משפחות־האדמה. אמן:

Creator of mercy and of blessings, be present in our prayers this Sabbath eve. Sabbath joy follows the working week, and our troubled minds find their comfort and rest. With prayers and thanks we turn to You to make this day holy. Wipe away our sins in Your mercy, and strengthen our work for good. Cleanse us from selfishness, and give us new longing for all that is good and true. Enlighten the darkness that lies within us, and bring a blessing to our homes and to those we love. So may we keep Your covenant forever, for Your help is sure.

May the blessing of this Sabbath come not for ourselves alone but for all. For it is in giving that we find contentment, in serving that we find our true freedom, and in blessing others that we ourselves are blessed. Through us may the promise be fulfilled "and all the families of the world shall bless themselves by You." Amen.

The third piece is also a lovely mood-setting one in preparation for the Sabbath.

רבון־כל־המעשים המשלתנו בעולמך לעבדו לשמרו וליהנות ממנו.
בששת־ימי־המעשה אנו אומדים ובונים. מחברים את־חשבון־עמלנו האמיתי
והמדמה. מעבירים את־יתרת־הצלחתנו ואת־מחירה:
אך בזה יום־השבת המציא לנו מנוחה:
בששת־ימי־המעשה אם אנו יגעים או רצוצים תחת־נטל־החיים. אם
נתחזה כענקים או נכאיב לאחרים. אין לנו רגע להרהר ולא פנאי להכיר
במה שצריכים אנו להיות באמת:
אך בזה יום־השבת המציא לנו הפוגה:
בששת־ימי־חמעשה אנו קרועים בין־תאוותנו אנו ובין־צרכיהם הדחופים
של־אחרים. בין־הטפלות הנשמעת באזנינו ובין־תפלת־נפשנו שבדממה דקה:
אך בזה יום־השבת המציא לנו הבנה ושלום:
עזר לנו יי להוסיף לקחי־המנוחה והפוגה ההבנה והשלום לששת־ימי־
המעשה הבאים ולכל־ימי־מעשה־ידינו למען נתברך בכל־חיינו. אמן:

Lord of all creation, You have made us the masters of Your world, to tend it, to serve it, and to enjoy it. For six days we measure and we build, we count and carry the real and the imagined burdens of our task, the success we earn and the price we pay.

On this, the Sabbath day, give us rest.

For six days, if we are weary or bruised by the world, if we think ourselves giants or cause others pain, there is never a moment to pause, and know what we should really be. On this, the Sabbath day, give us time.

For six days we are torn between our private greed and the urgent needs of others, between the foolish noises in our ears and the silent prayer of our soul.

On this, the Sabbath day, give us understanding and peace.

Help us, Lord, to carry these lessons, of rest and time, of understanding and peace, into the six days that lie ahead, to bless us in the working days of our lives. Amen.

In keeping with the prayer after the kindling of the candles on the eve of a Sabbath or Festival quoted above,[36] an engaging *kavvanah* with light as its main motif starts the entire Sabbath home ceremony. It begins typically in the manner of many a kabbalistic meditation: *hineni mukhan u-mezumman* ("Behold I am ready and prepared to fulfill the command of my Creator . . .") and modulates into

הנני מוכן ומזמן לכבד את־השבת בנאמנות אליך ואל־הדורות שקדמו
לי. הנני משליך מלבי כל־שנאה וכל־מרירות שנשתירו מהשבוע שעבר למען
תהיה רוחי שלוה ואקרא בשמך באמת: לאור־נרות־השבת רואה אני את־
המסובים בביתי כצון אותי לראותם. ומודה אני לפניך על־משפחה וידידות.
על־נאמנות ואהבה. בקדשי על־היין אביע לשלום השופע מקדשה ולשמחה
הנובעת מנדבת־הלב. באכלי את־פתי אכיר בחובתי לאחרים ואצפה ליום
שכלו שבת ושמחה ושלום לכל:

Meditation

Lord, I prepare to honour the Sabbath, keeping faith with You and the generations that have gone before. I cast away any hatred or bitterness that lingers from the week that is past, so that my spirit may be at rest, and I can truly speak Your name. I see those about me in the light of the Sabbath candles as You want me to see them, and thank You for family and friendship, loyalty and love. I make *kiddush,* and receive the gift of happiness, the peace that comes from holiness, the joy that comes from giving. As I eat the bread, I remember all I owe to others, and look forward to that great Sabbath when all shall find their joy and peace.

The preliminary prayers on Saturday morning are each assigned to six different services, each revolving on a distinct theme. The prayers, songs, and readings that lead the way to the Shema and its attendant benedictions for the most part spotlight a given theme; so does the excerpt from the Bible *before* the Taking Out of the Torah.

To illustrate, Sabbath Service III comes under the heading of "the

Future." Before the prefatory prayer after *mah tovu*— a fixture in every Sabbath and Festival service since the 1931 edition—is Shaul Tchernichowsky's sparkling and anthropocentric *tzaḥaqi, tzaḥaqi* ("You may laugh, laugh at all the dreams"). Later on, the appointed reading (preceded, in somewhat unconventional fashion, by the blessing *la-asoq be-divrey torah*) is taken from Maimonides' well-known portrayal of the messianic era in his *Mishneh Torah*.[37]

As alternatives to the traditional second and third paragraphs of the Shema (Deut. 11:13 21; Nu. 15:37–41), readings from Isaiah 55 and 56 and Jeremiah 31:30–33 are appropriated to fit the central theme of the service. The scriptural extract read just before the scroll is taken out of the ark is the eschatological Micah 4:1–4. And the prefatory prayer itself right after *mah tovu* is couched, innovatively, in the form of a *berakhah*:

יי מודים אנחנו לך על שטפחת בנו תקוה. עזנו היא בעת־צרה: למרות־
העול שבזמננו. האכזריות והמלחמות. נצפה לעולם שכלו שלום ושבו יגמלו
חסדים ואין מחריד: כל־עברה מעכבתו וכל־מצוה מקרבתו: נהיה־נא עדיך
ויברכונו דורות עתידים לבוא:
תן בלבנו להתפלל ולקות לעבוד ולזכות לבוא היום הנרמז על־יד־נביאך
וזרחה שמש צדקה ומרפא בכנפיה לכל־בריותיך. ברוך אתה יי מקוה־
ישראל. אמן:

Lord, we thank You for Your gift of hope, our strength in times of trouble. Beyond the injustice of our time, its cruelty and its wars, we look forward to a world at peace when men deal kindly with each other, and no-one is afraid. Every bad deed delays its coming, every good one brings it nearer. May our lives be Your witness, so that future generations bless us. May the day come, as the prophet taught, when "the sun of righteousness will rise with healing in its wings." Help us to pray for it, to wait for it, to work for it and to be worthy of it. Blessed are You Lord, the hope of Israel. Amen.

The Thanksgiving after Meals (*birkat ha-mazon*), here the most complete of all of the versions in *Forms of Prayer*, adds a nice touch towards the end between *magdil (migdol) yeshu'ot malko* and *adonay oz le-ammo yitten*, by substituting for the assorted biblical verses the following, which strives to sensitize those present to those in dire want.

אכלנו ושבענו. אל־נא נתעלם מצרכי־רעינו ואל־תאטמנה אזנינו מצעקתם
למזון. פקח עינינו ופתח לבבנו ונתחלקה במתנותיך למען חסול־הרעב
והמחסור מעולמנו:

We have eaten and been satisfied. May we not be blind to the needs
of others, nor deaf to their cry for food. Open our eyes and our hearts
so that we may share Your gifts, and help to remove hunger and
want from our world.

Attitude Toward Israel in the 1977 Rite

The Hebrew prayer for Yom Ha-Atzma'ut in the 1977 rite reveals a conspicuous change in attitude—while still acknowledging previous views on
the subject. Although Marks harbored no doubts about the Ingathering of
the Exiles, the Restoration of Zion, and even the Rebuilding of the Temple, his rabbinic successors from Morris Joseph on were not strong propo-
nents of the Zionist concept. By way of example, Reinhart and his editorial colleagues tailored the *retzeh,* the first of the Three Concluding
Benedictions of the *amidah,* to fit their neutrality, if not their actual inter-
mittent opposition to political Zionism, by changing its *ḥatimah,* or eulogy, from *ha-maḥazir shekhinato le-tziyyon* ("who restores His Presence to
Zion") to a spiritualized *ha-mashreh shekhinato al tziyyon* ("Blessed art thou,
O Lord, *who causest thy holy spirit to rest upon Zion"*). In this formulation,
religion outranks nationalism; and the endorsement of a wholesale Return
to Zion is plainly avoided.

A lukewarm acknowledgment that a Jewish homeland is currently a
reality and an ineluctable part of Jewish consciousness everywhere was
made in the shape of a weekly prayer for that country's spiritual and moral
well-being. As already pointed out, the editors of the latest Sabbath and
weekday prayerbook regarded the physical safety and political stability of
the State of Israel as an important object of concern and prayer. But perhaps the most definitive expression of Israel's acceptance by British
Reform Jewry appears in the leading prayer for Yom ha-Atzma'ut—
although here again, love for Zion and even pride in Israel's accomplish-
ments do not by any means presuppose the restitution of world Jewry to

its ancestral homeland. Without gnosticizing, or elevating the spiritual over all else, the new prayer implies a repudiation of a *Blut-und-Boden* mindset and stoutly validates the Diaspora and the Jewish people's abiding mission in the world. As a point of interest, the prayer is put in unmistakably literary Israeli Hebrew.

אלהינו ואלהי־אבותינו בידך גורל־עמנו ועתיד־כל־אומה ולשון: אתה הוא
המפזרנו בארצות־תבל ואתה הוא המקבצנו: אתה מנחינו מעבדות לחרות.
מצרה לשמחה. ואנו עדיך נאיר אורך בין־העמים: חזקנו־נא לעשות רצונך:

כאבותינו לפנינו לציון באהבה נפנה: זכרונותיה מקרבים אותנו זה לזה.
חזיונה מקרב אותנו אליך: זכנו לראות בבנין־ירושלים בימינו: יהיו־נא
חזקה במשפט הגנתה בצדקה ושכרה שלום:

לשמך נתן כבוד על־הנפלאות שראו עינינו כי תקוה קמה משואה. מעינות
בתוך בקעות־ציה נפתחו וערבה תפרח כחבצלת:

מבעד לצרות־זמננו שמענו דברי־נביאיך וראינו קיום־דברך: שוב פדיתנו
אדון־האמת: חזקנו ואמצנו לכלות מלאכתך ולפתוח שערי־פדות לישראל
ולעמים. אמן:

Our God and God of our fathers, in Your hand is the destiny of our people and the fate of all nations. You scatter us through the world and it is You who gather us in. You lead us through slavery and from pain to freedom and joy, to be Your light and witness among the nations. Give us strength to do Your will!

We turn to Zion in love, like our fathers before us. Its memories draw us nearer to each other, its vision draws us nearer to You. Give us honour to rebuild Jerusalem in our time. Let justice be its strength and righteousnessness its defence, and may its reward be peace.

We praise You for the wonders our eyes have seen: the hope that was born out of suffering, the springs that came to the dry sad valley, the rose that blossomed in the desert. In the troubles of our time we have heard the message of Your prophets and seen the fulfilment of Your word. Again You have redeemed us, Lord of truth. Give us courage to complete Your work, and bring redemption to mankind. Amen.

Similarly, the paragraph *u-veneh yerushalayim ir ha-qodesh* moves back to its hallowed location within Grace after Meals. So does the time-honored eulogy in the *retzeh* of the *amidah: ha-maḥazir shekhinato le-tziyyon.*

The 1985 *Prayers for the High Holy Days*

Although the 1985 *Forms of Prayer: Prayers for the High Holy Days* does not include as many new Hebrew compositions as some of the previous volumes, praise should be accorded its chief creators Lionel Blue and Jonathan Magonet and their many helpers. The new compositions in the prayerbook excite notice, and the return of three noteworthy items from the older liturgy (that Marks had omitted) deserve attention and appreciation.

For those congregations still uncomfortable with the literal Aramaic text of Kol Nidrey for its association with what is *ab origine* a legal proceeding, an all-Hebrew formula that brings out the spiritual import of the day is furnished as an alternative.[38] As for the *avodah,* the narrative portions between each of the three confessions by the High Priest, traditionally in abstruse and allusive paytanic style, here matches in essentials the account of the Service of the High Priest on the Day of Atonement as found in Leviticus 16. In the nineteenth century, Benjamin Szold followed the same tack for his all-Hebrew *avodah* in his *Pijutim, Gebete und Gesaenge* (Baltimore, 1862) and in his *Abodath Israel* (Baltimore, 1863) before changing the narrative portions into German and then English.[39] With regard to *u-netanneh toqef,* Ashkenazic in provenance, the text in the present British Reform maḥzor is the corrected version of the American Conservative *Mahzor for Rosh Hashanah and Yom Kippur* (New York, 1972), edited by Jules Harlow.

In different places the editorial staff did well to bring in Rabbinic passages (pp. 228, 324, 326, 412, 414 [uncited, however], 422, 484, 486, 572, and 580 [with a misprint]) as well as untapped scriptural ones, a piece from Ben Sira[40] (p. 616), a *baqqashah* and kind of *Benedicite omnia opera* by Sa'adiah Gaon (p. 376),[41] a martyr's prayer (p. 496), and verses by two Israeli poets, Rachel [Blumstein, 1890–1931] (p. 104) and Zelda

[Mishkovsky, 1914–1984] (p. 478)—all in the original Hebrew. This, however, is no more than a superficial listing of the veritable gold mine of Hebrew sources the prayerbook offers.

Also praiseworthy is the litany *mi she-anah...hu ya'anenu,* read or chanted during *seliḥot* and again on Kol Nidrey night. Rather than condense, the editors have actually spun out the traditional version and brought it up to date with the different ways God has dealt with His people after the biblical period and even to the present century. In place of Phinehas, Joshua, and Samuel, none of them particularly noted for restraint or moderation, the editors give greater prominence to peaceable historical figures from the days of Hannah and Rabban Yoḥanan ben Zakkai onward: Maimonides, the Besht, Moses Mendelssohn, Leo Baeck, Anne Frank, the *ḥalutzim,* and the survivors of the Shoah. All are accorded their rightful place in this liturgical chronicle of *magnalia Dei.*

הוא יעננו.	מי שענה לאברהם אבינו בהר המוריה
הוא יעננו.	מי שענה ליצחק בנו כשנעקד על גב המזבח
הוא יעננו.	מי שענה ליעקב בבית אל
הוא יעננו.	מי שענה למשה בחורב
הוא יעננו.	מי שענה לאהרן במחתה
הוא יעננו.	מי שענה לחנה בשלה
הוא יעננו.	מי שענה לדוד ושלמה בנו בירושלים
הוא יעננו.	מי שענה לאליהו בהר הכרמל
הוא יעננו.	מי שענה ליונה במעי הדגה
הוא יעננו.	מי שענה לדניאל בגב האריות
הוא יעננו.	מי שענה למרדכי ואסתר בשושן הבירה
הוא יעננו.	מי שענה לעזרא בגולה
הוא יעננו.	מי שענה ליוחנן בן זכי יום חרבן הבית
הוא יעננו.	מי שענה לרבי עקיבא בשעת נסיונו
הוא יעננו.	מי שענה לרבנו משה בן מימון עת דרשו בדרכי החכמה
הוא יעננו.	מי שענה לרבי ישראל בעל שם טוב שראה את־הקדשה בתוך החלין
הוא יעננו.	מי שענה לחלוצים שהפריחו את־השממה
הוא יעננו.	מי שענה למשה מנדלסון עת בקש להאיר אותנו באור ההשכלה
הוא יעננו.	מי שענה לליאו בק עת ירדה החשכה
הוא יעננו.	מי שענה לאנה פראנק שכבשה את־השנאה

הוא יעננו.
הוא יעננו.

מי שענה לפליטים אשר שבו ובנו חיי יהדות כקדם
מי שענה לצדיקים ולחסידים לתמימים ולישרים

He answered Abraham our father on Mount Moriah.
May He answer us.
He answered his son, Isaac, bound on the altar.
May He answer us.
He answered Jacob, praying at Beth El.
May He answer us.
He answered Moses at Mount Sinai.
May He answer us.
He answered Aaron bringing his sacrifice.
May He answer us.
He answered Hannah at Shilo[h].
May He answer us.
He answered David and Solomon his son in Jerusalem.
May he answer us.
He answered Elijah on Mount Carmel.
May He answer us.
He answered Jonah in the belly of the fish.
May He answer us.
He answered Daniel in the lions' den.
May He answer us.
He answered Mordechai and Esther in the city of Shushan.
May He answer us.
He answered Ezra the Scribe in exile.
May He answer us.
He answered Yochanan ben Zakkai when the Temple was destroyed.
May He answer us.
He answered Akiba in the hour of his martyrdom.
May He answer us.
He answered Maimonides who sought Him with reason.
May He answer us.
He answered the Baal Shem Tov who saw the holy in the profane.
May He answer us.
He answered the *chalutzim,* who made the desert bloom.

May He answer us.

He answered Moses Mendelssohn, who sought our enlightenment.

May He answer us.

He answered Leo Baeck as darkness descended.

May He answer us.

He answered Anne Frank who conquered hatred.

May He answer us.

He answered the refugees, who rebuilt their Jewish life.

May He answer us.

He answered the righteous and pious, the honest and the upright.

May He answer us.

Very likely the most revolutionary handling of a traditional liturgical text emerges in the prayers accompanying the three divisions of shofar blasts, the *malkhuyot-zikhronot-shofarot* complex. For each division the opening lines and the *ḥatimah* remain the same, but the ten verses, on the whole psalmodic in content, are not always scriptural or even hymnic. In several verses we find instead sentences by postbiblical Jewish writers— midrashic, medieval, Hasidic, and modern. In any event, the ten sentences all appear on the Hebrew side in the author's original wording (as for Sa'a-diah Gaon and Maimonides) or in Hebrew translation (as for Samson Raphael Hirsch, Morris Joseph, and Franz Rosenzweig). The same proce-dure is repeated in all three shofar sections. As a result, the theme of each is summoned forth in unexpected and provocative ways.

We reproduce the *shofarot* section:

אתה נגלית בענן כבודך על עם קדשך לדבר עמם. ובריות בראשית חרדו ממך. בהגלותך מלכנו על הר סיני ללמד לעמך תורה ומצות. ובקול שופר עליהם הופעת:

ויהי ביום השלישי בהיות הבקר. ויהי קלת וברקים וענן כבד על־ההר וקל שפר חזק מאד. ויחרד כל־העם אשר במחנה:

והיה ביום ההוא יתקע בשופר גדול. ובאו האבדים בארץ אשור והנדחים בארץ מצרים. והשתחוו ליהוה בהר הקדש בירושלים:

תקעו בחדש שופר. בכסה ליום חגנו. כי חק לישראל הוא. משפט לאלהי יעקב:

ענין השופר. להזכירנו מעמד הר סיני. ונקבל על עצמנו מה שקבלו אבותינו על עצמם:

תקיעת שופר בראש השנה גזירת הכתוב רמז יש בו כלומר עורו ישנים משנתכם ונרדמים הקיצו מתרדמתכם וחפשו במעשיכם וחזרו בתשובה וזכרו בוראכם:

בקרן הכבשים הכפוף כדי שיזכור האדם בראותו שיכון לבו לשמים:

תקיעת השופר בראש השנה מסמנת את־היום כיום הדין. כן מקדימים לעצם היום הזה את־תקופת הדין אשר אמורה לבוא רק בקץ הימים:

קול השופר מתריע את־הלב העקש. השופר הוא התקיעה של המצפון. המזהירה את־הנפש הרדומה על הסכנה העומדת לבוא:

קול השופר קורא לנו לעבודת הבורא. הוא קורא לעני ולעשיר גם יחד לחיי עשר של אמת. הוא קורא לתועה הנדח ביותר לחזור לביתו:

והעברת שופר תרועה. וקראתם דרור בארץ לבל־ישביה:

ברוך אתה יי. שומע קול תרועת עמו ישראל ברחמים:

You revealed Yourself through a cloud of glory over a holy people to speak to them. You manifested Yourself through Torah and commandments while Your creation stood in awe and trembling. Your might transformed them through the shofar blast.

On the third day, when morning came, there were peals of thunder and flashes of lightning, and a thick cloud upon the mountain, and a long shofar blast; and the people in the camp were terrified.

Exodus 19:16

On that day the great shofar will be sounded, and those lost in the land of Assyria will come, and those dispersed in the land of Egypt, and they will worship the Lord on the holy mountain, in Jerusalem.

Isaiah 27:13

Blow the shofar on the new moon, to proclaim the day of our festival; for this is a law of Israel, a decree of the God of Jacob.

Psalm 81:4 -5

The shofar . . . is to remind us of Mt. Sinai . . . and that we should accept for ourselves the covenant that our ancestors accepted for themselves.
Saadia Gaon

The shofar on Rosh Hashanah . . . says: Awake, you, sleepers, and consider your deeds; remember your creator and go back to Him in repentance.
Maimonides

The ram's horn should be bent, so that when we see it, we bend our hearts towards heaven.
Sefer Hachinuch

The shofar blown on the New Year's Day . . . stamps the day as a day of judgment. The judgment usually thought of as at the end of time is here placed in the immediate present.
Franz Rosenzweig

The shofar sounds the alarm for the wayward heart; it is the bugle-call of the conscience; it warns the slumbering soul of its peril.
Morris Joseph

The sound of the shofar calls us all to God. It calls poor and rich to true riches; it calls the most distant wanderer home.
S. R. Hirsch

Sound the shofar . . . and proclaim freedom on earth for all its inhabitants .
Leviticus 25:9f

Blessed are You Lord, who in mercy hears the shofar blast, the cry of His people Israel.

Conclusion

The survey above might be seen as a case study of how the Hebrew language has been used liturgically in one strand of non-Orthodox Judaism. The path taken by British Reform stands apart in that Reform/ Progressive/ Liberal Judaism of the twentieth century in the United States and in Continental Europe has generally focused on rephrasing classical Hebrew texts compatible with contemporary religious thinking in the vernacular rather than in the ancestral language of the Jewish people.

As we have seen, the style of Hebrew creativity in British Reform has fluctuated markedly since 1841, reflecting changing taste, education, and the national origin of the prayerbook revisers, as well as their understanding of the nature and raison d'être of Judaism. During the days of Queen Victoria, the Bible formed a universal staple whose diction and cadences infiltrated and shaped the English tongue in diverse ways. In the churches, established and Nonconformist, bibliocentrism reigned supreme. In their eagerness to prove themselves every inch as British as their Gentile compatriots, David W. Marks and the congregation he pastored all his adult life attest in their beloved *Forms of Prayer* a fervent attachment to the Bible they shared with their countrymen and their commitment to their own Hebrew tradition. Saturated and able as Marks was in the language of the Tanakh and the liturgy, he was not all that formally trained Judaically in the academic sense. Hence the structural changes he allowed were, from a scholarly standpoint, now and then arbitrary and erratic, and his Hebrew not free of desultory blunders. With the help of his learned assistant from Moravia, A. Loewy, many of his linguistic/stylistic drawbacks were set right. Several of Marks's own creations enjoyed remarkable longevity, even if all did not survive to the present decade.

The subsequent major revision of *Forms of Prayer,* the 1931 edition, while on balance loyal to the outlines of Marks's work, exhibits external influences. The English brand of spirituality evoked by Juliana of Norwich, George Fox, John and Charles Wesley, and Gerard Manley Hopkins, the advances made by American Reform, the inroads of biblical criticism, and wariness with respect to Jewish nationalism all affected the direction *Forms of Prayer* was to take. Sadly, the Hebrew of the prayerbook was stripped of biblical nuances, yet remained untouched by the growing vitality and malleability of the Hebrew evolving in the Palestine of the Yishuv era.

The post-war years posed a dry spell in liturgical terms, although during the war many issues of *The Synagogue Review* contained lengthy prayers, most of them penned by Reinhart, *pro Deo et pro patria,* appealing to God for victory in the Allied war effort.

In the war's aftermath, British Reform underwent some of its most profound changes due to the the the immediacy of the Holocaust, the influx and integration of its survivors (among them rabbis, teachers, and scholars), and the palpable reality of the State of Israel. The prayerbook mirroring the era, *Prayers for the Pilgrim Festivals,* benefited to a great extent from a resurgence or transplantation of *Wissenschaft des Judentums* on British soil, particularly with the new emphasis on textual and grammatical exactitude and historical continuity with Jewish liturgy of all lands and across the millennia.

Post-war momentum has been sustained in the succeeding decades, minus the strong, if in spots forced, classicism of the nineteenth century. After the somewhat shaky experimentation with contemporary Hebrew in *Funeral Service,* the Hebrew from the later seventies to the present is on firmer literary ground and true to the intrinsic nature of the *alt-neu* language of the Jewish people.[42] Even with its periodic prompting and propping up by the English language—and an assist from Israeli friends—a Hebrew liturgical creativity in one outpost of the Diaspora has been much in evidence.[43]

An earlier version of this chapter appeared in the *Hebrew Annual Review* 12 (1990): 49–90. © 1990 by the Melton Center for Jewish Studies, The Ohio State University. Reprinted with permission.

1. See chap. 4 above.

2. Jakob J. Petuchowski, *Prayerbook Reform in Europe* (New York, 1968), chaps. 9 and 12; Eric L. Friedland, *The Historical and Theological Development of the Non-Orthodox Jewish Prayerbooks in the United States* (Ann Arbor, Michigan, 1967), chap. 10.

3. Michael Leigh, "Reform Judaism in Britain (1840–1970)," *Reform Judaism: Essays on Reform Judaism in Britain,* ed. Dow Marmur (Oxford, 1973), pp. 3–50; Steven Singer, "Jewish Religious Thought in Victorian England," *AJS Review* 10 (Fall 1975): 181–210. For a complete history of Bristish Reform, see Anne J. Kershen and Jonathan A. Romain, *Tradition and Change: A History of Reform Judaism in Britain 1840–1995* (London, 1995).

4. Leonard G. Montefiore, "Reminiscences of Upper Berkeley Street," *The Synagogue Review* (June 1960):251–59; Leonard G. Montefiore, "David Woolf Marks (1811–1910): The First English Reform Minister," *The Synagogue Review* (November 1961): 67–72.

5. Leigh, op.cit., p. 17.

6. Nathan Marcus Adler, *The Second Day of the Festivals: A Sermon* (London, 1868).

7. Marks's rendition of the verse in the *yigdal,* "God hath given a law of truth to his people by the hand of his prophet, 'the faithful of his house'; and God will never alter this, nor change it for any other" was not understood in just a figurative sense. Nearly every one of Marks's sermons reveals that he took this poetic restatement of Maimonides' Ninth Principle of Faith quite seriously.

8. By the fourth edition of *Forms of Prayer, Vol II: Prayers of the Festivals* (London, 1921), the rite of *dukhan* had fallen by the wayside.

9. Cf. Jakob J. Petuchowski, "Karaite Tendencies in an Early Reform Haggadah," *Hebrew Union College Annual* XXXI (1960): 223–49.

10. Leonard G. Montefiore, "The Aramaic Kaddish and Mr. Marks," *The Synagogue Review* (February 1959): 146–47. In a letter to the West London Synagogue, the Liberal Rabbi Caesar Seligmann of Frankfurt am Main wrote (in translation from the German): "I am struck by the fact, not unfavorably—but I have noticed it in no other prayer-book— that you have translated all the Chaldaic portions of the liturgy back into Hebrew. This is an innovation at once correct in principle and worthy of imitation; for why should we, who live so far from the times when biblical Hebrew was replaced by the Chaldaic because that was then the vernacular, retain this Chaldaic or Aramaic in our prayers to-day?" [*West London Synagogue* 6 (1931–1932): 12–13].

11. "Loewy, Albert," *Jüdisches Lexicon* 3 (1929): 1235–36. In his *Response to Modernity: A History of the Reform Movement in Judaism* (New York and Oxford, 1988, p. 174), Michael A. Meyer mentions the cooperation with Marks of a Hyman Hurwitz, Professor of Hebrew at University College in London, in creating the movement's first prayerbook.

12. Philip Birnbaum, *Daily Prayer Book* (New York, 1949), p. 743; David de Sola Pool, *Book of Prayer* (New York, 1954), 2d ed., p. 415.

13. The Talmudic requirement is that those whose lives have been endangered and have been spared give thanks (Berakhot 54b). Later tradition made it mandatory that *birkat ha-gomel* be recited in the presence of ten (including two rabbis); and custom then had it *(ve-nahagu)* that such a person be called up to the Torah (Shulḥan Arukh: Oraḥ Ḥayyim 219).

14. In an egalitarian age, *The Book of Common Prayer* currently in use involves both parents, rather than just the mother, in what is more simply called "Thanksgiving for a Child."

15. Theodore H. Gaster, the noted Jewish anthropologist, who for a time served as minister in the British Reform movement, offers some illuminating remarks in this connection in his *Customs and Folkways of Jewish Life* [original title: *The Holy and the Profane*] (New York, 1955), p. 32.

16. Marks did not share the ancient Rabbis' qualms about reciting the Ten Commandments beyond the Temple's confines for fear of reinforcing the sectarian claim (*taromet ha-minim*) that the Decalogue forms the entirety of the Law (Berakhot 12a).

17. The Hamburg *Gebetbuch,* on the other hand, placed the choral rendition of the same Psalm aptly enough just before Joshua 1:8 9, which speaks of constantly meditating on and carrying out the dictates of the Law after all the Torah readings for the day are completed. In *Olath Tamid,* David Einhorn duplicated this arrangement. Whereas Einhorn made a point of having a haftarah read each Shabbat and Festival, the Hamburg Reformers did not.

18. "Shortened Services," *The Synagogue Review* (July 1947): 169–70.

19. The Sephardic and Yemenite (*tiklal*) rites go so far as to complete the alphabetic acrostic, e.g.. *le-ma'anakh shimkha eḥad lo titten kevodkha la-aḥerim, le-ma'anakh tokhen yeshu'ot le-hoshi'a am nivḥarim.*

20. The exchange of the Marks-Loewy *hosha na* for an even newer one took place in *The Prayers for the Pilgrim Festivals.* which will be treated more fully below.

21. While abreast of Jewish theological developments elsewhere, Marks with his "Mosaic" brand of orthodoxy was always more than a touch maverick.

22. Morris Joseph is perhaps best known for his inviting middle-of-the-road and heavily homiletical exposition of Judaism, *Judaism as Creed and Life,* which underwent several reprintings until as late as 1958. Harold Reinhart, "Morris Joseph: 1848-May 28, 1930," *The Synagogue Review* (June 1948): 149; Andre Ungar, "Morris Joseph Revisited," ibid. (September 1953): 9–12.

23. "Three Tributes to Rabbi Reinhart," ibid. (March 1954): 202–4; Jakob J. Petuchowski, "Harold F. Reinhart," *Yearbook of the Central Conference of American Rabbis* LXXX (1970):82–83.

24. Theodore H. Gaster, "The New Prayer Book," *The West London Synagogue Magazine* 5 (1930–31): 159–60.

25. Several remarks by different contributors to a special issue of *The West London Synagogue Magazine* (1930–31) make fairly clear that Joseph played a crucial part in the creation of the 1931 edition of *Forms of Prayer:* "Mr. Morris Joseph, whose sound scholarship and elegant expression are universally acknowledged, was the principal collaborator" (p. 136); "Probably the first thought . . . will be one of regret that the Rev. Morris Joseph, whose influence can be felt throughout the book, was not spared to see its completion" (the 1931–32 volume of the *Magazine,* p. 10). Some of the English prayers penned by Joseph first appeared in the *Order of Service* (2d ed. [London: Wertheimer, Lea & Co., 1903]) of the then-cross-denominational, experimental Jewish Religious Union, which ultimately became Liberal Judaism.

26. Marks and Loewy substantially retained just the Sephardic *ha-noten teshu'ah* for the government and *mi she-berakh* for the congregation.

27. It is here also, according to the Eastern European *minhag,* that Yizkor is held on hehalf of the departed on the concluding day of the Pilgrimage Festivals and on Yom Kippur.

28. *Prayers for The Pilgrim Festivals,* for instance, prescribes the psalms to be used on each of the *shalosh regalim:* for the eve of a holiday on the First Day of Passover it is Ps. 113; the Seventh Day, Ps. 148; on Pentecost Ps. 19; the First Day of Tabernacles, Ps. 15; on the Eighth Day of Solemn Assembly, Ps. 67; then on all of them, with the exception of the First Day of Passover, Ps. 122. During the *pesuqey de-zimrah* of the morning of the Festival, the following are read: the First Day of Passover, Ps. 105:1–15, 23–27, 37–45; the Seventh Day of Passover, Ps. 33 or 34; Pentecost, Ps. 19; Tabernacles, Ps. 100 or 96; Eighth Day of Solemn Assembly, Ps. 98 or 146.

29. Marks had a *havdalah,* albeit without wine, spices, and flame.

30. Cf. S. Singer, *Authorized Daily Prayer Book* (London: Eyre and Spottiswoode Limited, 1962), pp. 436–37; *Sabbath and Festival Prayer Book* (The Rabbinical Assembly of America and the United Synagogue of America, 1946), p. 224; Ben Zion Bokser, *The Prayer Book: Weekday, Sabbath and Festival* (New York, 1957), p. 258 (beginning with *av ha-rahamim*).

31. Bruno Italiener, "The Musaf-Kedushah," *Hebrew Union College Annual* XXVI (1955): 413–24; Gerhard Graf, "The Influence of German Rabbis on British Reform Judaism," *Reform Judaism: Essays on Reform Judaism in Britain,* ed. Dow Marmur (Oxford, 1973), 154–59.

32. The editors of the 1977 *Forms of Prayer* for Sabbath, weekday, and occasional use and the 1985 one for the High Holy Days have, however, come pretty much to ignore the boundaries between the *birkhot ha-shaḥar* and the *pesuqey de-zimrah*.

33. Happily, this prayer is preserved, though minimally adjusted for Shabbat, in the 1977 volume, with the addition of a nice modern *kavvanah* before the domestic Sabbath Eve celebration.

34. *Li-menuḥat ḥayyey ha-olamim* makes way for a not so high-flown *el beyt (olamo) (olamah)*; the lovely *ve-hastirehu (ve-hastireha) be-tzel kenafekha la-ḥazot be-no'am panekha u-le-hitanneg be-rov tuvekha asher tzafanta li-yre'ekha* is unfortunately plucked out; *la-aveley vanekha* fills in for *la-aveley yisrael;* the two concluding verses from Isaiah are reversed, and *uvi-yrushalayim tenuḥamu* is dropped.

35. The Reconstructionist editors excised *ule-khol aveley vanekha* from the clause *ve-shallem niḥumim lahem ule-khol aveley vanekha.*

36. Cf. the meditation after the parental blessing in Joseph H. Hertz, *The Authorized Daily Prayer Book with Commentary, Introductions and Notes,* rev. ed. (New York, 1948), pp. 402–3; and (without, however, the father saying the Priestly Benediction) in Birnbaum, op.cit., pp. 283–87.

37. Hilkhot Melakhim 12:4–5.

38. Petuchowski, *Prayerbook Reform in Europe,* chap. 15; Friedland, *Historical and Theological Development,* chap. 11.

39. Interestingly enough, both the first edition of *Abodath Israel* and the current edition of the *Forms of Prayer* for Rosh Hashanah and Yom Kippur both open the *avodah* with the *heilsgeschichtlich* Sephardic *attah konanta olam me-rosh*—showing their common descent in the Reform Hamburg *Gebetbuch* of 1819.

40. Ecclesiasticus 44:1–9.

41. I. Davidson, S. Assaf, and B.I. Joel, ed., *Siddur Rav Sa'adiah Gaon* (Jerusalem, 1963), pp. 378–79.

42. In his written response (October 6, 1988) to the author, Rabbi Jonathan Magonet, co-editor of the present-day British Reform rites and principal of the Leo Baeck College in London, explained the modus operandi in furnishing the Hebrew for the newly-couched prayers in English:

"How was the Hebrew text prepared for your funeral service (Tziduk Hadin)?" I presume you mean specifically the Hebrew translation. As I recall, the funeral book was required somewhat urgently so we produced it in the middle of our work on the Siddur. We asked ourselves what was the purpose of such a volume and felt that it had to meet the very particular needs of those in mourning and reflect the nature of the death—the same prayers could not be recited if a child died as when an adult died. The translations were, as with the Siddur, the results of a curious committee exercise. The Siddur introduction acknowledges the work of Rabbi N Ginsbury, Dr E Littman (Zal) and Naomi Nimrod. As I recall Dr Littman made some preliminary translations which were then looked at by Naomi Nimrod, a young Israeli, but these were in turn somewhat criticized and "improved" by Rabbi Ginsbury and may even have been subsequently changed by other advisers! The essential problem seemed to be the difficulty of choosing an appropriate Hebrew style for contemporary English prayers. Some wished to translate them into "mediaeval" Hebrew to conform with the classical liturgy, others felt that a modern Hebrew was more appropriate but that no current models existed, and that most attempts sounded like somewhat inappropriate technological language. Because of our dissatisfaction with them we tried to avoid the same problem with the Machzor, though there may now be people able to do a more appropriate job today. As to the text itself, most of the traditional elements were taken either from the West London Synagogue "Burial Prayers" or probably from Singer.

43. The latest *Forms of Prayer* volume (1995) is a 924-page revision and expansion of the 1965 *Prayers for the Pilgrim Festivals*. While the new prayerbook is decidedly Hebraic in tone and content—with many texts reproduced in the Hebrew—there are really no new Hebrew prayers as such.

6

Leo Merzbacher and an Unusual Reform *Eyn k-Eloheynu*

In the early part of this century, the number of standard Hebrew hymns included in liberal prayerbooks was minimal,[1] and the many English songs of praise in the old *Union Hymnal*[2] were depended upon to fill in the gaps. The one universal twentieth-century musical staple in Reform worship was *eyn k-eloheynu*—no doubt due to its easy lyrics and the stirring tunes to which it was set.

What will probably come as a surprise is that a number of nineteenth-century American liturgical redactors deliberately left out the popular hymn. One explanation may be the widely divergent traditional stipulations that governed its use.[3] In addition, no doubt David Einhorn, Isaac M. Wise, and Adolph Huebsch did not take kindly to the artless, tautological quality of its text—anything resembling liturgical doggerel was to be avoided at all cost. They preferred instead the lofty and tender *adon olam,* the quasi-catechetical *yigdal,* or the in-vogue hymnody from the Hamburg Temple *Gesangbuch.*[4] Leo (Ludwig) Merzbacher[5] took a different approach, augmenting the text of the old favorite so as to ensure its staying power.

A native of Fürth, Bavaria, Merzbacher (1809 or 1810–1856) obtained his *morenu* diploma from the learned Rabbi Moses Sofer in the Pressburg Yeshivah, though there remains some uncertainty as to whether he obtained his doctorate upon the completion of his studies at the Universities of Erlangen and Munich. After his immigration to America in the 1840s, Merzbacher served two congregations consecutively in New York City and ultimately assumed the pulpit of the congregation that eventually became known as Temple Emanu-El, where he served until his death from consumption in 1856, before his fiftieth year.

Even though Merzbacher has been classified as a moderate Reformer, his siddur bears several earmarks of what Jakob J. Petuchowski has called "Independent Reform." In the interest of avoiding a schism within the Household of Israel, Merzbacher strove to preserve the historical *matbe'a shel tefillah,* the trim core of Jewish public worship, as well as to maintain the essential Hebraic character of the prayerbook.[6]

The fact remains, nonetheless, that he made notable alterations in the

137

infrastructure of the worship service.[7] Ultimately, many of these compositional modifications—along with those from Einhorn's *Olath Tamid* and Huebsch's *Gebete*—entered the *Union Prayer Book,* preeminently through the editorial efforts of Isaac S. Moses.[8]

One of Merzbacher's innovations was the *Order of Prayer*'s provision in the evening *amidah* that only the introductory Three Benedictions, abridged, and the crowning Intermediate Benediction be said. This pattern was adopted in the *Union Prayer Book* from its very beginning, with, however, the *shalosh rishonot* intact.[9]

Another was his modification of the *aleynu* deleting the ethnocentric *she-lo asanu ke-goyey ha-aratzot* ("who hath not made us like the nations of other lands") and continuing with the words of the empyreal second paragraph *she-hu noteh shamayim ve-yosed aretz* ("who stretched out the heavens and laid the foundations of the earth"), after *yotzer bereshit,* ("who formed the world in the beginning"). Because the *aleynu* climaxes in *va-anahnu kor'im u-mishtahavim* ("Thus we bend the knee, prostrate ourselves"), Merzbacher termed the prayer, if a bit grandiloquently, *hishtahavayah* (on the English side, "Adoration"; but literally "prostration").[10] And it was this modified *aleynu* that Isaac M. Wise incorporated in all editions of *Minhag Amerika.*

Finally, Merzbacher was responsible for initiating the long-time standard operating procedure of interspersing between the various services on the Day of Atonement generous selections from the Psalter as fillers in place of the amplitude of *piyyutim* customarily inserted into the Ashkenazic High Holy Day and Festival *amidot.*[11]

But Petuchowski's notion of "Independent Reform" applies here only to a moderate degree. A typical Morning Service in *Order of Prayer,* whether for a Sabbath, a Festival, Rosh Hashanah, or a weekday, is basically made up of the so-called Shema and its Benedictions (starting with the *barekhu* [or *yotzer or*] through *ga'al yisra'el*), the entire *amidah,* the "Order of Reading the Law," *mizmorim* (viz. Psalm 145 or, anomalously enough here, on the holidays, the *hallel*), the *aleynu,* the Kaddish, and the closing hymn. Although there are serious omissions[12] from the technical point of view, mishnaically speaking the Morning Service may be regarded in halakhic terms as complete—and thus it was intended.[13]

As mentioned earlier, Merzbacher kept all the old hymnic standbys, *adon olam, yigdal,* and *eyn k-eloheynu*—but spread them out among an

Evening Service, a Sabbath Morning Service, and a Festival Morning Service respectively—to bring the various services to a satisfying and tuneful close. For the choral finish to the Rosh Hashanah Morning Service, however, he rescued from the banished *musaf* service the grand symphonic Hallelujah, Psalm 150.[14]

What makes the *eyn k-eloheynu* in Congregation Emanu-El's *Order of Prayer* so unusual is that it is an augmented version, penned by Leo Merzbacher himself. Surprisingly, *minhag* Merzbacher's sole reviser, Samuel Adler—especially given his tendency to abbreviate and curtail even further in the name of literary and theological consistency[15]—left the unprecedented hymn intact. It constituted a part of the Emanu-El rite until the congregation adopted the *Union Prayer Book*.[16]

Now for a closer look at Merzbacher's revision. First the Hebrew text; then Merzbacher's translation in verse—in the orthography and punctuation of the day.

שיר

אין כאלהינו. אין כאדונינו:

אין כמלכנו. אין כמושיענו:

אלהינו אחד נשגב לבדו. ואין שני להמשיל לו:

ואל מי תדמיון אל. ומה דמות תערכו לו:

מי כאלהינו. מי כאדונינו

מי כמלכנו. מי כמושיענו:

אדונינו גדול וקדוש שמו. ספרו בגוים כבודו:

הודו לאדני האדנים. כי לעולם חסדו:

נודה לאלהינו. נודה לאדנינו.

נודה למלכנו. נודה למושיענו:

מלכנו אמת אפס זולתו. ברוך שם כבוד מלכותו:

ברכו יהוה כל מעשיו. בכל מקמות ממשלתו:

ברוך אלהינו. ברוך אדונינו.

ברוך מלכנו. ברוך מושיענו:

מושיענו צדיק אין בלתו. ועד דר ודור אמונתו:

שירו ליהוה ברכו שמו. בשרו מיום ישועתו:

אתה הוא אלהינו. אתה הוא אדנינו.

אתה הוא מלכנו. אתה הוא מושיענו:

[I.a]
There is none like our God; there is none like our Lord;
There is none like our King; there is none like our Saviour.
[I.b]
Our God is one! he alone exalted supreme;
And there is none, who can be compared unto him
"To whom, then, will you liken God;
Or what likeness will ye compare unto him?"
[II.a]
Who is like our God? who is like our Lord?
Who is like our King? who is like our Saviour?
[II.b]
Our Lord is great, and holy is his name;
Among the nations his glory proclaim!
"O give thanks unto the Lord of lords
For his mercy endureth for ever."
[III.a]
We will give thanks to our God; we will give thanks to our Lord;
We will give thanks to our King; we will give thanks to our Saviour.
[III.b]
Our King is true, all others are but vain;
Blessed be the fame of the glory of his reign.
"Bless the Lord! all his works,
In all places of his dominion."
[IV.a]
Blessed be our God; blessed be our Lord;
Blessed be our King; blessed be our Saviour.
[IV.b]
Our Saviour is righteous, and there is none besides.
Unto all generations his changeless truth abides.
"Sing unto the Lord, bless his name;
Show forth from day to day his salvation."
[V.]
Thou art our God! thou art our Lord!
Thou art our King! thou art our Saviour!

As noted above, Merzbacher gave prominence to the *Stammgebete,* the quintessential elements of the classical Prayerbook, which meant that ancillary poetic creations, ancient and medieval, were either downplayed or ruled out.[17] It could well be that his muted psalmodic/paytanic sensibility reasserted itself in the *eyn k-eloheynu*.

Merzbacher interspersed his subjoiners in stanzas that alternate with the familiar verses of the hymn. His new stanzas always open with a name of God from the original *eyn k-eloheynu: eloheynu* (our God), *adoneynu* (our Lord), *malkenu* (our King) and *moshi'enu* (our Saviour) segueing into terse proclamations about God in biblical and liturgical phrases.

Each scriptural verse hints at the ensuing stanza by word or thought. The scriptural verse in the second line of the second stanza (I.b), from Isaiah 40:18, *ve-el **mi** tedamyun el, u-mah demut ta'arekhu lo?* ("To **whom** then will you liken God,") anticipates the *mi* of the third stanza: *mi- kh-eloheynu* ("**Who** is like our God?"). Similarly, the biblical verse in the second line of stanza II.b begins with *hodu* ("O give **thanks** unto the Lord of Lords . . ." [Psalms 136: 3]) to match *nodeh* ("Let us **give thanks**"), while the sixth stanza has, for the same spot, *barekhu adonay kol ma'asav* ("**Bless** the Lord all His works in all places of His dominion" [Psalms 103:22]) to presage *barukh eloheynu* ("**Blessed** be our God; **blessed** be our Lord"). It is worth noting that the literary technique Merzbacher employs here resembles the more intricate or involved style used by medieval versifiers such as the tenth-century Meshullam ben Kalonymos.[18]

The question then arises as to exactly how the embellished hymn was musically handled at Congregation Emanu-El and at other congregations using the Merzbacher rite. Unfortunately the musical scores available in print provide no real clues.[19] But the New York temple rightfully took pride in its eminent cantorial tradition,[20] and we can speculate that the well-known lines were sung by both the congregation and the choir, with the more elaborate ones by Merzbacher presumably sung by the cantor alone.

Merzbacher's reworking of the popular hymn is one more vivid illustration of Hebrew liturgical creativity within Liberal Judaism—in this case in a premier congregation during the earliest days of American Reform.[21]

An earlier version of this chapter appeared in the *CCAR Journal* (Fall 1994): 43–53. Reprinted with permission.

1. This is as opposed to the oldtime one- or two-line congregational responses in

Hebrew. The 1975 version of the *Union Prayer Book for Jewish Worship* I contains at the end of the volume a robust selection of songs and hymns, the Hebrew vastly outnumbering the English—in obvious contrast to what prevailed, for instance, in the twenties or thirties.

2. *Union Hymnal* (New York: Central Conference of American Rabbis 1897); *Union Hymnal: Songs and Prayers for Jewish Worship*, 3rd ed. (Macon, GA, 1932).

3. Seligmann Baer, *Seder Avodat Yisrael* (Roedelheim, 1868) p. 245; Eliezer Landshut, *Siddur Hegyon Lev* (Koenigsberg, 1845), pp. 323–24; Israel Davidson, *Otzar ha-Shirah veha-Piyyut: Thesaurus of Medieval Hebrew Poetry*, intro. J. Schirmann, 1970, vol. I, p. 142.

4. David Einhorn, *Olath Tamid, Gebetbuch für Israelitische Reformgemeinden* (Baltimore, 1858); Adolph Huebsch, *Seder Tefillah, Gebete für den Oeffentlichen Gottesdienst der Tempelgemeinde Ahawath Chesed* (New York, 1875); Isaac M. Wise et al., *Minhag Amerika: Daily Prayers* (Cincinnati, 1857).

5. So to differentiate the Emanu-El rite *Seder Tefillah, The Order of Prayer for Divine Service* [New York, 1855]) from another New York prayerbook, at first devised expressly for Congregation Ahawath Chesed and also designated in Hebrew as *Seder Tefillah* (see n. 4 for full title), I shall refer to Merzbacher's literary brainstorm (in point of fact the only one of his ever to be published) simply as *Order of Prayer.*

6. Merzbacher addressed the issue of balance between Hebrew and the vernacular in the twelve-page preface to *Order of Prayer*:

> The main feature of both these books [the Sabbath, Festival, Rosh Hashanah, and weekday volume and the one for Yom Kippur] consists in reducing the Hebrew part to the most essential prayers, and in supplying well-elaborated compositions in the vernacular language; so as to do equal justice to the claims of the past, and to the demands of the present. This compromise, however justified in principle and skillfully executed, seems in our humble opinion, unsatisfactory, for these reasons.
>
> In the first place, two languages in juxtaposition is an anomalous expedient in itself, and cannot be without injurious effect on either side. Those who feel themselves solemnly moved by the familiar sounds of the sacred language will be sensitively disturbed by the sudden intrusion of the vernacular accent; and those who pray devoutly in their native tongue will feel a disagreeable interruption by the approach of the foreign language: thus, attention will be diverted and divided. . . .
>
> The more appropriate remedy for our present exigency, it seems to me, will be found in retaining the Hebrew part of the Service, in its pure and perfect type, discriminately selected; and in annexing to the instruction in the vernacular tongue hymns and prayers, adapted to the particular wants of the congregation. In this way an ultimate conformity will be easily arrived at; as in regard to the Hebrew part, the diversity of opinion is narrowly limited by positive marks, and the general disposition is inclined to accept a moderate change. [*Order of Prayer,* 1855 edition, preface, p. xii; 1864 edition, preface, p. xv].

Also in W. Gunther Plaut, *The Growth of Reform Judaism: American and European Sources until 1948* (N.Y., 1965), pp. 297–98. Merzbacher then goes on to say, "Thus, peace and harmony will reign in Israel, and 'Behold! how good and how pleasant it is for brethren to dwell together in unity!'"

7. Significant modifications are most noticeable in the architectonic of the five services throughout the Day of Atonement.

8. Moses was a prolific hymnographer and liturgical synthesizer. The preliminary manuscript draft (1891) of the *Union Prayer Book* (*Tefillath Yisrael: The Jewish Prayer Book, Order of Worship for Sabbaths and Holiday* [Chicago, 1891]), presented to the Central Conference of American Rabbis' meeting in Baltimore in July 1891 for consideration was edited by him (Friedland, *Historical and Theological Development,* pp. 116–18).

9. The *shalosh aḥaronot* were thus dropped. Although either the *birkat me'eyn sheva* or *magen avot* as an *amidah*-abstract is the inspiration behind this abridgement, it is unclear why the Last Three Benedictions, however condensed, were excised. (It is to be recalled that in Rabbinic usage the evening *tefillah* came under the category of *reshut* rather than *ḥovah* [Berakhot 27b].) Cf. the treatment of *magen avot* as a possible alternative to the regular Sabbath Eve *amidah* in the old Reconstructionist *Sabbath Prayer Book* (New York: The Jewish Reconstructionist Foundation, Inc, 1945). Cf. Kaufmann Kohler's similar treatment in his *Sabbath Eve Service for Temple Beth-El,* (New York, 1891). It is interesting to observe that only four of the ten Friday Night Services in *Gates of Prayer* are missing two or more of the Three Concluding Benedictions from the Sabbath *amidah*'s Seven Benedictions. The varied fate of the Intermediate Benedictions in the weekday *amidot* of *Sha'arey Tefillah* is another subject with an interesting history of its own.

10. For an overview of the transmutations of the *aleynu* prayer in Reform rites, see chap. 9.

11. Cf. the much diminished psalmodic inserts in the 1922 edition of the *Union Prayer Book* II for the Atonement Afternoon Service, pp. 233–37, and for the Concluding Service, pp. 341–44.

12. Notably, there are neither the Preliminary Benedictions (*birkhot ha-shaḥar*) nor the benedictory casing of the Introductory Hymns and Psalms (*pesuqey de-zimrah*), to wit, the prefatory *barukh she-amar* and the terminal (*nishmat* through) *yishtabaḥ* And the Additional Service is set aside—except for Yom Kippur. For Rosh Hashanah, however, Merzbacher keeps the *malkhuyot-zikhronot-shofarot* aggregate under the rubric *seder teqi'at shofar* ("Order of Blowing the Shophar") rather than in the Additional Service. He places all of it after the Adoration (*malkhuyot* of course being its original matrix) and just before the Mourner's Kaddish that precedes the closing hymn. Oddly enough, though, none of the three units within the *malkhuyot-zikhronot-shofarot* complex ends in a *ḥatimah;* and for all of them together there is but a single series of shofar blasts (*teqi'ah, shevarim, teru'ah, teqi'ah*) and no more! By contrast, Adler dispensed with this triadic arrangement and provided instead a lone prayer prior to the penultimate Adoration, a smooth blend of motifs from the *zikhronot* and *shofarot* sections with a strong accent on universalism. Parenthetically, neither Merzbacher nor Adler kept the blessing(s) customarily said before blowing the shofar.

These material deletions and the nonadmission of any English (or German) prayers give the first volume of *Order of Prayer* its lean look. In response to a query from a New Orleans congregation in the making, Samuel Adler wrote on October 20, 1864 (the same year in which his third revision of *Order of Prayer* came out), "We now read the prayers in the books regularly in Hebrew; I, however, add a few prayers not printed, in German and on the day of Atonement some English prayers and bible-passages contained in the prayer-book for that day are read" (Herbert C. Zafren, "Samuel Adler: Respondent," *Essays in Honor of Solomon B. Freehof,* ed. Walter Jacob, Frederick C. Schwartz and Vigdor W. Kavaler [Pittsburgh, 1964], p. 314).

13. "So the 'Order of Prayer,' as presented in this publication, has been regulated in strict adherence to the ancient standard, retaining the essential parts intact, following the customary order, without any foreign interposition, and removing only the grievances complained of, with due regard to their justness and urgency."

14. The only edition of the *Union Prayer Book* to reproduce the psalm as the concluding hymn for Rosh Hashanah Morning was the revised 1922 version.

15. That he was a stickler for theological and liturgical consistency comes through in his fine-tuning of *Order of Prayer* (1864 edition) according to the recommendations of the German Rabbinical Conferences of the mid-1840s. As a case in point, in the *yigdal* hymn Adler reworded the hope for the Messiah's coming (*yishlah le-qetz yamin pedut olam*) and the ultimate resurrection (*ha-kol yehayyeh el be-rov hasedo*) in accordance with the classical Reform understanding. Adler's subtle rewrite of *yigdal* has been standard for American Reform from the 1894 edition of the *Union Prayer Book* through the 1994 edition of *Gates of Prayer.* It is to be recalled that Adler numbered among his close, like-minded colleagues the more "radical" Reform Einhorn, Bernhard Felsenthal, and Samuel Hirsch.

16. Rabbi of Emanu-El after Adler, Gustav Gottheil prepared a nearly all English and highly non-conformist *Morning Prayers* (New York, 1889), designed primarily for Sunday morning services. Interestingly, much of the English text found its way into the 1894 *Union Prayer Book* for the weekday morning services (an innocuous euphemism for Sunday morning worship). As noted earlier, the post-Kaddish word of assurance, "May the Father of peace send peace to all who mourn and comfort all the bereaved among us," is originally Gottheil's.

17. Nevertheless, an exception was made for Yom Kippur, when psalm and *piyyut* were made the most of, but, revealingly enough, always apart from the statutory prayers.The Sephardim are used to putting their *piyyutim* and suchlike outside the *Stammgebete,* either before *nishmat* or after the different *amidot* so as to avoid disjointedness or distraction.

18. E.g., *imeru l-elohim* or *ma'aseh eloheynu* chanted antiphonally in the Reader's Repetition of the *amidah* during the Atonement Morning Service (Philip Birnbaum, *High Holy-day Prayer Book: Yom Kippur* [New York, 1958], pp. 355–63).

19. There is no clue in either A. Kaiser and Wm. Sparger [for a while cantor at Emanu-El], *A Collection of the Principal Melodies of the Synagogue from the Earliest Time to the Present* (Chicago, 1893) or M. Goldstein, A. Kaiser, S. Wechsler and I. L Rice, ed., *Zimrath Yah: Liturgic Songs consisting of Hebrew, English, German Psalms and Hymns systematically arranged for the Jewish Rite with Organ Accompaniment* (New York, 1873).

20. Emanu-El engaged a cantor, Adolph Rubin, who arrived at the same time as Samuel Adler and served the congregation thirty-eight years. This was after a lackluster beginning, with "a boys' choir reinforced by a few adult male voices" that sang Sulzer "very poorly," according to the testimony of Isaac M. Wise, shortly after his arrival from Europe in 1846, when he dropped by either before or on Tish'ah be-Av. See James G.

Heller, *Isaac M. Wise, His Life, Work and Thought* (New York, 1965), p. 110; Nathan A. Perilman, "One Hundred Years of Congregation Emanu-EI" in *Moral and Spiritual Foundations for the World of Tomorrow* (New York, 1945), p. 202. Adler wrote of Cantor Rubin, "Our Congr., moreover, has also a Hazan of great ability" (Zafren, "Samuel Adler: Respondent," p. 314).

21. For Merzbacher's facility and flair with the Hebrew language in his subtle transformation of the Middle Benedictions of the *shemoneh esreh,* see chap. 4. One recent excellent example of modern Hebrew liturgical creativity is Chaim Stern's *yehi ratzon* prayer, in alphabetic acrostic, for *Sha'arey Selihah, Gates of Forgiveness* (New York, 1993), p. 42. In the CCAR's *Al Mezuzot Beytekha, On the Doorposts of Your House* (N.Y., 1994), examples can be multiplied.

7

The Yom Kippur Yizkor Service in the American Maḥzor

The claim is periodically made that Judaism does not have much of a theology to speak of—that it has not produced a large corpus of works, either of the scholarly or popular variety, or that the Jews lag behind their Christian counterparts in this area. To be sure, theological concerns have been raised and probed from the time of the Bible and the Talmud through the writing of the medieval classics to Rosenzweig's *Star of Redemption* and Soloveitchik's impelling occasional essays. Nonetheless, the fact remains that the overall output of *summae* and like treatises for a folk constantly on the move has been comparatively small. Where the issues are explicated, a certain laconicism marks the Jewish understanding of the realm beyond our mortal earthly existence. In his *Judaism: A Portrait,*[1] for example, Leon Roth remarks:

> The Rabbis retain their characteristic reticence. They give little description of the exact nature of future bliss. There is a saying, made much of later by the philosophers, that the righteous sit with their crowns on their heads and enjoy the brightness of the Divine Presence. . . . It is the everyday things and acts which, in a favorite Rabbinic phrase, lift the eyes to our Father in Heaven. The Rabbis seem to have been so full of the presence of God that they shied from the overtly transcendental.

In the introductory paragraph of his essay on Rabbi Abraham Isaac Kuk's views on death and immortality,[2] the Czech-born Israeli philosopher, Shmuel Hugo Bergman, commented in a similar vein:

הספרים, שנכתבו אצלנו בדור האחרון על עיקרי היהדות, אינם מאריכים
את הדיבור על שאלת הישארות הנפש והעולם הבא. מובן, שאינם
מכחישים אותם, אך משתדלים לתת לשאלה כולה מובן וכיוון מוסרי
ולהימנע על ידי כך מכל פירוש שיש בו משום הגשמה.

The books that have been written among us in the last generation about the principles of Judaism do not dwell on the question of the soul's immortality or the World-to Come. Obviously, they are not being denied, but the attempt is made to give the entire question an ethical meaning and direction and to avoid any interpretation smacking of materiality.[3]

To further explore whatever theology is implicit, two areas of Jewish literature deserve greater attention. One is the Jewish sermon, a largely untapped resource for the study of Jewish history and thought. Another is the Jewish prayerbook, where the abiding spiritual landmarks of Jewish life come into view. The prayerbook offers a bird's-eye view of Jewish history, religious poetry, ceremonial observances, sacred time—and, of course, quantitites of theology. Historical Jewish sensibilities regarding God, death, and ties to the deceased are especially revealed in Memorial Services on Yom Kippur in various mahzorim, particularly during the nineteenth century, the golden age of European and American liturgical reform. By considering the changing styles in the Yizkor service on the holiest day in the Jewish calendar, it is possible to realize how far and in what direction those Jewish theological attitudes have evolved.

Our focus in this study is in the United States, where that development was at its richest in the various prayerbooks published under the patronage of individual congregations, chiefly made up of those who had left Central Europe for the freer atmosphere of America. The Atonement Memorial Service was celebrated then amid much circumstance and solemnity, in ways previously unknown. Not only were Sephardic memorial prayers preferred over the more established Ashkenazic ones, but the service itself was conducted principally in the vernacular, even in synagogues where Hebrew otherwise prevailed. What is perhaps most surprising of all is that the climactic private Yizkor prayers in the vernacular, German or English, were as a rule addressed to the departed themselves.

The nineteenth-century American Memorial Services that are examined are those by Merzbacher, Einhorn, Wise, Huebsch, Krauskopf, and Levy on the Reform side, and those by Szold and Jastrow, of the Positive-Historical (later to become the Conservative) school. In briefer fashion the twentieth-century Conservative, Reform, and Reconstructionist High Holy Day liturgies in their various stages come in for scrutiny, and revealing comparisons are drawn with their nineteenth-century antecedents.

The Memorial Service in Merzbacher's Order of Prayer (1855)

Leo Merzbacher, as discussed in chapter six, was rabbi of the congregation that later grew into the renowned Temple Emanu-El in New York. He designed for his congregation a Hebrew *hazkarat neshamot,*[4] accompanied by English translation, for Yom Kippur between *minhah*[5] and *ne'ilah.* Merzbacher's revision amounts to little more than scant adjustment of the traditional Ashkenazic Yizkor prayer with its votive offering and the entreaty that the deceased kin be bound up in the bond of life with the Patriarchs or Matriarchs and with the rest of the Righteous in Paradise.

On the English side, however, the prayer is directed to the departed themselves and bears little connection to the Hebrew[6]—a departure for Merzbacher, whose renditions on the whole were fairly literal. The solemnities begin with the recitation of Psalm 90, followed by eight verses of *adonay, mah adam,*[7] here treated as an anthem. Then a sermon is delivered, making way for the rabbi or *sheliah tzibbor* to take a scroll of the Torah and hold it while pronouncing a *mi she-berakh*[8] on behalf of congregants committed to charitable contributions in memory of those called to their eternal rest. For whatever reason, the last-named Hebrew supplication appears neither with vowels nor in English. Afterwards the Yizkor is read by "the congregation in silent prayer," followed by a newly-composed (possibly by Merzbacher himself) prayer in good liturgical Hebrew, in memory of the patrons and supporters of the congregation:

> May the Lord remember the souls of all the righteous and good, who lived as benefactors in our midst, and were gathered to their people, and left a blessing to their name. . . . they rest in glory with imperishable renown *{shemam yikkon la'ad},* and their memory shall not depart from us.
> Happy are they who walk in their path. Amen![9]

The anthem *shivviti*[10] serves as a musical interlude, preceding both *mah rav tuvekha* and *menuhah nekhonah* and culminating in the Kaddish with the Reform *al yisra'el ve'al tzaddiqaya,*[11] all of the foregoing in accordance with the usage determined by the Hamburg Temple *Gebetbuch.*[12] Thus the prefatory portion of the Memorial Service here is mostly Ashkenazic in derivation, while the latter half, after the climactic Yizkor itself, is largely Sephardic, notably the *hashkavah* (in lieu of the Ashkenazic *el male raḥamim*).

The Todtenfeier in Einhorn's Olath Tamid (1858)

The next prayerbook of consequence to appear was the polished German-Hebrew *Olath Tamid* (1858) by David Einhorn (1809–1879). Here the *Todtenfeier* is implanted within the framework of an all-purpose Afternoon Service (*Nachmittagsgottesdienst*), an amalgam of elements drawn from *musaf* and *minḥah*, including an emended *u-netanneh toqef*, the *avodah*, and the afternoon Torah Service. The rites are performed almost exclusively by the rabbi (*Rabbiner*), in oratorical style. An unspecified German hymn introduces the Memorial Service, whereupon the cantor (*Vorbeter*) sings all eight verses of *adonay, mah adam*. From then on the entire service is conducted in German until the Kaddish,[13] which is of course read in the original Aramaic/Hebrew. Following the prelude is a prayer four and one-half pages long composed by Einhorn himself. Although the language is high-flown, it is nonetheless quite moving. A pair of extracts illustrates its skillful blend of biblical, Rabbinic, and original motifs. (The 1896 English translation, in brackets, is by Einhorn's son-in-law, Emil G. Hirsch, who on occasion, embellished it):

> Sie Alle trifft dasselbe Loos der Zeitlichkeit, sie Alle ziehen dahin wo der Erde
> Lust und Last für immer schwinden, wo Gross und Klein, Herr und Knecht, Wolf und Lamm friedlich neben einander rasten; sie zerreisst—die silberne Schnur, die Leib und Geist auf eine kurze Weile aneinander kettet, und zerbrochen wird der Krug an der Quelle. Dies ist nach Deiner unerforschlichen Weisheit, o Gott, unser Aller unausbleiblich' Ziel.
> [They journey thither where earthly pain and pleasure cease forever, where the great and the small, the lord and his servant, the wolf and the lamb, lie down to rest together in peace. Loosed is the silver cord that has held the spirit and body together for a brief while, and the pitcher is broken at the fountain. This, according to Thine inscrutable wisdom, O God, is the inevitable end of all men.]

Für den ist der Tod ein Hoherpriester, der bei seinem Erscheinen ein zweifaches Opfer darbringt, den Leib, den Nahrungsquell des sündlichen Verlangens, in die Wüste sendet, den Dir entstammten Geist aber leuchtend und flammend Deinem Altare weihet und zu Dir emporsteigen lässt, um Frieden zu finden und Seligkeit zu schauen für ewige Zeiten.

[For him, death is a high-priest, and in its advent a twofold sacrifice is offered to Thee. The body, the root and residence of sinful desire, he sendeth forth into the desert. The spirit, Thy child, he consecrateth a flaming offering on Thine altar to wing its way unto Thy light, to abide with Thee in the realms of beatified peace forevermore.][14]

A silent congregational reading of Psalm 23 comes after the rabbi's prayerful declamation. Then Einhorn does something rather unprecedented: he presses into service three medieval Hebrew poems[15]—excogitations on the flight of time and the sobering recognition of humankind's frailty and evanescence—which, as he points out in his introduction to *Olath Tamid,* are derived from Michael Sachs's *Die religiöse Poesie der Juden in Spanien* (Berlin 1845). The only other prayerbook that I am aware of that incorporates such brooding reflections from the Middle Ages in a Memorial Service for Yom Kippur is Benjamin Szold's 1863 and Marcus Jastrow's 1873 editions of *Abodath Israel.* One cannot help but wonder whether the more conservative Szold's utilization of an unspoken Psalm 23 and selections from Sachs's metrical rendition of *barekhi nafshi* was prompted by their prior use in the prayerbook of a rival, radical Baltimorean.[16]

The three aforementioned poems are followed by another inspired ruminative piece by Einhorn himself. This one is more personal, acting as a preface to the congregants' own prayers for immediate kin and friends who are gone. Two of the most touching sentences remind us not only of the Jews' frequently unsettled state but, no less poignantly, of the fact that the majority of the worshipers were immigrants to these shores who perforce left much behind not long before.

. . . Sie bleiben uns nahe—die geliebten Heimgegangenen, auch dann, wenn viele Jahre über ihren Grabeshügel dahingezogen; auch dann, wenn ihre Asche in weiter, weiter Ferne von uns ruhet. Selbst die wogenden Gewässer des Weltmeeres und eines sturmreichen Schicksals könnten unsere Liebe zu ihnen nicht auslöschen, nicht schmälern, die Stimme der Sehnsucht in unserem Herzen nicht übertäuben.

[These dear ones of ours are near us now, even though the snow of many circling winters has spread its white pall over their graves; even though the sun of a distant sky watches over the far-off spot where their mortal dust was laid to final sleep. The rolling waves of the dividing ocean, the shifting tides of a life beset by tempests, and the caprices of fortune have not quenched the fire of our love for them, nor the ardor of our longing.]

The concluding paragraph of this prayer is widened to embrace the Jewish victims of persecution in all lands over the millennia, in language reminiscent of the martyrological *av ha-raḥamin* prayer. A few lines capture a sense of the whole, this time just in Hirsch's paraphrastic rendition:

We know the names of only a few of this vast army of martyrs and heroes who in life and death clung unto Thee and Israel, and who, for the glorification of Thy name, displayed the daring and undaunted courage of the eagle, the fortitude and enduring strength of the lion. Our hearts treasure their unnamed memory; the glory of their lives, the grandeur of their deaths; Thou, who hast counted all their tears and weighed the deeds of the quick and the dead, hast given them place and name in the temple of Thy holy ones.[17]

After these, three Yizkor prayers in German are addressed directly to the deceased parents, children who are no more, and departed sisters, brothers, and other relatives. The wording of each is distinctive, apart from the closing wish that God would *wohlgefällig aufnehmen die Opfer, die ich in deinem Andenken ihm gelobe, um einst in immererwährender Glückseligkeit mit dir vereint zu werden!* ("willingly accept the offering that I pledge in your memory [after the phrase in Yizkor, *ba-avur she-ani noder tzedaqah}* so that I may be reunited with you in everlasting bliss"). Three of the English Yizkor prayers in the old *Union Prayer Book* II[18] are translations of Einhorn's originals. The rabbi resumes with a restatement of the Sephardic *mah rav tuvekha* and *menuḥah nekhonah* in German, drawing to a close with the Hamburg Kaddish. An undetermined hymn ends the Memorial Service.[19] Both Merzbacher's and Einhorn's prayerbooks share the unmistakable imprint of the Hamburg Temple *Gebetbuch* in their utilization of *al yisrael ve-al tzaddiqaya* for the Mourners' Kaddish and their adoption/adaptation of the Sephardic *hashkavah* to substitute for *el male rahamim.*

A curious note is struck in the abrupt appearance in *Olath Tamid* of an unvocalized, untranslated and, strictly speaking, redundant *el male rahamim*—beneath the translation of the Kaddish. The prayer is brought in, it can be supposed, as a halfhearted concession by Einhorn to the traditionally-inclined, who were reluctant to part with it and wanted it in the prayerbook.[20]

The Seelenfeier in Isaac M. Wise's Minhag Amerika (1866)

The first American prayerbook compiler to go his own way was Isaac M. Wise (1819–1900), principally responsible for the premier edition of *Minhag Amerika* for the Day of Atonement (1866).[21] Two features make its *hazkarat neshamot* stand out. First, the service is made into the focus and fulcrum of the Yom Kippur Eve Service by being positioned between the stirring *piyyut, ya'aleh tahanunenu,* and the finishing *aleynu.* Anomalous as the relocation may appear, it is not without precedent. The Sephardim have long carried the option of holding a Memorial Service of sorts, with its various *hashkavot,* just after the chanting of Kol Nidrey. The other unusual feature in the Wisean transformation is the absence of Hebrew, except for the prelude *adonay, mah adam.* This somewhat extraordinary Seelenfeier is given on the one side in English and the other in German; and the invitation to choose between the two is a bit unusual even for Wise, who as a rule sought to Americanize his immigrant congregation by furnishing an English translation for the Hebrew prayers, and keeping the German to a bare minimum. Apparently, for the Yizkor Service, linguistic consistency gave way to nostalgia and sentiments of yearning.

Interestingly, it is Wise's *Seelenfeier* that has outlasted all the other nineteenth-century versions—directly in the *Union Prayer Book* II and indirectly in the Conservative Morris Silverman's *High Holiday Prayer Book.*[22] *Minhag Amerika,* the *Union Prayer Book* II(1922), and *Gates of Repentance* (1978) versions are compared below to illustrate the style and flavor of the Wisean prototype and its influence on twentieth-century Reform prayerbooks.

MA (1866)

Das Auge wird des Sehens nicht satt, endlos sind des Herzens Wünsche. Noch hat kein Sterblicher genug Reichthum, Macht, Ansehen, Ehre, Wissen oder Weisheit gehabt, als der Tod sein Streben schloss. Auf den Gräbern von tausend getäuschten Hoffnungen dichtet neue Pläne der Erdensohn. Als Moses vollführt hatte das Werk der Erlösung und der Offenbarung, das grösste, das je ein Mensch vollbracht, da stand er noch unbefriedigt auf der Spitze des Berges Nebo und schaute wehmüthig hinüber ins, Land der Verheissung, das zu erreichen ihm Gott in seine Weisheit versagte. In Palästen wohnt die Unzufriedenheit wie des Bettlers Hütte, in der reich geschmückten Brust schlägt das unersättliche Herz, in der Mitte schäumenden Ueberflusses will der Mensch noch mehr. Und endlich endet der Tod Alles, den Kampf und das Ringen, die Leiden und die Lust, die Freude und den Schmerz, das gebrochene Herz hat genug der irdischen Güter, der Herr ist seinem Diener gleich, der Arme wie der Reiche, der Mächtige wie der Schwache, der Weise wie

The eye is never satisfied of seeing, endless are the wishes of the heart. No mortal one has yet had enough of wealth, power, respect, honor, knowledge or wisdom, when death closed his career. The son of man devises new schemes on the fresh graves of a thousand disappointed hopes. When Moses had accomplished the work of redemption and revelation, the greatest ever done by man, he stood dissatisfied on the summit of Mount Nebo, and beheld the promised land which to God in his wisdom had refused him. Discontentment abides in palaces as in the beggar's hut. An insatiable heart heaves in the breast richly decorated. More, still more man desires in the midst of the brightest opulence. Finally death closes all, the combat and the struggle, grief and joy, pain and delight. The broken eye is satisfied of seeing, the benumbed heart has enough of earthly possessions. The lord and his servant, the rich and the poor, the mighty and the feeble, the wise and the simple—death equalizes them all; the earth covers the remains of a king like those of a beggar.

der Thor, im Tode sind sie alle
gleich, die Erde bedeckt den
Leichnam des Königs wie den
des Bettlers.

UPB (1922)	*GOR (1978)*

The eye is never satisfied with
seeing; endless are the desires of
the heart. No mortal has ever
had enough of riches, honor and
wisdom, when death ended his
career. Man devises new schemes
on the grave of a thousand disappointed hopes. Like Moses on
Mount Nebo, he beholds the
promised land from afar, but
entrance into it he is denied.
Discontent abides in the palace
and in the hut, rankling alike in
the breast of prince and pauper.
Death finally terminates the
combat, and grief and joy, success and failure, all are ended.
Like children falling asleep over
his toys, man loosens his grasp
on earthly possessions only when
death overtakes him. The master
and the servant, the rich and the
poor, the strong and the feeble,
the wise and the simple, all are
equal in death; the grave levels
all distinctions and makes the
whole world kin.

The eye is never satisfied with
seeing; endless are the desires of
the heart. We devise new
schemes on the graves of a thousand disappointed hopes. Like
Moses on Mount Nebo, we
behold the promised land from
afar but may not enter it. Our
life, at its best, is an endless
effort for a goal we never attain.
Death finally terminates the
struggle, and joy and grief, success and failure, all are ended.
Like children falling asleep over
their toys, we relinquish our
grasp on earthly possessions only
when death overtakes us. Master
and servant, rich and poor,
strong and feeble, wise and simple, all are equal in death. The
grave levels all distinctions, and
makes the whole world kin.

Most nineteenth-century rites supplied a service for the House of
Mourning—generally a Morning, Afternoon, or Evening Service accompa-

nied by prayers of an obituary character.[23] True-to-form, Wise created a service of this nature, using the kind of Memorial Services we have been examining (*e.g.,* Merzbacher's) for either a *Jahrzeit* or a home service. He termed it, noncommittally, *tefillah la-avelim ule-Jahrzeit* and included elements normally appearing in a Yizkor Service: Psalm 90; *adonay, mah adam;* Yizkor in *the first* person (*ezkor, elohim, avi mori,* which Wise rendered "I do remember before Thee, O Lord, my dear and beloved father . . . ," in which, however, the deceased is not directly addressed); *shivviti; mah rav tuvekha;* and *menuḥah nekhonah,* ending with the Mourners' Kaddish. Considering that the rubrics in *Minhag Amerika* are routinely detailed to some degree, both in Hebrew and in translation, it is rather surprising that no directions are given for *tefillah la-avelim ule-Jahrzeit;* the latterday reader has no immediate way of knowing whether this is an appendix to a regular worship service or complete in itself. Nor is it clear whether this service was to be held amid a quorum and/or in private. Perhaps, by design, the author left these decisions entirely up to the solitary person or the specific group.

Now let us take a closer look at this maverick but moving *Seelenfeier.* Like his compeers in the field of liturgy-making, Wise starts off, after the introductory *adonay, mah adam* in Hebrew and in German (all eight verses), with a mood-setting discourse on the universality and inexorability of death. Between prose sections he regularly intersperses a choral refrain "What's man, the son of dust/What's man, O Lord?" The next paragraph beginning "The eye is never satisfied of seeing," quoted above, dilates on the inescapable struggles of life for one and all. "Death equalizes them all" (*Union Prayer Book* II; "All are equal in death; the grave levels all distinctions and makes the whole world kin"). Wise then describes the impact death has on survivors. Echoing for the second time the choir's antiphonal "What's man . . . ?" the ensuing section, the climax really, contains a liturgical attempt at a theodicy, a kind of *tzidduq ha-din.* Below is an excerpt from a longer passage as an illustration:

Thou art supreme goodness, O Lord, Thou hast not gifted us with this mighty yearning after thy light, this indomitable panting after the infinite, this restless longing after unattainable and indefinable ideals, this eternal dissatisfaction with the world, its treasures and charms, to disappoint us at last, and deliver us to the worms of the dust after a life of struggle, anxiety and pain. Thou hast inscribed our soul with the flaming characters of immortality. Thou deceivest not, Thou art the God of truth. Supreme justice art Thou, O Lord.

A hymn follows, on the German side as "Verklärt und hehr erscheinen"[24] and on the English side "Thy glory, Lord, surroundeth." This English hymn eventually was included in the High Holy Day volume of the 1894 edition of the *Union Prayer Book,* but discontinued thereafter.

To usher in *Minhag Amerika's* version of the Yizkor prayers themselves, in German and in English, Wise drew upon Isaiah 25:8 and 16:19, among the most eschatologically-oriented verses in the Isaian corpus. He might have derived the idea for the inclusion of these biblical verses from the *hashkavah* recited in the House of Mourning according to the Spanish-Portuguese rite. In addition, both the Ashkenazic and Sephardic rites designate the aforementioned scriptural sentences to be said at the washing of the hands upon leaving the cemetery. Wise has

> Our dead ones live, they awake and shout with gladness who repose in the dust. The dew of light is the dew of Thy promise, Thou eternal and incomprehensible God of life! The spirit is wedded to the spirit, when man rises above the dust of the earth, when the soul breaks asunder the fetters of mortality and soars aloft to eternal light.

This passage precedes the newly-composed Yizkor prayers in German and in English in which the deceased are tenderly and longingly recalled. Unlike anything Wise has done previously with the Yizkor prayer in his weekday, Sabbath, and Festival volume, in his maḥzor for Yom Kippur the congregants appeal directly to the dead in the first and second persons.

> Thy memory, dearly beloved father, which now entirely fills my soul, revives in me all the holy sentiments of love and affection which thou so often and so tenderly hast lavished on me, when thy parental hand still guided me, blessed and instructed thy child. For ever thine image will live in my soul and be my guiding star on the path of virtue in my pilgrimage to eternal life, that, arrived at the throne of mercy, I may be deemed worthy of thee in the presence of God.

This is one of Wise's two Yizkor prayers that found their way into the different editions of the *Union Prayer Book* II but not into the current *Gates of Repentance.* One more musical interlude by the choir ("Es leben deine

Todten"/"They live the life of glory") leads to a salutation to and communion with all the departed, including benefactors of humanity and lamented members of the temple family and of the Jewish people. Here are a few significant lines:

> We feel your presence and bless the hours you spent with us before God. O, be ye messengers of peace to us, distill consolation and heavenly solace into the hearts of the mourning; carry the voice of atonement into our souls; breathe angelic melodies on this congregation assembled before the Lord. They bless your memory.

Drawing the entire Memorial Service to a close, the minister calls upon the congregation to rise, not for the Kaddish, as one might expect, but for the *aleynu* that comes before it. We might wonder what Wise was trying to accomplish by this rearrangement and why he placed the concluding *qaddish yatom* for his *Seelenfeier* immediately *after* the *aleynu*. Perhaps he did it to eliminate the need for an extra Kaddish.[25] Perhaps he was also considering the eschatological character of both prayers, the first being fixed on the kingdom-to-come in a terrestrial dimension and the second in a cosmic sense (*yehe shelama rabba min shemaya; oseh shalom bi-meromav;* and, in the celebrated Hamburg interpolation, *ve-ḥulqa tava le-ḥayyey alma de-ate*).

In summary, the text and rearrangement in *Minhag Amerika* possessed in certain respects remarkable durability and left an indelible imprint on other prayerbooks.

The Memorial Service in Adolph Huebsch's Gebete (1875)

One discriminating nineteenth-century liturgiographer who took a very different approach from Wise on the Memorial Service was Adolph Huebsch, the Hungarian-born, Prague-educated rabbi of the "Böhmische Schule," i.e. Ahawath Chesed in New York City. Huebsch (1830–1884)[26] was no mean scholar, as evidenced by his exhaustive study of the Peshitta on the Five Scrolls.[27] Wise wrote in his *Reminiscences*[28]

> It was in the summer of 1857 that the *Minhag Amerika* finally appeared. For eleven years I had cherished the idea, now it was con-

summated; . . . It forced Szold and Huebsch to a like step, and made the use of the old ritual an impossibility in America.

Indeed, a comparison of individual benedictions in the weekday *amidah,* the *shemoneh esreh,* as it appears both in *Minhag Amerika* and in Huebsch's revised ritual, shows that, to a considerable extent, they are the same. But for his congregation Huebsch produced a trim and comely rite, *Seder Tefillah: Gebete für den öffentlichen Gottesdienst*—the first volume (1872) for Sabbaths, Festivals, and weekdays, and the second (1875) for the High Holy Days. Compared to Wise's *Seelenfeier,* Huebsch's Memorial Service for Yom Kippur, ensconced between the *musaf* and the Afternoon Services, is uncluttered and chaste, marked for its simplicity and restraint. The German text of the service is drawn in large part from the *Todtenfeier* in Holdheim's *Gebetbuch für jüdische Reformgemeinden* (2nd edition, Berlin, 1852).

Huebsch introduced here and there slight verbal changes and additions in the German. The soothing choral anthem, "Zum Land der Ruhe und der Stille," starts the service. Then the rabbi carries on with *adonay, mah adam* with all of its verses in poetic German paraphrase, followed by a temperate disquisition on the subject of immortality. A choral interlude ("Der Erdensohn und seine Pracht") intervenes, after which the rabbi resumes, this time invoking the memory of the deceased as an exordium to the silent individual prayers on behalf of kindred that are no more. An excerpt from Alexander Kohut's English translation[29] of "Ich gedenke dein . . ." conveys a sense of Huebsch's original literary treatment:

> On earth I can do no more for thee than to love thy memory, and pray for thy salvation.[30] May the merciful Father take thy soul unto His paternal keeping, into the fellowship of those who live eternally before Him, enjoy the splendor of His divine glory.[31] My sweet consolation is the unerring hope that I shall still be reunited to thee . . . in the world of eternity.

A modified *menuḥah nekhonah* ensues, rounded out by the recitation of the Hamburg Temple version of the Kaddish. The *Todtenfeier* for the Day of Atonement was not the only Memorial Service that Huebsch furnished for his ritual: he prepared one for the Seventh Day of Passover and Shemini Atzeret,[32] a condensed and lower-keyed version of the *hazkarat neshamot* on Yom Kippur, and reverted to the Ashkenazic *el male raḥamim* instead of the Sephardic *menuḥah nekhonah* for the concluding prayer.

In a footnote in the first volume, Huebsch leaves instructions to the effect that the service may be used, with negligible changes, in a *Trauerhaus,* a House of Mourning.[33] An unaffected quatrain (again in Kohut's translation) concludes the service.

> Those whom on earth we dearly love,
> But for a while they here remain;
> We meet them again above,
> Our souls forever life retain.

Hazkarat Neshamot in Abodath Israel by Benjamin Szold and Marcus Jastrow (1863 and 1873)

Written more than a decade earlier and a good deal more elaborate than Huebsch's *Todtenfeier* is the *hazkarat neshamot* in Benjamin Szold's *Abodath Israel* (Baltimore, 1863). Compared to other contemporary Yizkor services, Szold's is more heavily bilingual (Hebrew and German) and includes far more interplay among the rabbi, cantor *(Vorbeter),* congregation, and choir. As in the Hamburg Temple *Gebetbuch,* the Memorial Service follows the *musaf* and a singing of *yigdal.*[34]

The rabbi's opening prayer is fundamentally a discourse on theodicy and intimations of immortality. In the same lengthy oration he adumbrates the silent private Yizkor prayer by recalling parents, spouses, children, relatives, and friends who have gone to their eternal reward. Then the choir sings the eight-verse *adonay, mah adam,* which is succeeded by versions of the Yizkor prayer in Hebrew for father, for mother; and for grandparents, aunts and uncles, and siblings.

Each of these texts is accompanied by a corresponding *independent* prayer in the vernacular in which the deceased are spoken to directly (which is not the case in the Hebrew text). Prayers that are addressed to spouse and child are composed solely in German. All the Yizkor prayers in the revised English version (Philadelphia, 1873) by Marcus Jastrow appear only in English paraphrase of the German of his colleague and contemporary Szold. Many piteous lines stand out—such as these for the mother who might have died at childbirth or otherwise passed away before her time:

> O, allzufrüh hat der himmlische Vater dich, geliebte Mutter, mir entrissen; denn seitdem du nicht mehr um mich weilest, und ich

deiner Liebe und Theilnahme entbehre, fühle ich so ganz die schwere
Bedeutung deines frühen Heimganges.

which Jastrow renders:

> Oh, too soon has the heavenly Father taken thee away from me; for
> ever since thou hast ceased to dwell with me, and I am destined to
> live without thy loving sympathy, I am made to feel the great bitter-
> ness of thy early decease.

Then there is this tender, heartrending invocation of the child who prema-
turely predeceased his/her parents, reproduced here only in Jastrow's English, faithful to its Szoldian antetype.

> In this solemn hour, when the most earnest affections are roused in
> my bosom, and the dear departed seem to rise from their graves and
> appear before my mind as if in full life; thy sweet and lovely image,
> my dearly beloved Child, presents itself to my mental sight. I
> remember thee—a charming and tender flower which death has
> plucked, despoiling my garden of happiness. I still recollect the
> day—Oh, the sweet days—when I was yet permitted to delight in
> thy fair form, marking thy bodily and intellectual growth and cher-
> ishing the golden hopes I placed on thy future. The inscrutable will
> of the All-wise has torn thee from me to transplant thee into a fairer
> garden, and I have been left with a deepwounded heart from which
> thy memory will never be eradicated.—Still am I hopeful; for the
> bond, here broken asunder, connects my heart so much closer with
> the realms above. Thou wilt no more return to us, but I shall come
> to thee. In due time, I shall leave this vale of tears, and rise unto the
> light-beaming regions, where thy lovely and innocent countenance
> will look upon me smiling in serene joy. Until then, may our Heav-
> enly Father permit me to perform on earth many good deeds that
> will accompany me, when I leave for thy habitation. Amen.

At the conclusion of all the individual personal prayers for (really *to*) the
departed, there appears a general one for all the deceased. This prayer is
indistinguishable from a prayer of intercession—*i.e.,* those gathered to
their eternal home are asked to intercede on behalf of surviving kin and
loved ones—and might strike the modern Jew as similar to the Catholic

veneration of saints. Here is Jastrow's translation of Szold's summons to all of the departed ("O, meine Theuern"):

> O, my dear ones! From your celestial dwellings look down upon me in kindness, as your glances rested on me, ere the Lord removed you from our midst to receive you in his heights. (Accept my sincere thanks for your paternal solicitude, love and faithfulness, as well as for your mildness and indulgence, of which I received innumerable proofs. Pardon every offence I may have committed against you through rashness or thoughtlessness.) Remember me before the Lord; pray for me and all my kindred; pray that God may shield me, and keep far removed from me grief and affliction; that he may sanctify me through his commands, and aid me in every good work and noble undertaking,—that he may endow me with strength to resist temptation, and guard me against error and guilt. And when my career in this world shall end, and I shall be summoned to enter into my everlasting home: then may your loving kindness be my guide, that I may be received into the communion of the pious and just, there, in the realms of truth and peace. Amen.

Wise and Szold's respective all-embracing invocations to those who have gone to their eternal home are suggestive of this last supplication upon "quitting the Burial Ground," of which both the Hebrew and the English follow:

שלום עליכם נשמות הטהורות. נאצלות מזיו יוצר המאורות: הנני הולך
לדרכי. ונפשי את־יי ברכי. ולאל חי תפלתי. ישמר־בי נשמתי ורוחי. ישמע
עתירת דורשיו. ירבה כבוד שלמיו. יוסיף חן וחסד לעניו הקדושים עשי
מעוותיו....ובכן נוחו ישרים נוחו. עד יאמר מלך חיא מרא די־ארעא ודי־
שמיא. עמדו ישרים עמדו לתחיה: ואנחנו נכנס לחיים טובים ולשלום.
עד אשר יקרב הלם ציר נאמן ומשיח אלהי יעקב. והשיב לב אבות על־בנים
ולב בנים על־אבותם בלי עקב. וצדק יהלך לפנינו. ונהלל ונשבח לאלהינו
בכל מיני תהלה ופאר. כי הוא האל הגדול והגבור אדיר וחזק ונורא,
מחיה מתים במאמרו, עשה גדולות עד־אין חקר, ונפלאות עד־אין מספר.
ברוך מחיה המתים:

> Peace be unto you, ye pure beatified souls, emanations from the effulgence of Him Who created the luminaries. Behold I go my way, and my soul blesses the Eternal, the God of life, to Whom I direct my prayer. O may He deign to guard within me my soul and spirit;

may He hear the prayers of those who seek Him, increase the honour of His perfect ones, and heap grace and mercy on His pious and meek in the land, who perform His commandments; so that they may see their descendants grow strong in health, and in the fear of God, and cause them to behold the solemn assembly in the sacred temple. Thus rest, rest in peace, ye upright slumberers! Repose until the King of life, the Lord of heaven and earth, will exclaim, "Rise, ye upright ones! Rise to everlasting life!" Source of life! Grant that we may enter into a life of happiness and peace, until the faithful messenger will draw near, the anointed of the God of Jacob, and affectionately restore the hearts of parents to children, and the hearts of children to parents, and when righteousness will precede us. We will then praise and adore our God with all praises and glorifications; for He is great, mighty, and tremendous. He revives the dead by His mere word, "Who does great and unsearchable deeds; marvellous things without number." Blessed be He who reviveth the dead.

Interestingly, the practice of asking departed relatives to intercede on our behalf before God has many traditional Jewish antecedents: the Ashkenazim, and particularly Ashkenazic women, have played an estimable role in the creation of *tehinnot* (supplications), noted for their intimate, personal quality and frequent appeals to the deceased for intercession. Prior to the twentieth century, *tehinnot* have appeared in Yiddish, German, French, and English.[35] For a more recent example, a *Sefer ha-Ḥayyim,* dated 1863 in London and edited by B.H. Ascher, includes a number of rather affecting entreaties to the dead to be read at the grave—despite explicit cautionary instructions:

> Let no one, however, for a moment imagine that the prayers are directed to the departed, that they may assist the living, God forbid! but our supplication must be solely and entirely addressed to the All-merciful, that He may in His mercy, deign to receive our prayer, for the living and the dead.

The same volume presents an individual plea for a widow to her late husband—literate and fluent in both the Hebrew and English translation.

> שלום עליך Peace be unto thee, thou spirit of my beatified husband! Thou who hast been the prop of my house, and the delight of my dwelling. Thou who hast enlightened my darkness and cheered my

gloominess. Thou the crown of my glory, and the remedy for my affliction. But, alas! now my sun has gone down, and I, a bereaved widow, am left alone and destitute. My brightness disappeared, and my delight vanished. Alas! when I enter my house, when I look this way and that way and perceive thee not, I exclaim in the anguish of my heart, Where art thou? Wherefore has thou forsaken me, the grieved of spirit? Who will console me, who will heal my affliction, and who will stay the tears on my cheeks? I come to-day to the valley of the fountain of tears; to the cleft of the rock of the resting place of my delight and joy. I sought him and found him not; then I called out from distress, Peace be unto thee, and to thy purified soul. Mayest thou rest in, and be protected under the shadow of the Divine Glory, and ever be remembered for good.

I beseech Thee, O God! look on the affliction of Thy handmaid; behold my grief, my contrition, my crushed spirit, my troubled mind, and my great disquietude. [Behold, with whom hast thou left these sheep—mine and thine, lambs which thou hast left to themselves! Thou didst go to rest, but us thou hast left to sorrow. Who shall teach them knowledge, who make them that are weaned from the milk understand the ways of the living God, and the spirit of our inherited faith? Who will guide us in the path of rectitude, and who will teach us the right and proper use of time?] To whom hast thou entrusted thy sorrowful widow? Verily, if the death of a wife to a husband has been compared to one doomed to see the destruction of the glorious temple, then the death of a husband to a wife surely resembles the overthrow of the whole universe. Rise, therefore, beloved of my soul! pray, supplicate, and implore the mercy of the Most High and Holy One, the Father of the fatherless and the Judge of the widows, to have mercy on the remnant of thy flock; that He may deign to pardon my sins and to support my house that is broken down, to grant me a remedy for my sufferings, and to look down from His celestial abode with compassion on me, and on all those that depend on me. Heavenly Father! be Thou my comforter, my healer! Remove from me every disease and affliction, repair my ruin, and provide for me and my children our daily wants. Grant that they may grow up like the cedars, that their roots may strike, and their branches spread. May their remotest posterity be wise, understanding, honoured, attached to Thy Sacred Law, and devoted to piety and virtue, and may they spend long years in riches, honour, and ease.

Grant me Thy paternal aid; strengthen me in the fulfillment of my arduous task, for it is Thou Who protectest the weak, and raisest the drooping spirits of the fatherless, and never despisest the prayers of widows.

And thou, heavenly soul of my beatified husband! May God remember thee for good. May thy sacred ashes repose in peace, until thou art awakened to everlasting life, and to uninterrupted bliss, joy, and gladness. Amen.

For both his own *Sefer ha-Ḥayyim* (Baltimore, 1866) and his *Hegyon Lev* (Baltimore, 1867)[36] Szold adapted in smooth, pleasing Hebrew a general Yizkor, under the rubric *Allgemeines Gebet an den Gräbern,* to be intoned upon visiting the cemetery. Again, it should be observed, the deceased are the ones being addressed. The German translation is also Szold's.

Möge Gott stets deiner Seele zum Heile gedenken. Dein Körper schlummere sanft und liege in ungestörter Ruhe im Grabe. Deine Frömmigkeit schirme mich in Trübsals Zeiten und stehe zur Seite in den Tagen des Kummers und der Angst. Deine Seele weile ewig in dem Bund des Lebens, im Vereine mit den Seelen aller Frommen, in den Gefilden der Seligkeit. Amen Selah.

יזכור אלהים את נשמתך (נשמתך) לטובה. גופך (גופך) יישן שנת ערבה. וינוח בקבר במנוחה נכונה. זכותך (זכותך) יגן עלי בעת צרתי. ויעמוד לימיני ביום עברה. ונפשך (ונפשך) תהא צרורה בצרור החיים. עם נפשות כל הישרים והישרות שבגן עדן. אמן סלה:

For whatever reasons, in his revision of Szold's *Abodath Israel* in 1873 and *Hegyon Lev* in 1875, Jastrow no longer included a Hebrew Yizkor like the one above for the temple or the graveyard. Perhaps he thought it liturgically out of place or simply recognized that most congregants in his day and place were not proficient in the holy tongue.

After the general invocation in *Abodath Israel* to all the departed, Szold presents Sachs's prosodical German translation of Bahya's *barekhi nafshi*,[37] which Jastrow translated afresh for the 1873 version, keeping the same rhyme and meter. Szold continues with an interchange among the rabbi, cantor, choir and congregation for the recitation/singing of Psalms 23, 15, and 16. (Jastrow omits the last psalm and brings in Psalm 49:16–21 instead, to be sung in English as a hymn. It might be recalled that Psalm 49 is traditionally read in a House of Mourning.) Szold then provides, unvocalized, the text of *mi she-berakh*,[38] for worshipers making contributions in honor of those memorialized this day, and of *el male raḥamim*, couched in the singular, on behalf of individuals—neither of which Jastrow saw fit to retain. Szold proceeds with the choir's chanting of *mah rav tuvekha*, which again Jastrow does not have. Both liturgiographers however, go on with *ashrey adam matza ḥokhmah*, scriptural verses from the Sephardic rite by way of the Hamburg *Gebetbuch*, and *menuḥah nekhonah*, from the same source, including some new wording:

Be the portion, in the world to come, of all the righteous men and women that have performed acts of love and charity while on earth, and left blessing behind them, when departing unto their homes. Especially do we mention the name of _____ and _____. May their names flourish for ever, their rest be glorious, and their memory blessed. And let us say, Amen.	וחלק טוב לחיי העולם הבא. מנת הישרים והישרות. אשר עשו חסד וצדקה בארץ. והלכו לעולמם והניחו אחריהם ברכה: ובכללם יעלה לפניך זכרון . . . . וזכרון. . . . . מנוחתם כבוד. שמם ינון לעד. וזכרונם לברכה. ונאמר אמן:

While Szold draws it out through *melekh malkhey ha-melakhim be-raḥamav yaḥos . . . [Der König aller Könige erbarme sich ihrer in seiner Huld und berge sie . . .]*, also part of the Sephardic *hashkavah*, Jastrow does not. The rabbinic team prefaces the terminating Kaddish with *kol yisrael*, with very slight modifications, such as in not ascribing the biblical verse "Better is the fragrance of a good name than the perfume of precious oil; even better is the day of death (to him) than the day of birth" (Ecclesiastes 7) to King

Solomon, since to do so would only violate the canons of critical biblical scholarship, to which both men were loyal.[39]

Memorial Services by Joseph Krauskopf and J. Leonard Levy

The last of the nineteenth-century American memorial services to be considered are those by Joseph Krauskopf and J. Leonard Levy. The German-born Krauskopf (1858–1923) studied under Isaac M. Wise and was one of the four members of Hebrew Union College's first graduating class in 1883. In a sense he inherited Wise's visionary streak although he diverged from his mentor over the latter's proclivity toward compromise for the sake of a unified American Jewry. Despite Krauskopf's assertion in the Preface to *The Service Manual* that

> The fixed Order of Worship has been departed from in this manual, but merely in form. The spirit of the traditional service has been sacredly preserved. Its devotional sentiment has been brought nearer to the modern mind by the use of a number of the most approved liturgical aids . . .

a quick glance through the unique prayerbook will show that it is in many ways more radical than the ritual of Samuel Holdheim's *Reformgemeinde* in Berlin, which nonetheless basically traced the profile of the classical Siddur, including the fabric of the Rabbinic *Stammgebete*. In a nutshell, the typical worship service in *The Service Manual,* whether for a Sabbath or a Festival,[40] consists chiefly of short sermonic essays or discourses, ethical or religious in content, with hymns and sentences (sung by the choir) from the Hebrew Bible, the Apocrypha,[41] and the Talmud, usually to lend support and reinforcement to the point made in the discourse just read by the minister. As often as not these discourses, like the majority of the hymns in *The Service Manual,* are of Gentile authorship, adapted by Krauskopf for use in his synagogue. In both his preface and his index, Krauskopf gives credit to these contributors, who include Minot Savage (1841–1918), a Unitarian minister and preacher of note who, like Krauskopf, was a staunch advocate of the theory of evolution, and J.H.D. Zschokke (1771–1818), a Swiss novelist and playwright who also wrote books of religious meditation.

Krauskopf's younger colleague, J. Leonard Levy (1865–1917),[42] was an assistant (1893–1901) at Krauskopf's synagogue, Keneseth Israel in Philadelphia, before he assumed his own pulpit in Pittsburgh. His liturgical endeavors are no less a departure from the traditional norm than Krauskopf's, even though Levy came upon Krauskopf's revolutionary brand of Reform by a rather circuitous route. A native of England, Levy received his rabbinic training at Jews' College in London and, for a while prior to his emigration to the United States, served an Orthodox congregation in Bristol. Thus he seems to have taken a much longer journey doctrinally, than his seasoned, established senior did.

In 1892 Krauskopf came out with a Memorial Service of thirty-eight pages for the Day of Atonement. Ten years later, Levy's fifty-nine page service appeared. Both rituals present grandiloquent essays very much in the style of an Emerson, a Thoreau, or a Phillips Brooks work, where practically every sentence emerges as a finely chiseled aphorism. The rabbis' essays are interrupted at regular intervals by responsive readings of a biblical character and hymns. Especially in Levy's case, there are choral sentences made up of biblical verses.

Krauskopf's *Service Ritual* (Philadelphia, 1888), chiefly with a view to Sunday Morning Services, and his *Service Manual* (Philadelphia, 1892), specifically for Sabbath, Festivals and Hanukkah (but not Purim), are entirely in English, which was, of course, his adoptive tongue. Levy, a native Britisher, did his *Book of Prayer* (Pittsburgh, 1902) and his *Memorial Service for the Day of Atonement* (Pittsburgh, 1902) in a language already his from birth. This would doubtless account for a certain stiltedness—even grandiloquence—in Krauskopf's prayerbooks, compared to the smooth idiomatic flow in Levy's. Moreover, Krauskopf's openly appropriating from others—credit is given in his indexes—explains some of the occasional unevenness. Conversely, Levy's essays and prayers are all his own, even when he took up others' ideas. Unlike Krauskopf, who was not especially comfortable with overt expressions of Jewish ethnicity[43] in his liturgy, Levy was untroubled by such concerns, despite his undaunted universalism.[44]

A good illustration is the way each uses analogy and metaphor. On the whole, Krauskopf avoids imagery from classical Jewish tradition, whereas Levy freely integrates it into his devotional discourses and prayers. Our first example is drawn from *The Service Manual*:

[Suffering] strains and tortures almost beyond endurance, but it has the same result as has the musician's straining of the strings—it produces a sweeter melody. It shakes hard, but only to force a deeper and a firmer root;—the tree that is shaken most by storms roots the deepest and grows the strongest. It irritates, but only to effect what the oyster does with the irritating grain of sand that has entered its shell—it forms of it a beautiful pearl.

and our second one from Levy's *Memorial Service:*

How truly says the sacred writer, Man is born for trouble as the sparks are made to fly upward! Sadly the great Rabbi points out that without our consent were we created, without our consent were we born and without our consent do we live.

Our next set of examples, taken from a pre-Kaddish prayer that Krauskopf designated as "Remembering the Dead" and Levy "In Memoriam," speak of the sacrifices our ancestors made in the name of their faith and people. For this section Krauskopf tucks in the rubric "Here are read the names of illustrious benefactors of all nations and creeds who have died during the year," but not a word about the Jewish martyrs in all their unmistakable specificity!

And we remember also those heroes and martyrs of old who, for their faith's sake, for their advocacy of right and truth and justice, were frequently made to suffer ignominy, persecution, torture . . .

Levy is more explicit and makes no bones about pointing out the Jewishness of those whose lives were snuffed out *al qiddush ha-shem.*

Everywhere we find hallowed spots sanctified by the life-blood of heroes and martyrs who, for conscience's sake, suffered torture, endured ignominy, met death at the stake or on the scaffold. Thousands and tens of thousands of the House of Israel thus perished rather than be faithless to the high trust confided to their keeping, rather than be false to their mission of witnessing to the existence of the one, only God and of striving to establish on earth the kingdom of righteousness. To death went hoary-headed fathers and mothers in Israel; . . .

In this case, Levy's attitude resembles Szold's and Einhorn's far more than either Wise's or Krauskopf's.

Apart from these differences in style and emphasis, the Memorial Services for Yom Kippur by these two liturgiographers incorporate the same general themes—in the same order—to organize their services. There is no doubt that Levy borrowed and built upon Krauskopf's pattern. Both rites commence with *adonay, mah adam,* sung by the choir in English, and go on with the theme of the ubiquity of death and the evanescence of human achievements (Krauskopf's "Trials of Life;" cf. Levy's "What Is Our Life?" and "Through the Wilderness"). In *The Service Manual* the second reading division under the title of "Exhortation" and the subtitle "Darkness before the Dawn" addresses itself to the educative value of suffering, "the efficacy of suffering as character building"—similar to the prescription recommended by Job's comforters long ago. Levy's counterpart under the heading "The Meaning of Suffering" contains this sentence, coloring the entire section: "Our unavoidable sufferings have been one of the incessant goads to our minds to think, to our bodies to endure, to our hands to work, to our hearts to feel."

A two-page hymn in Krauskopf's prayerbook prepares the way for a piece called "The Fear of Death," according to which death inspires terror only among those who do not understand it, a point reinforced by the affecting if bathetic anthem based on Psalm 42, "Soul, why art thou troubled so?" (in three stanzas rather than the seven as in the *Hamburg Temple Hymnal),*[45] which he uses but which Levy does not. Coming next is an "Exhortation" with the subtitle, "The Mystery of the Hereafter," the crux of which is, in the words of the essay, "For man's good God kindled the hope of immortality in the human heart, and for man's good He does not permit it to be more than a hope." (Cf. Levy's "Over the future, near and remote, God has mercifully drawn the veil of uncertainty and for this act of mercy we should be eternally grateful.") Trailing another group of responses appears the meditation "Death Not Yet the End" (paralleling Levy's "Immortality") offering a series of six proofs substantiating the doctrine of immortality:

—whatever is, is forever
—superiority of mind over matter
—the theory of evolution
—the constant longing after perfection
—emancipation of the spirit
—belief in a God of justice.

Levy's arguments in support of the doctrine are not as extensive or as detailed as Krauskopf's, as the Pittsburgh rabbi confines himself to two proofs, namely the prevalence and antiquity of the concept ("The idea is as old as human civilization and was powerfully taught as early as the days of ancient Egypt.") and the "conservation of energy." ("Energy is indestructible, therefore life is indestructible.") Both seem to have been familiar with the demonstrations Moses Mendelssohn offered on behalf of immortality of the soul in his classic, *Phaedon.*[46]

Both Levy and Krauskopf were known for their skill in the art of oratory and, according to current fashion, prone to plentiful use of such standard rhetorical devices as the striking metaphor or emotive language. Although some of the techniques that were perfectly admissible at the turn of the century cause a present-day groan or scowl, we can appreciate how Krauskopf and Levy earned their reputations as compelling preachers. For instance, this sentence from Levy:

> We know that when our darlings come to us we place them in a cradle; we may hope that at death we are placed in another cradle, which we miscall a coffin, and are therein rocked to a higher life.

It is clear that Levy took the notion of postmortem existence very seriously and wanted his congregation to believe in it as well. In an unusual Passover haggadah[47] that he prepared for the members of Keneseth Israel, he devoted one-fifth of its pages to this very subject. As a matter of fact, the extract just quoted with the cradle/coffin/cradle simile in his Memorial Service made its debut in the aforesaid haggadah!

After all these lengthy learned disquisitions on death and the afterlife, our two author-preachers present memorial prayers leading into the English adaptations of Yizkor (in which, again, the deceased are directly addressed) and bringing their Memorial Services to a close with the recitation of the Kaddish.[48]

Comparisons with Nineteenth-Century European and Twentieth-Century American Atonement Memorial Services

Significantly, the nineteenth-century American Memorial Services that we have examined are constructed on a somewhat grander scale than their contemporary European correlates. Perhaps the elaborateness of the American Yizkor Service stemmed from an implicit wish to ward off or cleanse oneself of guilt. Most of those saying Yizkor or any of its variations were, after all, newcomers to these shores who had not long before left the parental hearth in the old country to try their luck across the seas where boundless opportunity beckoned. The departure from family, while encouraged and justified in any number of ways, could not fail to leave those who found success in their adopted country with a residue of guilt. The ceremonious nineteenth-century American Memorial Service—with its theological warrants and annual reaffirmations of family ties—no doubt satisfied a felt need for a *kippur* or *kapparah* between the generations. The same dynamics were to work again, only decades later, when the Jewish immigrants from eastern Europe were to tread the path beaten by their central European predecessors. Hence, from a psychological perspective, the amplified Memorial Service, in a profound sense, represented less of an intrusion into the daylong Yom Kippur liturgy than a level of wanted expiation that involved family and loved ones far away.[49]

This function of the Yom Kippur Yizkor Service as an occasion for catharsis was to last an entire century, chiefly because of the two major waves of immigration and their overlap. The early nineteen hundreds, however, saw slowly emerging changes, which can be noted in the Conservative *Festival Prayer Book* (New York, 1927) and subsequently in the *Sabbath and Festival Prayer Book* (New York, 1946) and in the Reconstructionist *Shir Hadash* (New York, 1939) and *High Holiday Prayer Book* (New York, 1948). In these transitional prayerbooks the Memorial Service, while enlarging on the Orthodox ritual, is briefer than the nineteenth-century productions that we have been examining. Although textually they dissociate themselves from the nineteenth-century proclivity toward the Sephardic version, doctrinally they are essentially at one, except for the Reconstructionist liturgy, with the Hamburg Temple *Gebetbuch*.[50] The sentimentalism of the older rites is in large measure muted; and prayers addressed to the deceased are all but revamped, the only lingering exception being in Morris Silverman's Conservative *High Holiday Prayer Book.*

What sets these transitional works apart from those that came before and afterwards are 1) the borrowing of the newly-composed, stylistically-successful introductory *av ha-raḥamim* prayer from the British Orthodox *Service for the Synagogue,* Day of Atonement II[51] (not to be confused with the entreaty of medieval origin), and/or 2) the Hebrew wording of the Yizkor prayer itself from the same source with no mention made of the Patriarchs or of oblations but, rather, with the biblically-inspired locution:

יזכר אלהים נשמת . . . שהלך לעולמו.
אנא תהי נפשו צרורה בצרור החיים. ותהי מנוחתו כבוד.
שבע שמחות את־פניך. נעימות בימינך נצח. אמן:

This version has gained supremacy in virtually every non-Orthodox prayerbook issued since.

When we turn to the latter half of our century, we find the *hazkarat neshamot* for Yom Kippur assuming a very different character and style, even though many of the old landmarks are kept or restored. The theological stance and the sensibility are profoundly altered, paradigmatically in the Conservative *Mahzor for Rosh Hashanah and Yom Kippur* (New York, 1972) and in the Reform *Gates of Repentance* (New York, 1978). Features that were everywhere to be found in the nineteenth-century prayerbooks have been systematically toned down or removed altogether. And those items that had been largely taken for granted as *idees* or *textes fixes* a hundred years ago are reevaluated, to wit:

1. Prayers directed to the deceased are turned to God instead.
2. The notion of joining the departed in paradisiacal bliss and communion goes unmentioned.
3. Prayers of intercession are not resorted to.
4. Victorian melodramatics are dismissed, almost as an embarrassment.
5. Talk about an afterlife is couched in cautious, circumlocutory terms. A kind of tactical agnostic language is adopted. In the new parlance, only *memory, values,* and *reputation* are eternal.[52]
6. Selections from Psalms occupy a bit more space, particularly those in which the proximity of God figures more prominently (*e.g.,* Psalm 63) than any dogmatic assertions about the life beyond.
7. The Sepharadizing tendency of former times initiated by the Hamburg Temple, while not completely tossed aside, has deferred to a positive reassessment of the Ashkenazic rite. The Sephardic *hashkavah* (*mah rav tuvekha* and *menuhah nekhonah*) in the nineteenth-century manuals has given way to the Ashkenazic *hashkavah, el male rahamim.*

8. Although the Six Million are mentioned in one way or another in the modern Yizkor Service, they are generally memorialized more extensively elsewhere in the maḥzor.[53]

9. The era of mass immigration, instead of invoking guilt in the worshipers, is recalled only nostagically. The feelings of guilt originally evoked by thoughts of family in the old country are now transferred to the Six Million.[54]

10. Memory takes on more of an existential cast. The older choral pieces in German or English and the discourses delivered in oratorical style are shunned in favor of plainer (and less theological) talk, Hebrew chants, and even an occasional ballad, of which the selection below might serve as an example:

In the rising of the sun and in its going down, we remember them.
In the blowing of the wind and in the chill of winter, we remember them.
In the opening buds and in the rebirth of spring, we remember them.
In the blueness of the sky and in the warmth of summer, we remember them.
In the rustling of leaves and in the beauty of autumn, we remember them.
In the beginning of the year and when it ends, we remember them.
When we are weary and in need of strength, we remember them.
When we are lost and sick at heart, we remember them.
When we have joys we yearn to share, we remember them.
So long as we live, they too shall live, for they are now a part of us, as we remember them.[55]

We see then in the vicissitudes of the Yizkor Service on Yom Kippur some notion of how American Jews, rabbinic and lay, have dealt religiously with concepts of death, the afterlife, and family memory. If little else, the interplay between tradition and change, abundantly evident in the oscillating fortunes of the Atonement Memorial Service, apparently continues without end.

An earlier version of this chapter appeared in the *Hebrew Union College Annual* LV (1984): 243–82. Reprinted with permission.
 1. (New York, 1972), p. 83.

2. "Mavet ve-al mavet be-mishnato shel ha-Rav Kuk," in *Sheviley ha-Emunah ba-Dor ha-Aharon,* ed. Ovadyah Margoliot, (Tel Aviv, 1964) pp. 285–91.

3. (Assen, The Netherlands, 1971), pp. 345–446. About the most broad-based, intensive treatment one can get on the subject is the careful, lucid study by Samuel S. Cohon in his posthumous *Jewish Theology* (Cincinnati,1987).

4. In the course of this study, the nomenclature for the Memorial Service, in Hebrew, English, and German will be used interchangeably: *hazkarat neshamot,* Yizkor Service, *Todtenfeier,* and *Seelenfeier.*

5. Or, as he takes us by surprise, his styling it "Vesper Service"; cf. the Hamburg *Gebet-buch's Vespergebet.*

6. The American Reform custom of apostrophizing the deceased, widespread through the nineteenth century, is unanticipated by the Hamburg Temple rite, the foremost liturgical influence of the century.

7. The biblical verses of which the prayer is made up are Pss. 144:3f; 90:5f, 3; Deut.32:29; Pss. 49:16; 37:37; 34:23; other prayerbooks have slight variations.

8. In Samuel Adler's 1863 revision, the *mi she-berakh* prayer is abandoned. Cf. Arthur Davis and Herbert Adler, *Service of the Synagogue,* Day of Atonement, Part II, London, 1905; and below, Szold's application of the same, pp.xxxxx.

9. The opening half of Merzbacher's public Yizkor is identical with the first half of the communal Yizkor as formulated by S.E. Blogg for the *Todtenfeier* in the latter's *Sefer ha-Hayyim* (Hannover, 1862), inasmuch as Blogg's second half is extracted from the Sephardic *hashkavah.*

10. Ps. 16:8—11.

11. From the pace-setting Hamburg *Gebetbuch* (1819); Jakob J. Petuchowski, *Prayerbook Reform in Europe* (New York, 1968), chap. 41, pp. 324–27.

12. A literal rendition of the Hamburg insert would read something like:

> Unto all Israel, and unto the righteous, and unto all who have departed from this world according to the will of God, may there be unto them abundant peace, a good portion in the world to come, lovingkindness, and compassion from the Lord of heaven and earth; and say ye, Amen.

13. See chap. 1 above for a discussion of Einhorn's Kaddish.

14. In his memorial tribute to the Hebrew poet, Hillel Bavli (1893–1961), Abraham J. Heschel used a similar homiletical image:

> That room in the hospital where he spent his last days was a sanctuary, with a High Priest preparing to celebrate the greatest ritual of all, the ritual act of reciprocity: to return the soul to Him who gave us a soul. We will think of the way in which he was taking leave of this world. All of life is a preparation. All of life one must learn how to die. Hillel Bavli walked away like a prince. ("Hillel Bavli: In Memoriam," *Conservative Judaism* XVIII [Fall 1961/Winter 1962], Nos. 1–2: 71.)

15. The poems that Einhorn picked from Sachs's work and translated himself are 1) *el beyt melekh,* by Abraham ibn Ezra, 2) *barekhi nafshi, oz tiderekhi,* a *tokhehah* by Bahya b. Joseph ibn Paquda, and 3) *shikhehi yegonekh,* also a *tokhehah,* by Solomon ibn Gabirol. All of these poems are identified by Israel Davidson in his *Otzar ha-Shirah veha-Piyyut, Thesaurus of*

Medieval Hebrew Poetry, Library of Jewish Classics, ed. Gerson D. Cohen, (1970 reprint). The only poem that the Memorial Service in the *Union Prayer Book* II, from the 1894 edition to the 1945 one, took over from *Olath Tamid* is *shikheḥi yegonekh* . Interestingly, during a special memorial service for Solomon Schechter at the Jewish Theological Seminary, that poem was chanted in its entirety by the officiating cantor. (Jewish Theological Seminary of America, *Memorial Exercises in Memory of Solomon Schechter,* [New York, 1916]).

16. It was during Einhorn's tenure at the Reform Sinai-Verein in Baltimore that the young Szold took his position as rabbi of the more traditional Oheb-Schalom-Gemeinde in the same city. It was around that time, in February of 1860, when Einhorn wrote his scathing *Abfertigung* (dismissal) of the new arrival and "Das Schicksal der Oheb-Schalom-Gemeinde in Baltimore." Szold responded promptly and vigorously.

17. This paragraph was resuscitated in somewhat altered form in the restored Memorial Service for the Seventh Day of Passover in the *Union Prayer Book* I (1940):

> Reverently we reflect upon the unnumbered hosts who lived and died for the sanctification of Thy name. We know the names of but few of the vast army of martyrs and heroes, who were swifter than eagles and stronger than lions in doing Thy will. We treasure their unnamed memory, the beauty of their life, the glory of their death.

18. I.e. the three editions of the *Union Prayer Book* II before the appearance of *Gates of Repentance,* the most recent edition of the *Union Prayer Book.*

19. In his translation of *Olath Tamid* (Chicago, 1896), however, Emil G. Hirsch does provide a particular hymn in English with which to close the Memorial Service and lead up to *ne'ilah.*

20. Cf. his treatment of the prayer before going to bed. The prayer before the nocturnal Shema is in broad paraphrase. However, for those accustomed to saying their nightly prayers in Hebrew, the compiler provides, in small type at the bottom of the page, once more unvowelled, the text of *ha-mapil ḥevley shenah—vi-yhi ratzon she-tashkhiveni.*

21. The full title of the Atonement volume of *Minhag Amerika* is *Tefillot Beney Yeshurun le-Yom ha-Kippurim, The Divine Service ol American Israelites for the Day of Atonement* (Cincinnati/New York, 1866).

22. The prayer's persistence comes through not only in the *Union Prayer Book* II itself but in other prayerbooks as well, Reform and non-Reform. The High Holy Day rites of British Liberal Judaism, the *Liberal Jewish Prayer Book* II (London, 1937) and *Gate of Repentance* (London, 1973), adhering to the basic scheme with some very English adjuncts (*e.g.,* Sonnet CXLVI by Shakespeare in the case of the former and an excerpt from Viscount Herbert L. Samuel of the latter) have kept this paragraph ("The eye is never satisfied with seeing . . .") pretty much intact. In the long-lasting *High Holiday Prayer Book* (Hartford, 1951), for use in Conservative congregations, Morris Silverman composed free verse highly reminiscent of Wise's piece (the italics are mine):

> Man is frail; his life is short and fleeting,
> Like an aimless cloud that drifts at noonday,
> Like the morning mists that rise and gather,
> Like the grass that sprouts and grows and withers.

With his sweat he daily wrests his morsel,
Wetting down with tears his every portion.
Wind and rain and sun arrayed against him;
Pestilence and war recur to plague him.
Vexed and harassed even from the cradle,
Stumbling, falls, and then resumes his struggle.
Ne'er content his eyes with all their seeing,
Nor his heart with all its endless wishes,
Seeking more and more of wealth and power
'Til at last death comes to overtake him.
Year by year, we see fresh blights of sorrow,
Pyres of blasted hopes that rise to mock us,
Bonds of love and friendship torn and severed,
Homes left desolate, bereft of dear ones.
Yet this sacred hour of cherished memories,
As the past and present merge together,
Is not meant to prove life vain and futile,
Nor to cast us down with hearts despairing.

Even the nontheistic Polydox *Funeral and Memorial Services* by Alvin J. Reines and Anthony D. Holz (Institute of Creative Judaism, 1979, p. 2), reproduces this paragraph by Wise
and ends in a newly-coined *berakhah:*

ברוך מקור החיים מעין ההויה,

אשר בכחו שופעת ושוקעת המציאות.

(Blessed is the source of life, fountain of being, by whose power existence flows and
ebbs.)

23. One of the most complete liturgical manuals from this period associated with
death and mourning is Aaron Wise's *Sefer ha-Ḥayyim. Ritual for Funerals and Prayers in the
House of Mourning and at the Grave* (New York, 1892). Rabbi Wise (1844–1896), then pastor of Temple Rodeph Sholom in New York City and one of the founders of the Jewish
Theological Seminary, was the father of Stephen S. Wise (1874–1949). Even an out-and-
out Reformer like Joseph Krauskopf provided a prayerbook of his own expressly for the
same purpose, *The Mourner's Service* (Philadelphia, 1895).

24. The Plum Street Temple, Wise's premier congregation in Cincinnati, was still
using the longer choral responsory, such as "Verklärt und Hehr erscheinen,"in German as
recently as the first or second decade of the twentieth century, long after the switchover to
English in spoken prose selections. So far as we can determine, that temple has been the
one congregation that has proven loyal to Wise's *Seelenfeier,* rather than to the compromised
conflated version in the *Union Prayer Book* II. Apart from the intrinsic merit of Wise's
perennial Memorial Service, the hold this rite has had on the congregation clearly is a lasting tribute to the man himself. As of 1982 in the booklet containing this service (with a
much improved translation), several new features make their appearance, like the "Parti-

sans' Song," special silent readings for the concluding days of the Festivals when Yizkor is customarily conducted, and *el male rahamim.*

25. For his first volume of *Seder avodah* (Philadelphia, 1951), Max D. Klein placed his Festival Yizkor Service just before the concluding Mourner's Kaddish.

26. Ahawath Chesed ultimately became known as the Central Synagogue. Its handsome edifice on Lexington Avenue has become a historical architectural New York landmark.

27. Avraham Yafeh, *Ha-Mekhuneh.* [designated]. Dr. Huebsch, *Hamesh Megillot im Targum Suri, Ha-Mekhuneh Peshitta* (Prague, 1866).

28. Trans. and ed. David Philipson (Cincinnati, 1901), p. 346.

29. While himself far to the right of his congregation in theology and ritual observance, Alexander Kohut furnished a faithful translation of the German text in Huebsch's Reform prayerbook (*Seder Tefillah le-Rosh ha-Shanah ve-Yom ha-Kippurim, Prayer for Divine Service of the Congregation Ahawath Chesed,* trans. Alexander Kohut, New York, 1889), a rendition that, in a matter of a couple of years, was displaced by an adaptation by Isaac S. Moses that reflected the influence of the then emerging *Union Prayer Book* in language and execution. One might justifiably ask why a traditionalist of Kohut's stripe would have taken it upon himself to translate a Reform prayerbook from German into English. In his account of Kohut's famous polemic/philippic against Kaufmann Kohler's brand of Reform, Barnett A. Elzas conjectured, "It is claimed that Kohut never saw the Prayer Book compiled by his predecessor prior to his arrival in America. Inasmuch, however, as he continued to use it without protest and later even put it in English garb for the use ot his congregation, we must assume that he regarded the *form* of the Prayer Book as non-essential" (Alexander Kohut, *Ethics of the Fathers,* ed. and rev. by Barnett A. Elzas, *with a Memoir and Appreciations by Various Writers,* New York: privately printed, 1920, p. xxxv, footnote). Among the *Tributes to the Memory of Rev. Dr. Alexander Kohut* (New York, 1894, p. 38) is a eulogy delivered by Stephen Wise, then rabbi at the Conservative Congregation B'nai Jeshurun in New York City. In his memorial sermon Wise quotes from the text of Kohut's first sermon at Ahawath Chesed upon his arrival in the United States, in which Kohut expressed his intention to be a "messenger of peace and unity":

> Insbesondere muss ein Rabbiner bemüht sein, stets die Bahnen des Friedens und der Wahrheit zu verfolgen, und ich werde stets bemüht sein, dass sie in mir einen Apostel des Friedens finden werden. Friede und Einigkeit in meiner Gemeinde zu bewahren wird mein stets Bestreben sein.

Wise notes that Kohut kept his word.

30. *Seelenheil.*

31. Cf. the classic Rabbinic phrase *nehenim mi-ziv ha-shekhinah.*

32. The Berlin Reformgemeinde also had a Memorial Service for the one day of Shavuot that it kept, a practice Huebsch's congregation chose not to adopt.

33. Incidentally, Kohut later produced a separate prayerbook, which he entitled *Allon Bakhut* (New York, 1892) for those sitting *shiv'ah.*

34. In the 1873 edition Jastrow shifted the Memorial Service back to the Morning Service *after* the Return of the Torah to the Ark. So, incidentally, did Max D. Klein in *Abodath Israel's* replacement, *Seder Avodah* II (Philadelphia, 1960).

35. Intercession is mentioned in Ta'anit 16a and Sanhedrin 44b. Moving *tehinnot* (Yid.: *tkhines*) by women may be found in *The Merit of Our Mothers: A Bilingual Anthology of Jewish Women's Prayers* (Cincinnati, 1992) in Yiddish, dating back to the seventeenth century; Fanny Neuda, *Hours of Devotion: A Book of Prayers and Meditations,* trans. M. Mayer (N.Y., 1866) from the German; and *Imrey Lev, Meditations and Prayers* (London, 1856), translated and adapted by a Danish Jewish woman, Hester Rothschild, from the French of Mr. J. Ennery.

36. Cf. wording in Seligman Baer, *Toze'ot Ḥayyim,* 2nd ed. (Rodelheim, 1862), p. 161.

37. Joseph Hertz, erstwhile chief rabbi of the British Empire and the famed commentator-editor of *The Pentateuch and Haftorahs* (1929–1936), used Jastrow's "noble version" of Bahya's *barekhi nafshi* for his (Hertz's) *Bachya, the Jewish Thomas à Kempis* (New York, 1898), pp. 19–20.

38. Cf. Merzbacher's handling of *mi she-berakh* on page 148 above; see n. 8.

39. In an overhaul of the Szold-Jastrow Memorial Service in his *Seder avodah* II, all Klein retrieved from the older prayerbook was *kol yisra'el yesh lahem ḥeleq* etc. He presented the Yizkor prayer mostly in the standard Conservative-Reconstructionist, though originally British Orthodox, diction—accompanied by English paraphrases in which God Himself is appealed to on behalf of the dead. He also restored *el male raḥamim,* framed in the plural for all the deceased (concluding, however, with Klein's own

ויהיה חלקם שלום ושלוה עם כל־הצדיקים
והישרים והתמימים שהלכו לעולמם

rather than the familiar וינוחו בשלום על משכבותם

40. *The Service Manual* was copyrighted in 1892, only one year before the first proposed draft of the *Union Prayer Book* by Isaac S. Moses appeared. A bit earlier, in 1888, Krauskopf issued his *Service Ritual* under a somewhat different format—including thirty distinct services (cf. the Berlin Reformgemeinde's nine 'cycles') intended primarily for Sunday morning services.

41. *Ben Sira* seems to have been a favorite of Krauskopf's, as apothegms from that non-canonical work are utilized with some frequency in *The Service Manual.* It was during the same time frame that Solomon Schechter discovered and deciphered portions of the original Hebrew *Ben Sira,* the *Vorlage* of *Ecclesiasticus,* in the Cairo Genizah. Solomon Schechter (in cooperation with Charles Taylor), *The Wisdom of Ben Sira,* Cambridge, 1899.

42. Solomon B. Freehof, *J. Leonard Levy, the Classic Reform Leader: Centennial Tribute,* (Pittsburgh, 1965); Rudolph L. Coffee, "Joseph Leonard Levy," *CCAR Yearbook* XXVIII (1917): 23–43.

43. This attitude also changed. In 1907 Krauskopf created a Sabbath Eve Service for the home before and after dinner. *(Kiddush, The Consecration of the Sabbath Eve at the Family Table,* Philadephia, 1907.)

44. In a biographical sketch and death notice of Leonard Levy before the Central Conference of American Rabbis in 1917, Rudolph Coffee had this to say:

> Some rabbis tried to reconcile traditional Judaism with modern life. Other colleagues held to a more conservative interpretation of the new view, but J. Leonard Levy, soon after coming to America, espoused the radical aspect of the new interpre-

tation. Though no longer believing in Orthodox Judaism, no rabbi spoke more reverently of it. He always said that the saintly lives of his dear parents were the product of that discipline, and he respected, though he could not accept it. He loved the
melodies and teachings of traditional Judaism, but he insisted that they could not
hold the rising generation in America. No Orthodox rabbi pleaded more earnestly
for Sabbath attendance. No minister could have objected more strongly to members
of his Temple keeping their places of business open on Yom Kippur. How deeply he
begged his people to observe the Sabbath eve and omit the New Year's dance, when
December 31 fell on the Sabbath eve. He never introduced Sunday service at the
expense of the Sabbath. He had a message for his people, and preached on Sunday
because people could then hear him. The man was intensely Jewish. Reform
Judaism did not spell convenience to him. It meant service to God through helping
his fellow-man. It spelled daily conduct along the highest ethical lines. [Rudolph L.
Coffee, "Joseph Leonard Levy," *Yearbook of the Central Conference of American Rabbis*
XXVII (1917): 238.]

As for Levy's no less ardent commitment to universalism, his latterday successor to the
pulpit of Congregation Rodeph Shalom in Pittsburgh, Solomon Freehof, remarked in a
centennial tribute:

What he did actually acomplish was this: When he came here, Judaism was still
what it had become through the passing centuries, the honored and beloved doctrine of a small group which maintained it through the generations and to which
they lovingly adhered. Judaism was the property and the preservative of the Jewish
people. What J. Leonard Levy did was to take Judaism, which had been confined to
the life of the Jews, and bring it into the life of the greater community. He made of
it a force in the ethics and in the idealism of the larger world. His achievement was,
therefore, not merely converting a small congregation into a great one; it was taking Judaism out of the backwater and leading it into the main stream of American
life. [Solomon B. Freehof and Vigder W. Kavaler, *J. Leonard Levy: Prophetic Voice*
(Pittsburgh, Rodeph Shalom Congregation, 1970), pp. 20–21.]

45. Krauskopf's *Service Manual* is probably the first American prayerbook to make consistent use of "Why art thou cast down, my soul?" as a major feature of its Memorial Service. Other non-Orthodox prayerbooks of the time did no more than place it in an appendix or a hymnal as one choice among others. When the hymn in its English guise caught
on in American rites, it eventually acquired a certain staying power.

The seven-stanza chorale originated in the *Hamburg Temple Hymnal (1833)*, but the
name of its composer went unrecorded. The full entry on the *Hamburg Temple Hymnal* is
Hamburg Tempelgemeinde, *Allgemeines Israelitisches Gesangbuch* (Hamburg, 1833); and the
hymn in question is on pp. 218–20. In the *Union Hymnal* (1932) the Hamburg *Gesangbuch*
is credited as the source of the German lyrics and the preacher and hymnodist James K.
Gutheim of its English version. However, in the Index to *The Service Manual* Krauskopf
lists an otherwise unidentified "Simms" as the translator. So does Gustav Gottheil (in his
Hymns and Anthems [New York, 1882]), rabbi of Temple Emanu-El, where Gutheim

preached in English during the term of Samuel Alder, Gottheil's predecessor. In his *Otzar ha-Shirah veha-piyyut,* Israel Davidson lists several *piyyutim* that start with the initial Hebrew verse of Psalm 42. One of these liturgical poems is *mah tehemi nafshi,* by Don Tadros ben Yehuda abu-l-'Afiah in his *Gan ha-Meshalim veha-Ḥiddot.* ed. David Yellin, Vol. I (Jerusalem, 1932), p. 65, no. 177. The theme and the drift of the *paytan's* lyric are suggestive of the *Hamburg Temple Hymnal's* own "Seele, was betrübst du dich!" The question we are left with is, Was the latterday hymnographer somehow acquainted with and inspired by the medieval Sephardic versifier?

Be that as it may, from its very inception "Why art thou cast down, my soul?" underwent one shift after another in the selection of its verses and in their arrangement, as with the fourth stanza (which in many an American prayerbook or hymnal often became the closing one):

Hamburg Gesangbuch	Service Manual (Simms)	*UPB* II (1922)
Seele, was betrübst du dich!	Soul, why art thou troubled so?	Why are thou cast down, my soul?
Was ist dir so bang in mir!	Why art thou so sore afraid?	Why disquieted in me?
Riss der Tod dir von dem Herzen	From thy heart has fatal death	Lo, thy dead live on immortal!
Heissgeliebte Wesen ab?	Torn the loved ones thou wouldst save	For God's messenger of love
Sahest du die unter Schmerzen	Sawest thou them, with anguished breath,	Them has guided through death's portal
Sinken in das finstre Grab!	Sink into the gloomy grave?	To the larger life above.
Angst und Noth bannt der Tod.	Death's last blow, Endeth woe;	No more strain, Travail, pain!
Seele, sei getröst im Herrn!	Soul, have comfort in the Lord!	Soul, find comfort sweet in God!
Weine nicht! Denn im Licht	Tears take flight,	For in light,
	For in light	Wondrous bright,
Wandelt die verklärte Schaar,	Walk the host that God adore,	Live the spirits, gone before,
Selig, selig immerdar.	Blessed, blessed evermore.	Blessed, blessed, evermore!

It is interesting to note that over the years the editors of the *Union Prayer Book* underwent a periodic change of heart about the hymn. Whereas the first edition (1894) limited itself to three out of the seven stanzas, the second edition (1922) kept three (the last two, however, having been altered and reordered). The third one (1945) retained only the opening stanza. To modern ears, the hymn no doubt sounds maudlin. Indeed, it has been completely omitted from the last edition of the *Union Prayer Book* II, *Gates of Repentance,* in favor of more Hebrew pieces in which assertions about the world-to-come are not given utterance so unequivocally. As a matter of fact, the vicissitudes of "Seele, was betrübst du dich!" parallel the changing fortunes of the renowned Hamburg Kaddish with its long fashionable *al yisrael ve'al tzaddiqaya* passage, which in recent decades has been gradually and irreversibly dropped in favor of the simpler and briefer traditional Mourners' Kaddish.

"Soul, why art thou cast down?" is really Krauskopf's only textual connection with other known Memorial Services of the time. While Levy did not incorporate this particular hymn, he chose another one that had a moderate, though shorter run among non-Orthodox High Holy Day prayerbooks, a gripping medieval poem introduced by David Einhorn for his *Olath Tamid,* Solomon ibn Gabirol's *shikhehi yegonekh,* in the English translation, "Forget thine anguish, /Vexed heart again!" by the poet Emma Lazarus. Is it more than a coincidence that ibn Gabirol's poem, which early found entry into American Reform rites like *Olath Tamid, Hymns and Anthems, The Service Manual,* and the *Union Prayer Book,* was printed to the full in Hebrew (along with Emma Lazarus' translation) and chanted at a special service of commemoration for the recently deceased Solomon Schechter? Cf. n.15.

46. Moses Mendelssohn, *Phädon oder Ueber die Unsterblichkeit der Seele,* 8th ed., Berlin, 1868; Moses Mendelssohn, *Phaedon; or The Death of Socrates,* trans. Charles Cullen, London, 1789 (reprint 1973).

47. J. Leonard Levy, *Haggadah or Home Service for the Festival of Passover* (Philadelphia, 1896).

48. It was apparently a "revised standard version" of the Kaddish, like the one formulated by the Hamburg *Tempelgemeinde,* and it left some cold in spite of its earlier popularity. Emil G. Hirsch was not alone when he said:

> But what about the "Kaddish?" I know to many this hoary formula is repulsive; and I must say we have made it so. We have given it the meaning of a "prayer for the dead." The origin of the custom to recite this prayer at the grave is unknown to me. It is very old, the treatise "Sopherim" knows of it already, I believe to see its cradle in old legends. Or perhaps—and the fact that the Sephardic version is the one used at the funeral leads me to make the guess—its introduction into the Jewish funeral service is due to non-Jewish influences. But take it by itself, and divest it of its tautology, it voices merely the old Jewish belief in Providence, the assurance of the coming of the messianic times. It is thus spoken in honor of parents, as a grateful acknowledgment of the child's adherence to the religion in which the father reared him. With this understanding, it may not be without inspiration for us, too. [Emil G. Hirsch, *How Shall We Bury Our Dead?* (Chicago, 1883–1895), p.11 (first sermon)].

There was not much one could do by way of corrective measures. For instance, one of the most Anglicizing of prayerbooks, Max Landsberg's *Ritual for Jewish Worship* (Rochester, New York, 1883), retained the Kaddish in its Aramaic-Hebrew entirety, with the Hamburg insert (the paragraph beginning *al yisrael ve'al tzaddiqaya).* Its hold on the average Jew a century ago was too persevering for any drastic changes to be tolerated. However, Krauskopf rewrote the Kaddish as an answer to the type of criticism raised by Hirsch:

KADDISH

Exalted and hallowed be the name of the Lord. Man is of few days, and full of trouble. He cometh forth like a flower, and is cut down; he fleeth as a shadow, and continueth not. All are of dust, and all turn to dust again. There the wicked cease from troubling, and there the weary are at rest. There the fettered are free; there they hear not the voice of the oppressor. The small and the great are there. The dust alone returns to dust; the spirit returns to God, who gave it. In the way of righteousness is life, and in the pathway thereof there is no death.

May the Lord of the Universe grant plenteous peace, and a goodly reward, and grace and mercy, unto Israel, and unto all who have departed from this life. Amen.
 May He who maintains the Harmony of the Universe vouchsafe unto all of us peace for evermore. Amen.

יתגדל ויתקדש שמה רבא:
אדם קצר ימים ושבע רגז
כציץ יצא וימל ויברח כצל
ולא יעמוד: הכל היה מן־
העפר והכל שב אל העפר:
שם רשעים חדלו רגז ושם
ינוחו יגיעי כח: יחד אסירים
שאננו לא שמעו קול נגש
קטן וגדל שם הוא: וישב
העפר אל הארץ כשהיה
והרוח תשוב אל האלהים
אשר נתנה: בארח צדקה
חיים ודרך נתיבה אל־מות:
על ישראל ועל־כל־מן
דאתפסר מן עלמא הדין
יהא להון שלמא רבא
וחולקא טבא לחיי עלמא
דאתי וחסדא ורחמי
מן־קדם מרא שמיא
וארעא. ואמרו אמן:
עשה שלום במרומיו
הוא יעשה שלום עלינו
ואמרו אמן:

Thus the Krauskopf Kaddish opens with the first clause of the traditional Kaddish and then brings in Job 14:L-2; Eccles. 3:20b,c; Job 3:17-19a; Eccles. 12:7; and Prov. 12:28. It concludes with part ot the Hamburg *al yisrael* and *oseh shalom,* but only through *aleynu* and *ve-imeru amen.* In the Preface to his earliest liturgical work, *The Service Ritual,* Krauskopf explains his rationale:

The compiler has taken the liberty of omitting parts of the time-honored *Kaddish,* and of substituting instead such Bible verses as are appropriate to the meaning which the *Kaddish* has acquired in our days, namely a *Prayer of Consolation.* An experience extending over a number of years has proven that appropriate *Introductions to the Kaddish* are a great comfort to mourners, and for that reason they are incorporated in this *Ritual*.

In the Preface to his *Book of Prayer,* Levy, who repatriated the Kaddish, makes his qualification in the following manner:

> The Kaddish [in this prayerbook] has been freely translated, the special object of the author being to make clear that it is a prayer sanctifying the name of God in the hour of trial, a prayer in memory of the dead, *and not a prayer for the repose of the soul of the dead* (emphasis mine).

49. Cf. the High Priest's confession during the *avodah* on behalf of his family and another for his clan.

50. The following excerpt from the Yom Kippur Yizkor Service in the Reconstructionist *High Holiday Prayer Book* (1948) is free of any assertion concerning *olam ha-ba,* either in the classical definition or in its accepted nineteenth-century meaning. Notice, however, how eternal life and infinitude are understood, particularly in the sense of intergenerational continuity:

> No longer can we express by deeds, from which they might benefit, our appreciation of all that they have done for us or meant to us. Only by thinking of their lives as part of Thine eternal life and of their love as part of Thine infinite love can we express our gratitude for the blessings that we enjoyed in our communion with them. Only by shedding love about us as freely as love was bestowed upon us can we discharge the debt we owe them. We are sustained and comforted by the thought that the integrity, generosity and courage they displayed are an enduring blessing which we can bequeath to our descendants. We can still serve our dead by serving Thee, by bringing to fruition those holy purposes and pious intentions which they cherished in life but could not carry to completion. We can show our devotion to them by persevering in the pursuit of those ideals which they acknowledged but which they, being human like ourselves and, like us, subject to weakness, error and sin, could not in their brief lifetime achieve.

In succeeding decades the doctrinal mood of the foregoing prayer insinuated itself into the liturgical works of both the Conservative and Reform movements. Creedal expressions about what happens after death reflect at most the ancient Rabbinic adage, "As for the world to come, no eye has seen what God has prepared for those who wait for Him" (Berakhot 34b).

51. Another Conservative High Holy Day prayerbook to adopt this *av ha-raḥamim* prayer is Ben Zion Bokser's *Ha-Maḥzor* (New York, 1959).

52. Even as early as 1945, the Memorial Service in the second volume of the *Union Prayer Book* showed signs of tempering its former certitude concerning the world to come with a mellow

> O God, who art Master of life and death, we know how limited is our wisdom, how short our vision. One by one the children of men, passing along the road of life, dis-

appear from our view. We know that each of us must walk the same path to the doorway of the grave. We strain our eyes to see what lies beyond the gate, but all is darkness to our mortal sight. Yet even the darkness of death is not too dark for Thee, O God, but the night shineth as the day, the darkness is even as the light. Thou hast created us in Thine image and hast made us share in Thine enduring righteousness. Thou hast put eternity into our hearts, hast implanted within us a vision of life everlasting. This hope we cherish in humility and faith, trusting in Thine endless goodness and Thy wondrous love. Into Thy gracious hands we commit the spirits of our dear ones who are gone from this earth, assured that Thou keepest faith with Thy children in death as in life. Sustain us, O God, that we may meet, with calm serenity, the dark mysteries that lie ahead, knowing that when we walk through the valley of the shadow of death, Thou art with us. Thou art our loving Father, in Thee we put our trust; Thou art the light of our life, our hope in eternity.

Cf. *Gates of Repentance,* pp. 482–83; Bernard Martin, *Prayer in Judaism* (New York, 1968), p. 243.

53. The Harlow maḥzor places it in the *eleh ezkerah* section during the repetition of the *amidah* for *musaf;* the *Gates of Repentance* in a martyrology after the *avodah* within the Afternoon Service; the Reconstructionist *High Holiday Prayer Book,* similarly, right after the *avodah,* seventeen pages in all; and Max D. Klein's *Seder Avodah* II after the scroll has been returned to the ark during *minḥah,* as a counterpoise to the Memorial Service in the morning after the return of the scrolls.

54. The Yizkor Service then and twenty to forty years into this century served, even if no more than on the psychological plane, as a communal-religious means of expiating that guilt. Nowadays a different picture emerges: there is less of a constraint among the third and fourth generations of American Jews to work off any remorse for such an abandonment. Most deceased parents and grandparents are interred on American soil. At any event, the geriatric sector of the Jewish population in the United States has grown exponentially. There is instead increased imputation of guilt in regard to the relative inaction and passivity shown by U.S. Jewry while the Six Million were being brought to their deaths, viz. the special original *al ḥet* litany ("We have sinned against You, and them, by refusing to hear") during the Additional Service in the Harlow maḥzor on pages 580–81.

55. Jack Riemer, ed., *New Prayers for the High Holy Days* (New York, 1971), p. 36; *Gates of Repentance,* pp. 490–91.

8

The American Reform High Holy Day Liturgy: Historical Notes

Both the High Holy Day *Sha'arey Teshuvah, Gates of Repentance* (1978)[1] and its companion commentary, *Sha'arey Binah, Gates of Understanding* (1984),[2] like all of the works in the *Gates* series, represent a watershed in the steady evolution of Reform Jewish worship and a useful gauge by which to measure the extent and depth of its theological and ethnic commitment. The movement's High Holy Day prayerbook may be its clearest statement of that commitment, if only because of the rite's highly concentrated character and religious intensity—which come out equally in the accompanying handbook explaining the prayerbook's layout, text, and rationale.

Doubtless because of the intended audience and limits of space, the editors did not dwell upon the historical vicissitudes of specific prayers in the Reform High Holy Day liturgy. Be that as it may, the details of their development deserve no less than the traditional forms to be reverently and proudly recorded for posterity. The Reform rite in the United States has a rich, variegated background that is waiting to be fully chronicled.

In the following pages I would like to discuss some of the ways in which certain prayers or sections of the liturgy for the *yamim nora'im* came to be as they are and to share some of my own personal reactions to the ways they have been incorporated. In a work on such a scale as the *Sha'arey Binah,* oversights and inaccuracies are amost inevitable.

For example, in note 71 on page 172, there is an error in the sentence, "Unlike the British *Liberal Jewish Prayer Book*[3] and *Gate of Repentance*[4] (p. 29), which place this passage *Meloch al kol ha-olam* in the *Kedushat Hayom* . . . we keep it in its traditional place. . . ." The traditional place happens to be *qedushat ha-yom.* The British Liberal prayerbooks went their own way by putting the passage in question in the *qedushat ha-shem* section instead.

And in note 64 on the previous page, in the emendation introduced by John Rayner and Chaim Stern for their *Petah Teshuvah, Gate of Repentance,* (1973) and subsequently taken over by the American *Gates of Repentance,* the second of the *u-vekhen* paragraphs in the High Holy Day *amidah* —different from all the prior editions of the *Union Prayer Book* II—has not as much to do with "and cause the light of redemption to dawn for all who dwell on earth" as with Rayner's and Stern's restoration of the traditional clause "fill Your land with gladness and Your city with joy." In contrast, a literal translation of the old *Union Prayer Book's* nonparticularist Hebrew rewrite of the traditional text would read something like "joy to all who dwell on earth and the sprouting of [messianic] might for those who proclaim the unity of Your name." Retaining Reform's universalism and leaving out reference to the Davidic Messiah, Rayner and Stern now recall Jerusalem, to a large extent in the language of the classical Maḥzor.

Finally, an opportunity missed: In continuity with the antecedent editions of the *Union Prayer Book* II, the *Gates of Repentance* concludes the daylong Yom Kippur services, after the last blast on the shofar and before *havdalah,*[5] with an apt benediction:

> And now, at the close of this day's service, we implore You, O Lord our
>   God:
> Let the year upon which we have entered be for us, for Israel, and for all
>   the world,
> A year of blessing and prosperity.
> *Amen.*
> A year of salvation and comfort.
> *Amen.*
> A year of peace and contentment, of joy and of spiritual welfare.
> *Amen.*
> A year of virtue and of reverence for God.
> *Amen.*
> A year that finds the hearts of parents united with the hearts of their
>   children.
> *Amen.*
> A year of Your pardon and favor.
> *Amen.*
> *Adonay yishmor tzetekha u-vo'ekha me-attah ve-ad olam.*
> May the Lord bless your going and your coming from this time forth
>   and for ever.
> *Amen.*

It provides the right touch. The benediction is actually an adaptation of the entreaty uttered by the High Priest as he quitted the Holy of Holies on this solemn day—with Psalm 121:8 tacked on. Unused in its proper place during the *avodah* in the *Union Prayer Book*, the 1894 compilers placed it at the end of Yom Kippur services, prefaced by "And now we implore Thee once more, O Lord, our God, at the close of this day's service, in the words of the high-priest of yore: / Let the year . . ." A word of explanation in *Gates of Understanding* II about this transfer would have no doubt evoked interest.

The Kaddish and Related Items

In line with the *Gates of Prayer's* reclamation of the *ḥatzi-qaddish* form and its placement before the *barekhu* in the Evening and Morning Services, *Gates of Repentance* carries on by reinstalling it before the *amidah* during *ne'ilah*.

Although the *Union Prayer Book* has always had a tender hymn on this spot, many a Reform temple reserved the right to have the *ḥatzi qaddish* chanted before the last *amidah* for the day, probably because of its special pleading and moving melody. Decades ago the Union of American Hebrew Congregations produced a recording, *Selected Liturgical Music for the High Holy Days*, in which Cantor Frederick Lechner of New York's Central Synagogue sings this *ḥatzi qaddish*. And in the original Hebrew/German rite[6] prepared by Adolph Huebsch (1830–1884) for this synagogue, the only *ḥatzi qaddish* to appear at all was the one chanted at that time in the service.

Thus both *Gates of Prayer* and *Gates of Repentance* go a long way toward correcting the popular misapprehension (strengthened by the former editions of the *Union Prayer Book*) that the Kaddish is only a prayer for the deceased. My reservation has to do with labeling the *ḥatzi qaddish* in English as the *Reader's Kaddish*, even though it is that, in addition to serving as a pause between one unit of Jewish worship and another. Granted, it is admittedly strange calling it a *Half-Kaddish* (as is commonly done), as if it were somehow worth half a mass or some such thing. The Sephardim have the good judgment to refer to it as *qaddish le'eyla*, which may be a solution to the oddity of using a numerical fraction for the name of a prayer. As for the designation *Reader's Kaddish*, it, strictly speaking, applies to the *qaddish titqabbel* (so called because of the extra paragraph inserted, starting with the word *titkabbel*), also tagged as *qaddish shalem*.

Gates of Repentance is the very first *Union Prayer Book* to actually have a *qaddish shalem,* though it is hard to ascertain why it is reintroduced on Yom Kippur, just before the final Shema. Is it perhaps because people are accustomed to hearing a Kaddish minutes before a service is over? Or is it a way of letting the worshiper know that there is even another category of Kaddish with its specific request that our "divine Parent accept the prayers and supplications" *(titqabbel tzelotehon u-va'utehon . . .)* intoned all this day? It is interesting that the *Union Prayer Book's* principal archetype, Einhorn's *Olath Tamid*[7] had only one other Kaddish of the non-mourning variety, a *qaddish titqabbel* as a kind of hiatus between the Morning and Afternoon Services.[8]

In *Gates of Understanding* II, Lawrence Hoffman sees an affinity between the Kaddish and the Lord's Prayer because both are eschatologically-oriented.[9] Similarly, the late American Sephardic Rabbi David de Sola Pool, in what was originally his doctoral dissertation on the evolution of the Kaddish, declared the *Paternoster* "the twin sister of the Kaddish."[10] I would offer an alternative theory—that the most celebrated prayer credited to Jesus corresponds more closely to the *tefillah qetzarah* or to any of those private prayers composed by Rabbinic Sages for their own personal use.[11] For in addition to looking forward to God's kingdom, the Kaddish, as a doxology, raptly heaps praises on God, which the Lord's Prayer does not. On the other hand, like the Rabbinic *tefillah qetzarah,* the Lord's Prayer does petition God to fulfill one's personal needs ("Give us this day our daily bread").

The Kaddish has been subjected to much tinkering in the past century. As discussed in chapter eight, the radical Joseph Krauskopf (1858–1923) substituted, in Hebrew and in English, biblical verses pertaining more directly to the themes of death and immortality.[12] Interestingly, this drastic liturgical overhaul was to last only during his rabbinic tenure at Keneseth Israel in Philadelphia. But it is remarkable that his Kaddish was the longest Hebrew prayer in his entire exceptional ritual. Incidentally, until little under a decade ago it was not all that unusual to hear in British Reform (as opposed to Liberal) synagogues the Kaddish recited wholly in Hebrew rather than in the traditional Aramaic.[13] Now only the Aramaic Kaddish is recited, and the Hebrew Kaddish, the British Reformers' or Krauskopf's, linguistically faultless as either one was, is no more than a passing curiosity. In the end, after enjoying unwonted staying power in non-Orthodox prayerbooks for nearly two centuries, the innovative paragraph *al yisra'el ve-al tzaddiqaya* (freely paraphrased in the old *Union Prayer Book* as "The departed whom we now remember have entered into the peace of life eternal . . . ") is all but passé. In the *Gates of Prayer* and *Gates of Repentance,* the Mourner's Kaddish is exactly the same as the Orthodox one.

Perspectives on Eternity

Vicissitudes in the Memorial Service on Yom Kippur reflect the changing Jewish views of death and afterdeath. For example, the last stanza of the perdurable *piyyut* sung on Kol Nidrey night, *ya'aleh tahanuneynu* ("Unto You with contrite spirits"), is rendered in the British *Petah Teshuvah* as

> May our supplications find You
> In the quiet of the eve,
> And Your hand with each new morning
> Send us succour and reprieve:
> That Your love and mercy guide us
> When our earthly home we leave.

A comparison of the introductions to the Kaddish in *Gates of Repentance* to either the older *Union Prayer Book* or *Petah Teshuvah* reveals the growing American hesitancy to be all that definitive about life beyond the grave. For example, not a single edition of the *Union Prayer Book* II, including the preliminary 1893 edition, was ever without the calming hymn at the start of *ne'ilah* as a rule immediately before the final *amidah* of the day:

> The sun goes down, the shadows rise,
> The day of God is near its close,
> The glowing orb now homeward flies
> A gentle breeze foretells repose;
> Lord, crown our work before the night;
> In the eve let there be light.
>
> While still in clouds the sun delays,
> Let us soar up, soar to heaven;
> That love may shed its peaceful rays,

New hope unto our souls be given.
O may the parting hour be bright:
In the eve let there be light.
And when our sun of life retreats,
When evening shadows 'round us hover,
Our restless heart no longer beats,
And grave-ward sinks our earthly cover.
We shall behold a glorious sight:
In the eve there shall be light.[14]

The fact that the hymn caught on as it did, even in liberal Conservative rites like Szold's and Jastrow's *Abodath Israel* and its successor, *Seder Avodah* (where the editor Max D. Klein translated the entire hymn into Hebrew, *ha-shemesh yifneh*[15]), points to its deep-seated esthetic, theological, and emotional drawing power. *Gates of Repentance,* on the other hand, presents the final stanza in more tentative hues, attesting American Reform's former certainty about the world-to-come ebbing into a class of pious ambiguity.[16]

And when the end of life draws near,
And darkness threatens to enfold us,
We shall not be dismayed by fear,
Our trust in You will still uphold us.
With You, eternity is bright:
In the evening there shall be light.

Aleynu

Drawing upon his expertise in Rabbinics and Gaonica, Hoffman presents in *Gates of Understanding* II a finely-tuned essay on the origins of the *aleynu.*[17] There is, however, scarcely a word on the prayer's ups and downs in the American Reform rite. Although there are basically three Hebrew versions of the *aleynu* in *Gates of Prayer,* only two of these find their way into *Gates of Repentance.* The missing version, namely the one from *Service of the Heart*[18] and *Petaḥ Teshuvah,* strikes the best balance between particularism and universalism without any of the negative language of the opening lines of the traditional *aleynu.* Since that third version is incongruously

translated in *Gates of Prayer (p.* 620), here is a fairly close, non-sexist translation as it appears in the Rayner/Stern *Siddur Lev Chadash* (1995):

> Let us now praise the Sovereign of the universe and proclaim the
> greatness of its Creator, whose unity it is our mission to make
> known, whose rule it is our task to make effective.
> We bow in awe and thanksgiving before the Supreme Sovereign, the
> Holy One, ever to be praised.

Sound as it is doctrinally and literarily, this emendation really should have
been allowed to stand in the English, along with the Hebrew.

Unlike *Petaḥ Teshuvah, Gates of Repentance* provides an *aleynu* not only at
the conclusion of the service, but also before the triad of shofar blasts and
before the *avodah.* New for a *Union Prayer Book* is the presence in *Gates of
Repentance* of an *aleynu* before the Blowing of the Shofar in the three shofar
sections traditionally found in the *musaf* for Rosh Hashanah. It is probably
not generally known that the time-honored *Union Prayer Book's aleynu* is
happily alive and well in *Gates of Prayer* (p. 617), going back not only to
Isaac M. Wise but also to the unjustly neglected Leo Merzbacher
(1810–56)[19] In their respective rites, the *aleynu* did not always go uncon-
tested. The provisional 1893 edition of the *Union Prayer Book* had for its
regular *aleynu* in English

> It is our duty to render praise and thanksgiving unto the Creator of
> heaven and earth, who delivered us from the darkness of false belief
> and sent to us the light of His truth.

which is based on Szold's and Jastrow's High Holy Day Hebrew *aleynu*

> Aleynu leshabe'aḥ . . . le-yotzer bereshit, she-beranu *li-khevodo, ve-
> hivdilanu min ha-to'im, ve-sam ḥelkenu be-torato, ve-goralenu ba-avodato.
> Va-anaḥnu kor'im . . . .*

The same 1893 edition's *aleynu* on the Hebrew side was the
Merzbacher/Wise formula that was to become ingrained, via translation, in
all subsequent editions of the *Union Prayer Book, Gates of Prayer* included.[20]
But an all-Hebrew *aleynu* in the special 1906 edition reads (alongside the
standard *Union Prayer Book* English version: "Let us adore the ever-living
God . . ."!) as follows:

It is our duty to praise the Lord of all . . . who has assigned our portion in His Torah *(she-sam ḥelqenu be-torato)* and our lot in His service
(ve-goralenu ba-avodato). And we bow . . .
[my translation]

This version is derived from the rite prepared by Adolph Huebsch for his
congregation, the aforementioned Ahawath Chesed. Apparently this same
aleynu was still chanted before the *avodah* at the Central Synagogue at least
until a short while ago. In the recording made by the Union of American
Hebrew Congregations alluded to earlier, the *aleynu* is none other than
that of Huebsch and the 1906 edition of *Union Prayer Book* II*!*

Kneeling

Unfortunately, *Gates of Understanding* II nowhere mentions the practice of
kneeling and prostration during the supreme moment of the *aleynu*—
whether done to launch the triple division of the shofar blasts or to lead
into the *avodah.* Its inclusion in the Szold-Jastrow *Abodath Israel* is not
unexpected, in light of that prayerbook's penchant for traditional forms.
Not only did the officiants kneel, but the congregation was expected to
follow suit, and the same movements and text have held on all the way
through Max D. Klein's left-of-center Conservative *Seder Avodah* II.

Since no instructions have been included, it is hard to verify what the
procedure was in most earlier American Reform rites. Although
Merzbacher's *Order of Prayer* does not stipulate any rubrics, Merzbacher was
responsible for coming up with the term "Adoration" for the *aleynu,* as
well as the term *hishtaḥavayah* (literally, "prostration") for his uncommon
title on the Hebrew side of his prayer text. The question is, for the pre-
avodah aleynu at least, was there actually a *hishtaḥavayah?*

Conversely, David Einhorn could always be counted on to furnish concrete guidelines as to what was to be said or done by whom and when. In
Olath Tamid, Einhorn had the congregation rise for the pre-*avodah aleynu*
quoted above. At the moment of *"va-anaḥnu kore'im,"* the *Vorbeter* (cantor
or reader) solemnly uttered each word one at a time, which the congregation and choir repeated. Ceremoniously as this *aleynu* was handled, kneeling was not indicated. This does not, however, mean that Einhorn, with

his aptitude for the dramatic, passed up the opportunity for liturgical choreography. He removed the *va-anaḥnu kor'im* verse from its *aleynu* matrix and placed it at the end of *ne'ilah,* just before the climactic Shema. Its particular solemnity at this point is undeniable. Einhorn heightened its effect by having the rabbi and then the congregation fall on their knees *(unter Kniebeugung).* For whatever reason, however, his son-in-law and translator, Emil G. Hirsch, decided against reproducing the directive about kneeling in the English version.

The Sounding of the Shofar

One of the prominent features of worship during the High Holy Day season is, of course, the Sounding of the Shofar *(teqi'at shofar)* The traditional Maḥzor has two shofar services, one after the Torah Reading *(teqi'ot meyushav)* and another, a threefold arrangement *(malkhuyot-zikhronot-shofarot,* sometimes referred to as *teqi'ot me'umad or teqi'ata de-rav),* during *musaf.*[21]

In the history of American Jewish liturgical change, the problem of handling the two traditional shofar services has generated some divergent solutions. Wise's *Minhag Amerika* upheld the distinction between the two and kept them in their proper places. However, after a German/English reading and a choral rendition of the quite appropriate, though previously unused in this context, Psalm 98, and a recitation of the two shofar blessings,[22] Wise brings in psalmodic verses *(adonai melekh . . . le-olam va'ed;* I Chronicles 16:15, Psalm 98, and, after the last set of shofar blasts, Psalm 89:16), adumbrating the themes of *malkhuyot-zikhronot-shofarot* in the *musaf* service. The verses were to be sung in Hebrew by the choir and to alternate with the three sets of notes on the shofar thrice-blown. The German instructions for the *Schoferblasen (sic!)* indicate that the choral rendition with an assist from the organ was to synchronize with the reader's summoning *(maqri)* the notes and the *ba'al teqia's* sounding them on the shofar.

In contrast, *Olath Tamid's* treatment of the *teqi'at shofar* startles by its summariness. Einhorn reserves his paraphrastic *malkhuyot* for the *tefillah (amidah)* in his Rosh Hashanah Evening Service (as part of *qedushat ha-yom),* zikhronot for the one in the Morning Service, and *shofarot* after the haftarah and before the sermon, a hymn, and the Return of the Torah to the Ark. His drawn-out forward-looking and universalist paraphrase of *attah nigleyta* (the *shofarot* section) culminates in one *teqi'ah, teru'ah, teqi'ah* on cornet and trumpets *(Horn und Trompetenklang),* and that's that!

To bridge the very dissimilar Wisean and Einhornian treatments, the editors of the provisional 1893 *Union Prayer Book* adopted *Olath Tamid's* distribution of *malkhuyot-zikhronot-shofarot* between the Evening and Morning Services of Rosh Hashanah. They included Wise's fortunate choice of Psalm 98, shortened Einhorn's marathon paraphrastic *shofarot,* and drew the section to a close with Wise's *teqi'ot meyushav* as described above. By the way, all these latter items were placed *after* the Return of the Scroll, even though neither of the introductory shofar blessings appeared and each of Wise's three sets of blasts was here done once rather than the accepted three times. Could it be that the arrangers of the preliminary 1893 text were content with the minimal halakhic requirement (Rosh Hashanah 4:9)? In any event, one of the subsequent editors of the 1894 version found this solution wanting and restored the original sequence of blasts.

Structurally, the British *Petaḥ Teshuvah* followed a different tack altogether in that *teqi'ot meyushav* and *teqi'ot me'ummad,* both trailing behind the Return of the Scroll, are kept. Separating the two are a meditation and *u-netanneh toqef,* the latter only through the climactic "But repentance, prayer and good deeds annul the severity of the judgment." In their resourceful fashion, Rayner and Stern turned the *malkhuyot* division into one extolling the sovereignty of God manifest in creation and reactivated a wonderful *piyyut* by Judah Halevi on precisely this theme, *elohim, el mi amshilekha?* ("O God, to whom shall we compare You?").[23] As for the *shofarot* section, they devoted it to the Redemption yet-to-be-realized, the Kingdom-to-Come. Hence the prayer ordinarily anchored in the *malkhuyot* section, *melokh al qol ha-olam* ("Our God . . . may You rule in glory over all the earth . . ."), is moved, because of its futuristic thrust, to the *shofarot* section. After the final shofar notes are sounded, the hymn "All the World Shall Come to Serve You" is sung, followed by another piece also originally from the traditional *malkhuyot* section, the *aleynu.* This sequence not only offers tighter thematic consistency but also leads to the high point, which also happens to be the concluding portion of the day's worship. Rayner and Stern created a similarly expectant rearrangement for the ending of their transformed *avodah.* Thus the *aleynu* in *Petaḥ Teshuvah* comes at the terminus of the Shofar Service on Rosh Hashanah and of the *avodah* on Yom Kippur instead of conforming to tradition as the preamble to each.

Basically the framework in *Gates of Repentance* is the same as in the first (1894) edition of the *Union Prayer Book,* where the pattern was to coalesce the two traditional blowings into one set of the *teqi'ot me'umad,* somewhat anomalously placed where the *teqi'ot meyushav* used to be. Their placement after the reading of the haftarah remains the same as always, but two new features differentiate this latest maḥzor from its *Union Prayer Book* forerunners: (1) *aleynu* is reintroduced at the beginning of the complex and (2)the classic Hebrew texts for *malkhuyot-zikhronot-shofarot,* slightly curtailed, are added in Service I, and borrowings from *Petaḥ Teshuvah* are added in Service II.[24] Thus the Sounding of the Shofar in *Gates of Repentance* recovers the unequalled majesty of the classical Hebrew texts in Service I and reproduces in large part the fluid prose of Rayner and Stern in Service II.

At first it struck me as curious that whereas the old *Union Prayer Book* adhered to the identical number of blasts for *malkhuyot-zikhronot-shofarot* as in the traditional Ashkenazic Maḥzor in fulfillment of the minimum requirement, *Gates of Repentance,* like *Petaḥ Teshuvah* tripled the number. Then I realized the blasts add up to 30, coinciding exactly with the obligatory *sheloshim kolot* according to the Talmud.[25]

Musaf and Minhah in Gates of Repentance

With *Gates of Repentance,* a full-blown *minḥah* for Yom Kippur is back in place, complete with its Torah Service and *amidah.* From its very inception the *Union Prayer Book* has always had an Afternoon Service for Yom Kippur, including a Torah Reading, but it could not exactly be called a *minḥah* since an *amidah* was lacking (although the temporary 1893 edition was outfitted with the initial Three Benedictions of the *amidah,* the last of which was the *qedushah* ordinarily earmarked for *musaf*). On the other hand, virtually all the precursors of the *Union Prayer Book,* even those that furnished no *musaf* and/or *minḥah* for Sabbaths and Festivals, made a point of accommodating both, especially for the High Holy Days.

The sole exception was David Einhorn's *Olath Tamid.* Einhorn followed his own bent and carved out something that was without equal. For Yom Kippur day he turned out only two *amidot,* one for the Morning Service and another for the Concluding Service, each of them, incidentally, technically complete and untruncated. In between, he deftly fused *musaf* and *minḥah,* bringing in, in conjunction with a quota of Psalms and *piyyutim,* the trademarks of each service—*u-netanneh toqef* (here foreshortened), an *avodah,* and the Torah Reading. Apart from the unexpected relocation of the Memorial Service *within* the Afternoon Service, Einhorn's layout has served as the dominant model for the *Union Prayer Book* II from which the latter did not stray since its premier 1894 edition.

What then distinguishes the current edition from its predecessors are (1) the restoration of a full *minḥah* with its own *amidah* and Torah Service, and (2) the placement of the *avodah* and Martyrology as parts of a synopsis of Jewish history up to its hoped-for eschatological conclusion—a *Heilsgeschichte* in a nutshell, so to speak. The *Union Prayer Book's* inspirational extras, readings in poetry and prose, were put in a section entitled "Additional Prayers"—in place of *musaf*—between the Morning Service and the Afternoon Service. The length of *Gates of Repentance's minḥah* may be attributed to the *avodah* and to a kind of multiform disquisition on the "Meaning of Jewish Existence" based on those readings.

As may be recalled, the traditional *avodah* starts out, in verse and acrostic, with the creation of the world. It proceeds then from the singling out of Abraham and his progeny, Israel, to the election of the Kohanim from the tribe of Levi for their service of atonement. Applying his forceful theology and daring exegetical originality, Einhorn recast the *avodah* as the occasion for explaining—passionately and eloquently—the destiny of the Jewish people as *Priestervolk* to the world:

> Not as a sinner, burdened with the penalty of his iniquity, did Israel go forth into the wider world, but his was the mission of the suffering Messiah. Leaving behind him his old home, the temple and its sacrificial cult, the pomp of the sacerdotal services; giving up the symbolism of the age of his preparation for his larger historic duty; he marched forth to found everywhere temples of a truer worship and a deeper knowledge of God and to lead by his self-sacrificing devotion *all mankind* to the spiritual altar of atonement. He was both priest and sacrifice, sent out like the sacrificial goat in the old ritual into the desert taking the sins of all men upon his own shoulders and *carrying them away.*
>
> [Hirsch's translation]

The fulfillment of the Jewish people's priestly/messianic mission is described in rhapsodic language:

> At last, Thy true sanctuary will arise spanning the wide limits of the earth, and at this, Thy true and only altar, atonement will be wrought not by the sevenfold sprinkling of blood but by the sevenfold rays of Sinai's sun.
>
> [Hirsch's translation]

The *avodah* in all the editions of the *Union Prayer Book* II stuck closely to Einhorn's text and theology—Jewish missiology, one may call it—with minor changes and much of the expansive language toned down.[26] The immediate predecessor of *Petaḥ Teshuvah,* the British *Liberal Jewish Prayer Book* II (1937), placed the *avodah* in its Additional—rather than Afternoon—Service and followed it up with a series of scriptural readings (mostly the "Servant of the Lord" passages in Second Isaiah) under the heading "The Meaning of Jewish History," ending on an affirmative note with a repositioned *aleynu,* Israel Zangwill's stirring translation of *ve-ye'etayu,* "All the World Shall Come to Serve Thee," and future-oriented biblical passages along with entreaties on behalf of the Jewish people and of all humankind.

Rayner and Stern have incorporated Mattuck's *avodah* and its sequel into the new maḥzor with impressive scope, movement, and spirituality. Among other components, the new *avodah,* entitled "From Creation to Redemption," includes the Martyrology, modern poems about the Shoah, allusions to Zion reborn, the Deutero-Isaiah Suffering Servant, and other scriptural passages. The result is a moving story about God's pilgrim people, marching on.

Gates of Repentance's Piyyutim

Hoffman provides a well-grounded summary on the development of the classical *piyyut.*[27] Since its beginnings, the *Union Prayer Book* II held no more than a half-dozen Ashkenazic liturgical poems for its Yom Kippur services, with such perennials as *ya'aleh* and *u-netanneh toqef*—although in its special 1906 edition some additional Ashkenazic lyrical favorites, in Hebrew, were included: the anonymous alphabetic acrostic *attah hu eloheynu* ("Thou art our God in heaven and earth") and Meshullam ben

Kalonymos' *imeru l-elohim* ("Say of God") and *ma'aseh eloheynu* ("Great are the works of our God"), the latter two abbreviated and all three left untranslated.

Gates of Repentance revives a number of Ashkenazic pieces: *omnam ken* ("Yes, it is true," pp. 376–77), *ki hineh ka-ḥomer* ("As a clay in the hand of the potter," pp. 381–82), and *le-el orekh din* ("Now all acclaim You king," pp. 401–2). The fact remains, nonetheless, that most of its *piyyutim* are substantially Sephardic-derived, most of them mediated by the standard-bearer, the Hamburg *Gebetbuch*[28] via its several nineteenth-century American liturgical heirs. They include: *yah shimkha, aromimkha* ("The Lord is Your name," pp. 471–74), and *mi yitteneni* ("O that I might be a servant unto Thee," pp. 395–96) by Spanish Jewry's medieval poet laureate Judah Halevi; and pieces like *malki mi-qedem* ("O Sovereign Source of salvation," pp. 396–98, which is really either Italian or Greek, as Stern informs us), *attah konanta* ("Author of life," pp. 410–11; the acrostic prelude to the *avodah), el nora alilah* ("God of awesome deeds," pp. 508–9), and *be-terem sheḥaqim va-araqim* ("The Lord will reign," p. 510)

The route taken by the acrostic *pitehu lanu sha'arey tzedeq* ("Open for us the gates of righteousness," pp. 517–18), a new revival, is just as oblique. It came by way of the Conservative Rabbinical Assembly's maḥzor, edited by Jules Harlow,[29] ultimately originating in the Sephardic *kaddish titqabel,* spun out specifically for Yom Kippur. A more apt choice could scarcely have been made: the last of a whole string of gates mentioned are *sha'arey teshuvah,* "the gates of repentance"!

Interestingly enough, little under a century ago the independent prayerbook creator, Joseph Krauskopf, finished his Yom Kippur services with this very Sephardic Kaddish insert as a parting benediction:

Minister: *(Facing the Congregation.)*
Te'anu be-raḥamim min ha-shamayim.
May God in mercy hear your prayer;
And answer your supplication.
With the opening of heaven's portals
To receive the earth-sustaining sun
May He also open unto you
The gates of light and of love,
The gates of knowledge and of truth,

The gates of atonement and of mercy,
The gates of help and of support,
The gates of peace and of plenty.
May He remove from your midst
Hatred and strife, envy and discord,
And grant you the noble wishes of your heart,
Now and for evermore. Amen

Choir:
Amen.—Hallelujah.

Conclusion

The foregoing notes on *Gates of Repentance* and *Gates of Understanding* II form only a digressive sketch of how aspects of the American Reform liturgy have taken shape, how internal and external influences have had their play, and how modernity continually interacts with tradition, often in surprisng directions. The more links with our liturgical past we establish, the more discriminating, mature, and lasting are our future efforts in the area of worship likely to be. An only-slightly-varnished mirror of who and where we were and are inwardly, the prayerbook examined in all of its multifarious stages and endless dimensions can illumine our path as we plot our way onward. In a sense, it is very much a *shomer she'erit am qadosh.*

An earlier version of this chapter appeared in the *Journal of Reform Judaism* (Summer 1988):57–74. Reprinted with permission.

1. Chaim Stern, ed., *Gates of Repentance (Sha'arey Teshuvah): The New Union Prayerbook for the Days of Awe* (New York, 1978).

2. Lawrence A. Hoffman, *Gates of Understanding* II *(Sha'arey Binah 2): Appreciating the Days of Awe* (New York, 1984).

3. Israel I. Mattuck, ed., *Liberal Jewish Prayer Book II Services for the Day of Memorial (Rosh Hashanah) and the Day of Atonement* (London, 1937).

4. John D. Rayner and Chaim Stern, eds., *Petaḥ Teshuvah, Gate of Repentance: Services for the High Holydays* (London, 1973). So as not to confuse the British *Gate of Repentance* with the American *Gates of Repentance,* I shall hereafter refer to the former by its Hebrew title, *Petaḥ Teshuvah.*

5. The last two items are later additions, the terminating *teqi'ah gedolah* in the 1922 edition and Havdalah in *Gates of Repentance.*

6. This was when the New York congregation bore its older name, Ahawath Chesed. Adolph Huebsch, ed., *Seder Tefillah le-Rosh ha-Shanah ve-Yom ha-Kippurim, Gebete für die Öffentlichen Gottesdienst der Tempelgemeinde Ahawath Chesed* (New York, 1875).

7. Cf. the *qaddish titkabbel* in the *ne'ilah* service in *Gates of Repentance.*

8. By contrast, Isaac M. Wise's *Minhag Amerika* (Cincinnati, 1857), like Benjamin Szold's and Marcus Jastrow's *Abodath Israel* (Philadelphia, 1873), always had all types of Kaddish, barring the *qaddish de-rabbanan* and the special funeral one, *qaddish ithadata.*

9. *Gates of Understanding* II, p. 47.

10. David de Sola Pool, *The Kaddish* (New York: Union of Sephardic Congregations, 1964), p. viii.

11. Berakhot 16b-17a; cf. Claude G. Montefiore and Herbert Loewe, *A Rabbinic Anthology* (Philadelphia, 1963), pp. 360–63.

12. Joseph Krauskopf, *The Service Manual* (Philadelphia, 1892), p. 38.

13. Ministers of the West London Synagogue, *Seder ha-Tefillot, Forms of Prayer for Jewish Worship* 6th ed. (Oxford, 1931), vol. I, p.10.

14. Although neither *The Hamburg Temple Hymnal* {=Hamburg Templegemeinde, *Allgemeines Israelitisches Gesangbuch}* (Hamburg, 1833) nor any of the works of the prolific hymnographer/liturgist Leopold Stein has the German original, Benjamin Szold's *Abodath Israel* (Baltimore, 1863) does—for all that, betraying no clue as to who wrote it.

15. Max D. Klein, ed., *Seder Avodah: Service Book for Rosh Hashanah and Yom Kippur* (Philadelphia, 1960), p. 808.

16. A more detailed study on the subject of American Jews' changing views regarding life beyond the grave as reflected in the Yizkor Service may be found in chap. 7.

17. *Gates of Understanding* II pp. 42–46.

18. *Siddur Lev Chadash: Services and Prayers for Weekdays and Sabbaths, Festivals, and Various Occasions* (London, 1995). Cf. John D. Rayner and Chaim Stern, ed., *Avodat ha-Lev, Service of The Heart Weekday, Sabbath and Festival Prayers for Home and Synagogue* (London: Union of Liberal and Progressive Synagogues, 5728/1967) p, 364. The Hebrew in each case is the same.

19. Leo Merzbacher, ed., *Seder Tefillah, The Order of Prayer for Divine Service* II, *Prayers for the Day of Atonement* (New York, 1855).

20. The Hebrew of the same was to show up in the *Union Prayer Book* II only for the *aleynu* before the *avodah.* Now of course it materializes in all the *Gates* prayerbooks as one of two or three versions of the Adoration in Hebrew. It is of more than passing interest that Einhorn's pre-*avodah aleynu* left no trace whatsoever in any edition of the *Union Prayer Book* II. Perhaps it was considered too unfamiliar even to be considered, consistent though it may be with Einhorn's theology:

> It is meet for us to worship before the Lord of the universe, to announce the greatness of its Creator who appointed the seed of Abraham to be a blessing unto all the families of the earth. And we bow down . . . [Emil G. Hirsch, trans., David Einhorn's *Olath Tamid, Book of Prayers for Jewish Congregations* (Chicago, 1896)]

21. Max Arzt explains briefly the reasons for the separate services in his *Justice and Mercy: Commentary on the Liturgy of the New Year and the Day of Atonement* (New York, Chicago, and San Francisco, 1963), p. 152. Although the Ashkenazic custom is for all to rise each time the shofar is blown, the Sephardim *sit* during the *teqi'ot meyushav* and stand for the ones during *musaf.*

22. It was not until as late as the 1945 edition that the *berakhot* before the blowing of the shofar were reinstated. The first *berakhah* is revised "Karaitically": *ve-tzivvanu lishmor et yom teru'ah* ("and commanded us to observe the Day of the Blowing of the Shofar"). The *Forms of Prayer* of the West London Synagogue had, for a long time but not now, also in Karaitic style, *ve-tzivvanu lehashmia qol shofar* rather than the Rabbinic *ve-tzivvanu lishmo'a qol shofar.* While the Torah prescribes *sounding* the shofar, the Sages of the Talmud were the ones who made a mitzvah of *listening* to its sounds.

23. Halevi's lofty poem appeared in Huebsch's *Gebete für die Öffentlichen Gottesdienst* as an introduction to the *qedushah* during the *amidah* of the Afternoon Service. The poem's 22nd line has Isaiah 6:3 ("Holy, holy, holy . . . "), the central verse of the *qedushah*. *Petah Teshuvah's* predecessor, the *Liberal Jewish Prayer Book* II(1937) placed the poem before the *barekhu* on Rosh Hashanah morning. The poem in its entirety may be found in Ḥayyim (Jefim) Schirmann, *Ha-Shirah ha-Ivrit bi-Sefarad u-ve-Provence, I* (Jerusalem and Tel Aviv, 1959), pp. 532–36.

24. As might be expected , this is not the first time that the somewhat abridged Hebrew texts of *malkhuyot-zikhronot-shofarot* turn up in the *Union Prayer Book.* In the 1906 edition, the whole fabric of the three blowings crops up in Hebrew with the shofar blessings *after* the close of the *malkhuyot* division. This is the scheme that *Gates of Repentance* — probably unwittingly—takes up again in 1978. *Union Prayer Book* II has always had a felicitous selection of mostly untapped biblical verses in Hebrew. Cf. *Petah Teshuvah's* even more opportune choices repeated in *Gates of Repentance* on pages 210–11, 213–14, and 216.

25. B. Rosh Hashanah 33b and 34b.

26. Compare the long Einhorn-derived penultimate prayer on pages 518–22 in *Gates of Repentance* with his German original, which covers over ten pages! For a discussion of Einhorn's influence on the Reform *avodah,* see chap. 1.

27. *Gates of Understanding* II, p.77.

28. S. J. Fraenkel and M.J. Bresselau, ed., *Seder ha-Avodah, Ordnung der Öffentlichen Andacht für die Sabbath-und Festtage des Ganzen Jahres Nach dem Gebrauche des Neuen-Tempel-Vereins in Hamburg* (Hamburg, 1819).

29. Jules Harlow, ed., *Maḥzor for Rosh Hashanah and Yom Kippur: A Prayer Book for the Days of Awe* (New York, 1973), p. 724.

9

The Maḥzor Twice Recycled:
High Holy Day Liturgy in Great Britain and Israel

Not very long after the appearance of the standard maḥzorim of the North American Conservative and Reform movements in the seventies,[1] the Reform Synagogues of Great Britain (RSGB) and the Movement for Progressive Judaism in Israel (*ha-tenu'ah le-yahadut mitqaddemet be-yisra'el*)[2] issued their respective High Holy Day prayer manuals, *Seder ha-Tefillot, Forms of Prayer for Jewish Worship: Prayers for the High Holydays,* (8th ed., London, 1985), and *Kavvanat ha-Lev* ("Devotion of the Heart") (Jerusalem, 1989). Each is a companion volume to a prayerbook for daily, Sabbath, and Festival use published just under a decade earlier: *Seder ha-Tefillot, Forms of Prayer for Jewish Worship: Daily, Sabbath, and Occasional Prayers,* 7th ed., (1977)[3] and *Ha-Avodah sheba-Lev* ("Service of the Heart"): *Siddur Tefillot li-Ymot ha-Ḥol, le-Shabbatot ule-Mo'adey ha-Shanah* ("Prayerbook for Weekdays, Sabbaths and Holidays") (Jerusalem, 1982).[4]

Both, of course, bear the unmistakeable imprint of the American rites and in general share common features: the constant interweaving of Ashkenazic, Sephardic and other liturgical strands; the use of a full-scale *musaf* where none is usually available for Sabbaths and Festivals; latitude with regard to the liturgical celebration of the second day of Rosh Hashanah; a newly-worded Hebrew Kol Nidrey[5] placed after the customary Aramaic one; the preference for Leviticus 19 and Deuteronomy 29–30 over the traditional lessons for the Torah reading on Yom Kippur;[6] and a full-fledged Memorial Service between the Afternoon and the Concluding Services on Yom Kippur. Nonetheless, *Forms of Prayer* and *Kavvanat ha-Lev* reflect dissimilar liturgical sensibilities—evident in the layout, content, theological orientation, literary quality, and mood of the two maḥzorim.

The Sephardic Influence

The difference in the Sephardic influence, for example, is largely one of degree. Long before the tercentenary of the Expulsion, Israeli society demonstrated a renewed and enthusiastic appreciation of the Sephardic factor in Jewish life, if only because a major segment of its population is of Mediterranean and Middle Eastern descent. Though the Progressive movement was principally begun by immigrants from Central Europe and supported by Jews from the English-speaking countries, now the children of *edot ha-mizraḥ* are making their liturgical presence felt within it. The Spanish-Portuguese influence, though not pervasive, can be detected throughout *Kavvanat ha-Lev* in such paytanic standbys as *ben adam, mah lekha nirdam*[7] during *seliḥot, ḥatanu lefanekha, raḥem aleynu*[8] as a closing hymn for the Evening Service on both Rosh Hashanah and Yom Kippur and elsewhere, and *eloheynu sheba-shamayim*[9] offered as an alternative to *avinu malkenu*.

The Sephardic roots of British Reform liturgy are far deeper and more extensive. The London Reformers who brought the West London Synagogue into existence in the 1840s were predominantly of Sephardic background, and chunks of Sephardic *piyyutim,* including cherished *pizmonim* (sung congregational refrains) from the Rosh Hashanah and Yom Kippur volumes of the original *Forms of Prayer* pervade the present single-volume edition:

Solomon ibn Gabirol's *keter malkhut;*[10] and *elohim eli attah*[11]

Ḥai Gaon's *{shema qoli asher tishma be-qolot . . . } aneh ani shefal kol ha-shefalim*[12]

David ben Baqudah's *ana be-qor'enu*[13]

Sa'adiah Gaon's *anshey emunah avadu*[14] and *be-terem sheḥaqim va-araqim nimtaḥu*[15]

Judah Halevi's *adonay negdekha kol ta'avati,*[16] *mi yitteneni eved elo'ah oseni,*[17] and *yah shema evyonekha*[18]

Solomon ibn Abun's *shofet kol ha-aretz;*[19] *atanu le-ḥallot panekha;*[20] the pre-Avodah *attah konanta olam me-rosh;*[21] *yisra'el avadekha le-fanekha ne'esafim*[22]

Ḥiyya's *lekhu nappil paneynu bi-nefashot ne'enaḥot*

Moses ibn Ezra's *el nora alilah.*[23]

Psalmody

Similarly, the selection of Psalms is far more extensive in the British rite than in the Israeli. Much more than the Ashkenazim, the Sephardim have been in the habit of picking distinct psalms for each of the Jewish holidays, a common practice in the liberal denominations of American Judaism (even, one might add, far more than has been the case on the European continent). *Kavvanat ha-Lev* generally settles, however, for those psalms used in the Ashkenazic *nusah,* notably in the Israeli Progressive rite's much-curtailed psalmodic section of the Morning Service, the *pesuqey de-zimrah.*

There are, to be sure, exceptions:

Ps. 81 for Rosh Hashanah Eve before *barekhu.*

Pss. 23 and 24 offered as admissible meditative options alongside *elohay netzor leshoni* at the end of the *amidah* in the same service.

On the morning of Rosh Hashanah, Ps. 130 figures unobtrusively during the meditation at the end of the *amidah.*

On Atonement Eve and Day, Ps. 130 during personal devotions before Kol Nidrey; Ps. 90 (which does not routinely appear in *Ha-Avodah sheba-Lev,* as it would in the traditional Prayerbook); Pss. 139 and 8 at the beginning of *minhah;* Ps. 130, again, as an option during the individual post-*amidah* meditation; and Ps. 121 to introduce the Concluding Service.

In contrast, there are twice as many Psalms in *Forms of Prayer* and the selection is richer and more sophisticated—no doubt due to British Reform's Sephardic birthright and its long-time biblicist and quasi-Karaizing bent. Figure 1 lists the Psalms in the 1985 edition. Those followed by 'Seph.' indicate those included in conformity with the Sephardic *minhag* and those followed by 'DWM' indicate choices first made by the minister of the West London Synagogue, David Woolf Marks (1811–1910), the first editor of *Forms of Prayer.*

Fig. 1
PSALMS IN FORMS OF PRAYER (HIGH HOLIDAYS)

Selihot *Service*	Pss. 134, 5 (vv.1–4), 39 and 130.
Rosh Hashanah Day	Pss. 103 (DWM) and 81 (DWM) during the *pesuqey de-zimrah.*

Yom Kippur Evening Service

Ps. 103 or Ps. 130 suggested for recitation just before *barekhu.*
(In his day Marks also pressed into service Pss. 38, 15, 39, 86, 85 and 4 [Seph.] during *ma'ariv.*)

Yom Kippur Day
  Birkhot ha-shaḥar

Pss. 103 (Seph.; DWM) and 90 (rather than *pesuqey de-zimrah,* as one might ordinarily expect);

Afternoon Service

Pss. 50 (DWM), 139 (DWM), 84 (Seph.; DWM) and 130 (DWM) in various spots.

Memorial Service

Pss. 121, 91 and 23

Ne'ilah

Ps. 32 (DWM).

Marks added and apportioned throughout the sacred day: Pss. 102 [Seph.], 25 [Seph.], 65 [Seph.], 6, 51 [Seph.] and 141.

The British Reformers were also influenced, as we recall (see chapter five) by the regnant Church of England. As discussed earlier, the *Book of Common Prayer* contains the Book of Psalms in its entirety, and a major portion of the Psalms occupy 77 pages of the 1931 *Forms of Prayer* and 153 pages of the 1977 edition.

Reconstructionist Influences

The Israeli rite borrows a fair number of pieces directly from the Reconstructionist maḥzor, often without acknowledgment[24]—even when sources are otherwise identified.

To specify, the *mi-peney ḥata'enu* proem to the Intermediate Benediction for the *amidah* during the *musaf* on Yom Kippur is superseded by a portion of the ethicized and decultified Reconstructionist version, in almost elegant modern Hebrew idiom, which on the English side of the Reconstructionist maḥzor reads somewhat platitudinously as follows:

> Shall we not feel impelled to devote of our
> substance to the service of God? Shall we not give
> of our store to the relief of suffering, the healing
> of sickness, the dispelling of ignorance and error
> . . . . In the word of Thy prophet: From Zion shall
> go forth the Law, and the word of the Lord from
> Jerusalem. Moreover it is said: The earth shall be
> full of the knowledge of the Lord, as the waters
> cover the sea.

Unlike *Forms of Prayer, Kavvanat ha-Lev* generally shares the Reconstructionist prayerbook's avoidance of the messianic metaphor.[25] For instance, as in the maḥzor edited by Mordecai Kaplan, Eugene Kohn, and Ira Eisenstein (and as in all American Reform versions of the prayer), the Israeli manual passes over the clause

> flourishing horn unto David Thy servant, and a rekindling of the lamp
> of Thine Anointed One, son of Jesse, speedily in our days

in the second of the High Holy Day *amidah*'s *uve-khen* triad.

The same treatment applies to the *ya'aleh ve-yavo* paragraph where "the remembrance of the Messiah son of David, Thy servant" goes wholly unremembered. However, both passages in *Kavvanat ha-Lev* restore Zion and Jerusalem to their full prominence and glow, as, for example, in the climactic *ve-timlokh* where once more we have

> Then Thou wilt reign over all Thy works in *Mount Zion, the abode of*
> *Thy glory, and in Jerusalem, Thy holy city* [italics mine].[26]

The Reconstructionists until now have pointedly dismissed any affirmation or discussion concerning a World-to Come or the postmortem fate of the soul. One vague but significant qualification to this avoidance of anything suggestive of a supernaturalist eschatology is *Kavvanat ha-Lev*'s mildly reworded *elohay neshamah* ("My God, the soul Thou hast given me"), where a doctrine of immortality is articulated: *ve-attah atid littelah mimmenni le-ḥayyey olam* ("and Thou wilt take it from me for life eternal") and where the close reads: *barukh attah, adonay, asher be-yado nefesh kol ḥay ve-ruaḥ kol besar ish* ("Blessed art Thou, O Lord, in whose hand are the souls of all the living and the spirits of all flesh").[27] Further, the editors of *Kavvanat ha-Lev* reproduced, to the letter, the Reconstructionist rite's selection of a meditation by Baḥya ibn Paqudah (really, extracts from his reflective, rueful *baqqashah*), another taken from Rabindranath Tagore's *Gitanjali,* in the tasteful Hebrew translation by David Frishman, and Hillel Zeitlin's immanentist *avi khol ba'esy olam* ("That We Be Reborn").

The core of the English Reform maḥzor is rather removed from the religious naturalism/humanism that bespeaks Reconstructionism.[28] Quite the contrary, *Forms of Prayer* is imbued with the pervasive Western European Jewish tendency to take the theological enterprise with all due seriousness and regard for the One who is at the center of it all. In any event, borrowings from the Reconstructionist liturgy may be found in both maḥzorim—and interestingly, in one case, by a rather circuitous route. *Kavvanat ha-Lev* contains a meditation from Joseph Marcus' flawless Hebrew rendering of the English original from the 1931 *Forms of Prayer* for the Sabbath and the weekday[29] (where its own forced Hebrew rendition of the English prototype falls short). We reproduce here first the 1931 *Forms'* English, then its Hebrew, and finally Marcus' transformed Hebrew:

> We come to Thee, O God, for thy gracious help. Give us strength to bear our load of care; give us clearness of vision, so that we may see the wisdom and the love which have laid it upon us. Help us to be true to our better selves, to discern our real work in life, and to do it with all our might [. . .] Help us to realize life's meaning, to understand its solemnity, so that each day we live may be yet another step leading us nearer to Thee. Amen.

1931

אלהינו עזרנו לשאת את־עולנו. הורנו להכיר
את־אהבתך גם מתוך תוכחתך. חזקנו לשמור על
אורך הגנוז בלבנו ולמצא את־תעודתנו האמתית בחיים:
היה אתנו בהתאמצותנו להתרומם על כל־חלשות
נפשנו ולהתקרב אליך בכל־יום תמיד: אמן:

THE RECONSTRUCTIONIST MARCUS HEBREW

אלהינו באנו אליך לבקש עזרתך. תן־לנו כח לנשא
ולסבל את־על ימינו. תן־לנו לב רואה נכחה להבין כי
בגדל אהבתך וחכמתך שת עלינו כפכה. שגבנו לעלות
במעלות רוחנו להכיר ולדעת את־תעודתנו בחיים ולמלא
אותה באמונה. היה עמנו ועמד לימיננו במלחמות לבנו
עת נשאפה להתגבר על־שגיאותינו ועל־חלשותינו. הורנו
להבחין את־תכלית החיים עלי אצמות. להשיג את־
רוממותם. למען נלך ונקרב אליך יום יום. אמן:

The prayer ultimately turns up in *Kavvanat ha-Lev* in Marcus' reworked Hebrew, without any attribution, just before the Preliminary Benedictions—intriguingly, the very spot for the prayer in the 1931 *Forms of Prayer*. The Reconstructionists had been accustomed to reciting it, or another similar mediation, as the Torah scrolls was returned to the ark, that is, before the singing of *uve-nuḥoh yomar*.

There is one additional Reconstructionist borrowing in the new English maḥzor: each scriptural reading is accompanied by a commentary culled from various Rabbinic, medieval, and modern sources. *Forms of Prayer* excerpts four glosses from those Reconstructionist prefaces for its own enterprising and fresh commentary.

The Conservative Influence

Although in their introduction the editors of *Forms of Prayer* go out of their way to acknowledge their debt to the American Conservative Movement,[30] that influence, like the Reconstructionist, is not that pronounced or profound. Essentially, there are three Conservative trademarks in the British rite:

1) The Precentor's Prayer, *hineni,* preceding the *amidah,* is presented[31] as an alternative to Marks's preferred Sephardic prefatory *atanu le-ḥallot panekha;*

2) *U-netanneh toqef* is emended grammmatically and orthographically, then followed by a transitional passage (*eyn qitzbaḥ li-*

shenotekha) and the grand entrance itself *(aseh le-ma'an shimekha)* to the *qedushah,* precisely as in the Rabbinical Assembly mahor;

3) The High Priest's entreaty at the end of the *avodah* in *Forms of Prayer* is the Ashkenazic formulation verbatim as in the Harlow rite.[32]

In addition, for both the Study Anthology and the Torah and haftarah commentaries, leading Conservative scholars and theologians are quoted extensively for light shed on Scripture, liturgy, ritual practice and doctrine: Max Arzt, Judah Goldin, Solomon Goldman, Julius Greenstone, Jules Harlow, Abraham J. Heschel, Abraham Millgram, Jack Riemer, Solomon Schechter, Harold Schulweiss, and Milton Steinberg. More rarely, apt borrowings from other sources via the Conservative mahzor are reproduced: for example, Leo Baeck's sage aperçu about the Kingdom enfolded in the human decision and deed[33] or Mosheh ha-Kohen Niral's incisive exegesis of the Thirteen Attributes.[34]

Other Conservative influences on *Forms of Prayer* are minor. *Kavannat ha-Lev,* on the other hand, is much more indebted to the movement's mahzor for a sizable portion of its liturgical text, starting with the positively-formulated matutinal *berakhot* ("who made me in His image," "who made me a Jew," and "who made me free") and the brief extracts from the Torah and the Mishnah in the course of the Preliminary Benedictions. (Lev. 19:1, 14–16 instead of the Priestly Benediction [Nu. 6:24ff] and Sanhedrin 4:5 and Yoma 8:9 instead of Peah 1)

The traditional *malkhuyot-zikhronot-shofarot* complex remains fundamentally intact in *Kavvanat ha-Lev.* As in the American Reform rite, however, it lacks its *amidah*-matrix, the First Three and the Last Three Benedictions. For those congregations that want it, nevertheless, a Silent *amidah* for *musaf* is furnished at the end of the volume.

The Israeli mahzor retains the Conservative modification that occurs in the last paragraph of the *shofarot* section. Whereas the Orthodox mahzorim all basically carry this wording (the Hebrew of course remaining uniform in all of them):

> Our God and God of our fathers, sound the great trumpet for our freedom, raise the banner to gather our exiles. Gather our dispersed from among the nations, assemble our scattered people from the ends

of the earth; and lead us to Zion, Thy city, with joyful song, and to Jerusalem, the abode of Thy sanctuary, with everlasting gladness; *and there we will prepare before Thee the offerings that are obligatory upon us as is commanded in Thy Torah through Moses Thy servant by the mouth of Thy glory, as it is said:* "And in the day of your gladness and in your appointed Feasts and in your New Moons you shall blow your trumpets *over your burnt offerings and over the sacrifices of your peace offerings;* and they shall be for you a memorial before your God. I am the Lord, your God" [Nu. 10:10]. For Thou dost deign to hear the sound of the ram's-horn and hearkenest to the trumpet-blast; and there is none like unto Thee. Blessed art Thou, O Lord, who in mercy hearest the sound of the trumpest-blast of Thy people Israel

the Conservatives changed the traditional text in 1972 to omit the lines italicized above, decultifying the prayer but retaining the "Zionist" emphasis. The expunged lines are replaced with

where our forefathers offered their sacrifices of well-being and their burnt offerings. And thus is it written in Your Torah: "On your joyous occasions, your fixed festivals and new moon days, you shall sound the trumpets. . . . They shall be a reminder of you before the Lord your God: I the Lord, am your God."

Kavvanat ha-Lev adopts this qualified version, leaving out, moreover, the citation from Numbers 10:10 entirely.[35]

Each letter of the Hebrew alphabet is used twice to begin the lines of the standard Ashkenazic Confession *al ḥet*. The Harlow rite cuts the prayer in half by using each letter only once, and this version is replicated in *Kavvanat ha-Lev*. In the same quarter of the Atonement liturgy, it also includes the Conservative version of the Thirteen Attributes of God (Ex. 34:6f), prefaced by *el melekh yoshev al kisse raḥamim* and accompanied by Mosheh ha-Kohen Niral's word-for-word exegesis during both *ma'ariv* and *musaf*.[36]

Another Conservative influence is in the Temple Service of the High Priest (*avodah*) in the middle of the *musaf*. Using neither the Ashkenazic *amitz koaḥ* or the Sephardic *attah konanta, Kavvanat ha-Lev*, like the Rabbinical Assembly maḥzor, explains the role and significance of sacrifices today. Afterwards, both provide the mishnaic account (in extracts from Yoma) concerning the Atonement Service in the Sanctuary of old, interspersed with the High Priest's Confession (*ve-khakh hayah omer*) for himself and immediate kin, for his tribe, and for all Israel.

Distinguishing the Israeli adaptation from the American model are 1) a short modern prayer before each pontifical act of confession and absolution ("*titharu!*"), 2) a reversion to the euphonious Sephardic version (with only slight modifications) of the High Priest's *yehi ratzon* prayer, and 3) the admission of a portion from Solomon's dedicatory prayer (I Kings 8:38–43; so as to include Gentiles), a usage that started in David Einhorn's *Olath Tamid* and continued up to the 1945 edition of the *Union Prayer Book II* and *Tokhnit Teqes ha-Tefillah le-Yom Kippur* (1964) for use in the chapel of the Hebrew Union College in Jerusalem. Before the universalizing Solomonic supplication, *Kavvanat ha-Lev* has this newly-composed plea in Hebrew. The translation that follows is mine:

אלהינו ואלהי אבותינו: עיני כל עמך ישראל תלויות בך היום
לבקש רחמיך וסליחתך. רוח נביאי ישראל מפעמת בתוכנו
עד היום הזה, להיות לך לעבדים ואור לגוים. וכשם שקדש
את היכלך שלמה בן־דוד עבדך ביום חנכתו, בתפלה על כל
באי־עולמך, כן נקדיש את מעשינו בימים הבאים עלינו,
לעשות ביתך בית־תפלה לכל העמים.

Our God and the God of our fathers, the eyes of all Thy people are turned to Thee today to seek Thy compassion and forgiveness. The spirit of Israel's prophets impels us to this day to be Thy servants and a light unto the nations. Just as David's son Solomon consecrated Thy sanctuary on the day of its dedication with a prayer for all humanity, so do we dedicate our deeds in the days to come to making Thy house a house of prayer for all peoples.

The familiar story of Rabban Yohanan ben Zakkai's consoling suggestion as to a substitutionary means of atonement,[37] quoted in the Harlow mahzor and repeated in *Kavvanat ha-Lev*, commands attention as the yearly symbolic reenactment of the *avodah* draws to a close.

The next major division of *Kavvanat ha-Lev* to bear the unmistakable imprint of the Conservative liturgy of the 1970s is the Martyrology, fused in the Israeli prayerbook with the Memorial Service. Borrowed from the Conservative *ellah ezkerah* are the 1) stories of Rabbi Akiba's and Rabbi Hanina ben Teradyon's martyrdoms, 2) Hayyim Nahman Bialik's "City of

Slaughter," and 3) Hillel Bavli's "Letter of the Ninety-Three Maidens" (which appeared for the first time liturgically in the martyrological section of the Reconstructionist 1948 Yom Kippur volume).

The Israeli Progressive ritual then brings in poems by Israelis such as Yosef Rakover, Shin Shalom, Avraham Shlonsky, and Ḥayyim Guri—as well as by Archibald MacLeish (in arresting Hebrew translation) as proxy for Anthony Hecht, Soma Morgenstern, and Nelly Sachs, which in the Harlow maḥzor are untranslated into Hebrew. There are also prose pieces by Anne Frank and Abba Kovner, a newly-coined Yizkor for Israel's fallen, two Conservative/Reconstructionist Yizkor prayers for parent, spouse, child and sibling with several additional phrases inserted, one of them being the typically Sephardic expression "May his/her righteousness go before him/her."

Gender Sensitivity

Although the literary contributions of Jewish women command more space in *Forms of Prayer* and *Kavvanat ha-Lev* than in any of standard prayerbooks issued before them, both maḥzorim are somewhat inconsistent in their approaches to gender neutrality. The Israeli *minhag* provides an alternative version of the opening *avot* section of the *amidah* for those Progressive congregations preferring the adjustment. The new variant mentions the four biblical Matriarchs as well as the three Patriarchs and broadens the terminating eulogy (*ḥatimah*) accordingly: *barukh attah, adonay, magen avraham u-foqed sarah*. Oddly enough, this is the only liturgical section in *Kavvanat ha-Lev* made completely gender-inclusive, apart from an unusual and unexampled litany addressed to the Shekhinah (God's indwelling, feminine aspect) with which a congregation might opt at one time or another to replace the established *avinu malkenu* or its Sephardic opposite, *eloheynu sheba-shamayim*. Here is the feminized, indeed maternal, litany, as it appears in *Kavvanat ha-Lev*, followed by my translation:

שכינה מקור חיינו

שכינה מקור חיינו – שמעי קולנו חוסי ורחמי עלינו.

שכינה מקור חיינו – זכרי כי בניך ובנותיך אנחנו.

שכינה מקור חיינו – חנכי אותנו להכיר במגבלותינו.

שכינה מקור חיינו – הדריכי אותנו בדרכי נעם.

שכינה מקור חיינו – למדי אותנו רחמים וצדקה.
שכינה מקור חיינו – עשי למען הנאבקים לשלום
ולצדק.
שכינה מקור חיינו – הפכי אבלנו לששון ויגוננו
לשמחה.
שכינה מקור חיינו – ברכי אדמתנו וכל מעשה ידינו.
שכינה מקור חיינו – קבצי בניך מארבע כנפות הארץ
לגבולם.
שכינה מקור חיינו –השלימי בנין ירושלים עיר
קדשנו.

Shekhinah, Source of our lives—hear (*shim'i*) our voice, have pity and have compassion upon us.

Shekhinah, Source of our lives—remember *(zikhri)* that we are Your sons and daughters.

Shekhinah, Source of our lives—train (*ḥannekhi*) us to recognize our limitations.

Shekhinah, Source of our lives—guide (*hadrikhi*) us in the ways of pleasantness.

Shekhinah, Source of our lives—teach (*lammedi*) us compassion and righteousness.

Shekhinah, Source of our lives—act (*asi*) on behalf of those struggling for peace and justice.

Shekhinah, Source of our lives—turn (*hifekhi*) our mourning to joy and our sorrow to gladness.

Shekhinah, Source of our lives—bless (*barekhi*) our soil and all the work of our hands.

Shekhinah, Source of our lives—gather (*qabbetzi*) Your children from the four corners of the earth to their borders.

Shekhinah, Source of our lives—consummate (*hashlimi*) the building of Jerusalem, our holy city.

As one would expect, *Kavvanat ha-Lev* also includes literary artifacts of Rachel (1890–1931), Zelda (1914–1984), and Ḥannah Senesh (1921–1944). The first Senesh excerpt below is handled as an exordium to the Mourner's Kaddish. (The English translation is borrowed from the close of *Forms of Prayer's* Yom Kippur Additional Service, where it serves, in a similar context, as a kind of postlude to an updated, much-expanded Martyrology.)

> There are stars whose light reaches the earth only after they them-selves have disintegrated and are no more.
>
> And there are men whose shining memory lights the world after they have passed from it.
>
> These lights that shine in the darkest night are those that illumine for us the path.

A second Senesh selection, disarmingly artless as it is, is from her diary. It is situated in that part of the *amidah* for *minḥah* reserved for private devo-tions ("*batar tzelota*"—*hityaḥadut shele-aḥar tefillat ha-amidah* ["After the Prayer"—Personal Communion after the *amidah*]):

> I always opposed religious forms devoid of content and sought gen-uine content, the pure morality that expresses itself in action. Obvi-ously I only sought and did not always find my way. But at least I tried. To pray according to routine I couldn't, and even today I can't and I don't want to. But man's conversation with his Creator about which the prophet preached I myself have found. I am searching for the inner and immediate connection, even if amid struggles and doubts. However, I will not make peace with an accepted dead rigid form of thought which is removed from me.

Withal, the all Hebrew High Holy Day volume willy-nilly remains textual-ly masculine. At the same time, the British maḥzor's selection of pieces com-posed by women is a good bit ampler, worldlier, and more challenging than that in *Kavvanat ha-Lev* —or in any other official *minhag,* for that matter.[38]

For example, the *seliḥot* Service incorporates women's insights as well as men's in two of the six inner-oriented passages : "God help me!" by Malka Heifetz Tussman and *ha-tishma qoli?* by Rachel. In addition, the litany *mi she-anah . . . hu ya'anenu* ("May He who answered Abraham [Isaac, Moses, Jonah, etc.] answer us!") is extended to include the likes of "Hannah at Shilo" and "Anne Frank who conquered hatred." Similarly, the readings in the Study Anthology section (pp. 710–12), offer three in a row by women, two of them German emigrees (a psychotherapist and a psychoanalyst) and one a philosopher and mystic (Simone Weil). All revolve around the vexed subject of prejudice and confront the individual conscience boldly and cut-tingly; and the British editors display rare sensitivity to true religiosity and the real meaning of the forgiving spirit mandated by the High Holy Days in their inclusion of the words of Mathilde Rathenau, who expressed compassion for the mother of her son Walter's assassin:

> In grief unspeakable, I give you my hand. You are the most pitiable of women; tell your son I forgive him in the name and spirit of the man he murdered; I forgive, even as God may forgive, if before an earthly judge he makes a full confession of his guilt, and before a Heavenly One he repents.

Innovation in Kavvanat ha-Lev

The Progressive prayerbook from Zion has a certain vibrancy exceptional in a siddur or maḥzor—owing doubtlessly to its creators being altogether at home in the Hebrew language and its literature across the millennia. Quo-tations from the Talmud, the Midrash and, strikingly enough, the Dead Sea Scrolls—all in the original Hebrew—are interspersed with moving poetic expressions of contemporary thought both from Israel and abroad. Like *Forms of Prayer,* it begins several of its services with readings. For instance, before the Yom Kippur *musaf* it presents a self-abnegating prayer by R. Naḥman of Bratslav; a saying by R. Mendel of Kotzk; an extract from Her-mann Cohen's famous essay on reconciliation; and trenchant verses from *The Manual of Discipline* 3 on how atonement is achieved.

The following are my translations of the two Hasidic pieces before the preludial *hineni:*

> Sovereign of the universe, Lord of peace, make me worthy of being truly a person of peace, that I merit becoming a lover and pursuer of peace always and wholeheartedly, that I never support controversy, even against those that disagree with me and those that rise up against me and try, Heaven forfend, to undermine me, and do to me what they do. May the Merciful One preserve me.

> Enable me not to be like them by doing to them what they do to me. On the contrary, may I judge them favorably and do for them all

manner of goodness. Be my help as I take great care not to shame or mock my friends or anyone in the world, even those who mock and shame me, even more so those who do not cause me shame. O Lord, guard and prevent me each time from embarrassing anyone in the world, small or great, intentionally and unwittingly, coercedly and willingly, because I have been caught thus [myself] several times.

R. Nahman of Bratslav

Why does the Creator seek sacrifices from humans and none from the angels? Is not the angelic deed purer than the human deed? It is not so much the deed the Lord seeks from us as much as the preparation. The holy angel can perform the deed, but cannot prepare itself. The preparation is a human concern: we are hampered by barriers which we must first overcome and free ourselves. This is the greatness of the human being.

R. Menahem Mendel of Kotzk[39]

Ze'ev Falk's sobering takeoff/gloss on the Kol Nidrey prayer, *Kol Nidrey sefateynu* is included in the Atonement Evening Service in the Rabbinical Assembly mahzor, where it is placed between *shema qolenu* and the verses beginning *al ta'azevenu ve-al titteshenu* (in Stanley Schachter's translation). Falk's poem shows up in *Kavvanat ha-Lev* as one meditational passage between the donning of the tallit and the chanting of Kol Nidrey, and another mimetic reinterpretation of the Aramaic formula by Mordechai Rotem serves as the subject for a post-*amidah* silent devotion. Both are reproduced below for comparison (the Rotem translation mine):

All the vows on our lips,
the burdens in our hearts,
the pent-up regrets about
which we brooded and spoke
through prayers without end on last Atonement Day
did not change our way of life,
did not bring deliverance
in the year that has gone.
From mountain peaks of fervor
we fell to common ways
at the close of the fast.

Will You hear our regret?
Will You open our prison,
release us from shackles of habit?
Will You accept our prayers,
forgive our wrongs,
though we sin again and again?

In moments of weakness
we do not remember
promises of Atonement Day.
Recall that we easily forget,
take only our heart's intent.
Forgive us, pardon us.

Ze'ev Falk

All the dreams, all the strivings, all the aspirations and hopes we have hoped, striven for, aspired to and hoped for from last Yom Kippur up to this Yom Kippur may they be firm and binding, may they gush, rise, triumph in our hearts even until next Yom Kippur. Let our dreams not be in vain, our strivings and our hopes not fail, until we merit turning them into a reality.

Mordechai Rotem

A similar type of adaptation is Rotem's rewording of the *avinu malkenu* litany into a series of intentionally blunt, but resultantly bland, questions and a summary petition:

Our Father, our King, light up for us the course of our lives.
Our Father, our King, how shall we have the strength not to get into a rut?
Our Father, our King, how shall we understand the purpose of our existence?
Our Father, our King, how shall we learn not to lead pointless lives?
Our Father, our King, how shall we emerge from our apathy?
Our Father, our King, how shall we distinguish between truth and falsehood?
Our Father, our King, how shall we find answers to our questions?
Our Father, our King, how shall we muster the strength to search for answers?

Our Father, our King, graciously answer us, fortify and embolden us,
   for in You and with You are the answers.

This unique recitation is treated in *Kavvanat ha-Lev* as one more alternative litany to the customary *avinu malkenu,* in addition to the Sephardic *eloheynu sheba-shamayim* and the feminist *shekhinah, meqor ḥayyenu* ("Shekhinah, Source of our lives"), quoted above.

Another innovation in the Israeli Progressive maḥzor is a guide
to observance of an old predominantly-Sephardic practice at dinner
on Rosh Hashanah Eve. The practice involves preceding the meal
with foods chosen for their symbolic value—dates, apple dipped in
honey, pomegranates, pumpkin or gourd, leek, beetroot, and sheep or
fish head.[40] Each item is to be eaten accompanied by a blessing and a
yehi ratzon entreaty, each of which entails wordplay of some kind.
For instance, the *yehi ratzon* for beetroot (*seleq*) reads: "May it be Thy
will, O Lord, our God and God of our fathers, that our enemies, our foes
and those seeking our harm be removed (*yistallequ*)"; while the one for
the fish head has "May it be Thy will, O Lord . . . that we be the head
and not the tail: 'The LORD will make thee the head and not the tail'
[Deut. 28:13]."

One might be taken aback finding in a non-Orthodox rite invidious
comparisons so overtly made between "us" and "them," even if only
metaphorically or semi-facetiously. In fact, the English, German, French,
Dutch, and American Sephardic High Holy Day *tefillot* edited by David
Levi, D. A. de Sola, Isaac Leeser, and Moses Gaster without exception
entirely omit this *seder leyl rosh ha-shanah* with its culinary tokens. Even
David de Sola Pool in his *Tefillot le-Rosh ha-Shanah*[41] tones down in his
translation the harsh negativity of the Hebrew text while playing up the
puns to the hilt: "As we bite the beet, may those who in the past have
beaten us or sought our harm beat to cover in the coming year."

Innovations in Forms of Prayer

Although both maḥzorim display creativity in the incorportion of widely
diverse materials, *Forms of Prayer's* innovations are exceptional and clearly
reflect British Reform's long-standing command of biblical scholarship, its

far-ranging and ongoing theological sophistication and European sensibility, and its rootedness in a century and a half of liturgical reform in Great Britain.

One new feature is "A Calendar of Repentance for the Month of Elul," which consists of a single Hebrew verse or phrase from either the Bible or the Jewish liturgy and a reading from a variety of Jewish sources, from Yoma and Maimonides to theologian and halakhist Eliezer Berkovits and *samizdat* poet Yuli Daniel. Appearing in the pages between the New Year Additional Service and the Atonement Evening Service, this *lectio divina* for each day of the month prior to Rosh Hashanah picks up again for each of the Ten Days of Penitence.

One model for the calendar is perhaps the various Protestant daily meditation manuals[42] with their scheme of a verse, usually scriptural in origin, followed by an excerpt of spiritual instruction and/or uplift by a saint, a divine, a religious thinker, or devout lay person. Even more likely, the calendar is modeled on the traditional Sephardic usage of *selihot* before the Morning Service from the second day of Elul until the day before Yom Kippur, a total of forty days.

Procedurally, of course, there are notable differences between the traditional and the English Reform practices. The Sephardic rubric specifies that *selihot* be said with a minyan prior to the mandatory morning prayers. In contrast, the British Reform rite suggests that the passages for study "can be used for private meditation, and they can also be inserted into the daily services." There are even special ones for the Sabbaths during Elul. In any case, the passages are to be preceded by the *berakhah* "who commands us to devote ourselves to the study of His teaching" (*ve-tzivvanu la-asoq be-divrey torah*).

Further, the editors of *Forms of Prayer* took liberties with the *piyyutim* that the Sephardic founders of the West London Synagogue would never have done, loath as they were to break up a classical prayer by interposing poetic compositions, or *qerovot*.[43] Specifically, *Forms of Prayer* transplants in the *yotzer* section for Shabbat Shuvah clauses from Solomon ibn Gabirol's "Royal Crown"—his *nifla'im ma'asekha*—and resurrects *az be-yom kippur*[44] from the Ashkenazic rite for the same section on Yom Kippur. One can speculate how Sa'adiah Gaon, who ostensibly opposed on principle admitting extracurricular verse into the prescriptive liturgical framework, would have felt upon seeing a substantial portion of his grand *magen u-mehayyeh*[45] annexed to a much-trimmed *nishmat kol hay* before *ha-el be-ta'atzumot uzzekha*.

Other noteworthy textual innovations in *Forms of Prayer* include a personalized *vidduy* attached to the (historically) Silent *amidah.* In the mostly English Confession it periodically inserts the traditional Hebrew refrain *ve-al kullam, eloaḥ seliḥot, selaḥ lanu, meḥal lanu, kapper lanu.* The "public" *vidduy* remains the consuetudinary Hebrew *al ḥet,* with the verses realigned somewhat topically rather than alphabetically.

The following is an example of the personal confession for the Atonement Evening Service:

> For the sin which we committed against You, through evading and
>   avoiding,
> because we could not face the truth.
> For our flight into hypocrisy and deception because we did not dare to
>   speak it.
> For the facts we dissembled, and all we glossed over, for the excuses we
>   made.
> *ve-al kullam . . .*
> For feeding our bodies and starving our souls.
> For interfering with the souls of others, and neglecting their needs.
> For shifting our responsibilities, for reproaches and recriminations.
> *ve-al kullam . . .*
> For our foolishness, our folly and false standards
> For seeing these things only in others, never in ourselves.
> For our complacency which blinds us, and our selfrighteousness which
>   lessens us.
> *ve-al kullam . . .*
> For calculating kindness and measuring out pity.
> For charity that is cold, and prayers without feeling.
> For sending in accounts for love.
> *ve-al kullam . . .*
> For the appeals that we ignored, and the people whom we refused.
> For the affection which died, and our love that became bitter.
> For the visions which faded, the ideals we neglected, and the opportuni-
>   ties we lost.
> *ve-al kullam . . .*
> For the fear of change and renewal, and our unbelief.
> For saying our prayers aloud, but refusing to listen.
> For being our own worst enemy.
> *ve-al kullam . . .*

Deserving of note are several prayers in much the same vein by co-editor Lionel Blue. Dispersed throughout the prayerbook, they are remarkably frank, direct and—when not coy—poignant, like this one at the start of the *seliḥot* section during *ne'ilah:*

Lord, I do not want to pester or repeat again or chant my list of sins once more. You knew the list before this day began. I recited them more for myself than for You. In fact, You know those which are still unknown to me, sins which I hid from myself or was too stupid to see.

I confess that I have been responsible for much that went wrong. I tried to get more out of life than I was willing to put into it. I never learned to ask the right question. I did not say, "What can I give life?" but "What can life give me?" Perhaps I cheated others. I certainly cheated myself of many things I could have had—friendship, love and self-respect.

I confess that a lot of my troubles came because I did not want to know the truths about myself or my life. I tried to buy what cannot be bought. I looked for permanence in passing things. I followed the crowd because I did not have the courage to stand alone.

And I also confess that I let my knowledge of You fade away. Many hopes and visions died because I did not trust them, though they were the signs of Your presence in my life. I have stumbled through so many prayers today, and uttered so many words that I have lost touch with much of their meaning. I am bewildered by their certainties and their demands. Let this confession at least be true and my own prayer.

For I confess that many confessions I made were not quite true. I blamed myself for the wrong things. I mentioned my failings but not my sins. I tried to pretend I was someone else, not the person You created.

I am too small to reach You and You are too great for me to comprehend. Therefore I shall try to be still, and in the stillness wait patiently for You to find me. You are so great, You can bend down to me, and the distance between us which my mind could not cover, Your love can bridge.

Forgive me, pardon me, and grant me atonement.

Finally, the overall plan of the English maḥzor is worth noting. Each service over the twenty-four hour period of Yom Kippur has its own particular emphasis.[46] The midpoint and climax of the five services is the *musaf,*
dwelling on the atoning and expurgatory effect of the *avodah* in ancient
times and, for the duration of a quadri-millennial Jewish existence, of martyrdom. The two services before the *musaf* serve as its preparatory stages,
while those following it gradually brace and guide the worshiping community back into the real world. As an example, the Atonement Afternoon Service brings home, especially through the *seliḥot* section and some
gripping literary excerpts, the necessity and solemn task of guarding and
nurturing the earth.

In light of the foregoing, there is little doubt that the British Reformers
have shown extraordinary resourcefulness and imagination in their reap-
propriation of a wide range of modern Jewish literary and theological creations into the Jewish liturgical tradition. While they may occasionally
borrow, they obviously neither imitate nor mimic.

A Few Drawbacks

Both the Israeli and the British liturgical creators are to be lauded for their
freshness and profound spirituality. This is not to say that there are no
flaws in *Kavvanat ha-Lev* and *Forms of Prayer.* A few of the shortcomings of
Ha-Avodah sheba-Lev, the earlier weekday/Sabbath/Festival companion volume of *Kavvanat ha-Lev,* have already been mentioned elsewhere,[47] and as
documented above, the central weakness of the Israeli maḥzor is perhaps
its overweening dependency on the American maḥzorim. Even with its
many wonderful novel touches here and there, it is hard to escape the
impression of a certain derivativeness.

As for the maḥzor from England, we merely spotlight a sampling of its
slight incongruities.[48] A string of biblical quotes will, curiously, be given a
source only for the last citation (pp. 422–25) or none at all (p. 650). Or we
are not told the derivation of more than one passage (p. 410). The method
of transliteration is inconsistent and irksome: the *khaf* yields an 'h' for
meḥilta, a 'ch' for *tashlich* and a 'kh' for *zikhronot.* "Shemoneh esray" may be
popular these days, but hardly accurate. Occasionally prayer units are trun-
cated or left dangling, like *el melekh yoshev* (missing its culminating—and

pivotal—absolution *ve-salaḥta la-avonenu ule-ḥatatenu u-neḥaltanu* ("Pardon Thou our iniquity and our sin, and take us for Thy heritage") or *shema qolenu* inexplicably abbreviated to two verses (p. 654).

But we quibble. The British Reform Movement, a minority within a beleaguered minority in the British Isles, took on a monumental assignment, gave its adherents an unparalleled syllabus for the spiritual life, bore abundant literary fruit, and set a shining example for Jewish liturgy for a long time to come. And the publication of *Kavvanat ha-Lev* marks a proud coming of age for the stalwart members of Israel's Movement for Progressive Judaism.

1. Jules Harlow, ed., *Maḥzor for Rosh Hashanah and Yom Kippur: A Prayer Book for the Days of Awe* (New York, 1972) [Conservative]; Chaim Stern, ed., *Sha'arey Teshuvah, Gates of Repentance: The New Union Prayer Book for the Days of Awe* (New York, 5738/1978) [Reform].

2. For an introduction to the British and Israeli varieties of Progressive Judaism, see David Geffen, *Har-El Jerusalem, A Vision Comes True: The First Thirty Years 1958–1988;* Izzy Mann, *Har-El Yerushalayim, Me-Ḥazon li-Metzi'ut: Sheloshim ha-Shanim ha-Rishonot 1958–1988* (Jerusalem; Dov Marmur, *Reform Judaism: Essays on Reform Judaism in Britain* (Oxford, 1973); and Michael A. Meyer, *Response to Modernity: A History of the Reform Movement in Judaism* (New York and Oxford, 1988), chaps. 4 and 10.

3. Lionel Blue, "The Background to the New Prayer Book" in Marmur, ibid., pp. 181–88; Eric L. Friedland, "Seder ha-Tefillot: Forms of Prayer for Jewish Worship" (review) in *Journal of Reform Judaism* (Fall 1978), pp. 91–93; Jonathan Magonet, "The New Reform Prayer Book" Judaism in Our Time pamphlet series (n.d.); Jakob J. Petuchowski, *Prayerbook Reform in Europe: The Liturgy of European Liberal and Reform Judaism* (New York, Ltd., 1968), pp. 66–70 and 140–41; see also chap. 12 above.

4. "A Rite from Zion," chap. 12 above; Yehoram Mazor, *Ha-Avodah sheba-Lev: Siddur le-Yahadut Mitqaddemet be-Yisrael: He'arot ve-Ha'arot* (Jerusalem, 5751 [1991]).

5. Both rites simultaneously use the version of Kol Nidrey in the 1904 edition of the Hamburg Temple *Gebetbuch* (Petuchowski, ibid., pp. 345–46).

6. Cf. *Seder Tefillot Yisrael, The Union Prayer Book for Jewish Worship II* (1945).

7. Cf. David de Sola Pool, ed., *Tefillot le-Rosh ha-Shanah, Prayers for the New Year according to the Custom of the Spanish and Portuguese Jews* (New York, 1937 [1985]), p. 1. For a closer look at the Sephardic hold on the non-Orthodox American siddurim, see chap. 13 above; and for an analysis of an indigenously lay-created, Sephardic-based ritual from the 1830s, *The Sabbath Service and Miscellaneous Prayers of the Reformed Society of Israelites* [of Charleston, South Carolina], see Eric L. Friedland, *The Historical and Theological Development of Non-Orthodox Jewish Prayerbooks in the United States* (Ann Arbor, Michigan, 1967), chap. 1, and a paper delivered at a conference of the National Association of Professors of

Hebrew, March 24–25, 1974 in Cincinnati, and published as "The Sabbath Service and Miscellaneous Prayers of the Reformed Society of Israelites," *Hebrew Abstracts* XV (1974), pp. 130–32.

8. Cf. David de Sola Pool, ed., *Tefillot le-Yom Kippur, Prayers for the Day of Atonement according to the Custom of the Spanish and Portuquese Jews* (New York, 1939 [1984]), pp. 185–86. It was pointed out to the author that certain Sephardic hymns like this one have gained popularity in Israel by being heard on radio and television.

9. Cf. Pool, *Tefillot le-Yom Kippur,* pp. 189–92.

10. Ibid., pp. 333a-34.

11. Ibid., pp. 129–31.

12. Ibid., pp. 23–24.

13. Ibid., pp. 52–53.

14. Ibid., p. 180.

15. Ibid., p. 183.

16. Ibid., pp. 128–29.

17. Cf. Ḥayyim Schirmann, *Ha-Shirah ha-Ivrit bi-Sefarad uve-Provence* II (Jerusalem/Tel Aviv, 1959), pp. 519–20; and *Gates of Repentance,* p. 390.

18. Cf. Pool, *Tefillot le-Yom Kippur,* pp. 175–76.

19. Cf. Pool, *Tefillot le-Rosh ha-Shanah,* pp. 163–64.

20. Cf. Pool, *Tefillot le-Yom Kippur,* p. 215.

21. Cf. ibid., pp. 226–30.

22. Cf. ibid., pp. 174–75.

23. Cf. ibid., pp. 294–95.

24. In his handbook on *Ha-Avodah sheba-Lev,* Yehoram Mazor makes a point of identifying the sources overlooked in the prayerbook itself. Perhaps eventually a comparable guide will be provided for *Kavvanat ha-Lev,* something on the order of a *Sha'arey Binah, Gates of Understanding* II (New York, 1984) for the High Holy Day *Sha'arey Teshuvah, Gates of Repentance.*

25. Mazor, ibid., pp. 78–79.

26. Remarkably enough, on theological principle, the British Reformers never tampered doctrinally with either of these texts in their maḥzor, though in their 1931 siddur the *ya'aleh ve-yavo* paragraph suffered a frightful dismemberment, that is, until the publication of the Assembly of Ministers of the Reform Synagogues of Great Britain's *Maḥzor le-Shalosh Regalim, Prayers for the Pilgrim Festivals* (Amsterdam, 1965). In this last-named rite the prayer's quondam eschatological and "Zionist" tone is unhesitatingly sounded anew.

27. This wording has existed uninterruptedly in both volumes of the *Union Prayer Book,* to replace the Orthodox "who restorest souls unto the dead." The employment here of the phrase from Job 12:10 goes as far back as the first official edition (1894) of the *Union Prayer Book.* It is reproduced, for instance, in the all-Hebrew New Year Morning Service for the chapel on the premises of the Jerusalem School of the Hebrew Union College-Jewish Institute of Religion, *Tokhnit Teqes ha-Tefillah le-Rosh ha-Shanah* (Jerusalem, 1964]). Interestingly, the Reconstructionists are now using the Reform version of *elohay neshamah*—conceivably by way of *Ha-Avodah sheba-Lev*—in their *Kol Haneshamah: Shabbat Veḥagim* (Wyncote, Pennsylvania: The Reconstructionist Press, 1994).

28. Cf. the almost stark entry in the Glossary of the 1985 *Forms of Prayer* under 'Reconstructionist Prayer Book' on p. 1036.

29. The prayer's original location was the exquisite *Order of Service of the Jewish Religious Union* (2nd rev. ed., London, 5664/1903). This pioneering English ritual is, it must be said, notable for its touching interior piety.

30. Credit is given expressly for the *musaf* Service.

31. Even to the point of including—in the Hebrew, literally—the cantor's request that his prayer be accepted as that of "an elder, experienced, well-mannered, with an ample beard and a pleasant voice."

32. And not the Sephardic recension, as favored for its lean, lucid literary style in many a non-Orthodox maḥzor.

33. *Maḥzor,* p. 234; *Forms,* p. 786. *Kavvanat ha-Lev* has a similar quotation by Leo Baeck, in Hebrew translation, concerning the ethical, universalist, theocentric aspect of *malkhut shamayim* —appropriately enough, right before the *aleynu* introducing the *malkhuyot* section in the *musaf* for Rosh Hashanah. Irving Howe's English rendition of the reference may be found in *The Essence of Judaism* (New York, 1948 [1961]), p. 243, beginning "If the kingdom of God represents . . ."

34. *Maḥzor,* p. 393; *Forms,* p 924.

35. By contrast, the nineteenth-century non-Orthodox prayerbooks, as by Abraham Geiger, Benjamin Szold, and even Isaac M. Wise, not only decultified but universalized this prayer—and kept the Numbers reference inviolate.

36. *Kavvanat ha-lev* uses it three times—during Evening, Morning, and Afternoon Services.

37. Avot de-Rabbi Nathan (vers. I), IV, 11a.

38. The 1995 edition of *Forms of Prayer: Prayers for the Pilgrim Festivals* goes a long way in using gender-neutral language, especially in the English. Best of all, its study anthologies and scriptural commentaries for each of the *shalosh regalim* include quality pieces by women for pondering and discussion. Special note should be taken, too, of such collections of women's prayers that have come out since, as Marcia Falk, *Sefer ha-Berakhot, the Book of Blessings: New Jewish Prayers for Daily Life, the Sabbath, and the New Moon Festival* (San Francisco, 1996); Tracy Guren Klirs, ed., *Bi-Zekhut Imahot, The Merit of Our Mothers: A Bilingual Anthology of Jewish Women's Prayers* (Cincinnati, 1992); Marcia Cohn Spiegel and Deborah Lipton Kremsdorf, ed., *Women Speak to God: The Prayers and Poems of Jewish Women* (San Diego, 1987); and Women of Reform Judaism, *Covenant of the Heart: Prayers, Poems and Meditations from the Women of Reform Judaism* (New York, 1993).

39. For another translation see Martin Buber, *Tales of the Hasidim: The Later Masters* (New York, 1948), pp. 276–77.

40. Shulḥan Arukh, Ḥoshen Mishpat: Hilkhot Rosh ha-Shanah, paragraph 583.

41. Pp. 91–93. For a more literal rendition of the "symbolic foods," see Nosson Scherman, trans. and ed., *Siddur Qol Ya'aqov, The Complete Artscroll Siddur* (Brooklyn, 1984), pp. 768–69.

42. For example, *Forward Day by Day,* issued quarterly by the Forward Movement Publications, an agency of the Episcopal Church. The Lubavitcher Hasidim have their *Ha-Yom Yom, From Day to Day* ["an anthology of aphorisms and customs, arranged according to the days of the year from the talks and letters of the Rebbe, Rabbi Yosef Yitzchak Schneerson of

Lubavitch"], arranged by Menachem Mendel Schneerson (Brooklyn, 1968). The American Reform movement produced something similar on a less dense scale in the 1920s when devotionalism was very much in the air: *Berakhah u-Tehillah, Blessing and Praise: A Book of Meditations and Prayers for Individual and Home Devotion* (Cincinnati, 1923).

43. This was a disinclination generally not shared by the Ashkenazim in bygone times. The way about it has been to place these lyrical grafts either outside the *Stammgebete* or between major prayer units. The definitive structure of the Jewish liturgy would thereby be left unharmed.

44. Philip Birnbaum, ed., *Maḥzor ha-Shalem le-Yom Kippur, High Holyday Prayer Book* (New York, 1958), pp. 287–91.

45. I. Davidson, S. Assaf and B. I. Joel, *Siddur R. Saadja Gaon* (Jerusalem, 1963), pp. 377–78.

46. Pp. 1943–44.

47. For an extended discussion of the Israeli daily, Sabbath and Festival volume, noting some of its shortcomings as well as its veritable merits, see chap. 12.

48. For an extensive, wider-ranging analysis of the British Reform liturgy over the last century and a half, see chap. 5.

10

Gates of Prayer in Historical-Critical Perspective

In a real sense *Sha'arey Tefillah, Gates of Prayer: The New Union Prayer Book* (1975), a collective endeavor of the American Reform rabbinate, is a result of trans-Atlantic collaboration. *Gates'* chief editor, Chaim Stern,[1] with the erudite John Rayner, produced two elegant prayer-books—*Service of the Heart* (1967, since replaced by *Siddur Lev Chadash,* 1995); and *Gate of Repentance* (1973)—both of which are updated, emended and transformed versions of Israel I. Mattuck's three-volume *Liberal Jewish Prayerbook* (1924–1926), designed for the Liberal and Progressive synagogues of Great Britain. All of these rites have left their mark on *Gates of Prayer.*

A Lithuanian-born product of the Hebrew Union College, Mattuck (1883–1954) served several American pulpits before emigrating to England and assuming the helm of its Liberal Jewish community. Dissatisfied with the limitations of the *Union Prayer Book* but without dispensing with it entirely, Mattuck created a liturgy known for its variety, its inclusion of many new prayers, its resuscitation of long-forgotten pieces in Jewish literature from all ages, and its utilization of prayers and poems by gentile authors. Whatever the shortcomings of his creative endeavors— and given the prodigious scope of his efforts, the shortcomings are many—Mattuck saw possibilities in the most unexpected places and blazed new paths that subsequent liturgiographers were to follow without ever knowing who the pathblazer was. With its variegated richness, the sensibility and ambience of his *Liberal Jewish Prayerbook* are decidedly of the first two or three decades of our century; and of this Stern and Rayner were keenly aware. Theirs was the huge task of bringing the Mattuck works into line with the demands and moods of the present generation, a task they executed quite commendably.

Earlier American Influences

In structure, theology, and language, the *Gates of Prayer* is a direct descendent of the *Union Prayer Book.* This entry in the notes is typical:

1087. 681 *May He whose spirit is with us* . . . adapted from SOH, p. 246, where it is slightly adapted from LJPB, p. 87 (which took it from an early edition of UPB; now in UPB,p. 130) and from LJPB, p. 115.

At first glance, however, the lines of continuity between *Gates* and the previous editions of the UPB may not be so clear-cut. *Gates'* size and its countless new features can easily obscure the base on which the UPB rested, as can be seen in both the few services that are essentially the old UPB staples and those services that are UPB-inspired, directly or in a roundabout way. The sparseness and symmetry of a typical service, hewing to the tannaitic *matbe'a shel tefillah,* much as the early American Reformers Leo Merzbacher, Samuel Adler, David Einhorn and Adolph Huebsch did, has held up remarkably well. The dimensions of the service, regardless of whether the individual components have been enlarged or shortened, have stayed fundamentally the same. For example, neither the *qedushah de-yotzer* nor the *musaf* has been restored in any of *Gates'* services.

The introduction of a section called "Special Themes," materially borrowed from *Service of the Heart,* forms the only significant exception to this rule concerning the proportions of a service. The segment in *Gates* labeled "Prayers and Readings for Special Occasions" may well be said to hark all the way back to Einhorn's all-German *Gebete beim öffentlichen Gottesdienste an besonderen Sabbathen* (which, however, were by design exclusively the Sabbaths of the *arba parashiyyot* and of Hanukkah, to be read after the haftarah.[2]) The augmented *birkhot ha-shahar* for the first Weekday and Sabbath Services respectively (always the most traditional of all the services) are really not anything new for the UPB: the tendency had already begun with the 1945 edition of the High Holy Day volume, UPB II. The preference for the Talmudic designation *tefillah* over *amidah* may well have been prompted by Einhorn's use of the Rabbinic label and his summoning the congregation to rise only for the First Three Benedictions *(shalosh rishonot,* also characterized by the Sages as *birkhot shevah)* rather than for the *amidah* in its entirety. It is interesting to note that a nineteenth-century antecedent of the Szold/Jastrow *Abodath Israel* (1873) treated the *tefillah* in precisely the same manner, instructing worshipers to be seated immediately after the *qedushah.* (It is to be recalled that for Szold and Jastrow there was no

Reader's Repetition.) Thus in this matter, the editors of *Gates* are reverting to older Reform usage.

The component benedictions of the *tefillah* are each accompanied by an appropriate heading, which is as a rule a traditional one. Occasionally, however, if a benediction of the weekday *shemoneh esreh* has been recast in such a way that the customary epigraph no longer tallies with the contents, an adjustment is made accordingly. The caption *qibbutz galuyot* comes to be *herut; boneh yerushalayim* (which Elbogen tells us was in former times variously known by other names) turns up in *Gates* as *shelom yerushalayim;* and *et tzemah* is correspondingly changed to *yeshu'ah.* It is perhaps more than coincidental that similar accommodations were made in Merzbacher's 1855 *Order of Prayer,* originally intended for New York's Temple Emanu-El. The Jerusalem one, to be cited shortly, is simply dropped in Adler's revision. The latter too suggested the phrase *mehayyeh ha-kol* for the Second Benediction of the *tefillah* in place of the Orthodox *mehayyeh ha-metim.* This is the emendation *Gates* adopted instead of UPB's Einhorn-based *note'a be-tokhenu hayyey olam,* which, nonetheless, is substantially kept in the last verse of *yigdal* in *Gates* (p. 731).

The UPB revisions prior to *Gates* in the main retained both the Hebrew and English texts of the preceding edition, with timely prunings. By way of example, the 1940 edition was disposed to preserve Kaufmann Kohler's "Now that the daily task is laid aside . . ." with its soothing if anachronistic "the brightness of the fireside shines forth to tell that a divine spirit of love holds sway"—with scarcely a change in wording from the 1895 version.[3] *Gates* is not so abjectly bent on saving the English text from alteration or excision; nor is it boldly or singlemindedly intent upon creating *ex nihilo.* The earlier editions provide abundant material to choose from, and quantities of it are put to imaginative use in new settings and freely adapted. (Rayner and Stern make a point of disclosing who the original authors were.) Although Gustav Gottheil's vintage preamble to the Kaddish[4] ("And now ere we part . . .," the only such pre-Kaddish prologue for Saturday morning) is cut, his crowning sentence of comfort is included in slightly altered form: "May the Source of peace send peace to all who mourn and comfort to all who are bereaved. Amen" (which, remarkably, seems to approach the classic *ha-maqom yenahem etkhem be-tokh aveley tziyyon vi-yrushalayim!*).

Missing Elements

Thus the links with *Gates'* predecessors, though not always made explicit in every instance, are, in the end, very much present. The nexus with the long and impressive train of prayerbook reform, European and American—and thereby ineluctably with the totality of Jewish liturgical tradition—might have been fortified even more had some of the older Reform and Liberal rites been considered a bit more thoroughly. Of all *Gates'* different recensions of the *birkat shalom* at the conclusion of the *tefillah*, not one matches the former UPB Hebrew version. That seems to me regrettable, partly because that adaptation was first composed for the 1857 edition of *Minhag Amerika* well over a hundred years ago. Isaac Mayer Wise and his collaborators gave us a reading that embodied the best elements of Tradition and Reform, Ashkenazic and Sephardic *(be-rov oz ve-shalom)* recensions, particularism and universalism *(ve-al kol yir'ey shemekha; ve-et kol ha-ammim),* the Babylonian and the Palestinian *(oseh ha-shalom).* The Reconstructionists liked Wise's formula so much that they have had it in all their prayerbooks—that is, until the appearance of *Kol Haneshamah.* For the more traditional services, greater use might have been made of the continental European Liberal prayerbooks that knew how to render historic forms compatible with Reform principles handily and gracefully. It was quite possible to *davven* out of these on the European side, and out of *Minhag Amerika* and *Abodath Israel,* on the American, while using the full regalia of tallit and tefillin. (All of the foregoing siddurim included Deuteronomy 11:13–21 and Numbers 15:37–41, as well as the *ve-ahavta* in their *qeri'at shema*) The Central European Liberal's moderating efforts might somehow have been incorporated at least in one *Gates* service, if only as an *ot zikkaron,* a kind of *Memorbuch,* for the martyred victims of the Shoah.

For a period of time the UPB passed through a stage of near-monolingualism, more in the way the text was read than in the actual text itself. Nevertheless, instances may be cited from the past, isolated as they are, when new Hebrew compositions were written, such as the imitation *piyyut* as a kind of peroration, composed by Max Margolis and translated by Henry Berkowitz, at the end of the 1908 *Union Haggadah.* Another is a piece newly-penned for the first edition of the UPB, in impeccable biblical Hebrew, a vestige of which is preserved just in English in the 1940 edition as a proem to the Kaddish for the House of Mourning. Initially, this prayer, modeled after the Talmudic *attem aḥeynu meyyuga'im* (Ketubot 8b), to be recited in the presence of the bereaved, served as the Intermediate Benediction of the *tefillah* for this very purpose. Could not this unique Hebrew prayer, unthinkingly dislocated in the 1940 edition, have been resuscitated in a prayerbook re-Hebraized? This gesture would have made clearer and stronger Reform's ties with its own creative past.

The Move to Embrace Kelal Yisra'el

The tendency for *Gates* to overlook portions of its variegated liturgical background may perhaps be understood by the desire to regularize the Hebrew text wherever possible to bring Reform into closer harmony with the rest of *kelal yisra'el*. The following are examples of prayers, abbreviated, altered, or hitherto absent in the UPB, that are reinstituted in several services (or at least in more than one):

1. *Ha-ma'ariv aravim*
2. *Hoda'ah,* or *modim,* with *ḥatimah*
3. Closing *retzeh* with *ve-teḥezenah*, alternating with *she-otekha lev-adekha be-yir'ah na'avod* as *ḥatimah*
4. Most of *ahavah rabbah* (e g., minus *mi-kol am ve-lashon;* cf., however, *attah veḥartanu* below)
5. *Tzur yisra'el* for Morning Services
6. *Hashkivenu* (both Ashkenazic and Sephardic renditions)
7. *Va-yekhullu* and *ve-shamru*
8. *Ve-zot ha-torah,* along with *hagbahah* (cf. the forced *torah tzivvah lanu,* a carry-over of Mattuck's reverse fundamentalism, on p. 429)
9. *Birkat ha-ḥodesh*
10. *Attah veḥartanu* in the Festival *tefillah*
11. *Netilat lulav* (with its *berakhah* but no *sheheḥeyanu*)
12. A fuller *hallel* with the prefatory *berakhah*
13. *Miqra megillah*
14. *Havdalah*

Several factors can undoubtedly explain this predilection for traditional forms, displayed by the Conservatively-oriented as well as the theologically radical and experimentally inclined. First of all, the third generation, as

may be expected, is not nearly so obsessed with flight from Jewish identity, though they are burdened perhaps with other ambiguities. Without
having vanished completely, the craving for acceptance in gentile society
does not prey on the mind as an overriding or compulsive goal, and the
assimilatory drive and pathetic apishness of yesteryear have lost much of
their edge. Maturity means recovery of roots and self-acceptance, and in
numerous ways Reform has come of age. Tradition, then, becomes a viable
option, and acts, time and again, as a principal ingredient in new forms of
Jewish expression.

A second explanation lies in improved knowledge of the liturgy's event-
ful history, shifting terrain, and enduring landmarks. In his day David
Einhorn had Leopold Zunz's scholarly researches in liturgical development
to fall back upon in constructing *Olath Tamid.* Unfortunately, neither Einhorn's contemporaries nor his followers were always secure in their understanding of the fabric or rationale of the traditional Siddur. Hence from
time to time they have perpetuated some egregious errors. A conspicuous
case in point is the *tefillah* which, until now, hardly ever appeared in the
UPB in other than a mutilated state. Einhorn was always scrupulous about
maintaining its structure—at least according to Zunz's understanding of
the time-sequence of its constituent parts. This included retention of the
First Three and Concluding Benedictions as well as the Intermediate
Benediction(s), which are frequently reformulated. As an out-of-the-way
illustration, one might compare the *tefillah* in *Olath Tamid* for *ne'ilah* with
the 1945 UPB II version, the English portions of which are roughly all
Einhorn-derived. The UPB lacks the terminating paragraphs of the
tefillah, while its nineteenth-century progenitor includes all of them.
Where, then, did the UPB go wrong? The unintending culprit is most
likely Merzbacher's *Order of Prayer,* another principal influence on the
UPB. For every evening *tefillah,* Merzbacher took advantage of the Talmudic permissiveness concerning its nocturnal recitation and reduced it to a
me'eyn tefillah (an *amidah* digest), leaving, however, the Intermediate Benediction whole, but somehow forgetting the expected Concluding Three in
either complete or condensed form. Since the early editors of the UPB
failed to catch on to what Merzbacher was trying to do—and bungled—
they restored the full text of the opening two (or, once in a while, three) of
the First Three and the Intermediate Benedictions, while failing to make
adequate adjustment for the Last Three.[5] This technical error, perpetuated

for three-quarters of a century, has been largely rectified for most of the Sabbath, all of the Festival, and two of the Weekly Services in *Gates*.

A third factor behind the return to more traditional forms is an obvious one, namely, the restoration of Zion in our day. The new prayerbook has special services for Yom ha-Atzmaut, as well as an insertion for the preceding Sabbath. In the *avodah* section (*retzeh* of the *amidah*), the Palestinian-derived UPB recension (*she-otekha levadekha*) takes turns with the long-suppressed *ve-tehezenah* (with its entreaty for the return of the Shekhinah to Zion), often followed by an interpretive and occasionally excusatory prayer in English on behalf of Zion along with the *golah*, in keeping with the outlook of an Ahad Ha-Am or a Simon Rawidowicz. A goodly number of the Hebrew selections in the "Songs and Hymns" appendix are for melodies emanating from Israel. These developments, of course, cancel Reform's nearly complete expurgation of Zion and Jerusalem from the prayerbook. The 1895 edition of the UPB contains a service "For the Anniversary of the Destruction of Jerusalem," all but steathily tucked away between '"Various Prayers" and "Prayers for Private Devotion." Earlier, Isaac M. Wise had a respectable and solid service for Tish'ah be-Av. So did Einhorn, but one drastically revamped according to his doctrinal specifications. Although Merzbacher included a benediction in his *tefillah* relating to Zion, Samuel Adler, his successor in the pulpit of Temple Emanu-EI, dropped it in toto.

The ensuing revised edition of the UPB (1918) turned out no such service for the Ninth of Av; and it has been that way ever since. The first hint of change appeared with its inclusion of *Hatikvah* in the *Union Hymnal* (1932) at the urging of Stephen S. Wise and over stormy opposition from the CCAR. Though the process was slow, it did not stop. The issuance of the Columbus Platform in 1937 fostered the reaffirmation of ties with the age-old fellowship of world Jewry—as reflected in the newly revised version of the UPB that came out three years later. Although *ahavat tziyyon* was proclaimed there in only a single prayer,[6] the snailpaced process of re-Zionization reached its climax all but ubiquitously in *Gates*. Both Jastrow and Einhorn in their day made use of *havinenu,* the traditional digest of the weekday *shemoneh esreh* (notably for private worship in the home, the *häusliche Andacht),* with the Messiah-Zion complex undone. The 1940 UPB availed itself of the device of an *amidah*-epitome and put it to use in a couple of unique ways.[7] As would be expected, both of these novel recensions go on being de-nationalized and de-eschatologized. By comparison, *Gates* retains the first of these in the form of a responsive reading and twice reactivates the traditional wording with the sole omission of the Davidic aspect of messianism. The reinstatement of Zion is thus presently a fait accompli.

The Inconstant Ḥatimah

The process of regularization is not, however, without its attendant difficulties. The most frequently encountered is the inconstant use of the *ḥatimah* that appears at the close of every *berakhah*. The previous editions of the UPB, while respecting the structure of the *Stammgebete* in essentials, showed a wanton disregard for the *ḥatimot*. *Gates* goes a long way toward restoring them, but not always consistently. Occasionally the *ge'ullah* section after the Shema[8] or any one of the benedictions in the *tefillah* (if not actually missing themselves as on p. 582) will run short of one. *Ribbon kol ha-olamim* ("Lord of all worlds, not in reliance . . . ") is missing one (*meqaddesh et shimkha ba-rabbim,* which is the *mission of Israel* in a nutshell!). On the other hand, the English meditation by Chaim Stern on p. 521 has a *ḥatimah* above and beyond the required seven for the Festival *tefillah*.

It is hard to know what to make of the responsive prayer that begins on the bottom of p. 692, which doubles as the Intermediate Benedictions for the *tefillah* in the fourth Weekday Service. In SOH this whole section formed a part of a "National Service." The prayer on the following page in *Gates* is awkwardly reminiscent of the beautiful prayer imputed to St. Francis of Assisi, "Lord, make us instruments of your peace. Where there is hatred, let us sow love; where there is injury, pardon . . ." Anomalously, *barukh she-amar* for the Weekday Morning Service has no psalms, much less a terminating *berakhah*, viz. *yishtabaḥ,* though for the first Sabbath Morning Service it does. In similar fashion, the Intermediate Benediction(s) suffer. For instance, in the service for Yom ha-Atzma'ut, none has a *ḥatimah*.

Adaptations and Innovations

The new prayerbook is filled with many novel features—many of which were inspired by the SOH—for example, those individual sections revolving on particular themes such as "Peace," "Doubt," and "Humanity." In

addition, some borrowings have undergone verbal modifications not only
for stylistic reasons (as in adjusting the British idiom to the American),
but in order to reflect new theological understandings and changing cultural mores, like the alteration of one title from "Brotherhood" to a non-
sexist "Unity." What a brainstorm it was to end the section on "Revelation," itself an SOH-engraftment, with the *qaddish de-rabbanan,* which
customarily climaxes a study session. In a slightly different vein, the *hatzi
qaddish* rounds out the section on "Doubt"—quite aptly, as the Kaddish is
a doxology that voices the perduring Jewish upbeat note of hope, even
amid grief and despondency.

Gates departs from the old UPB in refusing to cloak the anguish of
uncertainty, as in the following excerpt from the aforementioned section
on doubt:

> The way of God! How I would rejoice to be free of doubts and per-
> plexities, to know in my inmost being that I stand in the presence of
> the Most High all my days and nights. And I know how unclear is
> my vision of God, how uncertain are my words of praise when they
> are directed to the Highest. I pray therefore that I may learn to wor-
> ship, even as I hope to find a path to the nameless One, to the Power
> at the heart of life (p. 349).

Nor does it whitewash the the omnipresence of evil—hence the special
prayer for Shabbat Zakhor, the service "In Remembrance of Jewish Suffering," and the ones for Tish'ah be-Av and Yom ha-Sho'ah, bold departures
that carry on in the estimable tradition of medieval paytanic outpourings.[9]

An innovative tour de force that could easily wreak havoc if not used
with care is the uncommon way in which the Hebrew prayers and their
matching translations are interspersed. Our bilingualism is one of the key
differences between Jewish worship in the United States—Orthodox no
less than Reform—and American Christian liturgical usages—presentday
Catholic as much as Protestant. Whatever the degree of the Hebrew or the
English in actual use during services, there is the everpresent problem of
which language to use when. Accepting the premise that pluralism is now
a fact of life and that there is little point in bucking a potentially enrich-
ing current, the compilers of *Gates* allow for divergent approaches by frequently providing the translation for the Hebrew text line by line. Aside
from the general pedagogic value of a method suggestive of Magill's linear

cribs of decades ago, the lineup is especially effective when the attendant English is a latterday spinoff of the original Hebrew. Such interpretive paraphrases remind one of the method of the Targum—except that here, the congregation, cued by the prayerbook, is called upon to carry out the part anciently assigned to the *meturggeman.*[10]

In support of this system, one might cite the Rabbinic warrant, "When thou prayest, regard not thy prayer as a fixed mechanical task, but as an appeal for mercy and grace before the All-present."[11] On the other hand, in a goodly number of instances the integrity of a classical text no longer permitted to speak for itself is spoiled. In addition, without benefit of appendix or footnotes, congregants not well-versed in Hebrew must rely on intuition or guesswork to determine whether what they are reading is a fairly close rendition of the original, a broad paraphrase, or something entirely new. In contrast, SOH and GOR indicated non-literal translations with an asterisk and fully documented the details in the back of the book.

Fresh use of old materials should count among the many pleasing innovations of *Gates of Prayer.* Talmudic passages are forcefully and advantageously placed in unexpected but, as it turns out, quite appropriate settings. Prayers of ancient Palestinian provenance are represented, as in the recension of *ahavat olam* on p. 595.[12] The sense of the organic unity of all Israel is brought out in bolder relief than in any other Reform prayerbook and often in highly original ways with the reintroduction of prayers from kabbbalistic and Hasidic circles, such as *yah ribbon, berikh shemeih* (only the part that is generally sung), *yedid nefesh,* and others. The bucolic meditation attributed to Rabbi Nahman of Bratzlav[13] puts an agitated soul at rest. The modern preface, rhapsodic and numinous, to the *qedushah* on p. 373 has good pedigree among the votaries of the Jewish mystical tradition. It is good to see the Sephardic/Oriental usage of reciting the *hallel,* here abbreviated, during the Festival Evening Service offered as an option. All these examples exhibit the compilers' willingness not only to excise and reform when deemed imperative but to acknowledge and draw upon Judaism's rich and variegated tradition.

Another way in which traditional (aggadic and halakhic) and modern motifs are ingeniously interwoven may be found in "Havdalah II":

The Rabbis tell us: As night descended at the end of the world's first Sabbath, Adam feared and wept. Then God showed him how to make fire. and by its light and warmth to dispel the darkness and its terrors. Kindling flame is a symbol of our first labor upon the earth. Shabbat departs and the workday begins as we kindle fire. And we, who dread the night no more, thank God for the flame by which we turn earth's raw stuff into things of use and beauty.

The candle's double wick reminds us that all qualities are parted. We have the power to create many different fires, some useful, others baneful. Let us be on guard never to let the gift of fire devour human life, sear cities and scorch fields, or foul the pure air of heaven, obscuring the very skies. Let the fire we kindle be holy; let it bring light and warmth to all humanity.

Theology

Faithful as it is to the classical biblical and Rabbinic conceptual framework, the traditional Siddur has for its doctrinal content a theology remarkable for its breadth, reflecting the Prayerbook's rich evolution over the centuries. *Gates* furthers this thrust in the direction of theological pluralism. Just the same, as with the Siddur, *Gates* has its self-imposed limits, arrived at by a vague consensus. Preference is shown to an Elimelekh of Lizhensk over an Elijah Gaon of Vilna, to a Martin Buber, Elie Wiesel or Claude G. Montefiore over a secular Yiddishist or Hebraist (Shaul Tchernichovsky is a rare exception). Why are not the works of Hayyim Greenberg—essayist, orator, Labor Zionist, Socialist, humanist, and pacifist—included? Could not a mimeographed service pamphlet put out by a non-religious Kibbutz for Rosh Hashanah have been considered? It would be more catholic of us (in Schechter's sense, enlarged) to pay close attention to such earnest spiritual grapplings among the *lo-datiyim*. They too can help us in our quest after the Infinite.

The tenet concerning the Afterlife as couched in the 1940 UPB no longer satisfies many Jews today. That edition went only so far as to cross off "and good portion in the world to come" in the paragraph *al yisrael ve-al tzaddiqaya* of the old Hamburg Temple Kaddish. *Gates* divests itself of that venerable Reform paragraph-insertion altogether. Moreover, as mentioned earlier, it replaces Einhorn's long-established "who hast implanted within us immortal life" with Samuel Adler's *meḥayyeh ha-kol* (usually rendered in *Gates* as "Source of Life") in the Second Benediction of the *tefillah*. The eternity of the soul was a fixed postulate for the nineteenth-century Reformers, buttressed by utterances of the medieval Jewish thinkers (Solomon ibn Gabirol, Baḥya ibn Paqudah, and the Rambam, among others) and, of course, their leading elder contemporary, Immanuel Kant. Their Reform offspring of the present decade have a hard time with such an unhesitating statement of belief.[14] The theme of suffering is naturally related to the concept of an Afterlife by way of theodicy, justifying God's way to humankind. Given the meliorist position of pre-World War II American Judaism, the concept of suffering was nearly relegated to the past. The Shoah and related horrors have taught us otherwise. When the current revision of the UPB was in process, Daniel J. Silver wrote:

> Avodah in an age which has said Kaddish for the Six Million must find an occasion to say with the Psalmist: "Who knoweth the power of Thine anger and Thy wrath according to the fear that is due Thee." The sense of the tragic infuses our lives and no serious liturgy can avoid Job's encounter.[15]

In the service "In Remembrance of Jewish Suffering" strong language from the lone chapter in Obadiah (pp. 408–9), traditionally appointed for Shabbat Va-yishlaḥ and for a long time absent in the Reform haftarah lectionary, points the accusatory finger at the gentile world for its complicity, silent or undisguised, in the decimation of the Jewish people. Nevertheless, it is understood that the torment is not to lead to vengefulness or spite; the cry in the rest of the biblical chapter for the exercise of divine wrath and punishment goes unreproduced.[16]

Reflecting Modern Sensibilities

Despite an occasional honest mistake in spelling or grammar—*e.g.,* Habakkuk comes out as "Habbakuk" (p. 678) and the emended *u-va le-tziyyon* (p. 557) has a subject in a non-matching gender—the language of *Gates of Prayer* can be little faulted. On the contrary, improvements reflecting modern sensibilities are found throughout. Some of these are necessitated by modified theological and cultural perspectives. The section for Shabbat Shuvah (pp. 391–94) is worded in terms of human potential for growth and development; harping on guilt is recognized as leading easily to masochistic and self-defeating attitudes. Similarly, although inconsistent with what was said earlier, God is absolved of blame for evil in the world in the subtle but significant transmutation of the following passage from the last UPB's Service for the House of Mourning:

> We need fortitude and resignation under the chastening of the Lord; whence can these come save from Him who lays the burden upon us? (p. 300)

into *Gates'*

> We need fortitude and courage when pain and loss assail us; where shall we find them, if not in the thought of Him who preserves all this good from destruction? (p. 645).

Much has been said here and elsewhere about the removal of the sexist language that has plagued the older liturgies. Just as our Episcopalian neighbors were affected by similar considerations in the revision of the *Book of Common Prayer,* the language is appreciably modified in *Gates.* For example, this reformulation from the version in SOH (p. 231),

> As the swimmer gives himself to the sea, as the bird gives itself to the air

to

> As the fish gives himself to the sea, as the bird gives herself to the air, as all life gives itself to life, so may we give ourselves to You, O God. (p. 665)

In a similar vein, an old patriotic hymn like "God of Our Fathers," by Daniel C. Roberts, is made to read, "God of our People. " We are also treated to good poems by women, such as the seldom-encountered, controlled lyric on pp. 671–72 by the modern-day martyr Hannah Senesh. But the problem of sexism has not been completely set to rest. *Avinu malkenu* is left un-Englished. If the paternal is no longer tolerated, one might ask: What of the other figures of speech, as, say, "Rock of Israel"? If only there were some way to use the Kabbalists' implicative and cogent imagery of the masculine *and* feminine aspects of the Godhead, we could keep the fatherly associations and introduce the maternal. In today's divisive world we probably need to recite *le-shem yihud qudesha berikh hu u-shekhinteih* with as much fervor as our mystic forebears and our Hasidic counterparts.

Other stylistic alterations include the discarding of embarrassing anachronisms, such as the aforementioned *gemütlich* piece by Kohler (1940 UPB, pp. 62–63), much transformed as a meditation in *Gates* (p. 171). The generally near-literal translations, in many cases, have a new polish, and it is a relief to see that the Hebrew text is no longer invariably interdicted or buried beneath a barely recognizable paraphrase. One instance is the neat and only slightly anthropocentric rendering of the familiar and oft-quoted Amos 3:2: "You, of all the familes of all the earth, have known Me best; therefore I will hold you all the more accountable for your iniquities."

How to translate the typical *berakhah* formula with its simultaneous use of the second and third persons without giving the appearance of syntactical solecism has always been a knotty problem. The old UPB would render *barukh attah adonay* as "praised art Thou, O Lord" rather than as "blessed art Thou," leaving the benedictory activity to God Himself and the laudatory part to us mortals. In *Gates,* it is a question of grammar that concerns the editors, and it is disposed of by using in English the third person exclusively. While one may regret the subtraction of the intimate, personal note of *barukh attah* and the implicit dynamic between the transcendence and immanence of God, the pros and cons were weighed carefully in Talmudic times in a discussion between Rav and Samuel (J. Ber. 9: I). Another question might be raised as to why, if there are *haqqafot* for Simhat Torah, there are no *hoshanot* for Sukkot. Both *Minhag Amerika* and *Abodath Israel*—and, of all prayerbooks, the old whimsical British LJPB III—had them in one form or another. (Is it because this would entail more people acquiring lulavim and etrogim? Or because of the supernatural association with inducing rain?)

A minor aberration in *Gates* is the displacement of the holiday inserts *ya'aleh ve-yavo, al ha-nissim, tal,* and *geshem* from their customary positions, *e.g.,* the prayer for rain and dew that is commonly bracketed with the Second Benediction of the *tefillah* extolling the *magnalia Dei* in this terrestrial existence and beyond. In *Gates,* the prayer, now restored to the *tefillah* from its previous location before the Return of the Scroll to the Ark, is suspended between the Second Benediction and the *qedushah.* One is baffled in this connection by the presence of a Sephardic *tal,* captivating as it is, *at the beginning* of the Festival Morning Service for Passover (pp. 493–95) and a non-specific, all-purpose one (pp. 516–17), used also for Shemini Atzeret.

Another curiosity not satisfactorily explained is the near-total restoration of the Service for Tish'ah be-Av with provision made for a Torah reading but not a word about reading the Book of Lamentations! Also, what to call the morrow of the seventh day of Sukkot has always been a ticklish problem for those Reform synagogues that keep the biblical one day of *yom tov* and concurrently revive the practice of conducting *haqqafot,* this time on Shemini Atzeret rather than on the day following, the traditional date for Simhat Torah. (The pre-1940 UPB didn't go in for processions; and observing Simhat Torah at the end of a triennial cycle was deemed cumbersome.) The compilers of *Gates* came up with a solution of their own: Atzeret-Simhat Torah. No explanation is forthcoming as to why the "Eighth Day" was dropped or why the new label.[17] Would it have not been possible to use the terms Shemini Atzeret and Simhat Torah interchangeably? Is not Rosh Hashanah liturgically referred to as *yom ha-zikkaron,* the Day of Memorial? Confusion does not appear to have resulted on that account.

Leaving out the notes at the end of *Gates* marks a more serious problem. It is not just that credit is not being given where due, but ours is a time when few can aspire to be little more than *siddur-lamdanim.* For many the sole contact with the vast richness of Jewish tradition is through the medium of the prayerbook. Even more lamentable, the splendid notes, the fruit of immense assiduous labor, are appended only to the *Gates of the House* (for unknown reasons), thus putting them out of the reach of the average congregant and passing up a matchless pedagogic occasion.

High-caliber and thorough as the notes are on the whole, they are somewhat in arrears in acknowledging the full extent of the Conservative and Reconstructionist contributions to *Gates.* The Rabbinical Assembly's *Sabbath and Festival Prayer Book* is the source, albeit roundabout, of the Morning Benedictions in *Gates* on pp. 286–87. Another Conservative publication, the *Weekday Prayer Book,* provided several of the Hebrew rubrics in *Gates* for this section and elsewhere. Also insufficiently recognized is the Reconstructionist movement, which blazed trails in the area of American prayerbook reform, both by using biblical verses in novel ways and by resurrecting long overlooked prayers from the heyday of Sephardic Jewry in pre-Inquisition and pre-Almohade Spain.[18] These sporadic oversights notwithstanding, much encouragement is derived from the realization, as exemplified in *Gates of Prayer,* that an ecumenical trend looms large within the household of Israel, and that Isaac M. Wise's pious dream of a single rite serving a unified American—and, dare we hope, worldwide?—Jewry may not be all that remote after all or impossible to attain *ba-agala u-vizeman qariv!*

An earlier version of this chapter appeared in the *CCAR Journal* 24 (Autumn 1977): 1–16. Reprinted with permission.

1. The conscientious and accomplished Chaim Stern had a talent for joining together split pairs, the Ashkenazic and the Sephardic, Israel and the Diaspora, Tradition and Reform, and for orchestrating the polymorphous trends within Reform Judaism today— the naturalist, organicist, existentialist, traditionalist, classicist, non-theist, polydox, and process theologies. His was a more prickly task than that of the early unsung compiler of the UPB, Isaac S. Moses, who, too, wrote prayerbooks of his own before he was called upon to synthesize the labors of other men, such as Leo Merzbacher, David Einhorn, Isaac M. Wise, and others, into a single, uniform rite. It was a desirable move for the *New Union Prayer Book* to abandon the overlong policy of concealing its premier wordsmiths behind the veil of anonymity. Now we can give credit where due.

2. It is curious how Purim, here grudgingly accorded a nook after all these years, still encounters difficulties in gaining full recognition and status as a holiday, say, of the rank of Hanukkah. Like many of his confreres on this continent fifty years ago, Mattuck steadfastly refused to acknowledge Purim, with its hospitality to frivolity and comeuppance, in either his calendar or liturgy, as a holiday in its own right. Purim makes its full comeback in *Siddur Lev Chadash,* where the handling is remarkably balanced.

3. It originally appeared in Kohler's *Sabbath Eve Service* (New York, 1891).

4. From Gottheil's *Morning Prayers* (New York, 1889).

5. See pp. 19–25, 43–46, and 295–97.

6. UPB, pp. 68–69; cf. *Gates,* pp. 201 and 344.

7. Both on p. 349: (1) a broad English paraphrase of Adler's *havinenu* and (2) an admirable Hebrew one that sandwiches in a *tefillah qetzarah* taken from Berakhot 10a.

8. One even has the *ḥatimah* situated right in the middle of the section itself (p. 253).

9. Such as the medieval *anshey emunah avadu.* See translation, "The Men of Faithfulness Are Lost," in Joseph Heinemann with Jakob J. Petuchowski, *Literature of the Synagogue,* New York, 1975, pp. 241–42.

10. See the interesting example of the responsive reading beginning *attah gibbor* (pp. 356–57).

11. Ethics of the Fathers 11:18.

12. Incidentally, the Reconstructionists were the first in our time to seize upon this version as found in Sa'adiah Gaon's rite (cf. Heinemann and Petuchowski, ibid., pp.

217–18). Regarding this benediction immediately preceding the Shema, it should be noted how SOH improved the occasion by launching a unique *ahavah rabbah* (pp. 179f. and 108f.), in Hebrew and in English, entirely made up of scriptural verses, in the main from Ps. 119 in deep-felt praise of the Law, with Ps. 86:12 as the concluding eulogy. The remarkable thing about this, as it were, *alt-neu* prayer is that it dovetails with the way the Karaites created their prayerbooks, utilizing as a rule, and on occasion almost servilely, verses from the Bible. In this case, Rayner and Stern took advantage of a Karaite liturgical technique, thus doing honor to one of Israel's oldest and much-neglected living sects. *Gates* adopts this recreation by Rayner and Stern (p. 165, with something like it on p. 103f.) in English but wedged it in between the Hebrew verses of the Ashkenazic *ahavah rabbah!* The conclusion, again in English, is a *berakhah* revived from the Cairo Genizah. Each component is excellent in and of itself and self-sufficient; juxtaposed as they are, however, in *Gates,* they jostle needlessly .

13. Pp. 376–77; cf. pp. 173 and 187 which are also ascribed to the same *rebbe.*

14. Even their peers in the Conservative Movement are not without ambiguities on the issue, as is evident in Jules Harlow's rendition of the *ḥatimah* to the Second Benediction of the *amidah* as "Master of Life and Death," in his superb maḥzor. (Compare the pointed comments on the topic in *Judaism* (Fall, 1973) XXII: 432 and 448, respectively.) For a fuller discussion of this topic, see chap. 7 above.

15. "On the Union Prayer Book," *CCAR Journal* (January 1967): 17–18.

16. Cf. the deletion of the retributive verses 7–9 from Ps. 137, by now taken for granted.

17. H. G. Enelow wrote an illuminating scholarly essay on this very subject, "Atsereth Day," *Selected Works of Hyman G. Enelow,* Volume IV: Scientific Papers, privately printed, pp. 171–78.

18. Cf. *Gates,* pp. 501–2, with the Reconstructionist *Sabbath Prayer Book,* pp. 410–13.

11

Kol Haneshamah
"Let Every Living Thing Yah's Praises Sing":
Reconstructionist Rites of the Nineties

Ever since their *Shir Ḥadash* (1939)[1] and *New Haggadah* (1942), the Reconstructionists have been at the forefront of liturgical creativity, willing to try the new and unventured while reactivating material long forgotten. The entire Jewish world was their orbit, and the Hebrew language fervently maintained as the sovereign means of access to that rich world. The shapers of the rite were ordained at the Jewish Theological Seminary and versed in the critical handling of classical texts. However they may have been regarded by their Conservative colleagues, they were by and large committed members of the movement themselves, making up a good part of its liberal sector. Avoiding for decades the temptation to secede and form a separate denomination, they adopted instead the stance of a prod or a ferment within liberal American Jewry.

The creators of the first Reconstructionist siddur, *The Sabbath Prayer Book* (1945), maintained a basically traditional text for Shabbat Evening, Morning, and Afternoon Services, excising or rewording only those verses that, for its users, were doctrinally untenable (*e.g.,* the Chosen People concept, the privileged position of the *kohanim,* the rebuilding of the Temple, etc.), sharply curtailing the Preliminary Benedictions (*birkhot ha-shaḥar*), and all but entirely revamping the *musaf* service. Here and there new prayers in Hebrew and at times in English were inserted as possible alternatives. Its showpiece, however—and the showpiece of all subsequent Reconstructionist liturgical volumes[2]—was its Supplement, comprised of prayers, poems, hymns, and responsive readings from biblical times to the early 1900s and offering variations on the classic themes of God, Torah, Israel—and the American holidays!

The latest Reconstructionist prayerbooks—*Kol Haneshamah: Shabbat Eve* (1989), *Kol Haneshamah: Shirim Uvraḥot* [sic!] (1991), *Kol Haneshamah: Shabbat Veḥagim* (1994), and *Kol Haneshamah: Li-Ymot Ḥol* (1996)—thus have much upon which to draw. How have they met the twin challenges of their considerable legacy and the demands of the last decades of the twentieth century?

The feature of the new prayerbooks that will doubtless first capture the reader's attention is the layout. *Kol Haneshamah* is the first official American prayerbook to make use of illustrations in its pages. (The British Reform Movement has been doing this for the last twenty years in editions of *Forms of Prayer*). There are some good calligraphy and illustrative graphics, foremost of the latter being the stylized cityscape of Jerusalem (for the sabbatical/festal *hashkivenu*, which concludes "who spreadest the tabernacle of peace over us, over Israel, and over Jerusalem")[3] and an esthetically pleasing, exoteric, bilingual *mizrah* (or a *shivviti*, from the opening word of Psalm 16:8, "I have set the LORD before me continually"), which occupies a whole page. Positioned just before the *amidah*, this mandala-style meditation by Betsy Platkin Teutsch is aesthetically pleasing and thought provoking. Other graphics, as for each of the Festivals, are not nearly as successful and sometimes have a clumsy, amateurish look about them.

The Hebrew Text

The center of gravity of a prayerbook is its Hebrew text. Following in the footsteps of earlier Reconstructionist liturgists, the editors of *Kol Haneshamah* have, on the one hand, revived much that is traditional (*e.g.,* selections from the Song of Songs for *kabbalat shabbat*) and, on the other, gone a good deal further than their predecessors in textual emendation, largely in the way of addition.

The older Reconstructionist rites, for example, were wont to replace the second passage of the Shema (Deuteronomy 11:13–21), describing the meteorological consequences of the Israelites' ethical behavior, with Deuteronomy 11:21 and 28:1–6 (selected), promising length of days and the blessings of prosperity respectively. *Kol Haneshamah* removes 11:21, retains all of 28:1–6 (unexpurgated to the point of including "the LORD your God will set you high above all the nations of the earth," here palliated to "THE ULTIMATE will make of you a model for all nations of the earth"), and embraces 30:15–19. This last verse is the famous passage where the gauntlet is thrown before the people, and they are admonished *u-vaharta ba-hayyim,* "but choose life!"[4]

The most textual changes, however—more than in any previous Reconstructionist liturgical endeavor—occur in the *amidah.* As in the *Gates of Prayer,* Psalm 51:15 ("O Lord, open my lips . . .") is restored as a directive and foreword to the Seven Benedictions, or the Sabbath *amidah.* The first benediction joins the four Matriarchs with the Patriarchs and adjusts the eulogy, or conclusion, "Blessed are you, KIND ONE, Shield of Abraham and help of Sarah."[5] The second benediction, ordinarily on the theme of resurrection or immortality, is given a verbal twist similar to the locution in *Gates of Prayer* (deriving from Samuel Adler's revision in the 1864 edition of Merzbacher's *Order of Prayer* for New York's Temple Emanu-El and tracing ultimately to Nehemiah 9:6). Its eulogy, *barukh attah adonay, meḥayyeh kol ḥay,* is opportunely translated "Blessed are you, REVIVER, who gives and renews life." With our slowly awakening ecological sense, the editors were right to bring back the seasonal inserts, *e.g.,* "You make the wind blow and the rain fall."

The first of the concluding Three Benedictions, the *retzeh,* excludes any allusion to the resuscitation of sacrifices and adds the word *lahav* ("flame") to the old Reform/ Reconstructionist version. The addition lends an emotional, heartfelt quality to the blessing: "Lovingly accept their passionate prayer . . ." (*ve-lahav tefillatam be-ahavah teqabbel . . .*). Arthur Green's commentary on this phrase points to the connection between *lahav* and the Hasidic *hitlahavut* ("enthusiasm"). The latter can well fire up a worshiper's prayer-life, regardless of the branch of Judaism to which he or she is attached.

Ya'aleh ve-yavo, added during the week of a Festival, is closer to the traditional diction, by which not only the Jewish people and their ancestors are recalled, but Jerusalem and the Messiah (slightly rephrased) as well. (Green's comments *ad locum* "the memory of messianic hopes" are essentially modernist.) Finally, the prayer for peace applies not just to Israel but to "all who dwell on earth" (*yoshevey tevel,* first employed in this setting by Max D. Klein in his left of center Conservative *Seder Avodah* in the fifties and borrowed from the Rosh Hashanah liturgy).

The middle portion of the post-*amidah* meditation, *elohay netzor,* has been augmented by a single sentence containing an admirable peace-loving sentiment. Unfortunately, its syntax is convoluted. The same goes for a zigzag Hebrew text offered as an alternative to the Traditionalist or the former Reconstructionist opening paragraph of the *aleynu.* Perhaps prayerbook compilers should use literarily-inclined Israelis for the editing of Hebrew compositions by Americans—unless they can find someone of the caliber of Joseph Marcus, the Jewish medievalist and superb stylist who proofread and magically refashioned the new Hebrew texts in the Reconstructionists' 1945 *Sabbath Prayer Book.*

The compilers of *Kol Haneshamah* are to be thanked for bringing to our attention little known gems of Hebrew creativity from the past. As an available alternative to the *pesuqey de-zimrah* in the Sabbath and Festival volume, for example, they offer *pereq shirah,*[6] which contains nature's praise for the Creator and is reminiscent of the doxology in the apocryphal *Prayer of Azariah* and the *Song of the Three Jews* (verses 29–68).[7] Another interesting set of options are the Hebrew excerpts (regrettably uncited, except for one item) from Rabbinic literature ensconced between the benedictions *la-asoq be-divrey torah/ ve-ha'arev-na* and the *qaddish de-rabbanan.*[8] Other pleasant surprises in the same volume include the Rabbinic blessing from Berakhot 17a, which is offered as a blessing for a bar/bat mitzvah; an *ashrey ayin* for rain by the Sephardi Mosheh Gabbay in the Festival Evening Service for Shemini Atzeret; and portions of the Sephardic prayers for *tal* and *geshem* for the First Day of Passover and Shemini Atzeret, respectively, in place of the modernized and cultivated versions of the same by Eugene Kohn/Joseph Marcus for the 1958 Reconstructionist *Festival Prayer Book.* The reappropriated texts in *Kol Haneshamah,* though abridged, lend themselves more comfortably to a congregation's chiming in.

Ignoring precedent, *Kol Haneshamah* locates the Hebrew text on the left and the English translation on the right, conceivably to ease the transition from one language to another. Also without parallel is the extent to which transliteration is provided for the Hebrew texts that the congregation chants or reads aloud in unison or antiphonally. Obviously, a need is being filled, but at a price. Individual pages occasionally assume a busy cluttered look, leading to a measure of confusion. A single example should suffice: *emet ve-emunah,* which comes directly after the Shema and its attendant scriptural passages. The expanded Hebrew text runs to two pages, the English only one. An interpretive English version of *emet ve-emunah* faces the second half of the prayer. One not conversant in Hebrew but wishing to pick it up through the prayerbook thus has many back and forth eye motions to perform.[9]

Translation by Joel Rosenberg

The Englishing of the Hebrew text was left to the talented poet and Judaicist, Joel Rosenberg, whose renditions for the most part delight the eye and the ear. For example, how does a religious liberal render the second distich of the familiar but atavistic verse *hashivenu, adonay, elekha, ve-nashu-vah; haddesh yameynu ke-qedem* without fear of insincerity? Rosenberg hit upon an ingenious solution: "Renew our days, as you have done of old!"

In Rosenberg's English, Psalm 91 and *ashrey* recover the nuance and vivacity of the Hebrew. He transforms the verse that literally reads "And may [all] Israel, hallowers of Your Name, rest thereon" (*i.e.* the Sabbath), into a more universalist "Let all Israel, and all who treat Your name as holy, rest upon this day." He substitutes the more modern name "Matthew" for "Mattathias" in the *amidah* insert for Hanukkah, the *al ha-nissim* prayer. Both names go back, of course, to the Hebrew *Mattityahu* (the father of the Maccabee brothers; literally, "gift of the LORD"). Rosenberg's restatement of *aharitekha le-hayyey ha-olam ha-ba* as "may you be our link to future worlds" is probably the closest Reconstructionism can acceptably entertain concerning the Rabbinic Sages' notion of an Afterlife.[10]

Elsewhere, however, there are problems.[11] In the poet/translator's avidity to be politically correct, neither *adon olam* nor *yigdal* survives unscathed. Here are the opening and closing verses of the cherished first hymn, cleaned up and crippled:

> Crown of all time, the one who reigned
> before all mortal shape was made,
> and God's will brought forth all things
> then was the name supreme proclaimed.
> To God's kind hand I pledge my soul
> each time I sleep, again to wake,
> and with my soul, this body, here.
> Yah's love is mine; I shall not fear

And the degenderized English of the famous lines from Psalms 144:3–4 and 90:3, recited/chanted during Yizkor, descends to a new depth of prolixity and caricature:

> ALMIGHTY ONE, what are human beings
> that you take note of them,

the children of humanity
that you should think of them?
A human being is like a momentary breeze,
A person's days are but a passing shadow.
At dawn, life blossoms and renews itself,
at dusk, it withers and dries up.
You return a person unto dust.
You say: Return, O children of humanity![12]

For whatever reasons, the Sabbath Table Hymns (*zemirot*) in *Kol Hane-shamah's* Readings go untranslated. About the only translation of a Hebrew song that reads and scans nicely is the *cantabile* paraphrase of the mystical-amatory *yedid nefesh* by P'nai Or's Zalman Schachter-Shalomi—which the Conservatives have also done well to include in their *Siddur Sim Shalom*.

The Name of God in Kol Haneshamah

Interestingly, the very movement that has been criticized from both left and right for harboring a much-diminished God-concept devotes one-third of its *Sabbath Prayer Book Supplement's* pages to God—and none, strictly speaking, to Jewish peoplehood, ostensibly the heart of Recon-structionist theology. The most novel (non-)translation of the entire prayerbook is certainly the term *yah,* in Latin characters, for the sacrosanct Tetragrammaton (YHVH) in place of the customary LORD or KING (which really defines the surrogate name, *adonay,* rather than the unutter-able Name itself).

The reclamation of this ancient variant of the four-lettered name of God satisfies a fourfold need: using the specific name of God not shared, generi-cally, by any other deity; avoiding pronouncing the sacred Name in its entirety (in partial application of the Second Commandment); keeping away from terms suggesting male domination, like *Lord;* and putting to advantage the manifold mystical meanings that have come to be associated with the Name.

Many a Sephardic or Oriental prayerbook of Kabbalistic provenance would highlight the Name and insert particular markings as a way of indi-cating its significance in a given context, according to its position in the sephirotic realm. The creators of *Kol Haneshamah* have picked up on this method of unfolding its multiple latent meanings. Whenever the term *yah* appears, a divine attribute (not, however, always in the sephirotic scheme) is assigned underneath it, *e.g.,* YAH/BELOVED usually according to the context or theme of the liturgical or scriptural text in *Kol Haneshamah*. This inspired recovery of a traditional practice, begun by the sixteenth-century Safed mystics, unquestionably adds theological richness and sophistication to the prayerbook. At one level, one is prompted to think about those qualities that s/he would attach to divinity and seek to emulate.

In the succeeding volumes of *Kol Haneshamah,* the editors have chosen to dispense with this inspired if cumbersome tactic in favor of a compromise. Instead of using YAH whenever the Tetragrammaton appears on the Hebrew side, the editors rest satisfied with an epithet in caps (such as "Blessed are you, ALL BOUNTIFUL, who gives blessing to the years") in keeping with the content of the prayer (viz. *birkat ha-shanim/Blessing for Abundance*).

Supplement and Commentary

The Supplement (or *Readings,* as it is now called) and commentary in *Kol Haneshamah* are ensemble efforts, drawing upon the gifts of rabbis and laity, women and men, religionists and secularists. Although in the main the selections are scrupulously and becomingly made, the diversity of the contributors accounts for an inevitable unevenness in quality. The number of banal or affected passages can be counted on one hand; the others are notable for their ring of honesty and ability to stir the heart and mind.

In the last analysis the most moving and disarming for me was Edna Vincent St. Millay's "Dirge without Music" ("I am not resigned to the shutting away of loving hearts in the hard ground"), used here as one of a number of preludes to the Mourner's Kaddish. Then there are some astonishing layered pieces in Hebrew and Yiddish by authors as diverse as Solomon ibn Gabirol, Shemuel ha-Nagid, Leah Goldberg, Yehuda Amichai, Jacob Glatstein, and Aaron Zeitlin.

Some unexpected contributions are by the likes of Wendell Berry, Martin Luther King, Jr., Martin Niemoeller, Kenneth L. Patton and Albert Schweitzer. There are also eloquent, underused excerpts from the manifold writings of Mordecai M. Kaplan himself—recovered with the learned help of Mel Scult.

It is reassuring to see non-Orthodox religious Jews come up with commentary similar to the industrious, prolific offerings of Nosson Scherman and Meir Zlotowitz in the ubiquitous Artscroll siddurim. *Kol Haneshamah's* attractive and frequently original glosses provide instruction and uplift for late-twentieth-century sensibilities. The variety of rabbinic contributors to these glosses includes American *oleh* Levi Weiman-Kelman, Mordechai Liebling of the Reconstructionist Rabbinical College, pastor's pastor Sandy Eisenberg Sasso, poet Rami M. Shapiro, and editor-in-chief David A. Teutsch, to name but a few.

The discerning remarks of Arthur Green unfailingly offer wisdom and lucidity, even to those whose understanding of God may differ profoundly from his.[13] The following is an example of the tone and trend of Green's glosses to the words of the siddur—in this case, the phrase *ve-notenim be-ahavah reshut zeh la-zeh* in the *qedushah de-yotzer:*

> And lovingly they give to one another the permission. Here our text follows the Sephardic version [really the Hasidic, not the actual Sephardic] by adding the word *be'ahavah* (in love). It is only in our love for one another that we are truly capable of granting to each other "permission" to pray. A community of Jews who stand together in real prayer must be one where each individual is known and cared for as a person. Only when such exists among us are we a community whose members can truly "grant permission" to one another to seek or to sanctify God.

Gender Issues

For the first time ever in a denominational prayerbook, the homosexual community is allowed to enjoy modest recognition. *Kol Haneshamah: Li-ymot Ḥol* has in its Readings section two generalized muted prayers on the "Loss of a Gay or Lesbian Lover." The anonymous authorship attributed to the prayers indicates that acceptance of the gay lifestyle is less than total, even amongst liberal Jews.

Another striking aspect of *Kol Haneshamah* is its inclusion of many works by women, largely in the Readings supplement. To name but a few, there are Hebrew pieces by Leah Goldberg and Zelda, Yiddish ones by

Malka Heifetz Tussman and Kadia Molodowsky, and English ones by
Ruth F. Brin and Marcia Falk—all compelling and humanizing. Women
ordained at the Reconstructionist Rabbinical College are also represented
in the prayer-text and commentary. A disarming *kavvanah* by Sheila Peltz
Weinberg before the *amidah* reads:

> Dear God,
> Open the blocked passageways to you,
> The congealed places.
>
> Roll away the heavy stone from the well as your servant Jacob did
> when he beheld his beloved Rachel.
>
> Help us open the doors of trust that have been jammed with hurt
> and rejection.
>
> As you open the blossoms in spring,
> Even as you open the heavens in storm,
> Open us—to feel your great, awesome, wonderful presence.

In the Shabbat Eve volume, there is even an interpretive *amidah* by
Marcia Falk and two alternative ones as well. In all of them the fixed
frames of each of the seven benedictory units are basically degenderized in
the Hebrew (except for the *avodah* section, which refers to the *shekhinah*
and Her return).[14] The poems within each unit, chiefly by women, are of a
consistently high order. Two of my favorites are by Diane Cole and Malka
Heifetz Tussman, respectively:

> In many houses
> all at once
> I see my mother and father
> and they are young
> as they walk in.
> Why should my
> tears come,
> to see them laughing?
>
> That they cannot
> see me
> is of no matter:

I was once
their dream:
now
they are mine.

* * *

I know not your ways
A sunset is for me
A godset.
Where are you going,
God?
Take me along,
if, in the "along,"
it is light,
God.

I am afraid of the dark.
          (from the Yiddish)

Also noteworthy is a new Hebrew poem for *havdalah* by Reconstructionist
rabbi Leila G. Berner extolling Miriam (*miryam ha-nevi'ah*) to counterpoint
the popular *eliyahu ha-navi, eliyahu ha-tishbi*. (The musical setting for both
songs is the same.) Here is Arthur Waskow's rendition:[15]

Miriam! the dancing prophet,
In whose hands are strength and song
Miriam, come dance with us,

To lift up song for all the world.
Miriam, come dance with us,
To lift up song for all the world.

Speedily, in our own days,
Bring us to the healing waters
To the wells of liberation,
To the wells of transformation.

Miriam!—the dancing prophet,
In whose hands are strength add song
Miriam, come dance with us

To heal the hurts of all the world.
Miriam, come dance with us
To heal the hurts of all the world.

Yes, let's give Moses' sister her rightful place, especially when we intone the *shirat ha-yam* (for which she may well have been the spur and inspiration), whether in its entirety or in its two most familiar verses (*mi khamokhah ba-elim* and *adonay yimlokh* [Exodus 15: 11 and 18]). Yes, let's have more of the feminine in our liturgy. But must we remythologize in Berner/Waskow's quasi-eschatological fashion to counter the entrenched tradition of Elijah as male herald of the Messiah? It seems to me that in attempts to rectify a historic wrong, an overcorrection has been made. Why must the masculine be laundered out of existence—as it frequently seems in this volume—to make room for the feminine? The *animus* is no less indispensable than the *anima* for the healthy psyche and the healthy society.

Both women and men need to be heard, as Merle Feld intimates in the closing verse of "We All Stood Together," her poetic portrayal of a woman's fancied perspective, in contrast to her brother's recorded account, of what happened at Sinai:

If we remembered it together
we could create holy time
sparks flying.

Other Flaws

Regrettably, there are other flaws in *Kol Haneshamah*. Given the many truly admirable traits of the new prayerbook, it is troubling to espy the many orthographical mistakes and linguistic blunders that have crept in, particularly on the Hebrew side. The older Reconstructionist liturgies had the sure hand of Joseph Marcus to help proofread, revise, and compose Hebrew texts. While it is probably fair to say that someone on the present editorial staff has a discriminating and sound eye for selecting novel Hebrew (and Yiddish) readings, the same unhappily does not apply to the writing of new Hebrew prayers or to correct Hebrew spelling.

There are enough bloopers to make one cringe. The *shemoneh esreh* in the

1996 *Kol Haneshamah : Daily Prayer Book* has its unhappy share. In an effort to take some of the edge off the all-masculine imagery of God, the editors recast, however so slightly, the *berakhah* regarding repentance (Benediction V) by replacing "our Father" and "our King," respectively, with "divine source" (*meqorenu*) and "our sovereign (*atartenu*, literally "our crown"). The hitch is that the term *atartenu* is feminine, and all the verbs in the benediction, being masculine, do not match. (A similar mismatch can potentially occur in several of the suggested versions of *avinu malkenu*, on pages 140–43, for fastdays and the Ten Days of Penitence.) A single-*berakhah* alternative to the Intermediate Benedictions by Edward Feld, in place of the customary *havinenu*, is offered for those lacking in time or skill to recite all eighteen (or nineteen). The opening line in Hebrew reads *peqah eyni lire'ot be-tuv yitzrekha* ("Open my eye, that it may look upon the goodness of your plan"). Unfortunately, the term *yitzrekha* (*yetzer* = inclination, [evil] impulse, sexual drive) strikes one as most peculiar when applied to the Jewish concept of God.

Even the transliteration, which plays a very visible part in the new rite, has its share of inaccuracies. (The following infelicities are all taken from the 1994 *Kol Haneshamah: Shabbat Vehagim.*) Faculty and graduates of an institution of higher Jewish learning should know better than to spell Hanukkah with a *shuruq* rather than a *qubbutz;* to omit a *dagesh* within the second consonant of *ammekha (ammim), haggim* and *kallah;* to write out the months Adar and Tammuz with a *qamatz* under the first letter and to remove the *hataf patah* from under the *het* in *hatan ha-torah* in the Festival Evening Service. Fine points of grammar like the distinction between the *sheva na* and the *sheva nah* are lost on the transcribers in *vayhulu* [*sic!*] (p. 108), *ushavtem* [*sic!*] (p. 555) and *vaydaber* [*sic!*] (p. 590). The compilers' predilection for the diacritical *h* to serve for both *het* and *khaf* raises questions of another kind. Many of our Sephardic brothers and sisters are careful to distinguish between the two sounds. We probably should be too.

Luckily, cacography does not plague the English or Yiddish quite as much. But the second reformulator of the *aleynu* was the fellow-Philadelphian liberal Conservative liturgiographer, Max D. Klein, and not Max D. Kline. The last line of the first stanza of Kalia Molodowsky's winsome *Dos Gezang fun Shabbes* is smitten with two disconcerting typos (p. 734). And in the Hanukkah favorite "Rock of Ages," one wonders whether the spirit of the rabbi/hymn-writer and—to be unforgivably anthropomorphic—

God, too, are chagrined or tickled by the overeager patronymic umlaut in Gustav Göttheil.

Also, one can easily be put off by the recurrent tendency in the pages of *Kol Haneshamah* toward self-promotion. In the Sources, persons associated with the Reconstructionist Movement are listed expressly as "Reconstructionist rabbis" or "contemporary Reconstructionist scholars" while Alvin I. Fine, Lawrence Kushner, Richard Levy, Hershel Matt, Jack Riemer and Ruth Sohn are given the garden-variety designation "contemporary American rabbis."

Finally, there is the problem of acknowledgment. Although it is really not necessary to trace the origins of all practices in the rite to their creators (*e.g.* the positioning of titles of prayers or services at the foot of the page was started in *Siddur Sim Shalom*), it would surely have been an act of courtesy to acknowledge the Conservative prayerbook as the origin of the summonses to the Torah with panache on Simḥat Torah for both the end of Deuteronomy and the beginning of Genesis (the Shabbat and Festival volume, pp. 669–71; cf. *Siddur Sim Shalom,* pp. 554–57). And the perdurable Prayer for Our Country by Louis Ginzberg, graceful alike in Hebrew and in English, goes back to the first official liturgical text of Conservative Judaism, *The Festival Prayer Book* (1927), published under the auspices of the United Synagogue of America. There is nary a word of acknowledgment in the Sources. Instead, we are treated to an overblown retranslation of Ginzberg's stately Hebrew text.

Conclusion

But we cavil. The appearance of the *Kol Haneshamah* volumes is clearly a major literary/liturgical event. The impressive teamwork and esprit de corps among people from a wide theological spectrum but with shared principles—rabbis and laity, men and women, philosophers and poets—has yielded highly commendable results. Jews of every persuasion stand to gain from the new, indigenously American, *minhag.*

In the Introduction to the 1994 volume, David A. Teutsch gives expression to a wish no doubt shared by every prayerbook editor:

> The name of this prayerbook series comes from Psalm 150—*kol hane-shamah tehalel yah,* often translated, "Let every soul praise God." But

kol haneshamah could also mean, "all the soul." Let it be the soul's voice that offers praise.

Another appropriate wish would be the one voiced in the prayer with which Mordecai M. Kaplan, one of the first liturgiographers of the Reconstructionist movement, was accustomed to begin his classes. The prayer, which also appears in *Kol Haneshamah,* could serve as an encouragement and a caveat to all those striving to keep alive the ancient craft of siddur making:

> From the cowardice that shrinks from new truth,
> From the laziness that is content with half-truths,
> From the arrogance that thinks it knows all truth,
> O, God of truth, deliver us.

An earlier version of this chapter appeared in *Judaism* 39, 3 (Summer 1990): 339–44. ©1990, the American Jewish Congress. Reprinted with permission.

1. The book, a collection of prayers and readings for Rosh Hashanah or Yom Kippur, was to serve as a supplementary volume in conjunction with whatever maḥzor a congregation was using, "whether Orthodox, Conservative or Reformist." The material eventually wound up in the Reconstructionist *High Holiday Prayer Book* (1948).

2. As for the High Holy Days (1948), the Festivals (1958), and the Weekday (1963).

3. Oddly enough, the weekday *Kol Haneshamah* uses the same black and white of the Holy City in its diurnal *hashkivenu,* where Jerusalem is not mentioned at all.

4. This identical passage, with one extra verse about the "land sworn to the fathers," relieves the Shema's second paragraph, *ve-hayah im shamo'a,* in *Ha-Avodah sheba-Lev,* the liturgy of the Progressive congregations in Israel. This same Israeli siddur is the model for the update and amplification of the prayer unit that follows the Shema, *emet ve-emunah.* All mention of revenge is dropped, for the reasons explained in the commentary, but, perversely enough, terms for enemy keep cropping up in the expanded version of the prayer dealing with the Shoah and the Jewish state, which is far from the case in the Israeli analogue.

5. Members of the New-Age *P'nai Or* movement (or, as since renamed, ALEPH: the Alliance for Jewish Renewal) and rabbinical students and faculty worshiping in the Scheuer Chapel on the Cincinnati campus of the Hebrew Union College had been reciting the first section of the *amidah* in this gender-inclusive version for some time.

6. "Perek Shirah," *Encyclopaedia Judaica* 13: 273–75.

7. Nonetheless, my preference goes to the 1945 *Sabbath Prayer Book's* choice of the spirited, striking and tasteful *ezkor-na ma'asey-el* ("I would fain bring to mind God's works,/ And what I have seen I would recount") from Ben Sira 42:21–43:31, also from the Jewishly-little-used Apocrypha. The passage was suggested as an option for inclusion in the *yotzer* section under the theme of God in Nature.

8. No doubt the impetus for using Rabbinic sources other than the established ones comes from the Conservative *Maḥzor for Rosh Hashanah and Yom Kippur* (1972) and *Siddur*

Sim Shalom (1989) and that for including non-Rabbinic material from the British *Forms of Prayer for Jewish Worship* (1977 and 1985).

9. The disposition of text and translation in the *Daily Prayers* volume of *Kol Haneshamah* on pp. 456–57 takes the cake with the Yiddish of Hirsh Glik's *Partisanen-Lid* opposite Nachum Waldman's "To Touch Hands in Peace"—a typographer's *reductio ad absurdum* indeed.

More effective are the layouts in the British Liberal *Service of the Heart* and in *Gate of Repentance*—and to a lesser extent in its 1995 *Siddur Lev Chadash,* where the Hebrew and English appear together on a single page and are matched and aligned in remarkable proximity, line by line. The old Magill's linear cribs have been bested! To save space and add focus, perhaps a better model would be the Israeli Orthodox *Rinat Yisra'el,* which gives its biblical citations in the margins next to the verses quoted. To be sure, the overall look would be materially altered. However, the Hebraically-untutored congregant or visitor might thus be able to acquire some vocabulary and reading skills in our ancestral tongue, instead of falling on the mercies of the transliterator or being completely under the rule of rote.

10. Danny Siegel's broad paraphrase of the Talmudic benison [p. 785] in the Sabbath and Festival volume of *Kol Haneshamah* is affecting too in its own way. *Elohay neshamah* has made a comeback with a couple of verbal alternatives taken from the Israeli Progressive *Ha-Avodah sheba-Lev:* (1) *ve-attah atid li-ttelah mimmeni le-ḥayyey olam* and (2) the *ḥatimah, asher be-yado nefesh kol ḥay ve-ruaḥ kol basar.* The first to use the phrase from Job 12:10 as its *ḥatimah* was the 1945 edition of the *Union Prayer Book* II.

11. For the 1977 edition of the Episcopal *Book of Common Prayer,* the revisers called upon W. H. Auden, an upstanding Anglican in addition to being a noted litterateur, to act as a check on the stylistic soundness of the updated rite. Similarly, in the old days of the Reform *Union Prayer Book,* during the editorial stages, English literature specialists would be consulted on matters of English style.

12. By contrast, Chaim Stern is able in the Reform High Holy Day *Sha'arey Teshuvah* (1978; p. 480) to accomplish the same objective and keep the classic brevity of the Hebrew.

13. The theology of *Kol Haneshamah* deserves extended treatment in another article. It is rather revealing that, apart from the standard Hebrew prayers, God is nowhere mentioned in the Yizkor Service.

14. This transfigured *amidah* is now part of a more comprehensive and essentially feminist liturgy created by Marcia Falk, *Sefer ha-Berakhot, The Book of Blessings: New Jewish Prayers for Daily Life, the Sabbath, and the New Moon Festival* (San Francisco, 1996).

15. This is as it appears in another Philadelphia-based prayerbook still in the making, *Or Chadash* (more than incidentally, a guiding star to *Kol Haneshamah*) of the P'nai Or Religious Fellowship.

12

Ha-Avodah sheba-Lev (1982):
A Siddur from Zion

Considering the many hardcover, paperback, stapled, and looseleaf prayer manuals that are constantly being issued in the United States and England, one would probably assume that Jews in the English speaking countries are the only ones producing and conducting creative services. But our counterparts in the Israeli Progressive Movement (*tenu'ah le-yahadut mitqaddemet*) have also taken the initiative in the area of liturgical development. After a decade of relying on occasional mimeographed services and experimental/provisional editions of a comprehensive prayerbook, the movement in 1982 came out with a new siddur in which it may certainly take much pride.

Its title, appropriately, is taken from the Talmud:[1] *Ha-Avodah sheba-Lev,* "The Service from Within the Heart." There is, indeed, much in its 263 pages that touches the heart, some quite profoundly. As prayerbooks go, this one is lean and compact, yet substantial. Without presuming to aim at all-inclusiveness, it all but reaches the point of being a *kol-bo,* an all-purpose source of ready liturgical reference.

What will undoubtedly first strike the reader is the handsome type and spare appearance—all in Hebrew except for the Aramaic Kaddish and postprandial Sabbath hymn *yah ribbon olam,* both of which are accompanied by a Hebrew translation. The rubrics are discreetly few but couched in a flawless Hebrew after the classic style of the Mishnah; and the wide margins contain biblical or Rabbinic sources for a given prayer or psalm.[2]

Ha-Avodah sheba-Lev is obviously a home-grown product, even if subsidized in part by the World Union for Progressive Judaism and the Central Conference of American Rabbis. Its indigenous quality is shown, for instance, in its presentation of the Tetragrammaton, the unutterable four letter name of God, which appears in this rite invariably in all of its four consonants (*YHVH*) without the vowels.[3] By contrast, in most American manuals of prayer the sacred name has—in accordance with centuries-long usage—either the four consonants with the vowels for the substitute-term *adonay* supplied or simply two *yods* as an abbreviation for the ineffable

259

divine name. The unvocalized spelling has been the norm for a while now—both in Israeli prayerbooks issued under the aegis of the Israeli Ministry of Religions and in the Israeli-published Koren Bible, famed for representing the best and the latest scholarship on the Masoretic text.

Many modern prayerbooks devote an early section to tone-setting ruminations on the theme of prayer. The *Gates of Prayer,* and the British *Service of the Heart* after which it is patterned, both contain several pages for this purpose in which an extensive variety of sources are drawn upon. *Ha-Avodah sheba-Lev* includes a similar section, unique in that, aside from passages from the Talmud and Maimonides and an excerpt from that true *ba'al tefillah,* Abraham Joshua Heschel, its selections are all by residents of Eretz Yisrael, including the latterday Kabbalist and erstwhile chief rabbi Abraham Isaac Kuk and the contemporary religious thinker Eliezer Schweid.

There is no question that the Israeli experience has etched itself deeply in this prayerbook. The ravages of war and the county's embattled state are reflected prominently in the service for Yom ha-Zikkaron (Memorial Day) and in the *mi she-berakh* prayer for those entering the Israel Defense Forces. In a lighter vein, a unique service has been prepared for the planting of trees.

While there is no mistaking the prayerbook compilers' pride in the Jewish homeland and their taking for granted its part in the divine scheme of salvation, a recognition lingers that final Redemption has yet to come. The eschatological amalgam of the heavenly and the earthly Jerusalem still awaits realization. For example, the third blessing of the Grace After Meals is reworded, "Complete the building of Jerusalem Thy holy city (*ve-hashlem binyan yerushalayim . . .*). The Israeli religious progressives obviously take seriously the notion of the Ingathering of the Exiles as a prerequisite for the ultimate Redemption. In the Tenth Benediction of the weekday *amidah* they pray: *Gather our dispersed* (meaning those Jews still in the lands of dispersion, instead of the traditional "us") *from the four corners of the earth unto our land* (the last prepositional clause having been tacked on).

Similarly, in the paragraph before the morning Shema, the traditional "lead us" in *ve-tolikhenu qomemiyyut* is adjusted to read *and lead them upright to our land.* The plea heavenward that the "diasporates" be moved to come home—to make Aliyah—hardly corresponds with the nineteenth-century Reformers' doctrine concerning the *Endzeit,* to say the least!

A major concern of American and English non-Orthodox prayerbook editors has been how to bring variety into worship without marring its traditional structural fabric. To a significant degree, *Ha-Avodah sheba-Lev* has been able to break the monotony of doing the same service over and over again in more subtle and less grandiose ways than the American liturgies have.

As an example, it divides up a few of the longer prayer units such as the first blessing before the Shema (*yotzer or*) and the one after the Shema (*ge'ullah*), into shorter, self-standing paragraphs each separated by an asterisk, so that a choice may he made among them for reading or chanting. The authors take advantage of the optionality of the silent meditation at the close of the *amidah* and make available a number of old and new readings, some of them real gems, for private devotion within the context of public worship. On a rare occasion an alternate version of a given prayer is placed alongside the traditional text, to accommodate the sentiments of individuals and/or congregations within the Israeli Progressive Movement. For example, a revised *aleynu* accompanying the standard rendition has the following, with emended portion italicized:

> It is our duty to praise the Lord of all things, to ascribe greatness to Him who formed the world in the beginning *and who separated us from them that go astray and gave us the Torah of truth and planted everlasting life in our midst, for all the nations may walk in the name of their gods* (Micah 4:5), for we bend the knee . . .

Similarly, the siddur offers an optional replacement for the second paragraph of the Shema (Deuteronomy 11:13–21: "And if you will indeed hearken unto My commandments . . ."), with its promise of meteorological regularity in exchange for upright ethical behavior. In smaller type, one finds the alternative Deuteronomy 30:15–20[4]—which presents fewer problems for the religious liberal.

The Israeli religious progressives' apparent unconcern with gender terminology might reek of rank heresy to their American siblings. But what may appear to be indifference springs in part from the intrinsic character of the Hebrew language, where all nouns and verbs are either masculine or feminine and there is no neuter to speak of. An egalitarianism of sorts does, however, turn up occasionally—for example, in the *mi she-berakh* blessing offered on behalf of someone and usually beginning formulaically "May He who blessed our fathers Abraham, Isaac, and Jacob . . . .". Here, we note, the blessing also includes the matriarchs Sarah, Rebekah, Rachel, and Leah. The siddur also offers a unique *mi she-berakh* for a person just inducted into the Israeli Defense Forces. It begins, "May He who blessed our fighters [long ago] Joshua, David, and Judah, Deborah, Jael, and Judith bless . . ."

The creators of *Ha-Avodah sheba-Lev* also show their non-sexist sensibilities in launching the *birkat ha-mazon* with "*Friends* (rather than the customary *Gentlemen*), let us say grace." And they dutifully emulate the official rite of the Israeli Orthodox rabbinate's placement of a feminine *modah* alongside the fixed masculine *modeh* for the familiar *modeh ani* prayer upon arising in the morning—even if they slip up in the invitation to the *havdalah* blessings with inclusion of the traditional and unabashedly sexist phrase *savrey maranan,* which means something like "Sirs, may I have your attention?" But surely more significant than these minor textual matters is the inclusion of original poems and sundry pieces by women, spiritual outpourings and frank musings that appear in abundance in *Ha-Avodah sheba-Lev* and more than make up for its occasional male chauvinist lapses.

There are many other nice touches in the new prayerbook that might escape the attention of one casually thumbing its leaves: There is an unusual newly-composed Kiddush for the eve of Yom ha-Atzma'ut and another for the day itself. The *al ha-nissim* interpolations for Hanukkah, Purim, and Yom ha-Atzma'ut all close in Hebrew with a sort of update and flourish: "Even as Thou hast wrought miracles for the first generations, so mayest Thou work them for the last and deliver us in these days as of yore."[5] And every so often an ancient Palestinian wording of a given prayer appears in no more than a phrase or a clause, as in the Second Benediction of the *amidah* which starts off with "Thou O Lord art mighty forever. *Thou humblest and exaltest,* Thou art powerful to save." The italicized phrase, which is of Palestinian origin, here also happens to replace the long-since-standardized version "Thou revivest the dead," which troubles many non-Orthodox Jews. Further on in the *amidah* the compilers have affixed to the benediction *retzeh* (in its normal Liberal noncultic recension), the older Palestinian "Do Thou dwell in Zion and may Thy servants worship Thee in Jerusalem."

Another extra is a poignant blessing also taken from the Cairo Genizah and discovered by Solomon Schechter nearly a century ago. The blessing, at first intended as a prelude to the Shema, runs as follows:

> Blessed art Thou O Lord our God, King of the universe, who hath sanctified us with His commandments and commanded us concerning the

recitation of the Shema: to proclaim His sovereignty wholeheartedly, to affirm His unity unstintingly, and to serve Him in a willing spirit.

Ha-Avodah sheba-Lev places this blessing just before the weekday *barekhu,* the starting point for the principal portion of the service (*viz.,* prior to the Shema and its attendant blessings) and points out in a rubric that the worshiper may recite it when praying alone.[6] The beauty of the blessing lies in its setting the tone and priming the worshiper inwardly for a liturgical summit, the Shema itself. Likewise, the editors did well by inserting new verses in biblical idiom into the *ge'ullah* section after the Shema, thus adding instances of redemption closer to our own time to the account of Israel's redemption in the past.[7]

It is a welcome treat, too, to have a prayer appropriated from the Dead Sea Scrolls of the ancient semi-monastic Jewish sect at Qumran. Inserted for a domestic service on Shabbat Eve is the sect's touching adaptation of the well-known Priestly Blessing ("May the Lord bless thee and keep thee . . .")[8] Maybe before long we will feel more comfortable about including Falasha, Karaite, Samaritan. and other sectarian Jewish prayers in our siddurim. After all, Jewish identity embraces many besides Ashkenazim and Sephardim—and not just those whom the Chief Rabbinate adjudges eligible for inclusion in the fellowship of all Israel.

As might be expected, the impress of many prayerbooks ranging from the Traditionalist to the Reform, from the American and European to the ancient Palestinian and Yemenite can be spotted in the pages of *Ha Avodah sheba-Lev.* The weightiest liturgical influences upon it, however, are no doubt the American Reconstructonist rites, if only because they have always been theologically and liturgically forward-looking and loyally Hebraist. In addition, the Israeli siddur's inclusion of a variety of prayers, poems, and readings with which to leaven a fixed service goes back to the Reconstructionist *Sabbath Prayer Book* of 1945. And *Ha-Avodah sheba-Lev's* redefinition of the rationale for *musaf,* along with its inclusion therein of a series of essentially aphoristic ethical verses, harks back to the 1945 siddur—and also to Robert Gordis' superior meditations/*baqqashot* in the Conservative *Sabbath and Festival Prayer Book* of the following year (even though in the latter volume the chassis of the *musaf* stays undisassembled).

To illustrate, the following is my translation of the Israeli Progressive *musaf* (in which I have supplied all the scriptural citations but one):

May it be Thy will, O Lord our God and God of our fathers, that we recall before Thee the remembrance of our ancestors as they approached Thee in the days of old when they brought their obligatory offerings, the regular daily offerings and additional Sabbath offerings according to rule. Ever since our Temple hath been destroyed and we were exiled from our Land, the entreaty of our lips and the meditation of our hearts have become like unto the sacrifices our forebears offered up before Thee.

We have desired the nearness of God—how shall we come near? (cf. Isaiah 58:2)
We have sought to do His will—how shall we be reconciled?
For He is a God that hideth Himself, in the heights of the universe is His habitation
Every living thing is in His hand and His works are with every secret thing.
When He commanded us to keep His covenant to all generations:
Behold to obey is better than sacrifice and to hearken than the fat of rams (I Samuel 16:22)
And if thy brother becometh poor—thou shalt maintain him (Leviticus 25:35).
When a stranger sojourneth with thee—thou shalt love him (Leviticus 19:33–34).
To the hireling who is in thy house—thou shalt give him his hire on the day he earneth it (Deuteronomy 24:15).
And water drink from thine own cistern (Proverbs 5: 15)—and leave the community its own.
What hath passed thy lips do—and pay thy vows to the Most High (Psalms 50:14).
Years of life hath God given thee:
Bring thy sacrifice from thine hours.

May the words of my mouth and the meditation of my heart be acceptable unto Thee, O Lord, my Rock and my Redeemer. Thou who establishest peace (*on the Sabbath of Repentance:* the peace) in the heavens grant peace unto us and unto all Israel. Say ye: Amen.

There are other specific borrowings from the older Reconstructionist rites in *Ha-Avodah sheba-Lev* : several *mi she-berakh* prayers, such as the one spoken for a couple about to be joined in wedlock, are freely adapted from the *Sabbath Prayer Book;* and the service for Yom ha-Shoah—where the mood is at once both dolorous and undaunted—includes in Hebrew translation David Polish's powerful vindicatory poem "Resurrection," which appeared in 1948 in the Reconstructionist *High Holiday Prayer Book*.[9]

An older liturgical influence in *Ha-Avodah sheba-Lev* is David Einhorn's *Olath Tamid*. As in that nineteenth-century rite, the prayer for dew and for rain with their stirring melodies (that according to custom highlight the *musaf* service of the First Day of Passover and of Shemini Atzeret, respectively) are shifted to the *amidah* of the Festival Morning Service. In like manner, the *amidah* for the *musaf* on the Sabbath coinciding with the first day of the New Month is transplanted to the Morning Service, thus unseating the regular Sabbath Morning *amidah* and rescuing a quasi-festival from oblivion.

Ha-Avodah sheba-Lev is almost as exhaustive as a siddur should be. It covers domestic, private, and public worship for nearly all occasions, the Jewish festival calendar, and Israeli national life. Nonetheless, there are some surprising omissions, a few for which one could probably guess the reason and others that one might be at a loss to explain. Missing are texts for *avinu malkenu,* the litany said during the ten-day interval between Rosh Hashanah and Yom Kippur, and *tahanun,* the weekday morning penitential office.

More serious—and perhaps revealing—is the excision of services that one would expect as a matter of course in a prayerbook as omnibus as *Ha-Avodah sheba-Lev:* for a *berit milah,* a wedding, and the final rites. Could it be that the exclusion is due to the situation in Israel today, wherein the Orthodox exercise a virtual monopoly over the central liturgical events in its citizens' personal lives? If so, the absence of such services is a sad commentary.

One of the treasures of this prayerbook from Zion is its small collection of Hebrew poems, contemporary in provenance and profoundly religious in character, that are scattered throughout the second half of the book. The direct and penetrating pieces by Israeli poets, young and no longer so young, renowned and not so well known, *dati* and secularist, all evince the vigor, candor, and immediacy of the biblical psalmists.[10]

I have taken the liberty of translating just three into English in free verse, even where the Hebrew original is not. The first, *qinah* ("A Lament") by Zeev Falk is designated to be read on Tish'ah be-Av:

How shall we lament the Temple,
How bewail trees and stones.
Our ears tingling from a new cry:
The voice of myriads of burnt ones.

The destruction of a third of our people
Matches the loss of its two sanctuaries,
And what will the tabernacle of our God give
When there is no longer the people to enter its gates?

How shall we recount the pogroms of the enemy
How shall we describe the terror of war
Has not the destruction within the heart come first
Eaten from within the flesh of our nation?

The destruction going on now matches
All the falls of the past.
How then do we hope for a new House
For the people of the Lord, before it has returned?

This night we weep for the House of israel,
Over the ruin of the people in spirit and body
Over the hiding God, a world that suffers,
And everyone who goes hence without returning.

A no less touching selection, *eli, al tiqaḥ mimmenni et ahuvay,* comes from the pen of Tuviah Ruebner (b. 1924):

My God, do not take my loved ones from me
Do not let me be left alone!
Lonely people, their heart is hard
Like the bush in the wilderness.
They eat their bread in toil
With the bitter salt,
Until their tooth is set on edge
Until their voice goes hoarse
And is made dumb and unable to say: my God,
Do not take my loved ones from me,
Do not let me be left alone!

Finally, the speaker in *goral elohim*[11] by the prolific Yehuda Amichai (b. 1924), while grudging and ironic, also addresses the modern sensibility:

The fate of God
Is now like the fate of
Trees and stones, sun and moon
Which they stopped believing in
When they began believing in Him.
But He is compelled to remain with us:
At least like the trees. at least Iike the stones.
And like the sun and like the moon and like the stars.

It is obviously due season to steer such probing, plain-speaking talks with God from the "periphery to the center," from the world of secularity into the pages of the siddur and thus make worship truly come from the heart again.[12]

An earlier version of this chapter appeared in *Judaism* 33,1 (Winter 1984): 114–21. ©1984, American Jewish Congress. Reprinted with permission.

1. Ta'anit 2a: "'To love the Lord your God, and to serve Him with all your heart and with all your soul' (Deut. 11:13). What is this service of the heart (*eyzo hi avodah she-hi ba-lev*)? You must say: it is prayer!" Cf. I Chron. 28:9.

2. The Ashkenazic and Sephardic versions of the Israeli siddur *Rinnat Yisra'el* (1976), edited by Shelomoh Tal, served as a model in design, layout, and even typography.

3. Also a practice in *Rinnat Yisra'el.* The Reconstructionists are following suit in their *Kol Haneshamah* series.

4. *Kol Haneshamah* has this option too, as a first choice. However, it is preceded by Deut. 28:1–6.

5. Cf. the Sephardic close for the same: "and Thou hast performed for them miracles and wonders, and we give thanks to Thy great name."

6. Minus the *barekhu* versicle and response, which are ordinarily recited/chanted amid a quorum. Cf. *Gates of Prayer,* p. 165, where the blessing is positioned immediately before the Shema.

7. Cf. *Kol Haneshamah's* retreatment of *emet ve-emunah* along similar lines.

8. The Union of Progressive Synagogues's *Siddur Lev Chadash* (London, 1995) suggests nine different benedictions with which to conclude a worship service. This blessing from Qumran's Community Rule (2:2f) is the sixth one. Here is John Rayner's and Chaim Stern's gender-neutral translation:

May God bless you with all good and keep you from all evil. May God teach your heart the meaning of life (*sekhel hayyim*) and grant you knowledge of the Infinite (*da'at olamim*). May God reach out to you with tenderness, that you may have enduring peace.

9. Other Hebrew renditions that make their appearance in the pages of *Ha-Avodah sheba-Lev* are Archibald MacLeish's "The Young Dead Soldiers" for an Israeli Memorial Day Service and Yevgeny Yevtushenko's "Babi Yar" for a Yizkor Service.

10. Most of these poems and more may be found in a separate supplement, mimeographed still, put out by the Conservative-Reconstructionist Congregation Mevaqqeshey Derekh that *davvens* in Jerusalem. This superb anthology remains a strictly private, intra-congregational affair, but happily, several of its poems appear in translation in the Central Conference of American Rabbis' *On the Doorposts of Your House* (New York, 1994), particularly in the "Psalms, Poems, and Readings" section.

11. Another translation, "God's Fate," by Assia Gutmann, may be found in *Poems by Yehuda Amichai,* intro. Michael Hamburger (New York, 1968), p. 26.

12. For a discussion of the Israeli Progressive Movement's 1989 High Holy Day prayerbook, *Kavvanat Ha-Lev,* see chap. 9.

13

Sephardic Influences on
Non-Orthodox American Liturgy

There has hardly ever been a time when the Sephardic influence was not apparent in the Ashkenazic liturgical orbit. The Lurianic rite used by the Hasidim, for example, heavily interfuses Sephardic elements in an Ashkenazic *nusaḥ*. And in many Ashkenazic prayerbooks, Judah Halevi's *yom leyabashah nehepekhu metzulim* is found in the *ge'ullah* section for the Seventh Day of Passover.

Similarly, the Sephardic influence is evident in non-Orthodox rites today. Most obviously, it manifests itself in elements such as the zesty Israeli folksong *eyn addir k-adonay,* which has happily caught on in many an American synagogue. Probably less noticeable are contributions such as the Sephardic *hashkivenu* in one of the Friday night services from the *Gates of Prayer* or a version of the Sabbath and Festival Ashkenazic *hashkivenu,* shortened according to Sephardic specifications, in the Reconstructionist *Kol Haneshamah* (1989 and 1994).

One might easily grasp how catchy, singable, and short Sephardic pieces make their way into the non-Orthodox American siddur, particularly if they are seen as Israeli. But what of the more sophisticated selections? Since the 1940s the Conservative, Reconstructionist, and Reform rites have all carried Solomon ibn Gabirol's *shaḥar avaqqeshkha* ("Early will I seek Thee, my Rock and Refuge strong") to introduce Sabbath morning worship. They have also taken up Moses ibn Ezra's *el nora alilah*[1] for the Concluding Service on Yom Kippur. The Conservative Movement's maḥzor (1972) for the same service even presents the petition for the opening of the gates of blessing in a Sephardic-style alphabetic acrostic. According to Lawrence Hoffman, the *Gates of Repentance* borrowed this entreaty straight from the Conservative maḥzor, which in turn appropriated and extracted it from the Sephardic *qaddish titqabbel, te'anu ve-te'ateru,*[2] for the High Holy Days. Indeed, the *Gates of Repentance,* as a case in point, contains at least a half-dozen Sephardic liturgical poems—only slightly outnumbered by its Ashkenazic selections, a proportion that has existed since the second volume of *The Union Prayer Book* first appeared in 1894.

How did these Sephardic selections filter into the American prayerbooks? Seldom does anything quite happen overnight, appearances notwithstanding. The rule applies no less in the sphere of liturgical change, where the Sepharadizing tendency began in earnest almost two centuries ago and scholarly appreciation for the creative outpourings of Spanish Jewry came into its own several decades later. The extensive replacement of the standard Ashkenazic *piyyutim* with Sephardic ones, however, did not occur until a large segment of central European, German-speaking Jewry emigrated to the New World.

The first official non-Orthodox prayerbook, issued in 1819, was the famed Hamburg *Gebethbuch (Seder ha-Avodah)*. In part because of a Sephardic component in the German synagogue membership and in part because of a growing aversion to what were perceived as lengthy, unintelligible Ashkenazic *piyyutim,* the Hamburg Temple made a point of adopting as valid options the substitution of Sephardic *piyyutim* for the customary Ashkenazic ones. The temple also adopted Sephardic practices such as elevation of the unfurled Torah scroll *before* the reading of the weekly lesson—pretty much in accord with what was to be found in the Spanish-Portuguese synagogue at the time.

For example, *atanu le-ḥallot panekha,*[3] *addir ve-na'or {mi el kamokha},*[4] and *be-terem sheḥaqim va-araqim*[5] were staples repeated during two or more of the five services on Yom Kippur in the *Gebethbuch. Pizmonim* peculiar to each of the Atonement services are echoed in the its post-*amidah selihot* section, such as *yeratzeh am evyon* during the Evening Service, *le-ma'ankha, elohay, retzeh am lekha shiḥar*[6] in the morning, *yisrael avadekha lefanekha ne'esafim*[7] for *musaf,* and *yah, shema evyonekha*[8] for the Afternoon Service. Non-Ashkenazic litanies that found a niche here were *adonay, ḥonenu va-haqimenu,*[9] *adonay, aseh le-ma'an shemekha,*[10] *raḥum ve-ḥanun, ḥatanu lefanekha raḥem aleynu,*[11] and *eloheynu she-ba-shamayim.*[12]

One feature from the Sephardic prayerbook that the Hamburg *Gebethbuch* made equally its own was a set of memorial prayers that make up what is known as the *hashkavah.*[13] These prayers, placed before the regular Mourner's Kaddish—and preeminently during the Memorial Service—are *mah rav tuvkha, menuḥah nekhonah,* and *kol yisrael,* which more or less occupy the same position as *el male raḥamim* for the Ashkenazim. Surprising as it may seem, these Sephardic *in memoriam* prayers became de rigueur in virtually *all* of the nineteenth-century American non-Orthodox prayerbooks, Conservative as well as Reform, such as those compiled by David Einhorn, Leo

Merzbacher, Isaac M. Wise, Benjamin Szold (later joined by Marcus Jastrow), and Adolph Huebsch (English translation by Alexander Kohut). More Hebraically inclined American non-Orthodox rites followed another precedent set by the *Gebetbuch,* commencing the solemn *avodah* service on Yom Kippur with the Sephardic (though of unknown authorship) *attah konanta,*[14] rather than the abstruse prefatory *amitz koah*[15] by Meshullam ben Kalonymos. Indeed, even the most recent editions of the High Holy Day prayerbooks for both the American and British Reform Movements[16] include the Sephardic *attah konanta* as the poetic prelude to the *avodah.*

It must be recalled that the Hamburg *Gebetbuch* was largely the work of two dedicated, learned laymen, S.J. Fränkel and M.J. Bresselau. Their practical endeavors were followed by the groundbreaking labors of Leopold Dukes in his *Zur Erkenntniss der neuhebräischen religiösen Poesie* (1842), Michael Sachs in his *Die religiöse Poesie der Juden in Spanien* (1845), and, of course, the ever-prodigious Leopold Zunz in his *Die synagogale Poesie des Mittelalters* (1855). While Zunz certainly never belittled the devotional value of the Ashkenazic *piyyutim,* he joined Dukes and Sachs in spotlighting the matchless lyricism of the Jewish religious poets from Islamic Spain.

Individual traditional prayerbooks of the Sephardic *minhag* appeared in the United States between the decade before the American Revolution and the arrival of German-speaking Jews to these shores in the 1840s. As Israel Abrahams described in his *By-Paths in Hebraic Bookland* (Philadelphia, 1920), the first of these was Isaac Pinto's prayerbook (1761), which was no more than a literal English translation of the Sephardic rite, unaccompanied by any Hebrew text. The next American Sephardic prayerbook to be printed, in handsome Hebrew type and faithfully translated by Isaac Leeser, was *Siddur Siftey Tzaddiqim* (Philadelphia, 1837–1838).

On the non-Orthodox and non-Sephardic side, Leo Merzbacher, of New York's *Emanu-El-gemeinde,* produced a four hundred-page emended prayerbook for Yom Kippur, *Seder Tefillah, Order of Prayer,* in 1855, the same year Zunz's *Die synagogale Poesie* appeared. Among its dozen or more *piyyutim* of Sephardic derivation is Solomon ibn Gabirol's *elohim, eli attah (ashaharekha be-sod segullatekha),*[17] which was designated in Israel Davidson's *Otzar ha-Shirah veha-Piyyut* as a *reshut* for *nishmat* on Yom Kippur. Merzbacher placed it among the *piyyutim,* Ashkenazic and Sephardic, after the Morning *amidah* and the reading of selected psalms, where he also inserted, in its entirety, the beautiful introspective *lekha, eli, teshuqati,*[18] which Sachs classified among those of unknown authorship. Both *piyyutim* were subsequently included in the *Union Prayer Book* II, although only in English translation. Merzbacher also brought in ibn Gabirol's *shofet kol ha-aretz*[19]— minus, however, the hope for Temple and monarchy reinstated. This he accomplished by revising the fourth stanza from

הטיבה ברצונך את־ציון עיר קדושי. ונתת יד
ושם בביתך למקדשי. ועריכת נר לבן־ישי להעלת
נר תמיד.   כעלת הבקר אשר לעלת התמיד:[20]

to a more generalized but "enlightening" request in

הטיבה ברצונך . ישרשל ויהודה . ונתת יד
ושם . לתורה ולתעודה . וסר חשך ועלטה .
להעלות נר תמוד:

עולת הבקר אשר לעולת התמיד:[21]

In the post-*amidah* miscellaneous section of his *musaf* Service, Merzbacher also incorporated ibn Gabirol's *keter malkhut*,[22] the first poem extensively treated in Sachs's *Religiöse Poesie,* albeit stripped of the Andalusian poet's Ptolemaic planetary schematization.

Three years later, in 1858, David Einhorn's inspired German-Hebrew *Olath Tamid* was published in Baltimore. As he explained in his *Vorwort,* Einhorn strove to keep repetition of prayers to an absolute minimum in his High Holy Day services. No litanies are duplicated. To cite a solitary example, *avinu malkenu*[23] was to be recited on Yom Kippur *only* during the Morning Service, while for the Evening Service the Sephardic litany *eloheynu sheba-shamayim* (reduced to eleven verses) took its place. Einhorn shared the partiality of his contemporaries in preferring, in the language of his preface, "Pijutim von den berühmtesten spanischen Dichtern." By his own account he drew upon Sachs's *Religiöse Poesie* for such verses as ibn Gabirol's ruminative, monitory *shikheḥi yegonekh* (for his Memorial Service), the "charming" *(liebliche) yonah ḥafesah* by Isaac ibn Giat, and Judah Halevi's lofty *barekhi atzulah,* the last two for *ne'ilah.* All these pieces appear in *Olath Tamid* solely in German, as do ibn Gabirol's *el beyt melekh* and Bahya ibn Paqudah's "reproof," *barekhi nafeshi* (both of which materialize in Einhorn's rather long Memorial Service).

The one poem that entered the *Union Prayer Book* II and remained there until its 1945 edition is *shikhehi yegonekh* in English guise ("O soul, with storms beset,/ Thy griefs and cares forget!/ Why dread earth's transient woe") as a meditation before the personal English-language Yizkor prayers. Among the Sephardic items that show up in the Hebrew, on the other hand, are *adonay, honenu va-haqimenu,* during the Morning Service, and three during *ne'ilah: be-terem she-haqim va-araqim nimtahu* (missing, though, the last stanza); *el nora alilah* (much condensed); and *addir ve-na'or.* Except for *adonay, honenu va-haqimenu,* all these still thrive in the Reform rite, and *el nora alilah* is now rightfully restored to its original length.

A few years later Benjamin Szold, the younger Baltimorean who leaned to the right of Einhorn ritually and doctrinally, compiled *Abodath Israel* (1864). Despite the rivalry and recriminations between the two rabbis, Szold included nearly all of Einhorn's selection of *piyyutim*—for the most part, however, in the Hebrew original, with Sachs's German renditions. Szold was, however, more careful as to where he placed these. For example, he put the pieces by ibn Gabirol—*elohim eli attah, shahar avaqqeshkha, se'i ayin yehidati,* etc.—in the Morning Service, rather than in the morning, repositioning them all, in conformity to the poet's original intent, before *elohay neshamah.* Further, he imported *lekha, eli, teshuqati,* according to Sephardic custom, for reading before Kol Nidrey and Judah Halevi's *adonay, negdekha kol ta'avati* [24] as a meditation *(in stiller Andacht)* before the actual start of services on Yom Kippur morning.

Szold also included such Sephardic staples as *eloheynu sheba-shamayim* (as in Einhorn, for Yom Kippur Eve only), *shofet kol ha-aretz* in the Morning Service, *attah konanta olam me-rosh* as the preface to the *avodah,* and *yisra'el avadekha ne'esafim* during *musaf.* In his revision of *Abodath Israel* (1873), Marcus Jastrow made minimal changes in Szold's Hebrew text. Jastrow did, however, introduce metrical English translations, both his own and by others, of the *piyyutim* Szold chose, such as this portion of Bahya's *tokhehah* during the Memorial Service.

'Bless the Lord, O my soul, and all that is within me, bless His Holy Name!' My soul, step forth with victorious strength, sound thy Creator's praise with thy sweetest lays. Pour out before Him thy cares and vows; from thy slumber rouse! Think of thy home, keep in view the track, remember whence thou art come, whither thou goest back.

In addition to his known lexicographical skills, Jastrow had an aptitude for versification in his adopted tongue, as evident from his renditions of Moses ibn Ezra's *qedushah,* Halevi's *yah, anah emtza'ekha* and the much-beloved *adon olam* of still-anonymous authorship. These are found in his hymnal supplement to *Abodath Israel,* "Songs for Divine Services."

Adolph Huebsch's Hebrew-German prayerbook, *Seder Tefillah (Gebete für den öffentlichen Gottesdienst),* published in 1875 for his Bohemian Congregation Ahawath Chesed (now New York's Central Synagogue), assumed a theological and halakhic position between *Olath Tamid* and *Abodath Israel.* Incidental Sephardic touches can be detected here and there in the High Holy Day volume. Particularly striking is a *silluq* to the morning *qedushah* by Judah Halevi, *elohim, el mi amshilekha?*[225] that also appears in Sachs's *Religiöse Poesie.* Huebsch uses the first stanza of this captivating *piyyut* (up to "Holy, holy, holy is the Lord of hosts") as a preface to the *qedushah* of the afternoon *amidah* on Yom Kippur.

Finally, the Sephardic influence may also be traced in the Reconstructionist liturgy. A rich supplementary section of old and new material in its *Sabbath Prayer Book* (1945) offers a generous helping of poetic pieces by Solomon ibn Gabirol (most heavily represented, with eleven), Judah Halevi (four), and Baḥya ibn Paqudah (two)—the "constellation of three" (*das Dreigestirn),* as Elbogen once put it in a slightly different context.

I suspect several factors account for this predilection among the liturgy makers of early Reconstructionism for Sephardic religious poetry. Most obviously, it was readily available to them at the time. The first-rate bilingual volumes of the devotional poetry by Solomon ibn Gabirol, Judah Halevi, and Moses ibn Ezra were issued by the Jewish Publication Society in the 1920s and 1930s. Second, the *Sabbath Prayer Book's* compilers—Mordecai M. Kaplan, Eugene Kohn, Milton Steinberg, Joseph Marcus, and Ira Eisenstein—were no doubt influenced by the non-Orthodox prayer manuals discussed above, with which they were well acquainted. In addition, many of its prayers and meditations are taken from the 1931 *Forms of Prayer* of the West London Synagogue, the essentially Sephardic-based founding synagogue of the British Reform Movement. Third, the Reconstructionist movement was then very much in a state of ferment—even as it continues to be—with regard to its understanding of God. Fittingly, ibn Gabirol's poems bespeak the soul's profound yearning for and even constitutive identity with the divine.

Fourth, from the very outset, the Reconstructionist movement has been almost programmatically appreciative of Jewish literary, cultural, and spiritual endeavors in the Hebrew language throughout the millennia. And certainly not least of all, the Society for the Advancement of Judaism, the mother synagogue and original headquarters of the Reconstructionist Movement, was within a brisk walking distance of the famed Spanish-Portuguese Synagogue in Manhattan.

How can we explain the early attraction of certain Sephardic features in text and conduct of worship to *all* non-Orthodox branches of American Judaism? Surely the fact that medieval Spanish Jews in the Islamic milieu were as much at home in secular society as in the world of Jewish faith and culture offered post-Emancipation generations of Jews a model worth emulating. The Sephardic style did not appear to be limited to the halakhic mode of discourse. Perhaps the expansiveness of its sensibility provided a sense of release, an alternative, and a legitimation to Ashkenazim feeling oppressed or constricted by a tragedy-laden, impeditive tradition.

No doubt the new-found appreciation for the esthetic and decorous form in poetic word and liturgical execution among American Jews not long out of ghetto and shtetl was fortified by those who had cultivated that appreciation and skill ages ago. In addition, the Sephardic versifiers, several of whom were religious philosophers of the first order, addressed fundamental matters of God and the self, humankind, the moral life, terrestrial existence, faith, and immortality in ways that cut across boundaries of time, space, and *minhag* and even today strike a responsive chord among the spiritually attuned. Now that contacts between Ashkenazim and Sephardim extend beyond the sharing of revived old literary texts—especially in Israel———it should be quite interesting to see where Jewish worship and liturgy, non-Orthodox *and* Orthodox, Ashkenazic *and* Sephardic, American *and* Israeli, will lead us.[26]

An earlier version of this chapter appeared in *Shofar* 11 (Fall 1992): 12–21. © 1992, Purdue Research Foundation, West Lafayette, IN 47907. Reprinted with permission.

1. In a letter to the author, Bemard H. Mehlman, rabbi of Temple Israel in Boston, who initiated the singing of *el nora alilah* at his Reform temple during *ne'ilah,* mentioned

the fact that during his assistantship at Temple Sha'aray Tefila in New York City his senior, Rabbi Bern6ard Bamberger, was wont to chant this winsome *piyyut* during the last service for the Day of Atonement. It is hardly a coincidence that Bamberger's predecessor, Frederick De Sola Mendes—who pastored Sha'aray Tefila from 1874 to 1920 and who presided over the congregation's passage from the Historical School (= Conservative Judaism) to a traditionalist style of Reform—was, by lineage, a "true-blue" Sepharadi. The *piyyut* may be found in *Tefillot le-Yom Kippur: Prayers for the Day of Atonement, according to the Custom of the Spanish and Portuguese Jews,* edited and translated by David de Sola Pool (New York, 1939 [reprinted 1984]), pp. 294–95.

2. *Tefillot le-Yom Kippur,* pp. 327–28.

3. Ibid., p. 215.

4. Ibid., pp. 58–59.

5. Ibid., 183.

6. Ibid., pp. 173–74.

7. Ibid., pp. 174–75.

8. Ibid., pp. 175–76.

9. Ibid., p. 186.

10. Ibid., pp. 186–87.

11. Ibid., pp. 185–86.

12. Ibid., pp. 189–92.

13. Ibid.,, pp. 32–34.

14. Ibid., pp. 226–28 [-39].

15. Nosson Scherman and Meir Zlotowitz, ed., *Mahzor Zikhron Yosef: The Complete Artscroll Machzor* [Yom Kippur] (Brooklyn, NY, 1986), pp. 554–69.

16. Not only the Central Conference of American Rabbis' *Gates of Repentance* but *Seder ha-Tefillot: Forms of Prayer for Jewish Worship* III, Prayers for the High Holydays (London, 1985), put out by the Reform Synagogues of Great Britain, carry it.

17. *Tefillot le-Yom Kippur,* pp. 129–31.

18. Ibid., pp.21–22a.

19. David de Sola Pool, *Tefillot le-Rosh ha-Shanah: Prayers for the New Year according to the Customs of the Spanish and Portuguese Jews* (New York, 1937, repr. 1985), pp. 163–64 .

20. O deal in gracious favor with Zion's holy city. Give place and glory in Thy fame unto its hallowed priests. For David, Jesse's son, rekindle Thou the lamp, and the Temple's daily light as *"An offering of the morning to burn in our heart always."*

21. The translation there reads

Deal kindly in Thy favor with Israel and Judah, and confer strength and glory on Thy law and its mission, and let gloom and darkness vanish before it, that light may increase continually *Congregation: As* the regular burnt-offering in the morning.

With reinforcement from one of its two other liturgical predecessors, notably David Einhorn's *Olath Tamid,* only the 1894 edition of the *Union Prayer Book* II retained this *piyyut* in the Hebrew, with Merzbacher's graceful emendation just quoted.

22. *Tefillot le-Rosh ha-Shanah,* pp. 333a-43.

23. Sherman and Zlotowitz, pp. 436–39; *Tefillot le-Yom Kippur,* pp. 171–73.
24. Ibid., pp. 129–29.
25. Ibid., pp. 149–54.
26. Professor Jakob J. Petuchowski reviewed this essay and offered valuable pointers just weeks before his final illness and passing. His support and encouragement of colleagues and students always went beyond the call of duty. *Yehi zikhro varukh.*

14

Mystical Influences on Jewish Liturgical Renewal

With all the external and internal modifications of non-Orthodox worship during a major part of the nineteenth century and the first half of the twentieth, the outlines of the classical liturgy (Heb.: the *mathe'a shel tefillah*; Ger.: *Stammgebete),* as formulated by the ancient Rabbinic Sages, remained astonishingly intact: the Shema and its attendant benedictions, and the *amidah.* In keeping with the temper of the times, however, liturgical renewal tended to be marked by certain rationalizing tendencies, which meant that the mystical component in the Jewish tradition was either downplayed or removed altogether. Previously, scarcely a rite was without features drawn from the Kabbalah, operating as a kind of overlay upon the classic Rabbinic framework. Largely owing to abuses and aberrations that insinuated themselves into mystical belief and practice, the verdict was that kabbalistic teaching was little less than—in the words of the doyen historian at the time, Heinrich Graetz—*Schwärmerei* (excessive emotionalism). Since the appearance of the magisterial investigative, theological, and literary labors by the likes of Gershom Scholem, Martin Buber, and Abraham Joshua Heschel from the 1920s on, the liturgical revisers have been reevaluating the merit of the rich kabbalistic legacy and reappropriating many an abandoned prayer in the newer prayerbooks, often with good results.

Apart from the Psalms, known for their intimate contemplations of and heartfelt appeals to God, Jewish creativity in mystical prayer manifested itself not in the Bible but in the early Rabbinic period. Very sparingly but tantalizingly—lest these concepts be lamentably misconstrued and/or vulgarized—the Talmud and Midrash alluded to *ma'aseh bereshit* ("the Work of Creation" based on Genesis 1), which deals primarily with cosmology, and to *ma'aseh merkavah* ("the Account of the Chariot" deriving from Ezekiel 1), which is largely theosophical. Within the same time frame, into the Gaonic period, *heykhalot* literature appeared, telling us how the adept would enter several "palaces" by means of meditation and ecstasy until they experienced a vision of the Throne of Glory. A goodly portion of the lofty, rapturous *heykhalot* hymns[1] eventually found their way into the Ashkenazic High Holy Day prayerbook.

278

The next significant phase was the pietistic-mystical phenomenon of the twelfth- and thirteenth-century German Hasidim *(ḥasidey ashkenaz),*[2] under the leadership of Rabbi Judah ben Samuel the Pious *(he-ḥasid)* of Regensburg and his disciple Rabbi Eleazar ben Judah of Worms. From this circle came the devotional, ethical, and ascetic work *Sefer Ḥasidim,* which includes elements of letter and number mysticism and folk superstition. Medieval German Jewish Pietism was also responsible for the highly numinous *shirey ha-yiḥud,* ("Songs of Unity") for each day of the week, to be recited upon the completion of the statutory prayers. Highly allusive and arcane, they are only rarely translated, one exception being the well known *an'im zemirot,* which also has its own designation, *shir ha-kavod* ("Hymn of Glory") and which, in varying length, has come to new life in many a contemporary prayerbook.

This creative impulse in prayerful composition was to climax in sixteenth-century Safed, when exiles from the Iberian Peninsula established a community that gave prominence to the ascetic, consecrated devotional life based upon fulfillment of the mitzvot. One of its prime movers and leading lights was the sainted Rabbi Isaac Luria (the *Ari,* an acronym based on his name and title in Hebrew) and his key disciple Rabbi Ḥayyim Vital. The Ari's utterances—touching on his cosmology, theosophy, and understanding of the mitzvot—and his extraordinary deeds are hagiographically embellished and recorded in the works of his adherents. Directly from his own pen are some enchanting *zemirot* (Sabbath table hymns) that are replete with esoteric Kabbalistic references. They continue to be sung today by the Hasidim at each of the three Sabbath meals. The *kavvanot* (meditational aids for concentration during the recitation of given prayers)[3] and the performance of certain ceremonies are frequently ascribed to Luria.

More widely known among world Jewry are hymns by others of the Lurianic school, such as Solomon Alkabetz, who is the author of the strongly implicative and eschatological hymn at the commencement of Shabbat, the alluring and universally cherished *lekhah dodi* ("Come, my beloved, to meet the bride [i.e. the Sabbath]") and Israel Najara, composer of the Sabbath table hymn, *yah ribbon,* set to many different captivating melodies. Below is the entirety of *lekhah dodi* in Chaim Raphael's translation,[4] and the first three verses of *yah ribbon* in Philip Birnbaum's rendition:[5]

Lekha dodi

Come, my beloved, to meet the bride: come to greet the Sabbath.

"Keep" and "Remember," a single command, which God—in unity—
caused us to hear.

The Lord is One and His name is One, to His renown, His glory and
His praise.

Come, let us go to meet the Sabbath, for it is a fountain of blessing;
From the beginning, from of old, it was ordained; last in act, first in
thought.

The royal shrine, regal city, rise and come forth from destruction.
Too long have you dwelt in the vale of tears: now God will show His
pity on you.

Awake, arise from the dust; array yourself, O my people, in splendor;
At hand is Bethlehem's David, Jesse's son, bringing deliverance into
my life.

Awake, awake, for your light has come. Arise, shine !
Awake, awake, give forth in song; the glory of the Lord is revealed
to you.

Be not ashamed, be not confused; no longer humbled, no longer
sighing;
The poor of my people trust in Thee; and the city shall be builded on
her own mound.

They who spoiled you shall be spoiled, your devourers shall go far
away;
Then God shall rejoice over thee, as a bridegroom rejoices over his
bride.

You will break free, right and left; you will reverence the Lord;
Through the offspring of Perez, we also shall rejoice and be glad.

Come in peace, crown of her husband, in gladness and joy.
Amid the faithful of the treasured people, come O bride, come
O bride.

Yah ribbon

Lord, eternal Master of worlds,
Thou art the Supreme King of Kings.
Thy mighty acts and wondrous deeds
It is my pleasure to declare.
Lord, eternal Master . . .

Morning and evening I praise thee,
Holy God, who didst form all life:
Sacred spirits, human beings,
Beasts of the field, birds of the sky.
Lord, eternal Master . . .

Great and mighty are thy deeds,
Humbling the proud, raising the meek;
Were man to live a thousand years,
Yet he could not recount thy might.
Lord, eternal Master . . .

The Hasidic movement that arose in the eighteenth century, being essentially a populist and proletarian development and partial recasting of the mystical tradition, toned down the esotericism and elitism of the Lurianic Kabbalah and at the same time rendered its teachings accessible to the broad masses of Jews in Poland, Lithuania, Russia, and the Ukraine. With all its adaptations and transmutations, Hasidism was at bottom a remarkably faithful continuator of the Kabbalah as understood by the Ari and transmitted by his disciples. As an example, since their beginnings the Hasidim have been in the habit of using for their worship the rite established by the Lurianic school, the *nusah ari* or *nusah sepharad,* with its unique amalgam of the Ashkenazic and Sephardic prayers and *kavvanot.*

What differentiates Hasidic worship from its Kabbalistic forerunners are: I) its many written discussions of proper attitudes during prayer, 2) its creation of countless melodies, often joyous, to accompany individual prayers, 3) its individual cultivation of interiority during prayer, and 4) its fashioning of personal, private prayers (often in Yiddish rather than in Hebrew) by different tzaddiqim or rebbes.

The following are individual prayers[6] by two different tzaddiqim. The longer section afterwards, taken from Louis Jacobs' *Hasidic Thought,*[7] is an example of a tzaddiq's counsel regarding the proper conduct of prayer and fasting:

> Be it thy will
> to annul wars and the shedding of blood from the universe,
> and to extend a peace, great and wondrous, in the universe.
> "Nor again shall one people raise the sword against another
> and they shall learn war no more."
>
> But let all the residents of earth recognize and know the innermost
>   truth:
> that we are not come into this world for quarrel and division,
> nor for hate and jealousy, contrariness and bloodshed;
> but we are come into this world
> thee to recognize and know,
> be thou blessed forever.
>
> And let thy glory fill all our wits and minds, knowledge and hearts;
> and may I be a chariot for the presence of thy divinity.
> May I not again depart from the Sanctity as much as a hairsbreadth.
> May I not think one extraneous thought.
> But may I ever cling to thee and to thy sacred Torah,
> until I be worthy to introduce others into the knowledge of the truth of
>   thy divinity.
> "To announce to the sons of man thy power, and the honor of the glory
>   of thy kingdom."
>
>   Naḥman of Bratslav

> Guard us
> from vicious leanings and from haughty ways,
> from anger and from temper,
> from melancholy, talebearing,
> and from all the other evil qualities.
>
> Nor let envy of any man rise in our heart,
> nor envy of us in the heart of others.
> On the contrary:

put it in our hearts that we may see our comrades' virtue,
and not their failing.

Eliezer of Lizhensk

Since the Holy One, blessed be He, is so merciful and since there
is no limit to His power and since He demands from man only that
which man can do, it is possible that the Holy One, blessed be He,
does accept the fasting of some of these men who fast in an unsophis-
ticated way, even though they are insufficiently intelligent to carry
out the fast as it should be carried out so as to be acceptable to God.
As for men like us, however, who do know the truth, if we do not
fast in a manner acceptable to God there is no doubt that He will not
accept such a fast and it is as if the dogs had devoured it. Such a fast
goes to waste, God forbid, to the *kelipot,* called "waste." And this is a
total loss in many ways. The body loses since people in this generation are so weak, and the soul loses, for the faster loses his humility
since he imagines that by fasting he has repaid his debt. In reality he
has added to his transgression and prides himself to no avail. Now if
you are able to fast one day a week and your soul desires it, then do
it. But this is only helpful if you do as follows: Leave all your activities on that day and scrutinize your deeds in private. God forbid, do
not think that by doing so you have paid your debt, but trust in the
Lord who lets off those who sincerely repent, according to Rabbenu
Jonah's description of the various types of repentance. If you desire to
do more than this, do it, but take care that the defect does not out-
weigh the advantage. It seems to me, insofar as I have understood the
opinions of the holy men on earth I have mentioned, that in this
generation where there is so much weakness, if we fast we cannot
pray or study properly. It is therefore undoubtedly better to leave off
fasting, but instead to achieve whatever fasting is supposed to
achieve without fasting.

As for what fasting should achieve, the following are its desired
effects: (1) There must be remorse, as above; (2) breaking the heart
and the bodily energy which derives from the "Other Side"; (3)
breaking desire; (4) humility; (5) an increase of bodily heat, as it is

said, "Everything that may abide the fire, ye shall make go through the fire, and it shall be clean" (Numbers 31:23), as the *Reshit Hokhmah* states, and there are other things, too. But you can achieve all these things if you can compel your heart and the faculties of your body to offer your prayers with pure intention, which, as it is stated in the prayerbook *Shaarey Shamayyim,* is called *service.* For it involves great *service* to compel thought, busily occupied in worldly matters, to concentrate on the meaning of the words of the prayers. For this great strength is required, and this undoubtedly weakens all the limbs of the body. So if God helps you to pray occasionally with proper concentration you will undoubtedly feel remorse for your sins, your body will be broken, your desire humbled, and the burning flame that seizes hold of the heart in prayer purifies instead of the fire of fasting.

From the mid-nineteenth century through the 1930s, the revisers of the classical Jewish Prayerbook in divergent degrees hewed to the liturgical framework as outlined by the Rabbis of the Talmud but stripped away what they considered to be premodern excrescences, including kabbalistic and Hasidic material. By the middle of the twentieth century, we witness, little by little, a change of heart in the Reform *Union Prayer Book,* Conservative *Sabbath and Festival Prayer Book,* and Reconstructionist *Sabbath Prayer Book,* all of which incorporate in moderation selected items from the Kabbalistic tradition. Interestingly, with all their avowed rationalism, the Reconstructionists showed themselves the least hesitant to draw upon mystical devotional compositions—particularly the inner-oriented, contemplative prose and poetry of the Golden Age of Spanish Jewry—by including works by writers such as Baḥya ibn Paqudah, Solomon ibn Gabirol, and Judah Halevi.

Among the prayers of mystical provenance that were reinstated in the Reform *Union Prayer Book: Newly Revised* (1940) are a three-verse version of *ani'm zemirot,* attributed to Judah the Pious, to be sung in Hebrew or in Alice Lucas' English as an introductory hymn for a Shabbat Morning Service:

Sweet hymns and songs will I recite
To sing of Thee by day and night,
Of Thee who art my soul's delight.

How doth my soul within me yearn
Beneath Thy shadow to return,
Thy secret mysteries to learn.

And e'en yet Thy glory fires
My words and hymns of praise inspires,
Thy love it is my heart desires.

My meditation day and night,
May it be pleasant in Thy sight,
For Thou art all my soul's delight.

Another is the Sephardic *shaḥar avaqqeshkha* by philosopher-physician-poet ibn Gabirol—included both in the Hebrew and in the following metrical translation by Gustav Gottheil:

Early will I seek Thee, God, my refuge strong,
Late prepare to meet Thee with my evening song.
Though unto Thy greatness I with trembling soar,
Yet my inmost thinking lies Thine eyes before.

What this frail heart dreameth and my poor tongue's speech
Can they even distant to Thy greatness reach?

Because great in mercy, Thou wilt not despise
Praises which till death's hour from my soul shall rise.

The Conservative *Sabbath and Festival Prayer Book* (1946) recovered the same soulful piece by ibn Gabirol, albeit in an appendix and in English verse only, translated by Nina Salaman. It also resuscitated *an'im zemirot* and *berikh shemeih,* in Aramaic, taken from the Zohar, the classical text composed between the time of the German Jewish Pietists and the emergence of the Lurianic Kabbalah. Found in no other non-Orthodox prayer manual, however, is the Lurianic-style *kavvanah* recited before taking the lulav and etrog during the Feast of Tabernacles (on the basis of Leviticus 23:40). The meditation, from seventeenth-century Rabbi Nathan Hannover's *Sha'arey Tziyyon,* reads as follows:

I rise in reverence ready to fulfill the command of my Creator who hath enjoined upon us in His Torah: "And ye shall take for yourself on the first day the fruit of the goodly Hadar tree, branches of palm trees, a bough of the thick tree, and willows of the brook." As I wave them, may the blessing of God be vouchsafed unto me and may I be imbued with holy thoughts reminding me that God is the supreme Lord, whose divine rule pervades the earth below and the heavens above, and whose kingdom has dominion over all. May my observance of this commandment be accounted as though I had fulfilled it with whole-hearted devotion. And let the graciousness of the Lord our God be upon us; establish Thou the work of our hands; yea, the work of our hands establish Thou it. Blessed be the Lord forever. Amen.

The Reconstructionist *Sabbath Prayer Book* (1945) included *an'im zemirot* (only slightly condensed), *berikh shemeih* (a bit shortened), and *shahar avaqqeshksha*. Aptly included in the abundant supplementary section is "O Lord, where shall I find Thee?"by Judah Halevi. Like the verses above by ibn Gabirol, it stems from medieval Islamic Spain, when the mystically-tinged Neoplatonic influence permeated Judaism as well as Islam and Christianity. This translation is by Solomon Solis-Cohen.[8]

> O Lord, where shall I find Thee'?
>   Hid is Thy lofty place;
> And where shall I not find Thee,
>   Whose glory fills all space?
>
> Who formed the world, abides
>   Within man's soul alway;
> Refuge to them that seek Him,
>   Haven for them that stray.
>
> O, how shall mortals praise Thee,
>   When angels strive in vain;
> or build for Thee a dwelling,
>   Whom worlds cannot contain?
>
> Yet when they bow in worship
>   Before Thy throne, most high,
> Closer than flesh or spirit,
>   They feel Thy presence nigh.
>
> Then they, with lips exulting,
>   Bear witness Thou art one

That Thou art their Creator,
    Ruler and God alone.

Who shall not yield Thee reverence,
    That holdest the world in thrall?
Who shall not seek Thy mercy,
    That feeds and succors all?

Longing to draw near Thee,
    With all my heart I pray;
Then going forth to seek Thee,
    Thou meetest me on the way.

I find Thee in the marvels
    Of Thy creative might,
In visions in Thy temple,
    In dreams that bless the night.

Who says he has not seen Thee,
    Thy heavens refute his word;
Their hosts declare Thy glory,
    Though never voice be heard.

Dare mortal think such wonder?
    And yet, believe I must
That God, the Uncreated,
    Dwells in this frame of dust,

That Thou, transcendent, holy,
    Joyest in thy creatures' praise,
And comest where men are gathered
    To glorify Thy ways.

And where celestial beings
    Adore Thee, as they stand
Upon the heights eternal
    And Thou, above their band,

Hast set Thy throne of Glory
    Thou hearest when they call;
They sing Thine infinite wonders,
    And Thou upholdest all.

It was not until the fifties and the sixties that non-Orthodox Judaism gave a much wider berth to mystical outpourings, old and new—without, fortunately, yielding to defeatist or obscurantist sentiment, though an element of nostalgia can be detected. This was, we must recall, the period when the works of Buber, Scholem, and Heschel were widely read; when Middle and Far Eastern mysticism was both seriously and trendily studied; when Native American religion came to be appreciated anew; and when many felt that the scientific outlook scarcely explained everything or quenched the yearning soul and hungry heart.

The prayerbooks that have been published under the auspices of the main branches of American Judaism since that time generously help themselves to treasures of Jewish spirituality that had hitherto been regarded with suspicion and even disdain. What is of some interest is the kind of borrowing that has been done. Whereas the theurgic, metaphysical, speculative, or theosophical dimensions of the Kabbalah are still given little weight or even underplayed, the personal, emotional, evocative, and relational aspects are highlighted.

The *Gates of Prayer* (1975) retained all the mystical selections introduced in the 1940 *Union Prayer Book*. In addition, it included *yedid nefesh* ("Heart's Delight") by Eliezer Azikri, another sixteenth-century poet of the Safed community; two meditations ascribed to Rabbi Naḥman of Bratslav (one quoted above and another quoted below); and, in the supplementary section, the aforesaid table songs. After the manner of the Song of Songs and of mystics of all climes, the language of Azikri's poem is noticeably amatory and begins each stanza with a succeeding letter of the Tetragrammaton, YHVH. The English translation in the *Gates of Prayer* runs thus:

> Heart's delight, Source of mercy,
> draw Your servant into Your arms:
> I leap like a deer to stand in awe before You.
> Your love is sweeter to me
> than the taste of honey.

> World's light, shining glory,
> my heart is faint for love of You:
> heal it, Lord, help my heart,
> show me Your radiant splendor.

Let me return to strength
and have joy for ever.

Have compassion, O Faithful One,
pity for Your loved child:
how long have I hoped to see Your glorious might.
O God, my heart's desire,
have pity, hold back no more.

Show Yourself, Beloved, and cover me
with the shelter of Your peace.
Light up the world with Your presence,
that we may exult and rejoice in You.
Hurry, Loved One, the holy day has come:
show us grace as long ago.

A private meditation by Naḥman of Bratslav (1770–1811) stresses the
need for solitude in a natural setting, to be alone with God. In *Gates of
Prayer* it is included as a suggested reading after the regular *amidah:*[9]

Master of the universe, grant me the ability to be alone:
may it be my custom to go outdoors each day,
among the trees and grasses, among all growing things,
there to be alone and enter into prayer.

There may I express all that is in my heart,
talking with Him to whom I belong.

And may all grasses, trees, and plants
awake at my coming.

Send the power of their life into my prayer,
making whole my heart and my speech
through the life and spirit of growing things,
made whole by their transcendent Source.

O that they would enter into my prayer!
Then would I fully open my heart
in prayer, supplication and holy speech;
then, O God, would I pour out the words
of my heart before Your presence.

The Conservative *Siddur Sim Shalom* (1985) kept all that its immediate forerunner, the *Sabbath and Festival Prayer Book,* borrowed from the mystical tradition, with the exception of the *kavvanah* before waving the lulav and etrog during Tabernacles. Naḥman of Bratslav's prayer for world peace appears fittingly in the newer rite after the entreaties on behalf of the United States and of Israel. As in *Gates of Prayer, Siddur Sim Shalom* includes *yedid nefesh* in Hebrew, but the translation by Rabbi Zalman Schachter-Shelomi perhaps more optimally captures the mood and lilt of the original and is worth reproducing for comparison:

> Soul mate, loving God, compassion's gentle source,
> Take my disposition and shape it to Your will.
> Like a darting deer will I rush to You.
> Before your glorious Presence humbly will I bow.
> Let Your sweet love delight me with its thrill,
> Because no other dainty will my hunger still.
>
> How splendid is Your light, illumining the world.
> My soul is weary yearning for Your love's delight.
> Please, good God, do heal her; reveal to her Your face,
> The pleasure of Your Presence, bathed in Your grace.
> She will find strength and healing in Your sight;
> Forever will she serve You, grateful, with all her might.
>
> What mercy stirs in You since days of old, my God.
> Be kind to me, Your own child; my love for You requite.
> With deep and endless longing I yearned for Your embrace,
> To see my light in Your light, basking in Your grace.
> My heart's desire, find me worthy in Your sight.
> Do not delay Your mercy, please hide not Your light.
>
> Reveal Yourself, Beloved, for all the world to see,
> And shelter me in peace beneath Your canopy.
> Illumine all creation, lighting up the earth,
> And we shall celebrate You in choruses of mirth.
>
> The time, my Love, is now; rush, be quick, be bold.
> Let Your favor grace me, in the spirit of days of old.

The editors did well to restore the Lurianic custom of beginning each day's worship with the *kavvanah:* "I thereby accept the obligation of fulfilling my Creator's mitzvah in the Torah: Love your neighbor as yourself." They also added many excerpts from the literary output of Abraham Joshua Heschel who, though clearly a modern theologian, was very much the scion of a Hasidic dynasty. His readings are intended to facilitate the worshiper's entry into the mood of authentic prayer:

> The focus of prayer is not the self. A man may spend hours meditating about himself, or be stirred by the deepest sympathy for his fellow man, and no prayer will come to pass. Prayer comes to pass in a complete turning of the heart toward God, toward His goodness and power. It is the momentary disregard of one's personal concerns, the absence of self-centered thoughts, which constitute the art of prayer. Feeling becomes prayer in the moment in which one forgets oneself and becomes aware of God. When we analyze the consciousness of a supplicant, we discover that it is not concentrated upon his own interests, but on something beyond the self. The thought of personal need is absent, and the thought of divine grace alone is present in his mind. Thus, in beseeching Him for bread, there is one instant, at least, in which the mind is directed neither to one's hunger nor to food, but to His mercy. This instant is prayer. In prayer we shift the center of living from self-consciousness to self-surrender. God is the center toward which all forces tend. He is the source, and we are the flowing of His force, the ebb and flow of His tides.[10]

The Reconstructionists in their *Kol Haneshamah: Shabbat Eve* (1989) have gone perhaps a bit further. They include not only some of the items the other rites revived but also a running commentary that is by turns both openly rationalist and mystical; a *shivviti* illustration, with scriptural verses to aid the worshiper in focusing; and sections from the Song of Songs, which traditionally symbolizes the love between God and Israel/the individual and is, by custom in mystic circles, to be read on Shabbat Eve.[11]

All this goes to show that the mystical still appeals to the modern sensibility, and that the need for a more intimate relationship with God is an ongoing one. Recognizing that vital elemental need, the Jew on the verge of the twenty-first century can acclaim the secular world and the universe of science, but not without according the *mysterium tremendum* and the One who is at the heart of it full due and praise.

An earlier version of this article appeared in a special issue of *Marian Library Studies,* a Festschrift honoring Father Theodore Koehler, S.M., on his eightieth birthday. *MLS* 17–23: 684–97. Reprinted with permission.

    1. Gershom G. Scholem, *Jewish Gnosticism, Merkabah Mysticism, and Talmudic Tradition* (New York, 1960).

    2. Gershom G. Scholem, *Major Trends in Jewish Mysticism* (New York, 1965), pp. 80–118.

    3. Hyman G. Enelow, "Kawwana: The Struggle for Inwardness in Judaism," in *Selected Works of Hyman G. Enelow,* ed. Felix Levy (privately printed, 1935).

    4. Chaim Raphael, *Qabbalat Shabbat: The Sabbath Eve Service* (New York, 1985).

    5. Philip Birnbaum, *Ha-Siddur Ha-Shalem: The Daily Prayer Book* (New York, 1969).

    6. Nahum N. Glatzer, ed., *Language of Faith* (New York, 1947), pp. 314–17.

    7. Louis Jacobs, "How Should Man Worship God?" chap. 19 in *Hasidic Thought* (New York, 1976), pp. 149–54.

    8. Here is Marcus Jastrow's rendition, by way of comparison:

O Lord, where shall I find thee,
    Whose seat no eye espies?
And where, O Lord, not find thee,
    Whose throne is earth and skies?

Who dwell'st in hearts that fear thee,
    To worlds thou sett'st a bar;
Thou shield of all who're near thee,
    And staff of those afar!

O thou 'mong Cherubim dwelling,
    Enthroned in ether's light,
All praises they are telling
    Can never reach thy height.

And yet, midst sons of earth here,
    Should God dwell? Daring thought!
A dream how high aspiring
    Of man who is like naught!

Yet, where thy praise resoundeth,
    Thy majesty is near,
From heaven to earth reboundeth
    The song of holy fear.

    9. A portion of the Hebrew text is reproduced in the Readings section (on the theme of

Nature) in *Kol Haneshamah: Shabbat Vehagim* (Wyncote, PA 1994). A very similar translation there is attributed to Shamai Kanter. Comparable meditations by Hasidic masters have been garnered and becomingly translated into English by Arthur Green and Barry Holtz in *Your World is Fire* (New York, 1977).

10. Jules Harlow, ed. *Siddur Sim Shalom* (New York, 1989), pp. 850–851 (among others).

11. For examples of other mystical and New Age influences on *Kol Haneshamah*, see chap. 11.

15

Messianism in the Progressive Passover Haggadah

The most universally commemorated and celebrated event among Jews the world over, no matter what their level of ritual observance or doctrinal commitment, is the Seder on the eve of the first day of the pristine festival of Passover. Whether observed in the home or in a public place, the Seder serves as an unsurpassed opportunity for reunion and reaffirmation within the context of a joyous memorialization of a formative communal experience. Prayer, narrative, exegesis, symbol, memory, and song all play ineluctable parts in highlighting the Exodus experience and elucidating its significance over time and space. None of this of course is the special purview of any one segment of the Jewish community: the Passover experience belongs to all of Israel.

Countless traditions and practices have evolved and crystallized around the holiday, the preponderance of which have been maintained with remarkable earnestness and zeal by Orthodox Jewry. Inasmuch as modern Jews of other stripes have perhaps not been so exacting in all of the details that pertain to the one celebratory occasion they unanimously honor, the loving attention they do accord the Seder is certainly worthy of particular note. Proof of this lies in the abundance of haggadot produced by non-Orthodox Jews of every variety. And whatever the affiliation or belief stance reflected, nearly all these manuals adhere to roughly the same outline and feature a number of shared customs and motifs—most notably, the Four Cups, the Four Questions, the Cup of Elijah and the *nirtzah* (literally "accepted" or "acceptable," though it has been variously and loosely translated "conclusion," "close," "concluded," or "final benediction"). In addition, they all offer one or another expression of the unvarnished hope for the morrow that animates the proceedings and gives the occasion such lasting and widespread appeal. The one-time *pesah de-mitzrayim* ('Passover of Egypt'), in traditional parlance, has its assured correlate in a global *pesah de-atid* ('Passover of the future').

This being the case, a good way to trace what non-Orthodox Jews, both observant and non-observant, have asserted concerning the age-old messanic hope that informs the haggadah is to examine the various versions they have produced in the twentieth century—especially those sections that by design resonate messianically. These are 1) the invitatory *ha laḥma anya* ("This is the bread of affliction") 2) the Cup of Elijah, and 3) the *nirtzah*. The diverse treatments of these dramatic moments, perhaps better than any other modern text, uncover and announce expressly and intrepidly what the contemporary Jew espouses concerning the Age-Yet-to-Be.

The treatments examined here are from Reform, Liberal, Conservative, Reconstructionist and Polydox haggadot. Regrettably, those by women's groups, kibbutzim, Jewish vegetarians, and the like have not been included. The trademark of all the "denominational" groupings in contemporary Judaism is the conscious adaptation, in amenable fashion, of the millennia-old Jewish tradition to the modern age. The reader will undoubtedly be struck by the tenacity of the tradition even amid the mighty currents of change.

"This Is the Bread of Affliction": Ha laḥma anya

The opening stanza of the Seder, the *ha laḥma anya* in Aramaic, constitutes one of the oldest parts of the haggadah and is recited as the matzot are elevated. The traditional translation of the text runs as follows:

> This is the bread of affliction our ancestors ate in the land of Egypt. Let all who are hungry come and eat; let all who are in need come and share our Passover. This year here, next year in the land of Israel; this year bound, next year free.

"Next year in Israel," of course, is an expression of the classical yearning for the Return to Zion and an essential component of the eschaton. "This year slaves, next year free" recalls the midrashic statement, "Nisan is the month of redemption; in Nisan Israel was redeemed from Egypt; in Nisan Israel will again be redeemed" (Exodus Rabbah XV, 12).

How have Progressive haggadot handled this overture to the narrative on the Exodus (*maggid*) that addresses the themes of emancipation and homecoming? Nineteenth- and early twentieth-century Reform Judaism tended to steer clear of any hope for a massive return of scattered Jewry to its historic homeland and avoid any mention of that olden wish in the liturgy, for good reason. Reform saw the dispersion of the Jewish people not as cause for lament or ultimate redress but rather as the occasion for carrying out its assigned messianic task and spreading the good news of ethical monotheism throughout the world. Accordingly, the Central conference of American Rabbis in its 1908 and 1923 editions of *The Union Haggadah* replaced the traditional wording of "This year here, next year in the Land of Israel," both in the Aramaic and in the English, with the newly-formulated

> May it be God's will to redeem us from all trouble and all servitude. Next year at this season, may the whole house of Israel be free!

One of the first liturgical endeavors of the Reconstructionist movement, founded in the 1920s, was the widely-used and highly-influential *New Haggadah* (New York, 1941), which even today has lost little of its appeal. Although allowing for theological pluralism, Reconstructionism has taught and continues to teach God as Process and as "the Power that makes for righteousness," for creativity and for meaning—and Judaism as an "evolving religious civilization," in preference to a body of immutable truths and usages supernaturally revealed. *The New Haggadah* provides the traditional Aramaic *ha lahma anya,* but transforms its sense via the translation into a call for social consciousness followed by a forceful reading, "Let My People Go," on the various enslavements that continue to weigh heavily long after that first enslavement in ancient Egypt. Quoted below are, first, the English paraphrase with its changed emphasis and then the afterword to the dramatic reading:

> Behold the mazzah, symbol of the bread of poverty our ancestors were made to eat in their affliction, when they were slaves in the land of Egypt! Let it remind us of our fellow men who are today poor and hungry. Would that they could come and eat with us! Would that all who are in need could partake with us of this Pesah feast.
>
> How deeply these enslavements have scarred the world! The wars, the destruction, the suffering, the waste! Pesah calls us to be free, free from the tyranny of our own selves, from the enslavements of poverty and inequality, free from the corroding hate that eats away the ties that unite mankind.
>
> Pesah calls upon us to put an end to all slavery! Pesah cries out in the name of God, "Let my people go." Pesah summons us to freedom.

The Conservative movement was the next branch of American Judaism to issue a haggadah of its own (1959)—the editorial product of one very prolific compiler of liturgies, Morris Silverman. Like the Reconstructionists, Silverman sought and found a middle ground between Orthodoxy and Reform. Although his text follows the established Hebrew/Aramaic wording in its entirety, concessions to modernity are apparent not only in his translations but also in the explanatory notes and in the topical (for the 1950s) readings it offers. *Ha laḥma anya*, for example, is prefaced by an admonition in English to extend hospitality and a helping hand to those less fortunate and to rebuild the Jewish homeland for persecuted, dispossessed kindred. Although today one might be embarrassed by Silverman's watery brew of messianism stirred with dollops of American patriotism, vintage World War II, the admonition closes, almost histrionically, with

> As we celebrate our Seder as free men in a free land, let us pray for the day when all men shall be free, free from poverty, free from fear, free from bigotry and free from the ravages of war.

To be sure, the language here resembles that in the aforementioned Reconstructionist *New Haggadah,* but it is more than happenstance that the day of complete freedom programmatically acclaimed here echoes the Four Freedoms apostrophized by Franklin Delano Roosevelt.

More than the Reconstructionist version, Silverman's reflects a major qualification of the standard notion that in the Endtime all Jews will come back triumphantly to the Land of Israel. It is clear that the Conservative editor implicitly recognized the viability, indeed necessity, of a thriving Jewish community in the Diaspora along with one in Israel:

> Now we are here; next year may we observe Passover in the Land of Israel. Now many are still enslaved; next year may all men be free.

The last twenty years have seen a resurgence of creative activity in the making of non-Orthodox haggadot under the sponsorship of the rabbinical bodies in the United States and to a lesser extent in Great Britain, Holland, Israel, and Sweden. Standing on the shoulders of earlier haggadah-compilers, their editors have gone in unforeseen directions, allowing themselves to be immersed afresh in the tradition, reviving long-ignored Jewish theological concern, generously making room for original artistic expression, and welcoming all that is relevantly modern and serviceable.

The Central Conference of American Rabbis' 1974 (rev. 1975, 1982) *Haggadah shel Pesah: The New Union Haggadah,* edited by Herbert Bronstein, represents a giant leap away from the 1923 version. To characterize the profoundly enriched revision adequately would surely warrant a separate, full-length treatment. But a glimpse of the new Reform haggadah's metamorphosis can be seen in the way Bronstein restyled the *ha lahma anya* section, reverting to the customary text and thereby scrapping the old *Union haggadah's* doctored, "de-Zionized" wording. In addition, his compact preface trenchantly combines Jewish particularity with an embracing universalism and unhesitatingly sounds the prophetic note of social justice—cogently reminding us that these are necessary stepping-stones to the long-awaited Redemption.

Leader

[. . .] Among people everywhere, sharing of bread forms a bond of fellowship. For the sake of our redemption, we say together the ancient words which join us with our own people and with all who are in need, with the wrongly imprisoned and the beggar in the street. For our redemption is bound up with the deliverance from bondage of people everywhere.

Group
[Text of *ha lahma anya* in Aramaic]

This is the bread of affliction, the poor bread, which our ancestors ate in the land of Egypt. Let all who are hungry come and eat. Let all who are in want share the hope of Passover. As we celebrate here, we join with our people everywhere. This year we celebrate here. Next year in the land of Israel. Now we are all still in bonds. Next year may all be free.

Another leading modern haggadah, *Gates of Freedom* (1981, 1982), was edited by Chaim Stern, who is perhaps the most prolific non-Orthodox Jewish liturgiographer around. Although it bears similarities to the CCAR haggadah, *Gates of Freedom* was mostly derived from *A Modern Passover Haggadah* (1981), the earlier Passover domestic rite for the (British) Union of Liberal and Progressive Synagogues, on which Stern collaborated with John D. Rayner.

Although the *Gates of Freedom* text of *ha lahma anya* is the customary

Aramaic one, what sets it apart is the prefatory——and, in a Jewish context, a little short of astonishing—quotation from Mahatma Gandhi: "There are people in the world so hungry that God cannot appear to them except in the form of bread."

In the ULPS haggadah, Rayner offered the following gloss on "This year here, next year in the land of Israel":

'Here' is wherever any human beings are still enslaved, or deprived of their rights; 'the land of Israel' is the symbol of the hope of redemption. The journey of our ancestors is the journey of every people, and of every generation, until the Promised Land is reached by all, and freedom becomes the heritage of all God's children.

Interestingly, Stern does not reproduce this gloss in his American *Gates of Freedom.* Perhaps in his view each national journey is unique. As a kind of suggested postscript to and implied comment on *ha laḥma anya,* Rayner and Stern bring in a poem by Samuel Halkin, a Soviet Yiddish poet who was exiled to Siberia. The translation is by Stern:

Shall I celebrate the day of my birth?
>   Others know best—let them decide.
But that moment, the day they set me free
>   from the barbed wire of the prison-camp;
>   that hour not destined to arrive
>   did come in early March, in Siberian frost
>   bright with stars at high noon.
>   That hour I recited the blessing
>   not spoken since childhood.
Now I persuade myself: such an hour, such a day
>   will be bestowed at last on every human friend.
>   That festal day
>   will pass through every door
>   without the need to knock.

Another handsome haggadah with striking graphics and resplendent color is the Conservative *Passover Haggadah: The Feast of Freedom* (1982), adeptly edited by Rachel Anne Rabinowicz under the auspices of the Rabbinical Assembly. The comments, whether explanatory, edificatory, or homiletical, all appear in the margins, while the rubrics and incidental

readings in English accompany the haggadah text itself. Based on a wide
range of sources and, happily, with scarcely a hint of theological browbeat-
ing or condescension, the comments presuppose an educated readership
with a sense of literary appreciation. Directly after *ha laḥma anya,* for
example, is a newly-composed prayer in Hebrew, using all stock locutions,
on behalf of Jews "and indeed all humanity" who are persecuted and not
yet free. The first of the annotations illustrates its eschatological overtones:

> This is the bread of affliction. Why do we start this joyous celebra-
> tion with a pointed reference to the bread of affliction? Perhaps we
> do so to underscore that many of our fellow Jews are still afflicted,
> that there is still hunger in the world, and that we are still in *galut*
> (exile). This pivotal passage culminates in a confident assertion of our
> belief that the redemption will come and will come soon.

The Cup of Elijah

Perhaps the haggadah's most important focal point with a millennarian
theme is the open-door invitation to Elijah the Prophet after the *birkat ha-
mazon* and before the second part of the *hallel.* Although the traditional
haggadah makes no explicit mention of the prophet, the traditional rubric
directs that the door be opened for him and, in some communities, that he
be welcomed with a *barukh ha-ba!* Sadly enough, the scriptural verses to
be recited during his arrival are of an imprecatory character (Psalms
79:6–7; 69:25; Lamentations 3:66—directed towards godless Gentiles
who have done untold violence to the Jewish people). This entire section,
entitled *shefokh ḥamatekha,* is directed nowhere in the Mishnah and instead
represents an unfortunate byproduct of periodic outbreaks of persecution
during the Middle Ages.

Because the biblical Elijah is portrayed as the stalwart defender of the
faith who protects the oppressed and disadvantaged and who, in the end, is
mysteriously translated to heaven, the aggadic tradition has lovingly
embellished his traits—and his mention in Malachi 3:23—as the honored
herald to the Messiah. Liberal Judaism has thus been confronted with a
twofold problem: what to do with the inimical, if from hindsight under-
standable, sentiments in *shefokh ḥamatekha;* and with the mythical cast of
Elijah's personality in postbiblical Judaism.

The solution proffered by *The Union Haggadah* was either to leave out the section entirely (as in the 1908 version; cf. *Hagada: Liturgie für die häusliche Feier der Sederabende* [fourth edition, Frankfurt a/M, 1925], by C. Seligmann) or to open the door with the recitation/singing of the more buoyant, two-verse Psalm 117 (as in the 1923 edition). In any case, Elijah's Cup (*kos shel eliyahu {ha-navi}; der Kelch des Propheten Eliahu*) remained in its conspicuous place on the Seder table as a tangible symbol of the messianic hope, however redefined.

The Reconstructionist *New Haggadah* was the first to turn the spotlight on this section in an altogether positive fashion. It eliminated the maledictory scriptural verses and appropriated in their place *eliyahu ha-navi*, the nostalgic folk song from the *havdalah* service at the conclusion of the Sabbath. The lyric has caught on in nearly all Progressive haggadot ever since.

Unlike the haggadot it inspired, *The New Haggadah* presents the entire unit in the simplest manner possible:

> This cup of wine is called Elijah's cup. In Jewish tradition, the Prophet Elijah is the messenger of God appointed to herald the era of the Messiah, the era of perfect happiness, when the Jewish people and all peoples throughout the world shall be free.
>
> Let us sing together the song of Elijah, and we pray that we may soon see that happy world.
>
> [Hebrew of *eliyahu ha-navi,* followed by the English:]
>> Elijah the Prophet, Elijah the Tishbite,
>> Elijah, Elijah, Elijah the Gileadite,
>> Soon may he come, bringing with him the Messiah.

Another folksong, *tiqvat yisra'el* ("The Hope of Israel"), follows, but is found in no other haggadah before or since. Throughout the section, idealism and optimism prevail. The tragic note is muted and not sounded again until after the Holocaust.

Appropriately, seventeen years later, Silverman provided for his Conservative *Passover Haggadah* (1959) his heftiest readings in the vernacular for precisely this section. His prefatory explication on the role of Elijah in Jewish tradition is followed by the singing of *eliyahu ha-navi* and a paragraph outlining past woes beginning with the libelous host desecration and blood accusation and proceeding through subsequent calamities to the text of *shefokh ḥamatekha.* Then a responsive reading enumerates the

horrors that led to the annihilation of the Six Million, followed by a
singing of *ani ma'amin,* the twelfth of the Maimonidean Thirteen Articles
of Faith: "I believe with a perfect faith in the coming of the Messiah; and
though he tarry, nonetheless do I believe he will come!" The final responsive reading in the section is pitched in an upbeat tone, calling attention
to the bravery of the Righteous Gentiles and the Allied victors instrumental in saving the lives of Jews, and recounting the Ingathering of the
Exiles in a resurrected Zion—all viewed as anticipating the Age when
"nation shall not lift up sword against nation; neither shall they learn war
anymore" (Isaiah 2:4).

The haggadot of the seventies and eighties follow Silverman's structurally, with the content of their readings tempered by emerging percep-
tions of the enormity of the Holocaust, the fate of Israel's troubled existence, and, no doubt, America's internal and global fiascos. After the Third
Cup, *The New Union Haggadah ,* for example, introduces the section with
an explanation highlighting Elijah's role in "defense of justice," challenging power and bringing succor to the "humbled sick," "the widowed" and
"the weak." In the ensuing responsive reading, legendary motifs associated
with Elijah are interwoven in understated fashion with scriptural and
liturgical verses: First, Psalms 79:7; the line from *birkat ha-mazon:* "May
the All Merciful send us Elijah the Prophet to comfort us with tidings of
deliverance." Then Malachi 3:23–24, here, with a minor shift and in
degenderized language, transcribed as

> Behold, I will send you Elijah the prophet, and he will turn the
> hearts of the parents to the children and the hearts of the children to
> the parents before the great and awesome Day of God.

Then the climactic "I will bring you into the Land" (Exodus 6:8) and, to
draw the ritual to a dramatic close, the singing of *eliyahu ha-navi.*

In his British Liberal haggadah, John D. Rayner, theologically the
rationalist and verbally straightforward, transplanted the Opening of the
Door from immediately after the Third Cup to after the Fourth, before the
terminating *nirtzah,* tapping into the traditional view of Elijah as a forerunner of the Endtime. Interestingly, Rayner is one of the few who do not
include the song *eliyahu ha-navi.* Instead, citing the entirety of Exodus
6:6–8, which includes the pledge of Israel's entry into the Promised Land,
the fifth stage of redemption, he asks:

Should we then drink a fifth cup of wine? The Rabbis could not agree; so custom varied, and it came to be thought: Only when Elijah comes will the matter be resolved. The fifth promise is a promise of the future, when the Lord will bring our people, and all peoples, into the messianic land of freedom, harmony and peace.

Then Malachi 3:23f. is worked in, followed by

For Elijah we fill the fifth cup; but we do not drink from it, for the time of redemption has not yet come. We open the door to let it enter, though we know it may still be distant. We fill the cup and open the door with the faith that has strengthened our people throughout the ages: that the messianic age will come.

Subsequently a string of verses in Hebrew and in English translation not found in the traditional haggadah appears, including the subordinate clause of the twelfth Principle of Faith ("Though he tarry, we will wait every day until he comes"), rendered compatibly with classical Reform doctrine: "Though it [the Messianic Age, rather than the Messiah as such] tarry, yet we will daily wait for it."

The other familiar verses are scriptural: Zechariah 14:9, Isaiah 11:9, and Micah 4:4. While raising the Cup of Elijah, pointedly and poignantly the leader says, with the one and only phrase from *eliyahu ha-navi, bi-meherah ve-yameynu, amen* ("Speedily in our days. Amen."), as the door is closed.

In contrast, Chaim Stern, very much the poet, "remythologizes" what his colleague and frequent collaborator determinedly demythologizes. Like Rayner, Stern deals with the Cup of Elijah just before *nirtzah*. But, like Silverman, he traces the progression from Shoah to Rescue to Rebirth to Ultimate Redemption, vigorously involving all the Seder participants by 1) having the Cup of Elijah passed around, "with each person pouring a little wine into that cup," and 2) making a point of assigning reading parts to several people.

He rephrases Rayner's opening rhetorical question by the leader in this fashion:

But there is a fifth promise: ". . . and I will bring you into the land . . ." Should there then be a Fifth Cup? That question, says tradition, will not be answered until Elijah comes to proclaim the Messianic Time. Meanwhile it is a promise we remember with a cup from which we cannot drink, until all the world is redeemed from pain, injustice, denial of love.

Later in this expanded, seven-page section, Stern acknowledges the wondrous restoration of Zion, with Psalm 97:8, in Hebrew and in English, and then

Leader

But the full glory is still far from sight. Ignorance, prejudice, hatred; contempt for truth and justice; hunger and terror; the fear of a world-destroying war—these remain to plague the human race. To end these plagues, to summon Elijah—that is the task of all who care. It is our task, for we are the people who know the stranger's heart, the slave's aching bones, the shaking hands of the exile. When will Elijah come with the news of freedom? When we have called him by our deeds. Then we shall say:

All [in Hebrew and in English]

I will lift up the cup of salvation, and call upon the name of God. [Psalm 116:13]

Some verses later, all intone the sentences from Malachi, after which the leader says:

And on that day the promise of promises shall be fulfilled. As it is written:

All [in Hebrew and in English]:

And I will bring you into the land . . . Exodus 6:8

Leader:

Israel and all the world shall reach the Land of Promise.

All:

Bi-meherah ve-yameynu. Amen.

Speedily, in our days. Amen.

The door is closed.

All:

[*Eliyahu ha-navi* in Hebrew]

As a sequel, which may or may not be read at the Seder, Stern brings in a familiar passage from the Talmud (Sanhedrin 98a; the rabbis alluded to were second- and third-century teachers):

Rabbi Yehoshua [ben Levi] once came upon the prophet Elijah
at the entrance of the cave
of Rabbi Shimon bar Yochai,
Yehoshua asked:
When will the Messiah come?
Go ask him, said the prophet.
He sits at the gates of Rome,
like all the poor.
His body is covered with running sores,
as is theirs.
This is how you can tell him apart from them:
When they want to apply fresh bandages,
the others first remove all the old dressings.
Not so with him
he never changes more than one dressing at a time,
for he thinks:
I must be ready to answer the call without delay!
Rabbi Yehoshua went to Rome's gates and found him.
He said: Shalom to you, Master and Teacher! The reply was: Shalom
to you, Son of Levi!
Yehoshua then asked: Master, when are you coming?
And the answer was: Today!
Yehoshua left with a full heart,
and returned to his place.
But the day passed,
and with the fall of eve
no change could be seen.
Yehoshua turned to Elijah and wept:
The Messiah lied! Today! he said, yet he did not come . . .
But Elijah said: You must understand what he meant.
Is it not written?
"Today—if you will listen to God's voice." (Psalm 95:7)

The 1982 Conservative *Feast of Freedom* pulls out all the stops in staging
this segment of the haggadah, esthetically, folkloristically, textually, and
exegetically. Silverman's four-part scenario of Shoah-Rescue-Rebirth-
Redemption is taken up again, refined and elaborated upon (in twelve

pages, compared to Silverman's three). Rabinowicz partitions the section into three main subdivisions: 1) "In Every Generation," a small-scale anthology of readings about tragedy, struggle and triumph. 2) a striking illustration of the sun against a black backdrop spread over two pages, with *ani ma'amin* on the top righthand corner, and the affecting "I believe in the sun/even when it is not shining [. . .]" on the top lefthand side of the opposite page. 3) The Opening of the Door, with a rubric much like Stern's above: "The leader fills Elijah's goblet, or passes it around the table so that every participant can add some wine from his or her own cup to demonstrate that we must work together to bring about redemption."

Climactically, the traditional four verses of *shefokh ḥamatekha* then make their appearance, accompanied by an important qualifying commentary stretched over the whole length of the margin with lines such as

> We are forbidden to hate the Egyptians. Yet we are enjoined to remember the crimes of the Amalekites. We are commanded to feed our enemy when he is hungry. We are warned to leave the avenging to the God of justice. Remembrance. Gratefulness. Retribution. Restraint. Should we struggle to reconcile these complicated and conflicting emotions, or should we simply accept the fact that they coexist?

As if to allow those families not wishing to use the *shefokh ḥamatekha* passage in their Seder, the central portion of the ceremony that revolves around the figure of Elijah appears separately in the succeeding four pages.

Because of its significance as a kind of gauge and capsule summary of one Conservative position vis-à-vis the Messiah, it might be especially instructive to look at one sustained, telling commentary framing the text:

> *Even though he tarry.* And how long will he tarry? For millennia we have expected him momentarily. For millennia we have listened for his footsteps. For millennia we have lived in hope. Through fasting, through meditation, through prayer, through esoteric computations, the faithful have endeavored to accelerate his advent, or at least to arrive at the divinely scheduled date of his arrival. But this remains the best-kept secret of the ages. Like shooting stars, pseudo-redeemers rose and fell, leaving tragedy in their wake. Yet still the messianic hope blazed like a beacon through the gloom and doom of the exile.[. . . .] And when he comes, then what? "No hunger. No

warfare. No jealousy. No strife. Prosperity everywhere. Blessings in abundance. And the world will be wholly occupied with acquiring knowledge of God" [Moses Maimonides, *Mishneh Torah:* Hilkhot Melakhim 12:5].

And the same marginal gloss continues:

> Some believe that redemption—like revelation—is continuous and that every human being is intimately implicated in the process, endowed with the ability to help or hinder, advance or delay it. They see in every soul, in every action, a redemptive spark. So every one of us counts and everything we do matters. Together we can perfect ourselves, and complete creation. Together we can help to restore cosmic harmony. And bring about the beginning of the End of Days.

Thereupon the by-now standard sentences from Malachi are quoted. A novelty is the addition of Jeremiah 16:14–15, which speaks of another historical liberation, the restoration of the Jews from the Babylonian Captivity, brought into play, by implication, as a scriptural anticipation of the Ingathering of Exiles happening in our own time.

As the directions in *Feast of Freedom* explain, Deuteronomy 26:5–8 is recited during the Seder summarizing the Exodus event; now the culminating verse 9 is added as testimony to the realization today of the return to Zion foretold long ago:

> And He brought us to this place and gave us this land, a land flowing with milk and honey.

The singing of *eliyahu ha-navi* then rounds off the section, as the door is closed.

The all-Hebrew *Haggadah shel Pesah* (1989), edited by Yehoram Mazor under the aegis of the Israel Council of Progressive Rabbis (Maram = *mo'ezet ha-rabbanim ha-mitqaddemim be-yisra'el*) is an offshoot of the American Conservative haggadah by Michael Strassfeld (1979) and others. Here the Cup of Elijah ritual is less than two pages long, chiefly biblical in content, and with only one added reading. It opens with the normally sung epigram attributed to the Hasidic tzaddiq Rabbi Naḥman of Bratzlav, "All the world is a very narrow bridge, and the main thing is not be afraid at all," and ties in Psalms 83:2–5 (Strassfeld originally continued to verse

9), as a resolute reminder of the Holocaust. The eye-catching part of Mazor's retreatment of this segment is the placement alongside *shefokh ḥamatekha* of an alternative and far more irenic version of the same—borrowed, according to Mazor, from the sixteenth-century Worms Haggadah:

> Pour out [*shefokh*] Thy love [*ahavatekha*] upon the nations [*goyim*] who knew Thee, upon the kingdoms that call upon Thy name, for the kindnesses they do the seed of Jacob, and upon those who protect Thy people Israel from their devourers. May they be worthy of seeing the well being of Thy chosen ones and of exulting in the joy of Thy Gentiles [*goyekha*].

The *Maram* Haggadah proceeds, as in *Festival of Freedom,* with Jeremiah 16:14–15, followed by the idyllic-lyrical crowning prophecy of Amos (9:13–15) concerning the Land of Israel, in lieu of the expected sentences from Malachi regarding intergenerational amity. As a note to the traditional *shefokh ḥamatekha,* Mazor inserts Abraham Joshua Heschel's reply to the question whether it is possible to forgive the Nazis for their crimes against the Jews and others.[1] After the singing of *eliyahu ha-navi,* the section yearningly concludes with Isaiah 2:4: "Nation will not lift up sword against nation; neither will they learn war anymore."

"Accepted": Nirtzah

After the second half of the *hallel,* the antiphonal Psalm 136, and the prayer *nishmat* (the "Benediction of Song"), the traditional haggadah comes to a close with the Fourth Cup and the recitation of the following lines from the medieval liturgical poem, *ḥasal siddur pesaḥ ke-hilkhato* by Joseph ben Samuel Bonfils of eleventh-century France:

> Concluded is the order [*siddur*] of Passover
> According to its precept and custom.
> As we were fortunate to celebrate it,
> So may we merit performing it again.
> Thou Pure One, who dwells on high,
> Restore the congregation without count.
> Soon guide the offshoots of the stock Thou hast planted,
> Redeemed to Zion in happy song.

La-shanah ha-ba'ah bi-yrushalayim!
NEXT YEAR IN JERUSALEM!
(In Israel: Next Year in Jerusalem Rebuilt!)
Supplementary songs then follow.

How have non-Orthodox haggadot handled *nirtzah? The Union haggadah* of 1923 is graced with decorative borders, "based on material from Egyptian monuments and from ancient Jewish life," by Isadore Lipton. The illustration heading the page for *nirtzah* ("the Final Benediction")—a pictorial account of Isaiah 2:1–5 and Micah 4:1–4—shows in black tint a haloed King Messiah to the fore poised in front of an anvil beating a sword, while soldiers of different nationalities and climes with their weapons are lined up on either side of him about to hand over their implements of war. Meanwhile, behind him and in white relief, the peoples of the world are seen ascending Mount Zion to the Temple at its pinnacle. The concluding text includes a cadenced adaptation of the Priestly Benediction (Numbers 6:24–26) to be read aloud by all the company present, and ends with the *berakhah* over the Fourth Cup:

> The festive service is completed. With songs of praise, we have lifted up the cups symbolizing the divine promises of salvation, and have called upon the name of God. As we offer the benediction over the fourth cup, let us again lift our souls to God in faith and in hope. May He who broke Pharaoh's yoke for ever shatter all fetters of oppression, and hasten the day when swords shall, at last, be broken and wars ended. Soon may He cause the glad tidings of redemption to be heard in all lands, so that mankind—freed from violence and from wrong, and united in an eternal covenant of brotherhood—may celebrate the universal Passover in the name of our God of freedom.
>
> All read in unison:
>
> May God bless the whole house of Israel with freedom, and keep us safe from danger everywhere. Amen.
>
> May God cause the light of His countenance to shine upon all men, and dispel the darkness of ignorance and prejudice. May He be gracious unto us. Amen.
>
> May God lift up His countenance upon our country and render it a true home of liberty and a bulwark of justice. And may He grant peace unto us and unto all mankind. Amen.

[The blessing for the wine in Hebrew and in English.]
Drink the fourth cup of wine.

Characteristic of nineteenth- and early twentieth-century Reform, Zion and Jerusalem are buried under the wraps, except as a residual graphic metaphor.[2] In contrast, the Reconstructionists re-Zionized their *nirtzah* in *The New Haggadah* and soft-pedaled its eschatological thrust:

We are about to drink the fourth cup of wine. Let us say together:
[The *berakhah* for the wine in Hebrew and in English.]
Drink the wine.
THE CLOSE   NIRTZAH
Now we come to the close of our Seder Service.
Once again we have recited the age-old epic of Israel's liberation from bondage.
Once again we have chanted our Psalms of praise to God, the Redeemer of Israel and of all mankind.
We have learned the message of the Exodus for our day.
And we have rededicated ourselves to the cause of man's freedom from tyranny and oppression.
As we have celebrated this festival tonight, so may we celebrate it, all of us together, next year again, in joy, in peace and in freedom.
[*Ḥasal siddur pesaḥ* in Hebrew only.]
All say in unison:
La-shanah ha-ba'ah bi-yrushalayim
MAY THE COMING YEAR WITNESS THE REBUILDING OF ZION AND THE REDEMPTION OF ISRAEL.

Some thirty years later, Morris Silverman confronted the fact that *nirtzah* is said just before the beloved holiday melodies of medieval origin—thus lessening its dramatic impact as the Seder's end. As a partial solution, Silverman kept the traditional *nirtzah* as it stood but used the watchword *la-shanah ha-ba'ah bi-yrushalayim* as a point of departure (adding the "Zionist" Exodus 6:8) to create a new unit: a Fifth Cup, expressing "gratitude for the creation of the State of Israel" and culminating in a *berakhah* over wine (in a footnote: 'optional,' should one have halakhic qualms) and the psalmodic refrain, "Give thanks unto the Lord for He is good; His mercy is everlasting," in Hebrew and in English. The cherished Passover songs and madrigals are afterwards sung, upon the completion of which Silverman quotes the Philadelphia Liberty Bell in a brief, flag-waving homily on Leviticus 25:10, "Proclaim ye liberty throughout the land, unto all the inhabitants thereof."

The closing prayer is thematically not all that different from the English portion of the Reconstructionist *nirtzah* and, at the same time, a good bit more American-style patriotic and more inclusive, with a highminded resolve and determination to spread "the light of freedom" into "all corners of the world." It is noteworthy how a sublimated messianism tumbles into, or even becomes confused with, an American "Manifest Destiny."

> Our God and God of our fathers [. . .] May the memories of this night inspire us to cast off our own shackles of intolerance, greed, and hatred. May we here resolve to break the chains that fetter our minds and blind us to the glory, beauty and goodness which life offers in such abundance.
>
> Help us to realize that we cannot have freedom for ourselves unless we are willing to give it to others. Through our daily deeds and devotion, may each of us in our own way help to liberate all who live in fear, poverty and oppression. May the light of freedom penetrate into all corners of the world, and lift the darkness of tyranny until tyranny is no more, so that all men may be free. Amen.
>
> [The fourth stanza of "My Country, 'Tis of Thee."]
>
> [*Ha-tiqvah*, the Israeli National Anthem]

Going in a different direction and renaming this section *siyyum* (normally referring to the completion of the study of a tractate of the Talmud), John D. Rayner furnishes for the ULPS haggadah a simple "concluding prayer," comprised of *ḥasal siddur pesaḥ* (with a minor edit in the Hebrew, so as to avoid praying for the return of all Jews to the Land of Israel), a recap and appeal and, finally, the traditional *la-shanah ha-ba'ah bi-yrushalayim,* supplemented by an innovative *la-shanah ha-ba'ah kol ḥay nig'al* ("Next year in a world redeemed"), as a way of making explicit the implied universal in the word *Jerusalem.* Here is Rayner's prayerful "recap and appeal," in which the messianic tone is heard more distinctly:

> Our Seder is now completed; we have followed the order, told the story, performed the rites, prayed the prayers, sung the songs. Let us thank God that we have done so in freedom and safety, and let us pray for the Passover of the Future *{pesah de-atid}*, when all mankind will live in brotherhood and in peace.

Passing mention might be made here of a spare, essentially non-theist, Polydox haggadah, *A Passover Service for the Family* (Institute for Creative Judaism, 1976), created by Alvin Reines, which embraces a *nirtzah* of similarly compact proportions, minus both the Fourth Cup and *la-shanah ha-ba'ah bi-yrushalayim.* What makes it unlike any other is the personalized brand of existentialist humanism that informs the entire manual. Its low-key monolingual *nirtzah* bears quoting:

> In the joy of thankfulness, the Seder of Passover is now complete. The Torah states that the Israelites, in a covenant made at Mount Sinai, confirmed the new life their journey from bondage brought them. We, too, in this journey to freedom we have celebrated this night confirm a Covenant of Freedom. We rejoice in what we and others are, in the special and different person everyone is. By mutual affirmation of one another, in our uniqueness and personhood, we hallow life and receive the richness of creation. May the Covenant of Freedom forever guide our destinies and the future of all humankind.

The *New Union Haggadah* places its *nirtzah after* the customary songs and couches its conclusion in the form of a responsorial between leader and company. As in Rayner's haggadah, there is the recognition 1) of Jerusalem (and Zion) in its terrestrial particularity and in its universal dimension, and 2) of the Redemption ("God's highest blessing sealed") that has yet to be actualized worldwide.

Leader

As our Seder draws to an end, we take up our cups of wine. The Redemption is not yet complete. The fourth cup recalls us to our covenant with the Eternal One, to the tasks that still await us as a

people called to the service of God, to a great purpose for which the
people of Israel lives: The preservation and affirmation of hope.
[Hebrew of Exodus 6:7.]

Group

As it is written, "And I will take you to be My people."
[The Hebrew blessing over the wine in Hebrew and in Latin charac-
ters, translated:]
We praise Thee, our God, Sovereign of all Existence, Who has created
the fruit of the vine.
(All drink the fourth cup of wine.)

Leader

THE SEDER SERVICE NOW CONCLUDES: [*Ḥasal siddur pesaḥ*]
ITS RITES OBSERVED IN FULL,
ITS PURPOSES REVEALED.

Group

THIS PRIVILEGE WE SHARE WILL EVER BE RENEWED,
UNTIL GOD'S PLAN IS KNOWN IN FULL,
GOD'S HIGHEST BLESSING SEALED:

Leader

PEACE!

Group

PEACE FOR US! FOR EVERYONE!

Leader

FOR ALL PEOPLE, THIS, OUR HOPE:

Group

NEXT YEAR IN JERUSALEM! NEXT YEAR, MAY ALL BE FREE!
(Next year in Jerusalem is ever the hope of our people. Still we affirm
that all people will rejoice together in the Zion of love and peace.)
LA-SHANAH HA-BA'AH BI-YRUSHALAYIM! [Also in Hebrew
type.] [Closing hymn: *addir hu* ("God of Might").]

Nirtzah in Chaim Stern's *Gates of Freedom* rather resembles the one in the
New Union Haggadah. Nevertheless, a few features set them apart. First of
all, Stern's *nirtzah* comes *before* the songs, as in the traditional haggadah.

Second it will be recalled that Stern placed the Cup of Elijah, or Opening of the Door, just prior to *nirtzah,* possibly to create a dramatic climax to be followed by a denouement. One might thus say that Stern's Cup of Elijah provides the direct impetus for his *nirtzah,* at the beginning of which Stern brings forward several verses from the Torah that pertain to the recurrent mandate to empathize with and care for the stranger, the orphan and the widow, "for you were a slave in the land of Egypt" (Deuteronomy 16:11f.; Leviticus 19:34, 25:55). (These and related passages also appear in the Reconstructionist *New Haggadah,* albeit in a different location.)

Leader:
Our redemption is not yet complete, but as we raise the final cup of wine in remembrance of the fourth promise of redemption, our heart beats strong with hope. For it is said:
All:
[Hebrew and transliteration of Exodus 6:7, followed by translation:]
I will take you to be My people, and I will be your God.
[The blessing over the wine in Hebrew and in English.]

Finally, Stern follows Michael Strassfeld's example (preliminary edition of the Rabbinical Assembly *haggadah*) by borrowing a *berakhah* from the prefatory portion of the Morning Service as found in the Conservative and Reform rites. In *Gates of Freedom's nirtzah* it reads as follows:

Barukh attah adonay, eloheynu melekh ha-olam, she'asanu beney ḥorin.
[Translated as] We praise You, Eternal God, Ruler of time and space, who has made us to be free.
All now drink the fourth cup.

Leader:
[*Ḥasal siddur pesaḥ,* of which only the first four lines are reproduced.]
Our Seder now concludes,
its rites and customs done.
This year's task completed,
we look to a time yet unborn.
We look to the light of dawn,
tomorrow's promised Passover,
the days of peace, the days of love,
the time of full redemption.

> All:
>
> Tomorrow's promised Passover:
> the days of peace,
> the days of love,
> the time of full redemption.
>
> Leader:
>
> [The Hebrew of Micah 4:4, then its English:]
> Then all shall sit under their vines and under their fig-trees, and
> none shall make them afraid.
>
> All:
>
> FOR US AND ALL ISRAEL,
> *Lanu ule-khol beyt yisrael,*
> FOR US AND ALL HUMANKIND:
> *Lanu ule-khol yoshevey tevel:*
> NEXT YEAR IN JERUSALEM!
> *La-shanah ha-ba'ah bi-yrushalayim!*
> NEXT YEAR
> *La-shanah ha-ba'ah*
> ALL THE WORLD REDEEMED!
> *Kol ḥay nig'al!*

The watchful reader will probably quickly recognize the last three lines
from Rayner's haggadah, for which Stern composed the last two originally.

The last treatment for our scrutiny is the Rabbinical Assembly's *Feast of
Freedom,* which differs from all of the foregoing examples in that it retains
the traditional *nirtzah* intact, pure and simple. Its messianic mood is
intensified, though, by the rhapsodic commentary that abuts the text and
takes its cue from the custom of the pious to follow the Seder with a reading of Song of Songs 2:8–13.

> WHY do we read the Song of Songs (*Shir ha-shirim*) on Pesah? Coin-
> ciding with springtime, the earth's annual reawakening from its win-
> try slumbers, Pesah celebrates Israel's reawakening from its woeful
> winter of enslavement. *Shir hashirim* sings of spring, of flowering
> pomegranates and budding vines. It sings of love, a love that cannot
> be quenched, a love that is sweeter than wine and stronger than
> death. According to traditionalists, this is the eternal love between
> Israel and its Redeemer who came "leaping upon the mountains,"

leaping over space and time to hasten the liberation of His beloved people.

It is clear that most non-Orthodox Jews do not believe in a literal supernaturally-endowed Deliverer descendent from the line of David. On the other hand, our sampling of Reform, Reconstructionist, Conservative, Liberal, and Polydox haggadot suggests that the millennial hope, reconceptualized but often expressed in traditional language and metaphor, of a future world divinely and humanly transformed, is one that has now and then flickered but continues, withal, to burn brightly.

An earlier version of this chapter appeared in the *Jahrbuch für Biblische Theologie* 8 (1993): 251–71. Reprinted with permission.

   1. The moving story is repeated by Wolfe Kelman in his "A Tribute to Rabbi Heschel," John C. Merkle, ed., *Abraham Joshua Heschel: Explorations in His Life and Thought* (New York and London, 1985), pp. 32–34.

   2. Cf. C. Seligmann's *Schlussgebet* in rhyme which is de-eschatologized outright and in part charmingly and in part fatuously domesticated:

Möge draussen weiterklingen
Dieses Abends Melodie,
Die uns trug auf goldnen Schwingen
In das Reich der Poesie.
Möge seiner Gnade Walten
Uns beschützen immerdar,
Mög' er seine Huld erhalten
Uns auch in dem neuen Jahr.[. . . .])

16

"O God of Vengeance, Appear!"
Neqamah in the Siddur

The siddur in all its untold transmutations is a surprisingly functional gauge for assessing the inner state of Jewish folk and faith. Almost without fail, each new edition of the prayerbook makes some fresh disclosure about where we are at the moment theologically and attitudinally. Several of the prayerbooks that have latterly seen the light of day reflect the more obvious currentday issues such as pride commingled with continual concern for Israel, the quest for an adequate theodicy in the aftermath of the Holocaust, and, of course, the matter of sexism.

What is perhaps not quite so noticeable is a disturbing tendency of late, a recrudescence of an old sentiment that occasionally appeared in the classical Siddur—the collective desire for *neqamah* (vengeance), to be applied toward all those who have wronged the Jewish people. For well over a century it was the norm in virtually all non-Orthodox prayerbooks to consider all references to *neqamah* mean-spirited, jaundiced and, for that reason, unworthy of liturgical expression. There was good precedent in Leviticus 19:18: "You shall not take vengeance or bear a grudge against your kinsfolk, but you shall love your neighbor as yourself: I am the LORD."

Such being the case, the standard operating procedure was either to delete or to dilute all retributive phraseology in Jewish prayer. Once in a while an offending Hebrew text was altered. In the *Gates of Prayer* and in *Kol Haneshamah,* the verse "who wrought for us miracles and vengeance upon Pharaoh" in *emet ve-emunah,* which follows the Shema during any Evening Service, becomes a cleaned-up "He did wonders for us in the land of Egypt." In a similar vein, a left-of center Conservative prayerbook, *Seder Avodah* (ed. Max D. Klein, 1951), provides a tempered conclusion to its special *al ha-nissim* prayer for Purim:

> [Thou] didst save thy people Israel from [Haman's] power, as we read: And unto the Jews in the Persian Empire there was light and joy, gladness and honor." Therefore do we give thanks to Thy great name in each and every year

to replace the gloating traditional, "Thou didst frustrate Haman's design, and return his recompense upon his own head; and they hanged him and his sons upon the gallows." While leaving the latter Hebrew text intact, the current official Conservative weekday rites[1] euphemistically, if tamely, render the end of the same last sentence, "On the gallows he made for Mordecai, Haman, together with his sons, suffered death."

For Purim again, as custom has it, before the reading from the Scroll of Esther, three blessings are recited. So, too, another is said without delay after the reading is completed. The final blessing runs as follows:

> Blessed art Thou. O Lord our God, King of the universe, who dost plead our cause, judge our suit and avenge our wrong, who renderest retribution (*veha-noqem et niqmatenu*) to all that hate our soul, and on our behalf dealest out punishment to our adversaries. Blessed art Thou, O Lord. who on behalf of Thy people Israel dealest out punishment to all their adversaries, O God, the Savior.

To obviate the problem of *neqamah* here, more than one rite would simply leave the blessing unsaid. Conforming with almost all of the non-Orthodox prayerbooks in Continental Europe, the British Reform *Forms of Prayer for Jewish Worship* (1977) settles the difficulty by rewording the blessing in a more positive, nonretaliatory fashion:

> Blessed are you, Lord our God, King of the universe, who heard our plea and judged our cause. You are the one who has always saved us, our hope in every generation. May those who trust in You never be ashamed nor humiliated. Blessed are You Lord, the God who saves us.

We can see how a fairly uniform pattern has taken hold in most liberal prayerbooks.

In some recent rites, however, a subtle change seems to be taking place. A case in point: in 1984 the Reform movement put out a fine work, *The Five Scrolls* (ed. Herbert A. Bronstein and Albert H. Friedlander), providing in Hebrew each of the festival Megillot (Song of Songs, Ruth, Lamentations, Ecclesiastes, and Esther) with the cantillation notes (*te'amim*) and a translation adapted from the restrained and flowing English of the mid-nineteenth-century British *Jewish School and Family Bible.* In addition, worship services are supplied for each of the occasions when a scroll is read or chanted.

Here, too, the editors and their helpers gave good account of themselves in treating stock liturgical materials in unexpected and often impelling ways. On the other hand, the blessings before the Scroll of Esther are all there, according to time-honored usage. So is the one afterwards, unabridged! Interestingly, however, the English rendition of the same (p. 87) displays no clue that, in the Hebrew, *neqamah* has returned with a vengeance.

Not unexpectedly, a modern Orthodox prayerbook is not above putting the hex in no uncertain terms upon those who inflicted unspeakable harm upon our people in days gone by. The complete *Artscroll Siddur* (ed. Nosson Scherman, 1984) is handsomely produced and includes a bountiful range of traditional commentaries on the prayers and, by extension, on all facets of Jewish religious life and calendar. The modern reader can learn much from its pages, whatever one's ideological proclivities. Despite the strengths of the siddur, however, its punitive sentiments are distressingly aggressive. In its version of *el male raḥamim* ("O God, who art full of compassion"), for example, recited at Memorial Services on behalf of those martyred in the Shoah, it works in an "innovative" phrase bound by parentheses: "Through the hands of the German oppressors, may their name and memory be obliterated!"

These words raise some difficult questions. Did not other nationalitites have a hand in the atrocities of the infernal Kingdom of Night, *l'univers concentrationnaire?* Also—and here we are back to the notoriously difficult concept of collective guilt—is it just or fair to lump together indiscriminately all members of a people or a nation and to denounce them wholesale before the bar of divine judgment? By using the word "German" rather than "Nazi," we curse also the likes of Thomas Mann, Paul Tillich, and Heinrich Böll, all of whom represented what Buber called the *humanus* battling the Hitlerite *contrahumanus.*

To be sure, the concept of *neqamah* is not without its roots in our Hebrew Bible, where most of the references are somehow linked with the idea of justice (e.g., Isaiah 59:15b-18)—though there are, admittedly, instances where recompense sinks into vindictiveness and unremitting malice (e.g., Psalm 137:7–9). Though it is to be credited with breaking much new ground, the New Testament does not entirely avoid such language either (see Matthew 21:41 and Hebrews 12:29).

Thankfully, to counter these one comes across innumerable examples in the Torah, in biblical Wisdom literature, and in the Apocrypha of a more high-minded disposition toward the enemy. A piece of remarkable and, at the time, revolutionary ancient legislation emerges in the Covenant Code (Exodus 23:4–5):

> If you meet your enemy's ox or his ass going astray, you shall bring it back to him. If you see the ass of the one who hates you lying under its load, you shall refrain from leaving it there; be sure you help him with it.

The suggestive passage in Deuteronomy 23:8 and surrounding verses deserves special consideration. It bids us to refrain from loathing the Edomite and the Egyptian, sworn enemies of ancient Israel—that is, not to harbor inimical feelings towards, or bar for long from admission into the community of Israel, peoples who dealt cruelly with our biblical forebears. With this admonition we move, in our ethical concern, from the individual sphere to the collective one, which latter is usually considered to be more involved and problematic. The medieval commentators may have tacitly sensed the complexity of this shift to the much larger domain of relations between societies and nations, as witness Rashi's qualifying, if strained, glosses on the verse:

> *You shall not loathe the Edomite* entirely; and even though you are entitled to loathe him who came out with the sword to greet you; *you shall not loathe the Egyptian*—utterly; even though they threw your male offspring into the Nile. What is the reason? They were your hosts during a time of need.

Characteristically, Samson Raphael Hirsch, in his commentary to the Pentateuch *Terumat Tzevi,*[2] reminds us in this connection of the passage in the Mishnah (Yadayim 4:4) concerning the dislocation and blending of peoples during Sennacherib's conquests. The implication is that the demarcation made in our passage in the Torah between the Ammonites, Moabites, Edomites, etc., no longer applies because of the effects of miscegenation. Relying on the Rabbinic view just cited, Hirsch understands the passage to mean that the descendents of these peoples qualify, as a result, as willing candidates for admission into the Jewish fold.

Could we not revert to a position closer to the *peshat* (plain sense of the text) and at the same time push Hirsch's universalism a step or two further 1) by not restricting acceptance solely for the purposes of religious conversion, and 2) by dropping our grudges against the Ammonites and Moabites *et al.* (then and now!), in addition to the Edomite and the Egyptian already exempted in the Torah, commingled or no? In short, Deuteronomy 23:8 contains *in nuce* the promise of ending the stranglehold of long-drawn intergroup or international animosities—*neqamah* on the collective scale.

Further on in the Bible we read how, after Job's cronies had exhausted their suggested explanations for his tribulations, the book's author puts these words in the mouth of his patient/impatient hero as part of an impassioned self-defense (Job 31:29–30):

> If I have rejoiced at my enemy's ruin
> or exulted when trouble overtook him
> I have not allowed my mouth to sin
> by asking for his life with a curse.

A parallel mindset can also be found in a book never admitted to the scriptural canon—Ben Sira (or Ecclesiasticus) in the Apocrypha. Even though it was originally written in pure Hebrew and came out decades earlier than the biblical book of Daniel, it is certainly no less doctrinally orthodox than any canonical book of the Hebrew and is replete with noble utterances such as:

> He that takes vegeance will suffer vengeance from the Lord
> and he will firmly establish his sins.
> Forgive your neighbor the wrong he has done
> And then your sins will be pardoned when you pray.

> Does a man harbor anger against another,
> And yet seek healing from the Lord?
> Does he have no mercy toward a man like himself,
> Yet pray for his own sins?
> If he himself, being flesh, maintains wrath
> who will make expiation for his sins?
> Remember the end of your life, and cease from enmity; remember destruction and death, and be true to the commandments.
> Remember the commandments, and do not be angry with your neighbor;
> remember the covenant of the Most High and overlook ignorance.[3]

The Talmud, too, abounds in statements that resemble Jesus' radical admonition to love the enemy. Take the pithy, pungent simile (Yerushalmi Nedarim 9:15) of humankind's indivisibility in a comment on the verse in Leviticus (19:18) mentioned earlier:

> [One who takes revenge or bears a grudge is as] one who in cutting meat sticks the knife in his hand and now goes ahead and sticks it in the other hand

Avot de-Rabbi Nathan (chapter 23) answers the question,"Who is it that is most mighty?" with the gloss, "Mighty is the one who makes of an enemy a friend." Further on in the same extracanonical Talmudic tractate (chapter 41), we have a memorable instruction in self-denial:

> Rabbi Judah ben Tema used to say: Love Heaven and fear Heaven, tremble and rejoice an all the commandments. If you have done your neighbor a slight wrong, let it be in your eyes much; if you have done your neighbor much good, let it be in your eyes small. If your neighbor has done you slight good, let it be in your eyes much; if he has done you much evil, let it be in your eyes slight.

Perhaps the most oft-quoted Talmudic passage on the theme of self-abnegation or sacrificial love is this one from Shabbat 88b:

> Of them who are oppressed and do not oppress, who are scorned and do not scorn in return, who act only from love, and gladly bear their sufferings, the Scripture says, "They who love Him are like the sun when it rises in its might."

This tradition of selflessness was to be expanded and enlarged upon throughout the Middle Ages. In medieval Germany the pietistic *hasidey ashkenaz* engaged in devotional and theurgic mysticism. One of their leading lights, Eleazar ben Judah he-Hasid of Worms (c.1165–c.1230) not only suffered near-fatal injuries himself but endured the slaughter of his wife, son, and daughter at the hands of the Crusaders. We are told by Leo Baeck, himself a saving remnant of the latterday *hasidey ashkenaz,* that the pious Eleazar never wrote a word of hatred against his persecutors.

On the other hand, the same age produced the profoundly bitter *av ha-rahamim* ("Father of Mercies"), with its unsparing plea for divine revenge:

May the merciful Father who dwells on high, in His infinite mercy, remember those saintly, upright and blameless souls, the holy communities who offered their lives for the sanctification of the Divine Name. They were lovely and amiable in their life, and were not parted in their death. They were swifter than eagles and stronger than lions to do the will of their Master and the desire of their Stronghold. May our God remember them favorably among the other righteous of the world; may He avenge the blood of His servants which has been shed, as it is written in the Torah of Moses, the man of God: "O nations, make His people joyful! He avenges the blood of His servants, renders retribution to His foes, and provides atonement for His land and His people." And by thy servants, the Prophets, it is written: "I will avenge their blood which I have not yet avenged; the Lord dwells in Zion. And in the holy writings it is said: "Why should the nations say, 'Where then is their God?' Let the vengeance for thy servants' blood that is shed be made known among the nations in our sight." And it is further said: "The avenger of bloodshed remembers them; He does not forget the cry of the humble." And it is further said: "He will execute judgment upon the nations and fill [the battle-field] with corpses; he will shatter the [enemy's] head over all the wide earth. From the brook by the wayside he will drink; then he will lift up His head triumphantly."[4]

It should not be too hard to see why religious liberals and some traditionalists have excised or downplayed such exceptional passages in the prayerbook. In the years following the Emancipation, they no doubt reasoned, how would it look if we continued to nurse ill feelings towards those who gave us freedom from the ghetto but whose forebears brutally victimized our forebears in the not so distant past? Would we not be biting the hand that feeds us? And would not our misanthropy only prove us undeserving of acceptance by gentile society? Heirs of the Emancipation thus adopted the tactic of accentuating those aspects of the Jewish tradition that promoted nonviolence, forbearance, and *ahavat ha-beriyyot* (love of humankind).[5]

The Shoah has, of course, evoked second thoughts about our conciliatory attitudes. But is *neqamah* the alternative we want to foster? To be sure, at one level the notion stems from powerlessness. If there was no available means of redressing indignities, our tortured ancestors doubtless consoled themselves in thinking that, in the fullness of time, the "God of vengeance" and of justice would give all the wrongdoers and the wronged their due recompense.

But the wish for *neqamah* serves as just one response to the calamities that befall a helpless people. Post-Holocaust Jews have rejected the passivity of powerlessness as out of keeping with the modern Jewish self-image. Self-assertive and self-respecting, the new Jew insists that no minority should ever again be compelled to reconcile itself to the unwarranted abuse Jews have had to take for so long. This assertiveness notwithstanding, a part of us admits that there is something self-transcending, inspiring, and invincible in the manner in which Eleazar of Worms and Jewish martyrs of all time refused to flinch in the face of adversity or to return evil for evil in feeling or in act. Can we not, with reservations, call this a high form of civil disobedience, religious nonconformity, or passive resistance?

We understand that when our ancestors prayed that God's wrath be poured on the heads of their foes, it was their need to vent their anger before the Divine Hearer of their woes. But we must wonder how appropriate such retributive talk is in a liturgical setting. The old estimable principle of the link between *lex orandi* and *lex credendi* still holds: what we ought to pray implies what we ought to believe. If our prayers indeed delineate the values by which we aspire to live, is *neqamah* the religious ideal we want to set before ourselves? If so, we dismiss that prominent strain in the Jewish ethical tradition that forcefully promotes *ahavat ha-beriyyot* and ultimately run the risk of experiencing a rude awakening similar to that of Elisha, the victim-turned-executioner, in Elie Wiesel's *Dawn*.

The spoken or written word, if repeated often enough, leaves an unmistakable imprint on our attitudes. We cannot help internalizing the attitudes and values exalted by the siddur, however frequently or infrequently we may use it. Do we want our rites to emblazon, "O God of vengeance, O LORD; O God of vengeance, appear!" (Ps. 94:1) and drown out *olam ḥesed yibbaneh* (Ps. 89:3), interpreted by the Rabbis to mean that "the world is built on steadfast love"?

Without extenuating the horrors and losses inflicted on our people or simply letting bygones be bygones, we must not allow vigilantism to replace vigilance or *neqamah* and other forms of sweeping hatred to impair our ethical style and sensitivity. We must not lose our moral and spiritual temper as a *goy qadosh,* a holy people.

An earlier version of this chapter appeared in *Judaism* 37,1 (Winter 1988):73–80. © 1988, American Jewish Congress. Reprinted with permission.

1. *Weekday Prayer Book* (1961),*The Bond of Life* (1975), and *Siddur Sim Shalom* (1985), all of them under the imprint of the Rabbinical Assembly.

2. Ed. Ephraim Oratz, trans. Gertrude Hirschler (New York, 1986).

3. Ecclesiastes 28:107 (Revised Standard Version). Compare the biblical Prov. 20:22 and 24:7.

4. Benjam Szold was the sole American liberal liturgist to keep *av ha-raḥamim* in his prayerbook, but only through "May You remember them for good among the righteous of the world." The Reformers, Reconstructionists, and Max D. Klein chose to leave it out entirely, while the mainstream Conservatives have let it stand, with none of the usual detailed rubrics as to when it was to be recited, suggesting the prayer's optionality. But surprisingly, it has found its way back into the Reform High Holy Day prayerbook with an interesting change of venue (*Gates of Repentance* [1978] pp. 434–35, in the middle of its Martyrology).

5. To temper the harsh tone of the verses beginning with *ve-yinqom* [May He exact retribution], the *Artscroll Siddur* has the ensuing comment based on what Samson Raphael Hirsch wrote in accord with the Zeitgeist: "We do not pray that we be strong enough to avenge the martyrs; Jews are not motivated by a lust to repay violence and murder with violence and murder. Rather we pray that God choose how and when to atone for the blood of his fallen martyrs. For the living, decency and integrity remain the primary goals of social life."

17

Tish'ah be-Av Services: A Recommendation

In many ways the 1985 *Siddur Sim Shalom* is the *kol bo/vade mecum* Conservative Judaism has lacked for quite a while. It effectively fulfills personal, domestic, familial and communal liturgical needs—at times in refreshingly unexpected ways. For the first time, for example, one of the movement's prayerbooks acknowledges both Yom ha-Shoah and Yom ha-Atzma'ut as full-fledged sacred days in the Jewish calendar. Complete as it seems to be, one might ask then why it provides neither a *seder berit milah* (must it appear only in a rabbi's manual?) nor a funeral service (does this too always require the benefit of clergy?). No less disconcerting is the lack of any fullscale treatment of Tish'ah be-Av in its pages.

To be sure, since the appearance of the *Weekday Prayer Book* (1961), *anenu* has been added to the diurnal *amidah* and there is a revised *nahem* for *minhah*—both on the fast day. Rubrics prescribe that *tahanun* not be recited on this day, and the special Tish'ah be-Av Torah and haftarah portions are duly included.

One finds, however, no distinct readings for the occasion, much less a single *qinah*—that unique literary and devotional genre to which Leopold Zunz directed a goodly portion of his *wissenschaftlich* investigative energies. To be sure, the 1946 *Sabbath and Festival Prayer Book* provides an abbreviated version of Judah Halevi's Zionide, *tziyyon ha-lo tish'ali*,[1] presumably for the Sabbath before the fastday. And both the 1946 rite and *Siddur Sim Shalom* contain responsive readings based on scriptural verses about Zion and Jerusalem, again without stipulating when or where these are to be said.

The Reconstructionists, in their 1945 *Sabbath Prayer Book,* may have been more resourceful in this regard by providing separate material for both Shabbat Ḥazon and Shabbat Naḥamu, much in keeping with the traditional themes and moods of the Sabbaths before and after the solemn day. For their *Daily Prayer Book* (1963), by contrast, the distinction between the sense of tragic foreboding and the supervening motif of comfort and consolation was to be conflated in one Evening Service for the entire day of mourning. Undoubtedly for sound Reconstructionist reasons, they include neither an *anenu* nor a *nahem* to speak of—let alone Torah and haftarah lessons for the morning or afternoon of Tish'ah be-Av, although a reading of one or more chapters from *eikhah* is recommended, almost in passing.[2]

In the last fifty years Reform Judaism has had a gradual but decided change of heart as regards the Ninth of Av. In light of calamities that have befallen the Jewish people, the movement has arrived at the sobering realization that the eschaton may be taking a bit longer than anticipated. Of course the rebirth of the Jewish state has also tempered Reform's *quondam* wholesale universalism. Its 1975 *Gates of Prayer* reflects this turnaround by furnishing an interchangeable service for Tish'ah be-Av and Yom ha-Shoah, after Reform's doing without a Ninth of Av service for over seventy years. Interestingly, the Reform prayerbook now contains both *anenu* and *naḥem* in the context of a modified *amidah*. In its special haftarot section, the 1981 *Torah: A Modern Commentary* (UAHC) offers the traditional prophetic readings for the morning and afternoon of Tish'ah be-Av, and the lectionaries at the end of the 1977 *Gates of the House* and the 1994 *On the Doorposts of Your House* (CCAR) cite the Torah Readings for those times as well.

Has the Conservative movement ever created anything special for the Ninth of Av? Back in 1955 Rabbis Morris and Hillel E. Silverman put out an aptly black-covered pamphlet titled *Tish'ah be-Av Eve Service,* which includes little more than the *ma'ariv* service as found in the *Sabbath and Festival Prayer Book* along with the text of the Book of Lamentations in Hebrew and in translation. After the *shemoneh esreh* and *qaddish shalem,* the booklet provides a prayer in English recounting, somewhat matter-of-factly, the destruction of Jerusalem and its Temple, the restoration of Zion in our time, and the loss of the Six Million. Just before Lamentations is to be chanted, the opening line of Psalm 137 ("By the waters of Babylon") is to be said, and after it a dramatic responsive reading that recapitulates the horrors of the Holocaust leading to the miracle of Israel reborn, a recitation taken, strangely enough, almost wholly from the 1959 Silverman *Passover Haggadah* and readjusted minimally to fit the Black Fast. After this, four verses of *eli tziyyon ve-areha,*[3] the dirge in alphabetic acrostic, follow in Hebrew, with the climactic verses of the aforesaid psalm, "If I forget thee, O Jerusalem. . . . If I do not set Jerusalem above my greatest joy."

The Silverman effort hardly takes wing and is bare-boned by comparison with the services for Tish'ah be-Av in those European rites closest to those of the American Conservative movement, notably the many German Liberal *Gebetbücher* published through the early years of the Third Reich—

particularly in terms of the balance and proportion between traditional liturgical text/usage and modern sensibilities.

Practically every *Gebetbuch* gave an honored place to *neunten Aw*. It is thus illuminating to compare and contrast the recurrent features of three such siddurim: 1) the third (1893) edition of the *Israelitisches Gebetbuch* by Rabbi Manuel Joel of Breslau, 2) the (1910) *Israelitisches Gebetbuch* by Rabbi Caesar Seligmann of Frankfurt a. M., and 3) the fourteenth (1927) edition of the *Gebetbuch für die neue Synagogue zu Berlin*.

The most traditional of the three is the one by Joel; the most free-handed by Seligmann. Both the Joel and the Berlin rites divide up the reading of Lamentations, two chapters for the Evening Service and the remaining three for the Morning Service. The Seligmann rite is a bit more selective in that it calls for reading only chapters 1, 3 (verses 1–40), and 5 (verses 19–22).

Joel's prayerbook has the most *qinot*: El'azar ha-Qalir's *be-leyl zeh yivkayun ve-yeylilu*[4] and Solomon ibn Gabirol's *shomeron qol titten*[5] for the evening; and Halevi's famed *tziyyon ha-lo tish'ali,* Meir of Rothenburg's contemporaneous and possibly eye-witness *sha'ali serufah va-esh*[6] (uncannily presaging the *Kristallnacht*), and *eli tziyyon ve-areha* for the morning. The only elegy among these not to find its way into the doctrinally and liturgically moderate Berlin manual is Qalir's dialogical *qinah*.

Provision is made for the reading of the Torah and haftarah for the morning, though none for the afternoon, despite the fact that *naḥem* is pointedly included for *minḥah*. Taking more liberties with the text, Seligmann's prayerbook interposes a new, poised, reflective prayer to be said by the *Rabbiner* between a German paraphrase of the weekday *amidah* and the reading of Lamentations. W. Gunther Plaut includes a translation of this prayer from the German in his *Growth of Reform Judaism* (1965; p. 302). Plaut also brings in Seligmann's poignant insert from the bilingual *shemoneh esreh* for Tish'ah be-Av morning that was to reappear not long afterwards in the combined prayerbook for all of German Liberal Jewry, the sadly shortlived *Einheitsgebetbuch* (1929):

> Heavenly Father, deeply moved Israel turns today its eye backward to a past full of misery and oppression. Our souls are filled with sorrow as we contemplate all the suffering which Thou, O God, didst bring upon our fathers. But never did Thy hand lie as heavily upon us as on

the ninth of Av, on that day of horror on which three times Israel's pride sank into dust and ashes. On the ninth of Av Babylon's warlord destroyed Jerusalem, laid the Temple in ashes and drove Israel from its home. A half millennium later, on the ninth of Av, the Roman threw his incendiary torch into the new Sanctuary and Israel was cast out amongst all the peoples of the earth. On the ninth of Av the day of misfortune rose upon Spain which was once was so blessed, where our fathers had found a new and happy home. They were exiled and nowhere since did the Jew enjoy the glory which for centuries was his in that land.

In remembrance of all this misfortune our souls are full of sadness, but the past full of sadness and of woe also contains the comfort which our heart in all the manifold trials of the present needs so dearly. Babylon and ancient Rome are gone, the sun of Spain has set, but Israel and Israel's holy faith still live, for Thou, O Almighty One, wast our light during the night, our shield in our need. Therefore they could torture but not destroy us. O remember Thy people that everywhere where Thy sun is shining the sun of peace and human brotherhood may also warm the hearts of men, so that Israel may be aided and the day of remembrance of the month of Av may be changed into a day of happiness and joy through Thy grace. Amen. [Ibid., pp. 303–4]

Relatively independent as the Frankfurt rite was textually, it embraced *all* of Halevi's Zionide and the better part of *eli tziyyon ve-areha* (barring seven verses) and was chanted in Hebrew by the cantor (*Vorbeter*).

Historically considered, it is not surprising that Benjamin Szold's proto-Conservative 1864 American rite, *Abodath Israel*—designed for new arrivals from Central Europe—should hew to similar lines as the aforenamed Liberal *Gebetbücher*. As discussed in chapter three above, Szold was, like Manuel Joel, a product of the Positive-Historical Jewish Theological Seminary in Breslau founded by Zacharias Frankel. His one-volume siddur/mahzor, before undergoing broader changes at the hand of his colleague from Philadelphia, Marcus Jastrow, is essentially the classical Prayerbook, stripped of all petitions for the sacrificial cult and accompanied by sparing alterations in the Hebrew text and sporadic prayers and hymns in the vernacular.

Szold's handling of Tish'ah be-Av merits consideration here. The compact instructions for the occasion read:

Am neunten Ab werden beim Abendgottesdienste nach dem Gebete der 18 Benedictionen die Elegien Jeremiahs vom Vorbeter recitirt. Beim Morgengottesdienste wird nach der Vorlesung aus der Thora folgende Zionide recitirt.

(On the Ninth of Av during the Evening Service after the Eighteen Benedictions the Elegies of Jeremiah [the book of Lamentations] are recited by the Reader. At the Morning Service after the reading of the Torah the following Zionide is recited.)

Then the full texts of *tziyyon ha-lo tish'ali* and *teraḥem tziyyon* appear. Szold supplied only an abbreviated Reader's *anenu* and a complete *naḥem*, without necessarily specifying it for *minḥah*. Szold's more "radical" contemporary, Isaac M. Wise, proved more conservative in his 1857 *Minhag Amerika* by including *sha'ali serufah va-esh* and *eli tziyyon ve-areha* in addition to *shomeron qol titten* and *tziyyon ha-lo tish'ali*—though not in the 1872 edition, where Tish'ah be-Av is dropped altogether.

Another siddur, the 1982 Israeli Progressive *Ha-Avodah sheba-Lev,* models itself in several respects after the American Conservative and Reconstructionist rites. By far the least conventional and most biblically-centered of all the treatments reviewed so far, its Tish'ah be-Av service is markedly similar to the 1977 xeroxed pamphlet prepared by Yehoram Mazor for the Israeli Congregation Emet va-Anavah entitled *Tiqqun le-Leyl Tish'ah be-Av.* To a lesser degree, it resembles Jakob J. Petuchowski's interesting all-Hebrew 1970 booklet *Tefillah al Har ha-Tzofim.*

Biblical passages in the *Avodah sheba-Lev* service include I Kings 6:1, II Kings 25:1–11, Jeremiah 31:15, Lamentations 1:1–5, Psalms 137:1–6, Leviticus 26:44, Ezra 1:1–6; 6:15–16, 18, I Kings 6:13, Lamentations 5, Leviticus 26:44 (as a kind of reprise), Zechariah 8:1–5, 7–8, and Micah 4:1–5. Beyond these, it also offers *tziyyon ha-lo tish'ali* (selected verses); an extract from *emet me-eretz titzmaḥ* by Aḥad ha-Am; *eikhah,* a poem by Ze'ev Falk;[7] a passage from *Ḥurban u-Telishot* by Berel Katzenelson; excerpts from Josephus, *The Jewish War* 6:4; four verses and the refrain from *eli tziyyon ve-areha;* and the following passage (translated here for the first time), from Petuchowski's *Tefillah al Har ha-Tzofim:*

You are a God who hides Himself, the God of Israel, and You are the God who saves. You hid Your face, we were dismayed, and by Your favor You established us as a strong mountain. What generation like ours has seen the grievous wound of our people? What generation like ours has merited the consolation of Zion and the rebuilding of Jerusalem? What sorrow is like our sorrow and what rejoicing like our rejoicing? But we have not yet come into the rest and the possession. Plowshares are still being beaten into swords and pruning-hooks into spears. The Land still yearns for complete redemption.

Conclusion

While it is true that the old all-purpose Ashkenazic prayerbooks did not customarily make a point of including complete services for Tish'ah be-Av, we have seen examples of such in nineteenth-century American non-Orthodox rites that leaned significantly on traditional forms, in European Liberal (roughly equivalent to the American Conservative) prayerbooks before the Shoah, and in a new Israeli Progressive *minhag.*

Tragedy has long been embedded in our historical existence as a people and community of faith. The age-old awareness of this tragic element is bound up with the unshakable conviction that redemption will ultimately come. Thus a mature prayerful recognition of the alienation and suffering that have been the lot of the Jewish people and fellow denizens of the globe should help in some measure and in some undefined way toward bringing in the long-awaited *tiqqun.* A fitting and well-grounded observance of the Ninth of Av can encourage and enable the contemporary Jew to take this point truly and tellingly to heart. As we can see from the above, a new liturgy for that Tish'ah be-Av observance would have a fair amount of authentic textual resources upon which to draw.

An earlier version of this chapter appeared in *Conservative Judaism* XLIV 3 (Spring 1992): 56–61. © 1992 by the Rabbinical Assembly. Reprinted by permission.

1. Cf. Abraham Rosenfeld, *The Authorized Kinot for the Ninth of Av* (London, 1965), pp. 152–53.

2. The 1996 Reconstructionist *Kol Haneshamah: Daily Prayerbook* has a section for Tish'ah be-Av with items that are basically interchangeable with those for Yom ha-Atz-

ma'ut: Isaiah 40:1–5, 9–11; Avigdor ha-Me'iri's poem, *me-al pisgat har ha-tzofim;* and Psalm 126. The only elements that offer any clue of the day's tragic associations are Psalm 137 (mistakenly given here as 136):1–6 and Primo Levi's universalist "Song of Those Who Died in Vain." *Kol Haneshamah: Shabbat Vehagim* (1994) has a special Torah Readings list, in which the traditional Torah and haftarah lessons for the fastday are offered. These selections are normally assigned for the Morning Service. There is no citation of any of the readings for the Afternoon Service; and Lamentations goes completely unmentioned.

3. Rosenfeld, op.cit. p. 176.

4. Ibid., p. 36.

5. Ibid., pp. 37 and 177.

6. Ibid., pp.161–62

7. See p. 266 above (chapter 14) for my translation of Falk's poem.

Bibliography

While by no means exhaustive, the following bibliography is intended to be comprehensive. It lists not only nineteenth- and twentieth-century liturgical and liturgiological material, but premodern works as well, for the requisite textual and theological background they provide. To show the prodigious range and volume of contemporary liturgical productivity in recent decades, examples of parallel creative developments are included.

CLASSICAL JEWISH PRAYERBOOKS

Abudarham, David. *Seder Abudarham,* ed. S. A. Ratheimer. Usha, 1961/62.

Baer, Seligmann, ed. *Seder Avodat Yisra'el.* Roedelheim, 5628/1868.

Buber, Salomon and J. Freimann, eds. *Siddur Rashi kolel Pisqey Dinim va-Halakhot.* Berlin, 5672/1911.

Davidson, Israel, Simchah Assaf and B. I. Joel, eds. *Siddur Rav Saadja Gaon.* Jerusalem, 5723/1963.

Goldschmidt, Daniel, ed. *Maḥzor la-Yamim Nora'im.* Jerusalem, 5730/1970.

—————. *Maḥzor Sukkot, Shemini Atzeret ve-Simḥat Torah lefi Minhagey Beney Ashkenaz le-khol Anefeyhem,* completed by Yonah Frankel. Jerusalem/New York, 5741/1981.

—————. *Seder Rav Amram Ga'on.* Jerusalem, 5733/1973.

The Jewish Theological Seminary of America. *The Rothschild Maḥzor.* New York, 5744/1983.

Kuk, Abraham Isaac ha-Kohen. *Seder Tefillot im Perush Olat Re'ayah: Tefillot le-Shabbatot u-Mo'adim,* II. Jerusalem, n.d.

—————. *Seder Tefillot im Perush Olat Re'ayah: Tefillot li-Ymey ha-Ḥol. Berakhot, Rosh Ḥodesh, Ḥanukkah u-Furim,* I. Jerusalem, 5723/1963.

Landau, Avraham. *Tzelota de-Avraham.* 2 vols. Tel Aviv, 5723/1963.

Landshuth, Eliezer, ed. *Siddur Hegyon Lev.* Koenigsberg, 1845.

Rosenfeld, Abraham, ed. *Seder Qinot ha-Shalem le-Tish'ah be-Av, The Authorized Kinot for the Ninth of Av.* London, 5725/1965 [Ashkenazic].

—————. *Seder Seliḥot ha-Shalem le-khol ha-Shanah. The Authorized Selichot for the Whole Year.* 2nd ed. London, 5717/1957.

Shne'ur Zalman. *Seder Tefillot mi-kol ha-Shanah al pi Nusaḥ Arizal.* Brooklyn, 1965.

Siddur ha-Tefillot ke-Minhag ha-Qara'im. 4 vols. Gozlav, 1836.

AMERICAN PRAYERBOOKS, DEVOTIONALS, HYMNALS, AND HAGGADOT

Birnbaum, Philip. *Maḥzor ha-Shalem: Nusaḥ Sepharad, High Holyday Prayer Book.* 2 vols. New York, 1958.

———. *Siddur le-Shabbat ve-Yom Tov, Prayer Book for Sabbath and Festivals.* New York, 1964.

Bokser, Ben Zion. *Ha-Maḥzor le-Rosh ha-Shanah ule-Yom Kippur, The High Holyday Prayer Book,* with the help of an editorial committee appointed by the Rabbinical Assembly of America and the United Synagogue of America. New York, 1959.

———. *Pirqey Tefillah u-Qeri'ah le-Yom ha-Atzma'ut, Prayers and Readings for Israel Independence Day.* New York, 1967.

———. *Seliḥot la-Yom ha-Rishon, Seliḥot Service.* New York, 1955.

———. *Ha-Siddur, The Prayer Book: Weekday, Sabbath and Festival.* New York, 1957.

Bosniak Jacob. *Tefillot Yisra'el, Prayers of Israel.* 2 vols. Brooklyn, NY, 1925.

Brin, Ruth F. *Harvest: Collected Poems and Prayers.* New York, 1986.

Bronstein, Herbert A., ed. *Haggadah shel Pesah, The New Union Haggadah.* New York, 1974, rev. 1975, 1982.

——— and Albert Friedlander, eds. *The Five Scrolls.* 1984.

Browne, Edward B. M. *Tefillat Yisra'el kolel ha-Tefillot mi-kol ha-Shanah ke-Minhag Qehillah Qedoshah Sha'arey Tiqvah, Prayers of Israel Containing the Divine Services of the Entire Year arranged for the American Reform Services of the Temple Gates of Hope.* 2nd ed. New York, 1885.

Central Conference of American Rabbis. *Berakhah u-Tehillah, Blessing and Praise: A Book of Meditations and Prayers for Individual and Home Devotion.* Cincinnati, 1923.

———. *Rabbi's Manual.* Cincinnati, 1952.

———. *Rabbi's Manual,* rev. ed. New York, 1961.

———. *Seder Tefillot Yisra'el, The Union Prayer Book for Jewish Worship,* I. New York, 1895.

———. *Seder Tefillot Yisra'el. The Union Prayer Book for Jewish Worship,* II. Cincinnati, 1894.

———. *Seder Tefillot Yisra'el. The Union Prayer Book for Jewish Worship,* rev. ed., I. Cincinnati, 1924.

———. *Seder Tefillot Yisra'el, The Union Prayer Book for Jewish Worship,* rev. ed., II. Cincinnati, 1922.

———. *Seder Tefillot Yisra'el. The Union Prayer Book for Jewish Worship,* newly rev. ed. I Cincinnati, 1940.

———. *Seder Tefillot Yisra'el. The Union Prayer Book for Jewish Worship,* newly rev. ed. II. New York, 1945.

———. *Shir u-Tefillah. Union Songster: Songs and Prayers for Jewish Youth.* New York, 1960.

———. *The Union Haggadah: Home Service for the Passover Eve.* Cincinnati, 1908.

———. *The Union Haggadah: Home Service for the Passover.* Rev. ed. 1923.

———. *The Union Home Prayer Book.* Philadelphia, 1951.

———. *Union Hymnal.* New York, 1897.

———. *Union Hymnal: Songs and Prayers for Jewish Worship,* 3rd rev. ed., 1932.

Chiel, Arthur A. *Megillat Ḥanukkah.* New York, 1980.

[Congregation Emanu-El] *Order of Prayer in the House of Mourners.* New York, 1871.

Congregation Mickva Israel. *Seder Tefillah, Order of Prayers.* Savannah, GA/New York, 1891.

Cronbach, Abraham. *Prayers of the Jewish Advance.* New York, 1924.

Einhorn, David. *Olath Tamid, Gebetbuch für Israelitische Reform-Gemeinden.* Baltimore, 1858.

Elzas, Barnett A., ed. *Festival Prayer Book.* New York, 1915, 2nd ed. 1923.

———. *Prayer Book for New Year and Day of Atonement.* New York, 1927.

———. *Prayer Book for the Sabbath.* New York, 1914.

———. *Prayer Book for the Sabbath: Order of Service, arranged for the use of the Synagogue, Long Branch, N.J.* New York, 1916.

———. *The Sabbath Service and Miscellaneous Services, adopted by the Reformed Society of Israelites, founded in Charleston, S.C., November 21, 1825,* reprinted with an introduction. New York, 1916.

Fisher, Adam. *An Everlasting Name: A Service for Remembering the Shoah.* West Orange, NJ, 1991.

———. *Seder Tu bi-Shevat, The Festival of Trees.* New York, 1989.

Goldfarb, Israel and Israel H. Levinthal. *Zemirot ve-Tishbaḥot le-Leyl Shabbat, Song and Praise for Sabbath Eve.* Brooklyn, 1920.

Goldin, Hyman E. *Ha-Madrikh, The Rabbi's Guide: A Manual for Jewish Religious Rituals and Customs,* rev. ed. New York, 1939 and 1956.

Goldstein, M., A. Kaiser, S. Wechsler and I. L. Rice, eds. *Zimrath Yah: Litur-*

gic Songs consisting of Hebrew, English, German Psalms and Hymns systematically arranged for the Jewish Rite with Organ Accompaniment. New York, 1873.

Gottheil, Gustav. *Morning Prayers.* New York, 1889.

Greenberg, Sidney and Jonathan D. Levine, eds. *Likrat Shabbat.* Bridgeport CT, 1971.

The Isaac Harby Prayerbook, manuscript form prepared by Isaac Harby for the Reformed Society of Israelites founded November 21, 1824. Charleston SC: K. K. Beth-Elohim, 1974.

Harlow, Jules, ed. *Bi-Tzeror ha-Ḥayyim, Bond of Life: A Book of Mourners.* New York, 1975.

————. *Liqqutey Tefillah, Rabbi's Manual.* New York, 5725/1965.

————. *Maḥzor for Rosh Hashanah and Yom Kippur.* New York, 1972.

————. *Siddur Sim Shalom: A Prayer Book for Shabbat, Festivals and Weekdays.* New York, 1985.

————. *Yearnings: Prayer and Meditation for the Days of Awe.* New York, 1968.

Havurat Shalom Siddur Project. *Siddur Birkat Shalom.* Somerville, MA, 1993.

Hirsch, Emil G., trans. and ed. *Dr. David Einhorn's Olath Tamid: Book of Prayers for Jewish Congregations.* Chicago, 1896.

Hopp, David Ian. *High Holy Day Services,* Creative Symbolism Series. Cincinnati, 1977.

Huebsch, Adolph. *Divine Service for the Congregation Ahawath Chesed-Sha'ar Hashamayim,* rev. Isaac S. Moses. New York, 1916.

————. *Seder Tefillah le-Rosh ha-Shanah ve-Yom ha-Kippurim, Prayer for Divine Service of Congregation Ahawath Chesed,* trans. Alexander Kohut. New York, 1889.

————. *Seder Tefillah le-Rosh ha-Shanah ule-Yom ha-Kippurim, Gebete für den öffentlichen Gottesdienst der Tempelgemeinde Ahawath Chesed: Gottesdienst für Neujahr und Versöhnungstag.* New York, 5635/1875.

————. *Seder Tefillah le-Shabbat, Shalosh Regalim ve- Ḥol, Gebete für den öffentlichen Gottesdienst der Tempelgemeinde Ahawath Chesed: Gottesdienst für Sabbath und Festtage.* New York, 5635/1875.

Hyman, A. *Seder Tefillot le-Shabbat ve-Yom Tov, Conservative Sabbath and Holiday Prayer Book.* New York, 1925.

Idelsohn, Abraham Z. *Sefer Shirat Yisra'el, The Jewish Song Book for Synagogue, School and Home,* ed. A. Irma Cohen and Baruch J. Cohen. Cincinnati, 1951.

Institute for Creative Judaism. *A Book of Common Service: Experimental Edition* Cincinnati, 1976.

Jacobs, Henry S. *Tefillat Arvit le-Veyt ha-Avel, Evening Service for the House of Mourning* [for Congregation B'nai Jeshurun]. New York, 5644/1884.

Jewish Ministers' Association of America. *Jewish Home Prayer-Book: A Manual of Household Devotion.* New York and Cincinnati, 1887–88.

Jewish Theological Seminary of America. *Memorial Exercises in Memory of Solomon Schechter.* New York, 1916.

JWB Commission on Jewish Chaplaincy. *Siddur Tefillot le-Ḥayyaley Tzeva Artzot ha-Berit, Prayer Book for Jewish Personnel in the Armed Forces of the United States.* New York, 5744/1984.

Kaiser, Alois and William Sparger. *A Collection of the Principal Melodies of the Synagogue from the Earliest Time to the Present.* Chicago, 1893.

Kalechofsky, Roberta. *Haggadah la-Seh ha-Meshuḥrar, Haggadah for the Liberated Lamb.* Marblehead MA, 1988.

Kaplan, Mordecai M., Eugene Kohn, Jack J. Cohen and Ludwig Nadelman, eds. *Maḥzor le-Shalosh Regalim, Festival Prayer Book with Supplementary Prayers and Readings.* New York, 5718/1958.

———, Eugene Kohn and Ira Eisenstein, eds. *Maḥzor le-Yamim Nora'im, High Holiday Prayer Book: Prayers for Rosh Hashanah,* I. New York, 5708/1948.

———. *Maḥzor le-Yamim Nora'im, High Holiday Prayer Book: Prayers for Yom Kippur,* II. New York, 5708/1948.

———. *The New Haggadah for the Pesaḥ Seder.* New York, 1941.

———, Eugene Kohn, Ira Eisenstein and Milton Steinberg, eds. *Seder Tefillot le-Shabbat, Sabbath Prayer Book with a Supplement containing Prayers, Readings and Hymns.* New York, 5705/1945.

———, Eugene Kohn, Ira Eisenstein, Jack J. Cohen and Ludwig Nadelman, eds. *Seder Tefillot li-Ymot ha-Ḥol, Daily Prayer Book with a Supplement containing Prayers, Readings and Hymns.* New York, 5723/1963.

Klein, Max D. *Hymns of Praise and Prayer Compiled for the Use of Congregation Adath Jeshurun.* Philadelphia, 1926.

———. *Prayers for Use in the Jewish Home.* Philadelphia, 1921.

———. *Seder Avodah: Maḥzor le-Yamim Nora'im, Service Book for Rosh Hashanah and Yom Kippur.* Philadelphia, 5720/1960.

———. *Seder Avodah: Tefillot le-Shabbat, le-Shalosh Regalim ule-Ḥol la-Tzibbur vela-Yaḥid, Prayer Book for Sabbath, Festivals and Weekdays for Use in Synagogue and Home.* Philadelphia, 5712/1951.

Kohn, Eugene, ed. *Shir Ḥadash: New Prayers and Meditations for Rosh Hashanah and Yom Kippur.* New York, 1939.

Kohut, Alexander. *Allon Bakhut.* New York, 1892.

Krauskopf, Joseph. *Kiddush, The Consecration of the Sabbath Eve at the Family Table.* Philadelphia, 1907.

————. *The Mourner's Service.* Philadelphia, 1895.

————. *The Service Manual.* Philadelphia, 1892.

————. *The Service Ritual.* Philadelphia, 1888.

Leeser, Isaac, ed. *Siddur Divrey Tzaddiqim, The Book of Daily Prayers.* Philadelphia, 5608/1848 [Ashkenazic].

————. *Leyl Tish'ah be-Av/Service for the Eve of the Fast of Ab.* New York, 1963 [Sephardic].

————. *Siddur Siftey Tzaddiqim, The Form of Prayers according to the Custom of the Spanish and Portuguese Jews.* 6 vols. Philadelphia, 1837–38.

Levine, Elizabeth Resnick, ed. *A Ceremonies Sampler: New Rites, Celebrations and Observances of Jewish Women.* San Diego, 1991.

Levy, J. Leonard. *A Book of Prayer.* Pittsburgh, 1902.

————. *Haggadah or Home Service for the Festival of Passover.* Philadelphia, 1896.

Levy, Richard, ed. *Ma'aley Tefillot, On Wings of Awe: A Maḥzor for Rosh Hashanah and Yom Kippur.* Washington, DC, 1985.

Merzbacher, Leo, ed. *Seder Tefillah, The Order of Prayer for Divine Service,* I. New York, 1855.

————. *Seder Tefillah, The Order of Prayer for Divine Service,* 3rd rev. ed. Samuel Adler, I. New York, 1864.

————. *Seder Tefillah, Order of Prayer for Divine Service: Prayers for the Day of Atonement,* 2nd rev. ed. Samuel Adler, II. New York, 1863.

Mihaly, Eugene, ed. *Service of Inauguration for Alfred Gottschalk as the Fifth President of the Hebrew Union College-Jewish Institute of Religion.* Cincinnati, 1972.

———— and Jakob J. Petuchowski, eds. *Service of Dedication of the Scheuer Chapel.* Cincinnati, 1975.

Moses, Isaac S. *Tefillat Yisra'el, Order of Prayers and Responsive Readings for Jewish Worship,* 2nd rev. and corrected ed. Milwaukee, 1887.

New Jewish Agenda. *The Shalom Seders: Three Haggadahs Compiled by New Jewish Agenda.* New York, 1984.

Petuchowski, Jakob J., ed. *Shaḥar Avaqqeshkha, A Weekday Morning Service Based on the Traditional Birkhot ha-Shaḥar.* Cincinnati, n.d.

————. *Tefillah al Har ha-Tzofim.* Jerusalem, 5730/1970.

————. *Tefillat Ma'ariv le-Shabbat le-Erev Shabbat Shuvah, Sabbath Eve Service for the Sabbath of Repentance.* Laredo, TX, 5752/1991.

————. *Tefillat Musaf le-Yom ha-Kippurim, Sample of a Revised Atonement Afternoon Service.* Cincinnati, 1970–71.

————. *Tefillat Shaharit le-Hanukkah, A Hanukkah Morning Service for the Synagogue of the Hebrew Union College. Cincinnati.* Cincinnati, n.d.

————. *Tefillat Shaharit le-Shabbat.* Cincinnati, 5730/1970.

P'nai Or Religious Fellowship. *Or Chadash: A Second Draft Edition.* Philadelphia, 1989.

Polish, David, ed. *Ma'aggeley Tzedeq, Rabbi's Manual, with Historical and Halachic Notes by W. Gunther Plaut.* New York, 5748/1988.

Pool, David de Sola, ed. *Seder ha-Tefillot, Book of Prayer according to the Custom of Portuguese Jews: Daily and Sabbath.* New York, 1941.

————. *Tefillot le-Yom Kippur, Prayers for the Day of Atonement according to the Custom of the Spanish and Portuguese Jews.* New York, 1939.

————. *Tefillot la-Mo'adim, Prayers for the Festivals according to the Custom of the Spanish and Portuguese Jews.* New York, 1947.

————. *Tefillot le-Rosh ha-Shanah, Prayers for the New Year.* New York, 1937.

Raphael, Chaim. *Qabbalat Shabbat, The Sabbath Eve Service.* New York, 1985.

The Rabbinical Assembly of America and the United Synagogue of America. *Seder Tefillot Yisra'el le-Shabbat ule-Shalosh Regalim, Sabbath and Festival Prayer Book.* New York, 1946.

The Rabbinical Assembly. *Selihot.* New York, 5724/1964.

Rabinowicz, Rachel Anne, ed. *Haggadah shel Pesah, Passover Haggadah: The Feast of Freedom.* 1982.

Reines, Alvin J. *A Ceremony of Baal(at) Mitzvah.* Creative Symbolism Series. Cincinnati, 1976.

————. *Haggadah: A Passover Service for the Family.* Creative Symbolism Series. Cincinnati, 1973.

————. *A Rosh Hashanah Service for the Family.* Creative Symbolism Series. Cincinnati, 1973.

————. *A Yom Kippur Service for the Family.* Creative Symbolism Series. Cincinnati, 1974.

———— and Anthony D. Holtz. *Funeral and Memorial Services.* Cincinnati, 1979.

———— and Joel L. Levine. *An Equivocal Havdalah Service.* Creative Symbolism Series. Cincinnati, n.d.

Riemer, Jack, ed. *New Prayers for the High Holy Days.* New York, 1971.

Ritual Committee of the Central Conference of American Rabbis. *Tefillot Yisra'el, The Union Prayer Book.* Chicago, 1892.

Ritual Committee of Congregation Beth El of Sudbury River Valley. *Vetaher Libenu.* Sudbury, MA, 1980.

Ritual Committee of Congregation Sha'ar Zahav, ed. *Maḥzor u-Vaḥarta ba-Ḥayyim, Therefore Choose Life!: Prayerbook for Yom Kippur.* San Francisco, 1983.

Roekard, Karen G. R. *The Santa Cruz Haggadah: A Passover Haggadah, Coloring Book, and Journal for the Evolving Consciousness.* Capitola CA, 1991.

Rosenau, William, ed. *Sefer Tanḥumot, Book of Consolation.* Baltimore, 1914.

Scherman, Nosson, ed. *Siddur Qol Ya'aqov The Complete Artscroll Siddur: Weekday, Sabbath, Festival: Nusaḥ Ashkenaz.* Brooklyn, 1984.

———— and Meir Zlotowitz, eds. *Siddur Imrey Efrayim, The Complete Artscroll Siddur: Nusaḥ Sepharad.* Brooklyn, 1985.

Silberfeld, Julius, ed. *Tefillat Shabbat, The Sabbath Service.* New York, 1905.

Silberman, Shoshana. *Tik'u Shofar: A Maḥzor and Sourcebook for Students and Families.* New York, 1993.

Silverman, Morris, ed. *Haggadah shel Pesaḥ: Passover Haggadah with Explanatory Notes and Original Readings.* Hartford, 1959.

————. *Maḥzor le-Rosh ha-Shanah ule-Yom ha-Kippurim, High Holiday Prayer Book.* Hartford, 1951.

————. *Simḥat Torah Service.* Hartford, 1941.

————. *Tefillot le-Shabbat ve-Shalosh Regalim, Sabbath and Festival Services* Hartford, 1936.

————. and Hillel E. Silverman, eds. *Seliḥot: Prayers for Forgiveness.* Hartford, 1954.

————. *Tishah B'Av Eve Service.* Hartford, 1955.

Singer, Isador, ed. *Sha'arey Tefillah, Rabbinical Assembly Manual.* New York, 1952.

Spiegel, Marcia Cohn and Deborah Liopton Kremsdorf, eds. *Women Speak to God: The Prayers and Poems of Jewish Women.* San Diego, 1989.

Stern, Chaim, ed. *Haggadah shel Pesaḥ, Gates of Freedom: A Passover Haggadah.* Chappaqua, NY, 1981, rev. 1982.

————. *Sha'arey ha-Bayit, The New Union Home Prayerbook: Prayers and Readings for Home and Synagogue.* New York, 5737/1977.

————. *Sha'arey Tefillah: Gates of Prayer, The New Union Prayerbook/ Weekdays, Sabbaths, and Festivals, Services and Prayers for Synagogue and Home*. New York, 5735/1975.

————. *Sha'arey Selihah. Gates of Forgiveness: The Union S'lichot Service*, gender-sensitive ed. New York, 5753/1993.

————. *Sha'arey Tefillah, Gates of Prayer*. New York, 1975.

————. *Sha'arey Tefillah le-Shabbat, Gates of Prayer for Shabbat: A Gender Sensitive Prayerbook*. New York, 1992.

————. *Sha'arey Tefillah le-Shabbat ve-Yom Hol, Gates of Prayer for Shabbat and Weekdays: A Gender Sensitive Prayerbook*. New York, 5755/1994.

————. *Sha'arey Teshuvah, Gates of Repentance: The New Union Prayerbook for the Days of Awe*. New York, 5738/1978..

————. *Tefillot le-Hol uve-Veyt ha-Avel, Gates of Prayer for Weekdays and at a House of Mourning: A Gender Sensitive Prayerbook*. New York, 1992.

————. *Tefillot le-Yom Hol, Gates of Prayer for Weekdays: A Gender Sensitive Edition*. New York, 1993.

———— (with Donna Berman). *Sha'arey Simhah, Gates of Joy*. Hoboken, NJ, 1991.

———— (with Donna Berman, Edward Graham and H. Leonard Poller), ed. *Al Mezuzot Beytekha, On the Doorposts of Your House: Prayers and Ceremonies for the Jewish Home*. New York, 5755/1994.

Strassfeld, Michael, ed. *Haggadah shel Pesah, A Passover Haggadah:* Preliminary Edition. New York, 5739/1979.

Szold, Benjamin, ed. *Abodath Israel, Israelitisches Gebetbuch für den öffentlichen Gottesdienst im ganzen Jahre*. Baltimore, 5624/1864.

————. *Abodath Israel, Israelitish Prayer Book for the Public Services of the Year,* rev. ed. Marcus Jastrow. Philadelphia, 1873.

————. *Hegyon-Lev, Israelitisches Gebetbuch für häusliche Andacht*. Baltimore, 1867.

————. *Qodesh Hillulim: Pijutim, Gebete und Gesänge*. Baltimore, 1862.

————. *Sefer ha-Hayyim: Andachtsbuch zum Gebrauche bei Krankheiten und Sterbefallen, und auf dem Friedhofe*. Baltimore, 1866.

———— and Marcus Jastrow. *Abodath Israel, A Prayer Book for the Services of the Year at the Synagogue*, rev. and enlarged ed., I. Philadelphia, 1934.

Teutsch, David A., ed. *Kol Haneshamah: Li-Ymot Hol, Daily Prayerbook*. Wyncote, PA, 1966.

————. *Kol Haneshamah: Erev Shabbat, Shabbat Eve* . Wyncote, PA, 1989.

————. *Kol Haneshamah: Shabbat ve-Ḥagim.* Wyncote, PA, 1994.

————. *Kol Haneshamah: Shirim u-Verakhot, Songs, Blessings and Rituals for the Home.* Wyncote, PA, 1991.

Tolley, Jacquelyn, ed. *On Our Spiritual Journey: A Creative Shabbat Service.* San Diego, 1988.

Vidaver, H., ed. *Sefer ha-Ḥayyim, The Book of Life: Services and Ceremonies Observed at the Death-bed, House of Mourning and Cemetery together with Prayers on Visiting Graves.* New York, 5649/1889.

Wiesel, Elie and Albert H. Friedlander. *The Six Days of Destruction: Meditations toward Hope.* Mahwah, NJ, 1988.

Wise, Aaron, ed. *Shalhevet Yah, The Temple Service for the Sabbath and the Festivals.* New York, 1891.

Wise, Isaac M., ed. *Minhag Amerika: Tefillot Beney Yeshurun le-Rosh ha-Shanah, The Divine Service of American Israelites for the New Year.* Cincinnati, 1866.

————. *Minhag Amerika: Tefillot Beney Yeshurun le-Yom ha-Kippurim, The Divine Service of American Israelites for the Day of Atonement.* Cincinnati, 1866.

————, W. Rothenheim and I. Kalisch, eds. *Minhag Amerika: Tefillot Beney Yeshurun, The Daily Prayers of American Israelites.* Cincinnati, 1857.

Women of Reform Judaism. *Covenant of the Heart: Prayers, Poems and Meditations from the Women of Reform Judaism.* New York, 1993.

EUROPEAN AND ISRAELI PROGRESSIVE PRAYERBOOKS, HYMNALS, AND HAGGADOT

Assembly of Ministers of the Reform Synagogues of Great Britain, ed. *Maḥzor le-Shalosh Regalim, Prayers for the Pilgrim Festivals.* Amsterdam and Tel Aviv, 5725/1965.

————. *Tefillat Arvit le-Shabbat, Sabbath Evening Service: Introductory Format.* London, 5730/1970.

————. *Tzidduq ha-Din, Funeral Service.* London, 5735/1974.

Blue, Lionel and Jonathan Magonet, eds. *Seder ha-Tefillot, Forms of Prayer: Daily Sabbath and Occasional Prayers,* 7th ed., I. London, 5737/1977.

————. *Seder ha-Tefillot, Forms of Prayer for Jewish Worship: Prayers for the High Holydays,* 8th ed., III. London, 5745/1985.

————. *Seder ha-Tefillot, Forms of Prayer for Jewish Worship: Prayers for the Pilgrim Festivals,* 2nd rev. ed., III. London, 5755/1995.

————. *Seder ha-Tefillot, Forms of Prayer for Jewish Worship: Shavu'ot,* introductory format. London, 1988.

Fränkel, S. J., and M. J. Bresselau. *Seder ha-Avodah le-Shabbetot ha-Shanah u-Mo'adey Adonay Miqra'ey Qodesh, Ordnung der öffentlichen Andacht fur die Sabbath- und Festtage des ganzen Jahres nach dem Gebrauche des Neuen-Tempel-Verein in Hamburg.* Hamburg, 5579/1819. ["Hamburg Temple *Gebetbuch*"].

Gebetbuch für jüdische Reformgemeinden: Allwöchentliche Gebete und häusliche Andacht, 3rd ed., I. Berlin, 1859.

Gebetbuch für jüdische Reformgemeinden: Die Festgebete, 3rd ed., II. Berlin, 1858.

Hamburg Tempelgemeinde. *Allgemeines Israelitisches Gesangbuch.* Hamburg, 1833.

Ḥugim le-Yahadut Mitqaddemet *Siddur ha-Tefillot le-Shabbat,* temporary edition. Jerusalem, 5722/1962.

The Jewish Religious Union. *A Selection of Prayers, Psalms and Other Scriptural Passages and Hymns,* 2nd rev. ed. London, 5664/1903.

Joel, Manuel. *Seder Tefillah li-Ymot Ḥol ule-Shabbatot ule-khol Mo'adey ha-Shanah, Israelitisches Gebetbuch für die öffentliche Andacht des ganzen Jahres,* 3rd ed., I. Breslau, 1893.

Klenicki, Leon, ed. *Libro de Oraciones.* Buenos Aires, 5733/1973.

Lattes, Dante. *Bircat Hammazon con Canti e Salmi secondo il Rito Italiano.* Florence, 5699/1938.

Liberaal-Joodse Gemeenten in Nederland. *Seder Tov le-Hodot: Gebeden voor Rosj Hasjanah en Jom Kipoer.* 5725/1964.

————. *Seder Tov le-Hodot: Gebeden voor Sjabbat en Festdagen.* 5724/1964.

Mattuck, Israel I., *Liberal Jewish Prayer Book: Services for the Day of Memorial (Rosh Hashanah) and the Day of Atonement,* rev. ed., II. London, 1937.

————. *Liberal Jewish Prayer: Services for Passover, Pentecost and Tabernacles,* III. London, 1926.

————. *Liberal Jewish Prayer Book: Services for Weekdays, Sabbaths,* etc., rev. ed., I. London, 1937.

Mazor, Yoram, ed. *Haggadah shel Pesaḥ.* Kibbutz Yahel, 5749/1989.

————. *Tiqqun le-Leyl Tish'ah be-Av.* 5737/1977.

———— and Mordekhai Rotem. "Ki ha-Adam Etz ha-Sadeh": *Tiqqun Tu bi-Shevat.* 5753/1993.

Ministers of the Association of Synagogues in Great Britain. *Seder Ha-*

Tefillot: Tefillat Arvit, Forms of Prayer for Jewish Worship, First Supplement to Volume I: Evening Prayers. Oxford, 5712/1952.

The Ministers of the Union of Liberal and Progressive Synagogues. *A Book of Prayer and Meditation.* London, 1951.

Ministers of the West London Synagogue of British Jews. *Seder ha-Tefillot, Forms of Prayer for Jewish Worship: Daily, Sabbath and Occasional Prayers,* 6th ed., I. Oxford, 1931.

Ministers of the Congregation. *Seder ha-Tefillot, Forms of Prayer used in the West London Synagogue of British Jews: Prayers for the Festivals,* 4th ed., II. London, 5682/1921.

Petuchowski, Jakob J., ed. *Le-Ovdekha be-Emet, "Dass Wir Dir in Wahrheit Dienen": Ein jüdischer Gottesdienst für den Sabbatmorgen.* Aachen, 1988.

Rayner, John D. ed. *Haggadah shel Pesaḥ, Passover Eve Service for the Home,* rev. ed. London, 1962.

———— and Chaim Stern, eds. *Avodat ha-Lev, Service of the Heart* London, 1967.

———— and Chaim Stern, eds. *Petaḥ Teshuvah, Gate of Repentance.* London, 1973.

———— and Chaim Stern, eds. *Siddur Lev Chadash, Services and Prayers for Weekdays and Sabbaths, Festivals and Various Occasions.* London, 5755/1995.

———— and Chaim Stern (with Julia Neuberger), eds. *Haggadah shel Pesaḥ A Modern Passover Haggadah.* 1981.

Seligmann, Caesar. *Hagada: Liturgie für die häusliche Feier der Sederabende,* 4th ed. Frankfurt a/M, 1925.

————. *Israelitiches Gebetbuch: Sabbat, Festtage und Werktag,* I. Frankfurt a/M, 1910.

————. *Neues Gebetbuch für Neujahr und Versöhnungstag.* Frankfurt a/M, 1904.

————, Ismar Elbogen, and Hermann Vogelstein eds. *Tefillot le-khol ha-Shanah/Gebetbuch für das ganze Jahr: Neujahr und Versöhnungstag,* II. Frankfurt a/M, 1929 ["Einheitsgebetbuch"].

Soetendorp, J., ed. *Haggadah shel Pesaḥ Hagadah voor Pesaḥ.* Amsterdam/The Hague, 5730/1970.

The South African Union for Progressive Judaism. *Seder Tefillot Yisra'el, The Union Prayerbook for Jewish Worship.* Newly rev. ed., I. Johannesberg, 1957.

Stern, Herman [Chaim], ed. *Sabbath Services: Experimental Edition.* London, 1964.

Ha-Tenu'ah le-Yahadut Mitqaddemet be-Yisra'el [Israel Movement for Progressive Judaism] ed. *Ha-Avodah sheba-Lev: Siddur Tefillot li-Ymot Ḥol, le-Shabbatot ule-Mo'adey ha-Shanah.* Jerusalem, 5742/1982.

―――. *Ha-Avodah sheba- Lev, Siddur Tefillot li-Ymot Ḥol, le-Shabbatot ule-Mo'adey ha-Shana,* rev. ed. Yehoram Mazor. Jerusalem, 5751/1991.

―――. *Kavvanat ha-Lev: Maḥzor ha-Tefillot la-Yamim ha-Nora'im.* Jerusalem, 5749/1989.

Union of Liberal and Progressive Synagogues. *Services and Prayers for Jewish Homes,* 2nd ed. London, 1955.

Vardi, Dov, ed. *Haggadah shel Pesaḥ, Pesach Haggada.* Tel Aviv, 1979.

West London Synagogue. *Hymnal.* London, 1938.

West London Synagogue of British Jews, ed. *Seder ha-Tefillot, Forms of Prayer used in the West London Synagogue of British Jews and its Associated Synagogues: Prayers for the Day of Atonement,* 7th ed., IV. Oxford, 1958.

―――. *Seder ha-Tefillot, Forms of Prayer used in the West London Synagogue of British Jews and its Associated Synagogues: Prayers for the Day of Memorial* (New Year), 6th ed., III. Oxford, 1958.

Ydit, Me'ir, ed. *Haggadah Yisre'elit le-Seder Leyl Pesaḥ.* Jerusalem, 5725/1965.

STUDIES ON JEWISH LITURGY, ACADEMIC AND DEVOTIONAL, SCHOLARLY AND POPULAR

Abrahams, Israel. *A Companion to the Authorized Daily Prayer Book.* London, 1922.

―――. "Some Rabbinic Ideas on Prayer," *Jewish Quarterly Review* XX (1908).

Agus, Jacob B. "The Meaning of Prayer" in Abraham E. Millgram, ed. *Great Jewish Ideas.* Washington DC, 1964.

Angel, Marc D. *Thoughts about Prayer.* New York, 5743/1983.

Arzt, Max. *Joy and Remembrance: Commentary on the Sabbath Eve Liturgy.* New York and Bridgeport, 1979.

―――. *Justice and Mercy: Commentary on the Liturgy of the New Year and the Day of Atonement.* New York, 1963.

Baumel, Judith T. *Qol Bekhiyyot: Ha-Sho'ah veha-Tefillah.* Ramat Gan, 5752/1992.

Baumgard, Herbert M. *Judaism and Prayer: Growing Towards God.* New York, 1964.

Bemporad, Jack, ed. *The Theological Foundations of Prayer.* New York, 1967.

Berkovits, Eliezer. "Prayer" in Leon D. Stitskin, ed. *Studies in Torah Judaism* (New York, 1969), pp. 81–189.

Blumenthal, David. *God at the Center: Meditations on Jewish Spirituality.* San Francisco, 1987.

Bokser, Baruch M. "Ma'al and Blessings over Food: Rabbinic Transformation of Cultic Terminology," *Journal of Biblical Literature* (December 1981): 557–74.

―――. *The Origins of the Seder.* Berkeley, 1984.

Bradshaw, Paul F. and Lawrence A. Hoffman, eds. *The Changing Face of Jewish and Christian Worship in North America.* Notre Dame and London, 1991.

――― and Lawrence A. Hoffman, eds. *The Making of Jewish and Christian Worship.* Notre Dame and London, 1991.

Casper, Bernard M. *Talks on Jewish Prayer.* Jerusalem, 5723/1963.

Central Conference of American Rabbis. *Commentary to Union Prayer Book,* vol.4, newly revised: *First Evening Service for the Sabbath, Experimental Edition.* New York, 1962.

Cohen, Jack J. *The Religion of the Jewish Prayer Book.* New York, 1942.

Cohen, Jeffrey M. *Blessed Are You: A Comprehensive Guide to Jewish Prayer.* Northvale NJ and London, 1993.

―――. *Horizons of Jewish Prayer.* London, 1986.

Cohn, Gabriel H. and Harold Fisch, eds. *Prayer in Judaism: Continuity and Change* Northvale, NJ and London, 1996.

Davidson, Israel. *Otzar ha-Shirah veha-Piyyut. Thesaurus of Medieval Hebrew Poetry.* 4 vols. New York, 1970.

Davis, Moshe. *The Emergence of Conservative Judaism: The Historical School in 19th Century America.* Philadelphia, 1965.

Dembitz, Lewis N. *Jewish Services in Synagogue and Home.* Philadelphia, 1898.

Dienstag, Jacob I. "The Prayer Book of Moses Maimonides" in Menahem Kasher, ed. *The Leo Jung Memorial Volume.* (New York, 1962), pp. 53–63.

Dresner, Samuel H. *Prayer, Humility and Compassion.* Philadelphia, 1957.

Elbogen, Ismar. *Jewish Liturgy: A Comprehensive History,* [based on *Der jüdische Gottesdienst* and *Ha-Tefillah be-Yisra'el,* below] trans. Raymond P. Scheindlin. Philadelphia, New York and Jerusalem, 5753/1993.

————. *Der jüdische Gottesdienst in seiner geschichtlichen Entwicklung.* Frankfurt a/M, 1931.

————. *Ha-Tefillah be-Yisra'el be-Hitpattehutah ha-Historit* [Heb. translation of *Der jüdische Gottesdienst* above], ed. J. Amir, I. Adler, A. Negev, J. J. Petuchowski and H. Schirmann. Tel Aviv, 1972.

Enelow, Hyman G. "Kawwana: The Struggle for Inwardness in Judaism" in *Jewish Studies in Honor of Kaufmann Kohler,* (Berlin, 1913), pp. 82–107.

Fields, Harvey J. *Be-khol Levavkha, With All Your Heart: A Commentary.* New York, 1976.

Finkelstein, Louis. "The Birkat Ha-Mazon," *Jewish Quarterly Review* XIX (1929): 211–62.

Fleischer, Ezra. *Shirat ha-Qodesh ha-Ivrit bi-Ymey ha-Beynayim.* Jerusalem, 1975.

————. *Tefillah u-Minhagey Tefillah Eretz-Yisre'elim bi-Tequfat ha-Genizah.* Jerusalem, 1988.

Freehof, Solomon B. "Devotional Literature in the Vernacular," *Yearbook of the Central Conference of American Rabbis* XXXIII (1923): 3–43.

————. "Hazkarath Neshamoth," *Hebrew Union College Annual* XXXVI (1965): 179–89.

————. *In the House of the Lord: Our Worship and Our Prayerbook.* New York, 1951.

————. *The Small Sanctuary: Judaism in the Prayerbook.* New York, 1942.

Friedland, Eric L. *The Historical and Theological Development of Non-Orthodox Jewish Prayerbooks in the United States.* Ann Arbor, MI, 1967.

————. "Loose Ends," in *Manna* (Spring 1996): 1518.

Gaon, Solomon. *Minhat Shelomoh: A Commentary on the Book of Prayers of the Spanish and Portuguese Jews,* ed. Gertrude Hirschler. New York, 5750/1990.

Garfiel, Evelyn. *The Grace,* Jewish Tract Series. New York, 1968.

Gaster, Theodore H. "The New Prayer Book," *The West London Synagogue Magazine* V (1930–1931): 159–60.

Glatzer, Nahum N. *Language of Faith: A Selection of the Most Expressive Jewish Prayers.* New York, 1947, rev. 1967.

Goldberg, P. Selvin. *Karaite Liturgy.* Manchester, 1957.

Goldschmidt, Daniel. *Mehqerey Tefillah u-Fiyyut.* Jerusalem, 5739/1978.

Goldschmidt, E. D. "Studies on Jewish Liturgy by German-Jewish Scholars," *Year Book of the Leo Baeck Institute* II (1957).

Gordis, Robert. "A Jewish Prayer Book for the Modern Age," *Conservative Judaism* II (October 1945): 1–20.

Green, Arthur and Barry W. Holtz. *Your Word Is Fire: The Hasidic Masters on Contemplative Prayer.* New York, 1987.

Greenberg, Moshe. *Biblical Prose Prayer: A Window to the Popular Religion of Ancient Israel.* Berkeley, Los Angeles and London, 1983.

Habermann, A. M. *Toledot ha-Piyyut veha-Shirah.* Ramat Gan, 1970.

Hammer, Reuven. *Entering Jewish Prayer: A Guide to Personal Devotion and the Worship Service.* New York, 1994.

Harlow, Jules. "Introducing Siddur Sim Shalom," *Conservative Judaism* XXXVII (Summer 1984): 5–17.

Havazelet, Me'ir. "Qeri'at 'Azharot' be-Hag ha-Shavu'ot bi-Ymey ha-Ge'onim," *Ha-Doar* LIV (28 Iyyar 5735/May 9, 1975): 409.

Heinemann, Joseph. *Iyyuney Tefillah,* ed. Avigdor Shinan. Jerusalem, 5743/1983.

————. *Prayer In the Talmud: Forms and Patterns* [English translation by Richard Sarason of *Ha-Tefillah bi-Tequfat ha-Tanna'im veha-Amora'im*]. Berlin, 1977.

————. *Ha-Tefillah be-Mahshevet Hazal.* Jerusalem, 5720/1960.

————. *Ha-Tefillah bi-Tequfat ha-Tanna'im veha-Amora'im.* Jerusalem, 1964.

———— (with Jakob J. Petuchowski). *Literature of the Synagoque* New York, 1975.

Heschel, Abraham J. *Al Mahut ha-Tefillah.* Jerusalem, 5720/1960.

————. *Man's Quest for God.* New York, 1954.

————. "Perush al ha-Tefillot," in *Qovetz Madda'i le-Zekher Mosheh Schorr.* New York, 5705/1945, pp. 113–26.

————. "The Spirit of Prayer," *Proceedings of the Rabbinical Assembly of America* XVII (1953): 151–215.

Hoffman, Lawrence A. *The Art of Public Prayer: Not for Clergy Only.* Washinghton, D.C., 1988.

————. *Beyond the Text: A Holistic Approach to Liturgy.* Bloomington and Indianapolis, 1987.

————. *The Canonization of the Synagogue Service.* Notre Dame, 1979.

————. *Sha'arey Binah, Gates of Understanding: A Companion Volume to Gates of Prayer.* New York, 5737/1977.

————. *Sha'arey Binah II, Gates of Understanding 2: Appreciating the Days of Awe.* New York, 5744/1984.

Idelsohn, Abraham Z. *Jewish Liturgy and Its Development.* New York, 1932.

Italiener, Bruno. "The Musaf-Kedushah," *Hebrew Union College Annual* XXVI (1955): 413–24.

Jacobs, Louis. *Hasidic Prayer.* The Littman Library of Jewish Civilization. New York, 1973.

————. *Jewish Prayer.* London, 1955.

Jacobson, B. S. [Yissakhar]. *Netiv Binah.* 5 vols. Tel Aviv, 1968–83.

Kadushin, Max. *The Rabbinic Mind,* 2nd ed. New York, 1965.

————. *Worship and Ethics: A Study in Rabbinic Judaism.* Evanston IL, 1964.

Kaplan, Aryeh. *Jewish Meditation: A Practical Guide.* New York, 1985.

Kieval, Herman. *The High Holy Days,* I. New York, 1959.

Kohler, Kaufmann. *The Origins of the Synagogue and Church.* New York, 1929.

————. "Wesen und Wirkung des Gebetes: Predigt zum Vorabende des Versöhnungstages," *The Jewish Times* [German Section] (October 25, 1872): 697–98.

Kohn, Eugene. "Prayer and the Modern Jew" in *Proceedings of the Rabbinical Assembly of America* XVII (1953): 179–81.

Levi, Eliezer. *Yesodot ha-Tefillah.* Tel Aviv, 1965.

Luzzatto, Samuel David. *Mavo le-Maḥzor Beney Roma.* Livorno, 1856. [Reissued with annotations by E. D Goldschmidt and a bibliography by J. J. Cohen. 1966].

Mann, Jacob. "Changes in the Divine Service due to Religious Persecutions," *Hebrew Union College Annual* IV (1927): 241–310.

Martin, Bernard. *Prayer in Judaism.* New York, 1968.

Mazor, Yehoram. *"Ha-Avodah sheba-Lev": Siddur ha-Tenu'ah le-Yahadut Mitqaddemet be-Yisra'el, He'arot ve-Ha'arot.* Jerusalem, 5751/1991.

Meyer, Michael A.. *Response to Modernity: A History of the Reform Movement in Judaism.* New York and Oxford, 1988.

Michelson, A. Elihu. *Toward A Guide for Jewish Ritual Usage.* New York, 1941.

Milgram, Abraham E. *Jewish Worship.* Philadelphia, 1971.

Montefiore, Leonard G. "The Aramaic Kaddish and Mr. Marks," *The Synagogue Review* (February 1959): 146–47.

Munk, Elie. *The World of Prayer: Daily Prayers* I. New York, 1953.
————. *The World of Prayer: Sabbath and Festival Prayers* II. New York, 1953.

Nulman, Macy. *The Encyclopedia of Jewish Prayer: Ashkenazic and Sephardic Rites.* Northvale, NJ, 1993.

Pel'i, Pinḥas. "Al Ba'ayat 'ha-Yaḥad' bi-Tefillah: Iyyun le-Dugmah bi-Dynamiqah shel Ma'arekhet ha-Yeḥasim she-beyn Halakhah u-Meta-Halakhah," *Proceedings of the Rabbinical Assembly of America* (1980): 319–32.

Perath, Meyer J. *Rabbinical Devotion: Prayers of the Jewish Sages.* Assen, 1964.

Petuchowski, Jakob J. "Abraham Geiger and Samuel Holdheim:Their Differences in Germany and Repercussions in America," *Yearbook of the Leo Baeck Institute* XXII (1977): 139–59.

————. "Conservative Liturgy Come of Age," *Conservative Judaiism* XXVII (Fall 1972): 3–11.

————. *Contributions to the Scientific Study of Jewish Liturgy.* New York, 1970.

————. "From Censorship Prevention to Modern Theological Reform," *Hebrew Union College Annual* XL-XLI (1969–70): 299–324.

————. *Guide to the Prayerbook.* Cincinnati, 1967.

————. "Karaite Tendencies in an Early Reform Haggadah," *Hebrew Union College Annual* XXXI (1960): 223–49.

————. *Prayerbook Reform in Europe.* New York, 1968.

————. "Reflections of a Liturgist," *Proceedings of the Rabbinical Assembly* (1986): 4–13.

————. *The Sabbath Prayer Book of the Hebrew Union College/Jerusalem: A Description.* Jerusalem, 1964.

————. *Theology and Poetry: Studies in Medieval Piyyut.* London, 1978.

————, ed. *Understanding Jewish Prayer.* New York, 1972.

———— and Ezra Fleischer, eds. *Studies in Aggadah, Targum and Jewish Liturgy in Memory of Joseph Heinemann.* Jerusalem, 1981.

Pool, David de Sola. *The Kaddish.* Leipzig, 1909.

Reif, Stefan C. "Darko shel Meḥqar ha-Tefillah ha-Yehudit," *Proceedings of the Eighth World Congress for Jewish Studies,* III (1982): 175–82.

————. *Judaism and Hebrew Prayer: New Perspectives on Jewish Liturgical History.* Cambridge, 1993.

————. "Some Liturgical Issues in the Talmudic Sources," *Studia Liturgica* XV (1982–83):188–206.

Response: A Contemporary Jewish Review. [Special Issue on Prayer] XIII (Fall-Winter 1982).

Sarason, Richard. "On the Use of Method in the Modern Study of Jewish Liturgy," in William S. Green, ed., *Approaches to Ancient Judaism: Theory and Practice* (Missoula MT, 1978), pp. 97–172.

————. "Religion and Worship: The Case of Judaism," in *Take Judaism, For Example: Studies Towards the Comparison of Religions,* ed. Jacob Neusner (Chicago, 1983).

Schechter, Abraham I. *Lectures on the Jewish Liturgy.* Philadelphia, 1933.

Schirmann, Ḥayyim [Jefim]. *Ha-Shirah ha-Ivrit bi-Sefarad uve-Provence* I. Jerusalem and Tel Aviv, 5719/1959.

Schorsch, Ismar. "Moritz Steinschneider on Liturgical Reform," *Hebrew Union College Annual* LIII (1982): 241–64.

Silberman, Lou H. "The Union Prayer Book: A Study in Liturgical Development," in Bertram W. Korn, ed., *Retrospect and Prospect* (New York, 1965), pp. 46–80.

Simon, Ernst. "On the Meaning of Prayer," in Alfred Jospe, ed., *Tradition and Contemporary Experience: Essays on Jewish Thought and Life* (New York, 1970).

Slonimsky, Henry. "Prayer," *Essays.* Chicago, 1967.

Weinberg, Dudley. *The Efficacy of Prayer.* New York, 1965.

Weintraub, Simkha Y., ed. *Healing of Soul, Healing of Body: Spiritual Leaders Unfold the Strength and Solace in Psalms.* Woodstock, VT, 1994.

Weiss, A. *Women at Prayer: A Halakhic Analysis of Women's Prayer Groups.* Hoboken, NJ, 1990.

Werner, Eric. *The Sacred Bridge: Liturgical Parallels in Synagogue and Early Church,* I. New York, 1970.

————. *The Sacred Bridge: The Interdependence of Liturgy and Music in Synagogue and Church during the First Millennium,* II. New York, 1984.

Wertheimer, Jack, ed. *The American Synagogue: A Sanctuary Transformed.* Cambridge, 1987.

Wiener, Shohama Harris and Jonathan Omer-Man, eds. *Worlds of Jewish Prayer: A Festschrift in Honor of Rabbi Zalman Schachter-Shalomi.* Northvale, NJ, 1993.

Zahavy, Tzvee. *Mishnaic Law of Blessings and Prayers: Tractate Berakhot.* Brown Judaic Series. Decatur, GA, 1987.

Zunz, Leopold. *Ha-Derashot be-Yisra'el ve-Hishtalshelutan ha-Historit,* ed. Ḥanokh Albeck and trans. M. Jacques. Jerusalem, 5714/1954.

———. *Die gottesdienstliche Vorträge der Juden,* 2nd ed. Frankfurt a/M, 1892.

Index of Prayers, Piyyutim, and Hymns Cited

Index of Persons Cited

Tishby, Isaiah, 15n.11

Ungar, André, 134n.22

Vincent St. Millay, Edna, 250
Vital, Ḥayyim, 279

Waldman, Nachum, 258n.9
Waskow, Arthur, 253–54
Wechsler, S., 144n.19
Weil, Simone, 214
Weiman-Kelman, Levi, 251
Werner, Eric, xii
Wesley, Charles, 131
Wesley, John, 131
Wiener, Max, 67n.6
Wiesel, Elie, 237, 324
Wise, Aaron, 10
Wise, Isaac Mayer, 10, 11, 12, 18, 19,
    43n.4, 44n.7, 50–54, 58, 61, 64, 66,
    72, 73, 76, 78, 79, 82, 84, 86, 87, 89,

137, 138, 142n.4, 191, 193, 194,
    200n.8, 225n.35, 230, 233, 242,
    242n.1, 270, 330
Wise, Stephen S. 233

Yafeh, Avraham, 177n.27
Yannai, 2
Yellin, David, 179n.45
Yevtushenko, Yevgeny, 268n.9
Yoma, 219

Zafren, Herbert C., 143n.12, 144n.20
Zangwill, Israel, 197
Zeitlin, Aaron, 250
Zeitlin, Hillel, 207
Zelda, 213, 251
Zlotowitz, Meir, 251, 276n.15, 277n.23
Zschokke, J. H. D., 166
Zunz, Leopold, xii, 9, 15n.6, 16n.24, 21,
    24, 26–27, 35, 45n.25, 45n.27,
    46n.35, 68n.17, 232, 271, 326